ESSAYS IN SOCIOLOGY
OF THE LONG RUN

Macrohistory

ESSAYS IN SOCIOLOGY
OF THE LONG RUN

RANDALL COLLINS

Stanford University Press
Stanford, California

Stanford University Press
Stanford, California
© 1999 by the Board of Trustees
of the Leland Stanford Junior University

Printed in the United States of America

CIP data appear at the end of the book

Acknowledgments

I AM INDEBTED for comments and suggestions to Charles Tilly, Jack Goldstone, Michael Mann, Arthur L. Stinchcombe, John A. Hall, Hans Joas, Dietrich Rueschemeyer, Robert Wuthnow, Susan Watkins, Samuel W. Kaplan, Michael Hechter, Alexandra Maryanski, Joseph M. Bryant, Jonathan Turner, Albert Bergesen, Koya Azumi, Stephen Kalberg, Johan Goudsblom, Orlando Patterson, Kenneth Barkin, Glenn Firebaugh, and to colloquium participants at International Christian University and Joetsu University. David V. Waller, Jie-li Li, and Rebecca Li were close participants and discussants in the development of several of these papers. Robert Hanneman and Gabriele Mordt, who originally cowrote the appendix on computer simulation, are owed special thanks for their collaboration.

Contents

Figures

Macrohistory

ESSAYS IN SOCIOLOGY
OF THE LONG RUN

Introduction: The Golden Age
of Macrohistorical Sociology

HISTORY, ÉMILE DURKHEIM remarked, should be sociology's microscope. Not that it should magnify the tiny, he meant, but that it should be the instrument by which structures are discovered invisible to the unaided eye. The program Durkheim put forward in the *Année Sociologique* did not go far with this research; it sketched static structures more than the dynamics of structural change. The charge still remains: whatever is large and widely connected can be brought into focus within no perspective but one larger still. Political and economic patterns, especially as they encompass states and the strains of war, property systems, and markets, can best be seen in the study of many interconnected histories over a long period of time. What Durkheim wanted for sociological theory was not a microscope, but it might well be called a macroscope.

Two opposing views on history dominated the twentieth century of the Christian calendar still in use in the post-Christian West. On one hand, it was the century of macrohistory par excellence, the first in which a comprehensive history of the world became possible. G. W. F. Hegel, writing in the generation when professional historiography was being established, knew just enough about the cycle of Chinese dynasties to posit that only the West had a history. By the time of World War I, Oswald Spengler, Max Weber, and a little later Arnold Toynbee were surveying the civilizations of China and India, Egypt and Mesopotamia, Persia and the Arab world, and sometimes Mexico, Peru, and Polynesia, as well as making the more familiar comparison of Greco-Roman antiquity with medieval and modern Europe. The view of twentieth-century intellectuals has been to recoil from these global vistas in favor of the argument that history shows us no more than ourselves hopelessly contextualized in patternlessness. In the epistemological version of a familiar phrase, all that we learn from history is that it is impossible to learn from history. Let us briefly explore the two sides of this century of historical consciousness.

Cumulating Strands of Analytical Macrohistory

Early recognition of patterns crystallized in the ambiguous insight that "history repeats itself." Toynbee began his search for the pattern of all civilizations because the world wars of Britain and Germany reminded him of the death struggle of liberal Athens and authoritarian Sparta. Spengler collated evidence of repeated sequences of cultural efflorescence and decadence throughout the world, each distinguished by its unique mentality like a melody played in different keys. Karl Marx, whose knowledge of non-European history was not far beyond Hegel's, depicted its static nature in materialist form as Oriental despotism, a model elaborated in the 1950s by Karl Wittfogel. Bracketing the non-Western world, Marx started from the insight that the class conflict of the Roman world was repeated by analogous classes in medieval feudalism and in modern capitalism. The Marxian school of historical scholarship is largely an intellectual movement of the twentieth century. It presents a materialist parallel to Spengler's observations, discerning abstract sequences repeated in distinctive modalities. Instances of history repeating do not necessarily imply cycles like the turning of a wheel; later generations of scholars began to see that what repeats can be treated more analytically and that multiple processes can combine to weave a series of historical tapestries, each peculiar in its details.

Of all the macrohistorians of the pioneering period, Weber has survived best. In part this is because it took scholars most of the twentieth century to appreciate the scope of his work. His Protestant ethic argument was famous by the 1930s, but not until the 1950s and 1960s was there much recognition of his comparisons among the world religions, designed to show why Christianity, continuing certain patterns of ancient Judaism, gave rise to the dynamism of modern capitalism whereas the civilizations of Confucianism, Buddhism, Hinduism, and Islam did not. Weber's method of showing how multiple dimensions of social causality intertwine has also gradually become influential. Scholars almost everywhere now concede that the three dimensions of politics, economics, and culture must be taken into account in every analysis, although, as structuralist Marxists of the 1970s argued, one of them may be given primacy "in the last instance." There is also a negative side to Weber's preeminence. Peeling the layers of Weber's concepts has provided a field rich in scholarly niches, and the opportunities for developing Weberian ideas in one direction after another have given Weber the great classic reputation in sociological macrohistory. The very process of uncovering Weber as a multisided icon has made it difficult to see just what it takes to go beyond him. Only now, as we are becoming able to see Weber's full achievements, are we able as well to see his limits. These limits are not so much in his analytical apparatus as in his view of world history. For all his disagreement with Hegel and Marx, Weber shares with them a Eurocentric view: for all important purposes, the histories of what lies east of Palestine and Greece are taken as analytically static repetitions, while the only dynamic historical transformations are those of the West. In some of the essays collected here, I suggest how Weber's analytical tools can be used to take us beyond Weber's Eurocentrism.

The period of scholarship from the mid-1960s onward, continuing into the present, can appropriately be called the Golden Age of macrohistory. The crudities of the generation of pioneers have been surpassed; fruitful leads have been taken up, and a generation of scholars has built a set of new paradigms. Analytically, the principal style of this period is an interplay of Weberian and Marxian ideas. Although dogmatic loyalty to one or another of the classics exists in some scholarly camps, across the creative core of this Golden Age the approach has been pragmatic. The Marx/Weber blend has earned its prominence because key ideas from these traditions have proven fruitful in unanticipated directions.

The most striking accumulation of knowledge has taken place on Marx's favorite topic, revolution. By broadening the focus on economic causality, researchers have created a paradigm revolution in the theory of revolution. Barrington Moore and Arthur Stinchcombe, followed by Jeffrey Paige and Theda Skocpol, noted that the epoch of revolutions was not so much industrial capitalism but the preceding period of agrarian capitalism. Agricultural production for the market was the locus of class conflicts from the English revolution to the Vietnam revolution, and the work relations and property patterns of agricultural capitalism have set modern politics on transformative paths to the left, right, or center. Going further, Skocpol and Jack Goldstone have shown that class conflict alone is insufficient for revolution and must be accompanied by a fiscal crisis of the state as well as a split between state elites and property owners over the repair of state finances. Skocpol's work marks the paradigm shift to what might be called the state-breakdown theory of revolution. Skocpol and Goldstone elaborate a common model of state breakdown into alternative chains of causes further back, focusing respectively on geopolitical strains and population-induced price changes.

Another direction of research has continued a purer Marxian line. Here the premise of economic primacy has been preserved by shifting the arena of application from the traditional focus on a nation-state to a capitalist world system. This resuscitation of Marxism has been helped by a diplomatic marriage with the Annales school. Fernand Braudel's 1949 work, *The Mediterranean and the Mediterranean World in the Age of Philip II*, wove a grand historical tapestry from the patiently accumulated scholarship on the material conditions of everyday life and the flows of trade and finance. Braudel depicted the first of the European world-system hegemonies, the Spanish/Mediterranean world of the sixteenth century. Immanuel Wallerstein, in a multivolume series begun in 1974 and still in progress, theorized Braudel's world in a Marxian direction. Wallerstein has spearheaded a world-system school that describes expansions of the European world system around the globe through successive crises and transfers of hegemony. World-system scholarship has served as a central clearinghouse for the scholarship of the world, giving a theoretical resonance to work by regional specialists on topics ranging from the trade of the Malacca Straits to commodity chains in Latin America. Like the Annales school, the world-system camp is a strategic alliance of detailed and specialized histories. The Golden Age of grand historical vision has come about by combining the researches of a century of historians. The expanding population of universities and historians was the base for the Marxian revival in mid-twentieth-century scholarship, and world-system Marxism has provided the vehicle by which otherwise obscure specialties could join in a grand march toward paradigm revolution.

All active intellectual movements have their inner conflicts and unexpected lines of innovation. The world-system camp has not remained conceptually static. The earliest period, epitomized by André Gunder Frank's dependency theory, stressed that underdevelopment, the world-system equivalent of the immiseration of the proletariat, is created by and grows apace with the penetration of world capitalism. This assertion has been attacked on factual grounds, and dependency theory has retreated to the stance of dependent development, that although development can occur under capitalist dependency the gap between metropole and periphery continually widens. Moreover, there are cases of upward mobility in the world system, from periphery to semiperiphery into the core, sometimes (like the North American region that eventually became the United States) even into hegemony within the core. Given a structuralist interpretation, a capitalist world system is a set of positions that can be filled by different geographic regions. There is room only for a small hegemonic zone surrounded by a limited core region where capital, entrepreneurial innovation, and the most privileged workers are concentrated. There are always gaps in wealth between this region and the semiperiphery and periphery subservient to the capital flows and technical and labor relations shaped at the center. The structuralist version of world-system theory holds that social mobility may occur upward and downward within the system, but the relative privilege or subordination of the several zones always remains. As I write in the late 1990s, this remains a hypothesis without conclusive evidence to support or disprove it. On similar ground are suggestive theories about expansive and contractive waves of the world economy and the pattern of hegemonic wars and shifts in hegemony (Sanderson 1995, Arrighi 1994, and Chase-Dunn 1989 provide useful overviews). Even more speculative remains the old Marxian prediction recast in world-system guise, that the future holds a crisis of such proportions that the capitalist system itself will be transformed into world socialism.

For all these uncertainties, world-system research contributes energy and vividness to the activity of this Golden Age of macrohistory. It broadens and integrates the many strands of specialized and regional history, even if the conceptual model is not as well grounded as developments within the narrower compass of the state-breakdown model of revolutions.

Another direction of creative development from the world-system model has come from questioning its Eurocentric starting point. Wallerstein, like Marx, conceptually distinguished large regional structures that are static and incapable of self-driven economic growth (referred to as world empires) from capitalist world systems, balance-of-power regions among contending states that allow a maneuvering space in which capitalism becomes dominant. In practice, the latter category is European capitalism, while the structural stasis of world empires brackets the ancient Mediterranean and the non-Western world. Wallerstein's starting point for the capitalist world system is the same as Weber's, Europe in the sixteenth century. Other scholars have applied the model of a capitalist world system farther back in time or farther afield to zones of trade that were initially independent of the European world system. Janet Abu-Lughod depicts a superordinate world system of the Middle Ages that linked a series of world-system trading zones from China through Indonesia, thence to India, to the Arab world centered on Egypt, and finally to the European zone. Abu-Lughod reverses the analytical question, asking how we can explain not so much the rise of the West as the fall of the East. Braudel, too, in his later work, describes a series of separate world systems in the period 1400–1800, including not only those in Abu-Lughod's medieval network but also Turkey and Russia. Braudel suggests there was a rough parallel in economic level among all of them from before the industrial revolution until they were upset by a late European intrusion.

Other scholars have applied the logic of world-system models farther back in time. Chase-Dunn and Hall (1991, 1997) argue that even stateless tribes and the earliest states known through the archeological record never developed in isolation but relied on regional world systems with cores and peripheral trading zones. These efforts to extend the model backward in time have shifted the analytical emphasis of world-system research. Some consider the specifically capitalist character of world systems to have been unessential; others believe trade relations were the crucial feature rather than property, labor relations, or modes of production. What is seen increasingly as central in the model are its dynamic properties: the Kondratieff-like waves of expansion and contraction over periods of approximately one to two centuries, punctuated by hegemonic crises and shifts in core dominance. Gills and Frank (1991) have schematized such cycles from 3000 B.C. to the present. Generalizing world-system models to all times and places deemphasizes other questions, above all what causes changes in the character of economic and political systems as different as stateless kin-based tribal networks, agrarian production coerced by military elites, and the several kinds of capitalism. This recent phase of omni-world-system theorizing is bound to be supplemented by other models.

These controversies occupy the immediate foreground of attention. More significant for the trend of contemporary thought has been a permanent gestalt switch in the way we do macrohistory. The subject of analysis can no longer be taken as the isolated unit, whether it is the isolated tribe of structural-functionalist anthropology, the isolated civilizations of Spengler's era, or the nation-states beloved of national historians. These units exist in a world of like and unlike units, and their pattern of relations with each other makes each of them what they are. This is not to say that for analytical purposes we cannot focus on a single tribe, cultural region, or national state. But explanations of what happens inside these units, abstracted from their world-system context, are not merely incomplete; that might be of relatively small consequence, since explanations always abstract from a mass of detail in order to focus on what is most important. The world-system viewpoint makes a stronger theoretical claim: to ignore this external context is to miss the most important determinants of political and economic structures. In crucial respects, all social units are constituted from the outside in.

This gestalt switch to an outside-in causality, pioneered by contemporary neo-Marxism, has been paralleled on the neo-Weberian side. This is my way of referring to the primacy that has been given, during the contemporary Golden Age of macrohistory, to explaining states by their interstate relations, which is to say, by geopolitics. Here too there is a prehistory. The concept of geopolitics developed at the turn of the twentieth century in an atmosphere associated with nationalistic military policies. Halford Mackinder in Britain, Alfred Thayer Mahan in the United States, and Friedrich Ratzel and Karl Haushofer in Germany argued over the importance of land and sea power and about the location of strategic heartlands on the globe whose possession gave one state dominance over others. The topic of geopolitics acquired a bad odor with the rise of the Nazis and still more during postwar decolonization. But gradually the historical sociology of the state made it apparent that geopolitics could not be overlooked. The old confusion between recognizing geopolitical processes and advocating military aggrandizement has dissolved. Contemporary analytical geopolitics is more likely to emphasize the costs and liabilities of geopolitical overextension. The old geopoliticians tended to particularize their subject, as, for ex-

ample, Mackinder asserted that hegemony depended upon controlling a geographic heartland at the center of Eurasia. Contemporary geopolitics shows
instead that the expansion and contraction of state borders is determined by
the geopolitical advantages and disadvantages of neighboring states, wher-
ever they may lie on the globe.

One influence in the revival of geopolitical theory has been the world
history of William McNeill. McNeill's *The Rise of the West* (a deliberately
anti-Spenglerian title), published in 1963, represents the maturity of world
historiography, the point at which enough scholarship had been accumulated so that the history of the globe could be written in conventional narrative form without resort to metaphor. In comparison with the flamboyant
efforts of the generation of pioneers, McNeill's world history is that of the
professional historian, extending routine techniques and building on knowledge that had accumulated to the point where a world history was no longer
a miraculous glimpse of a conjectured past. This maturing of world historiography can be seen too in the contemporaneous appearance of other mon-
umental works on non-Western history: Joseph Needham's multivolume
Science and Civilization in China (1954–) and Marshall Hodgson's *The Venture
of Islam* (1974). McNeill succeeds in decentering world history from a European standpoint, giving pride of place to the process by which "ecumenes"
of intercivilizational contact have been widening gradually for several thou-
sand years. McNeill shows the significance of geopolitical relationships in
the expansion of empires, their clashes and crises. He presents a wealth of
examples from the far east to the far west of states that were invaded from
their marchlands, overextended their logistics to distant frontiers, or disintegrated in internal fragmentation. The military side of the state may have
been a passing concern in McNeill's early work, but it grows into explicit
importance in his later works, especially *The Pursuit of Power* (1982), which
documents the world history of the social organization of armaments and
their impact on society.

Another type of compendium fostered the modern scholarship on
geopolitics. This is the comprehensive historical atlas, such as the series
edited by McEvedy (1961, 1967, 1972, 1978, 1982). The publication of such
atlases is an indication of the synthesis now possible through the accumulation of historical scholarship. The endless complexities of state histories
come into visual focus when we can examine maps that show sequentially
how state territories changed. The difficulty of comprehending all this material in purely verbal form is one reason why older narrative histories either
fragmented into specialized studies or glossed over the general pattern by
reference to an unrealistically small number of great empires. Historical atlases published in the 1960s and 1970s marked the consolidation of information upon which more explicit theorizing could take place.

The geopolitically oriented or military-centered view of the state has become increasingly important through the convergence of three areas of scholarship: geopolitical theory, the state-breakdown theory of revolution, and the historical sociology of the modern state as an expanding apparatus of military organization and tax extraction.

From the 1960s through the 1980s, an analytical theory of geopolitics began to take shape. Arthur Stinchcombe, Kenneth Boulding, George Modelsky, Martin van Creveld, Paul Kennedy, and others developed a co-herent set of geopolitical principles.[1] In my synthesis, these comprise the dynamics of relative economic and material resources of contending states; geographic configurations affecting the number of potential enemies on their borders; and the logistical costs and strains of exercising the threat of force at varying distances from resource centers. In contrast to the older geopolit-ical theories of the pioneering age, contemporary geopolitical theory has be-come multidimensional: there is no single overriding cause of state expan-sion or decline but a combination of processes that can produce a wide range of outcomes. Although there remains a natural tendency to concentrate on the fate of the great hegemonic states, geopolitics applies analytically not merely to single states but to regions of state interrelations, and encompasses times and places where small states and balances of power exist as well as hegemonies and major wars. Since war and peace are analytically part of the same question, geopolitics implies a theory of peace as well as its opposite.

A second strand of research elevating the importance of geopolitics is the state-breakdown theory of revolutions, especially in Skocpol's formulation. The fiscal crisis at the heart of major revolutionary situations has most com-monly been brought about by the accumulation of debts through the largest item of state expense, the military. The previous links in the chain of causes are the geopolitical conditions that determine how much a state has been fighting, with what costs, what destruction, and what recouping of resources through military success. I have argued that the Skocpolian model of state breakdown meshes not only with geopolitical theory but also with a neo-Weberian theory of legitimacy. The state-breakdown theory is resolutely material, emphasizing hard-nosed military and economic conditions. There remains the realm of belief and emotion, the cultural and social realities that many sociologists argue are primary in human experience, a realm of lived meanings through which material conditions are filtered in affecting human action. In my argument, the theoretical circle is closed by taking up the Weberian point that the power-prestige of the state—the prestige deriving from its power—in the external arena, above all the experience of mobiliza-tion for war, is the most overwhelming of all social experiences. The legit-imacy of state rulers comes in considerable part from their people's sense of geopolitics as it affects their own state. Militarily expanding states and pres-tigious actors on the world scene increase their domestic legitimacy and even help create it out of whole cloth. Conversely, states in geopolitical straits not only descend the slope toward fiscal crisis and state breakdown but also follow an emotional devolution that brings about delegitimation. Geopolitics leads to revolution by both material and cultural paths.

A third strand of contemporary research has shown that the modern state developed primarily through the ramifications of its military organization. Historians and social scientists have documented the "military revolution," the huge increase in scale of armies that began in the sixteenth and seventeenth centuries. In its train came organizational changes: weapons were increasingly supplied centrally by the state instead of through local provision; logistics trains became larger and more expensive; armies converted to close-order drill and bureaucratic regimentation. Two summary works may be singled out: Michael Mann's *The Sources of Social Power* (two volumes thus far, 1986 and 1993), shows how prominently military spending, along with debts incurred from previous wars, has loomed in the budgets of modern states. Mann goes on to show that increases in the scale of military expense, the first at the time of the military revolution and the second around the Napoleonic Wars, successively motivated the penetration of the state into civil society: in part to secure funding, in part to mobilize economic resources and military manpower. This distinctively modern penetration of society by the state has proven to be a two-edged sword: it has created national identities and loyalties, but it has also mobilized classes to participate with the full weight of their numbers in an overarching arena and to struggle for political representation and other concessions in response to fiscal demands. Mann plays a neo-Weberian trump card on the Marxist theory of class mobilization: in the state-centered model, the development of the state through the expansion of its own specific resource, the organization of military power, determines whether classes can be mobilized at all as political and cultural actors. The same process of state penetration into society simultaneously mobilizes nationalist movements. We could add here another Weberian point: once the military-instigated penetration of society has occurred, processes of both bureaucratization and interest mobilization are set in motion; the organizational resources of the modern state now can be used for purposes far removed from the original military ones, ranging from the creation of the welfare state to experiments in socialism or cultural reform.

The other modern classic summarizing the military-centered theory of state development is Charles Tilly's *Coercion, Capital, and European States, A.D. 990–1990*. Marshaling the wealth of scholarship now available, Tilly shows how the pathways of states diverged as they underwent the military revolution. Depending upon which kinds of economic organization were in range of their forces, states relied on extracting money from urban merchants or from the conquest of agrarian territories. The availability of these bases determined the difficulty of the fiscal task and the kinds of opposition rulers faced in raising funds for their armies. As the large number of small medieval states was winnowed down to a few through geopolitical processes, modern states crystallized into a range of democratic and autocratic polities, shaped by their differing fiscal bases. The historical pathways of state military organization mesh with their external geopolitical experiences and their internal struggles over taxation and representation. The result was to instigate revolutions and to shape the constitution of the various kinds of modern states.

The areas of scholarship I have just reviewed are prime evidence for my claim that we are living in the Golden Age of macrohistory. Not all problems have been solved, but no period of creative work ever solves all its problems—to do so would bring innovation to a standstill, and creative scholars always generate new issues as they go along. What we can say is that the range and depth of our vision of world history has permanently widened. I believe we have the firm outlines of some important analytical tools—the state-breakdown theory of revolutions, the world-system gestalt in the most generic sense of looking for causal processes from the outside in, the elements of geopolitical processes, the military-resource trajectory of the development of the modern state. I have given pride of place to political and economic topics of macrohistorical sociology because these topics have seen the most sustained research and the most cumulative theorizing. I must neglect, in a discussion of this scale, many other areas in which the maturing of modern social history has reached a critical mass, or at least passed the threshold into considerable sophistication. Let me mention just a few of the advances that have been made: in the historical study of the family, the Laslett school and the comparative works of Jack Goody; in the history of civilizing manners, the works of Norbert Elias, Stephen Mennell, and Johan Goudsblom; in the macrohistory of diseases and the environment, the works of McNeill and Alfred Crosby; in the macrohistory of art, the works of Arnold Hauser and André Malraux. Other work proceeds apace in the history of gender, sexualities, and material culture. There is every indication that the Golden Age of macrohistory is continuing. Approaches pioneered for European societies are just now being used in depth elsewhere (such as Eiko Ikegami's work on the civilizing process in Japan). Durkheim's sociological microscope on becoming a macroscope has accumulated a first and second round of discoveries; another round surely lies ahead.

Critics of Macrohistory

Having viewed one side of the twentieth century's love affair with macrohistory, let us turn now to the opposing side. Alongside the development of world-encompassing and analytically illuminating history there has been a persistent countertheme attacking its misuses and denouncing its epistemology. Here too we can schematize the account into two waves, which correspond to the pioneering generation of macrohistorians and to the late-twentieth-century wave of sophisticated reflexivity.

In the 1930s and 1940s, grand historical visions were repudiated on many grounds. Spengler's vague poetic metaphors and Toynbee's religious pronouncements were taken as the sort of flaws that are inevitable in works of pretentious scope. Karl Popper, in revulsion to Nazism and Soviet totalitarianism, claimed that what his idiosyncratic terminology labeled the "historicist" mentality (i.e., the search for historical laws) was at the root of antidemocratic movements. In a narrower professional sphere, anthropologists reacted against the earlier generation that had approached ethnographic materials in a comparative and historical light, construing items of culture against the template of what kind of "survival" they represented from the earlier track of evolutionary development. In contrast, the structural-functional program held that an entire society must be studied in depth as a kind of living organism, which would reveal how institutions meshed with one another as an integrated system operating in the present.

The first wave of objections to macrohistory proved ephemeral, and a newer generation of historians and comparative sociologists began to publish during what I have referred to as the Golden Age. On the anthropological side, the tide turned again as well. Beginning in 1949, and with increasing prominence in a series of works in the 1950s and 1960s, Claude Lévi-Strauss took a new approach to writing the history of "peoples without histories"—that is, tribal societies without written records and hence without the explicit consciousness of a historical frame of reference. Lévi-Strauss proposed to read their implicit historical memory by cracking the symbolic code in which mythologies are recollected. The method led him to reconstruct events of epoch-making importance such as the practice of cooking, which differentiates humans from the animals that they eat. Lévi-Strauss's *Mythologiques* parallels his earlier work on the structural patterns of kinship, in which he attempted to reconstruct the pattern of a kinship revolution by which some family lineages constituted themselves as an elite, breaking with primitive reciprocity and leading to the stratification of the state. Lévi-Strauss's structuralism had an ambiguous relation to history. Its affinities to structural functionalism and to other static structuralist theories like Chomskyian linguistics gave the impression that it too dealt with unchanging structural relationships. At the same time, he depicted structures as dynamic relations, systems in disequilibrium, which both motivated historical changes and left symbolic residues by which we can memorialize them. Lévi-Straussian structures are both historical and suprahistorical in much the same way that language is.

Via this ambiguity, the receding wave of enthusiasm for structuralism flowed directly into a wave of poststructuralism. Lévi-Strauss had shown no reliable way either to decode symbolic history or to correlate symbols in a straightforward Durkheimian way with social structures. In the French intellectual world, the failure of Lévi-Strauss's project was taken as a warrant for historicizing all the codes. The notion was retained that we live in a world structured by codes and that we see the world only through the lenses of our codes. But what we see through them is shifting and unreliable, like eyeglasses made of flowing water.

The attack on macrohistory, as well as on substantive sociological theorizing of wide analytical scope, has been fed by several streams: the influence of later generations of phenomenological philosophy; the extension of Hegelian reflexivity in Michel Foucault's expansion of the history of psychiatry contextualizing and relativizing Freud; the 1960s generation combining mind-blowing psychedelic "cultural revolution" with political radicalism tied no longer to industrial workers but to movements of student intellectuals; the anti-Westernism of ethnic insurgencies; and feminist-intellectual rebellion against the dominance of male textual canons. Together these have constituted a formidable alliance of political and intellectual interests. There is also an implicit rivalry inside the world of scholars, between specialists concerned with their own niches and synthesizers drawing specialized research into broader statements.

A common denominator of this contemporary attack on macrohistory is the priority of contextuality and particularism. This antihistorical consciousness nevertheless arises from the same circumstances as its opposite. Today's antihistorians arise from a surfeit of history. Postmodernist thinking might perhaps be described as a kind of vomiting up of history, a choking fit that began in disillusionment with Marxism and to some extent with Freudianism, which in certain fashionable circles had been considered the only Grand Narratives worth knowing about.

Both the macrohistorians of the current Golden Age and the anti–grand historians who are their contemporaries are products of a rising tide of consciousness of our location within history. All of us, those who write history and those who write against it, exist and think within history. A future intellectual history will doubtless be written about the late twentieth century, just as it is about everything else. Our ideas, our very language, are part of history. There is no standard outside of history by which anything can be judged. Does this recognition weigh in favor of macrohistorians or condemn them? If there is no escape from the prison of contextuality, what follows?

Theory and Analytical Particularism

Let us bring the two positions into close confrontation. I have emphasized that the Golden Age of macrohistory in which we are living rests upon the accumulation of scholarly work by generations of historians. In today's fashionable philosophies, is this not warrant for dismissing macrohistory as nothing but naive empiricism? My response would be simply that we are intellectually constituted by a community of thousands of historians and social scientists who have been working for several centuries, and whose accumulated archives have been tapped by McNeill, Wallerstein, Mann, Tilly, and others, just as the spottier archives were tapped years ago by Weber and Toynbee. It is a polemical simplification to suppose that attending to empirical research makes one oblivious to theoretical activity. It is equally arbitrary to assume that the development of theoretical interpretations proceeds by reference to nothing but other ideas, much less by mysterious ruptures in the history of consciousness. In the social reality of the intellectual world, today's hyper-reflexive philosophies and advocates of narrow contextuality are products of the same accumulation of historical archives as the macrohistorians. The only difference is that one group specializes in the history of intellectual disciplines, literary criticism, and linguistics, whereas the other has drawn upon the histories of economies, polities, and religions.

The answer to conceptual embeddedness in historical contexts is not less theory, but more. Falling back on local contextuality is often a way of begging questions, leaving us not with greater sophistication but with implicit dependence upon unexamined theories encoded in the very language one uses. All history is theory-laden. Any effort to disguise this fact results in bad history and bad theory.

There is no such thing as purely narrative history. It is impossible to recount particulars without reference to general concepts. Nouns and verbs contain implicit generalizations ("another one of *those* again"). Even proper names are not as particularistic as they might seem, for they pick out some entity assumed to have enduring contours over time and contain an implicit theory of what holds that "thing" together: an innocuous reference to "France" or to "Paris" is laden with assumptions. To impose a name, whether abstract or particular, is to impose a scheme of what hangs together and what is separated from what. By this route, rhetorical devices become reified, and multidimensional processes are construed as unitary. And narrative is always selection. From the various things that could be told, some are focused upon as significant, and their sequence implies what is supposed to cause what consequences.

Let us take an example from what is usually regarded as the most mindlessly event-driven particularistic narrative, traditional military-diplomatic history: "Napoleon marched his battle-hardened veterans all day, surprising the Austrians in the late afternoon with 6,000 men. By the end of the battle, Austrian control of Italy had been lost." This has the sound of a narrative in which history is made by heroic individuals, but its effects are achieved by abstracting the individual from the organizational context. It assumes a world in which troops are organized into disciplined armies in such a fashion that a commander can exercise centralized control over rapid organizational response. It further assumes a theory of combat, such that large numbers of troops amassed on certain kinds of terrain win victories, previous combat experience makes troops more capable of such maneuvers, and the speed and timing of troop movements determine battlefield outcomes. These assumptions may or may not be generally true; there now exists an extensive military sociology that explains the social and historical conditions under which such things do or do not come about. Napoleon's organizational preconditions would not have existed at the time of the Gauls, and they would fail again in several particulars by World War I. The narrative also assumes a theory of the state, in which decisions are driven straightforwardly by military outcomes. Again this may be true under certain conditions, but only if we specify the organizational context—victory by Visigothic armies in 410 did not result in a Visigothic empire taking control of Italy, unlike the way Napoleon's victory in 1800 resulted in building a French empire.

The extent to which the narrated sequence of events makes a coherent story—an adequate explanation—cannot be judged merely by examining one single narrative. My point is not that narrative histories of the Napoleonic type are inherently wrong, but that we only know why and to what extent they are right in the light of our more general theoretical knowledge. Such knowledge does not come out of thin air. It comes in part from having studied a wide enough range of other histories that we can tell what the central conditions are and which are local concomitants with no important effect on the particular outcome. What sociological theory does is to cumulate what we have learned from history.

Specialized, locally contextual histories are not immune to theory. Their atheoretical assertions mean that the theories they implicitly assume are only those old enough to have passed into common assumptions. As we shall see in Chapters 4 and 5, histories of democracy in particular are vitiated by the unconscious acceptance of popular ideological categories. Sociological macrohistorians have the advantage of being able to check whether their models of large-scale processes in time and space are coherent with what we have learned from other areas of sociological research. The battlefield processes mentioned above are more securely understood to the extent that we find them consistent with analysis of organizations and their breakdowns, face-to-face violence, and emotional solidarity within groups. The sociologist devoted to exposing the dynamics that underlie historical narratives generates more confidence that she or he is on the right track to the extent that she or he can cross-integrate historical patterns with other parts of sociology.

The end product need not be theory in itself. In the light of such cumulation of sociological knowledge via explicit theory, we are better able to produce new histories. These are not necessarily new comparisons or new cases (which is fortunate, since the amount of history is finite and the distinct cases of macrophenomena are soon exhausted), but studies that select new facets of our previously studied narratives for analysis with greater depth and fresh insight. (For instance, there is considerable overlap among the cases studied by Moore 1966, Skocpol 1979, Goldstone 1991, and Downing 1992.) It is an old story that theory and research recycle through each other, but true nevertheless, and it is indispensable advice even when fashionable metatheories hold that one or the other pole is irreducibly autonomous. When history or general theory goes its own way without the other, it is really shadowed by what it has vaguely and unconsciously accepted from the other. The result is bad history and bad theory.

Overview

This book comprises a collection of my own efforts to practice macrohistory in the full consciousness that it is a theoretical task and that theories always build incrementally and critically upon their predecessors. These are essays, not treatises. I have not attempted to review the literature and to give each rival position its due, even if that were possible. Instead, I sketch in broad strokes, perhaps in overbold outline, some further directions of argument.

The first chapter surveys how far we have come in the state-centered theory of revolution and the related topic of ideologies—that is, what the Golden Age has done with the archetypal Marxian concerns.

The following three chapters trace some implications of the geopolitical perspective of viewing states and societies from the outside in. The state-centered theory, linked to the geopolitical theory of military vicissitudes, implies that revolutions are in principle predictable from geopolitical conditions. Chapter 2 discusses the collapse of the Soviet Empire and the revolutions of the Communist bloc at the turn the 1990s. It is also a retrospective discussion of the geopolitical theory by which I predicted the breakup of the Soviet Union at a time when the conventional wisdom was sharply to the contrary. Chapter 3 combines geopolitical principles with the Weberian theme that legitimacy is shaped by the power-prestige of states. Extending this principle, we can say that the legitimacy not only of rulers is affected, but also the legitimacy of dominant ethnic groups. The essay goes on to argue that ethnicity is far from primordial but is constituted by the path of history, which can either split off smaller ethnic identities (which I refer to metaphorically as "Balkanization") or amalgamate them into a larger ethnonational identity (emblematically, "Americanization"). Which direction is taken is crucially influenced by whether the geopolitical condition of the state is declining or expanding.

Chapter 4 presents a theory of democratization. It argues that most such theories are vitiated by the selective slicing up of history into expanses of time and terrain that are teleologically biased, and by smuggling assumptions of what is to be proven into their very units of analysis. Democratization cannot be reduced to a unidimensional process because it in fact comprises two distinct processes—the mobilization of people into the political franchise, and the shaping of collegial structures of shared power within which mobilization might occur. Collegially shared power is not a phenomenon of modernization, although the widening franchise is. Collegial structures have typically been constituted by geopolitical processes that favor permanent federations and alliances rather than centralized states. I attempt to demonstrate this by a series of comparisons ranging across the medieval papacy, the medieval German Empire, and the formation of the United States of America. I go on to suggest some applications of geopolitical theory to the future prospects for collegial democracy in the former Soviet bloc.

Chapter 5 further explores the theme that the received concepts of modernization distort the phenomenon by forcing a multidimensional process into a single dimension of development. An iconoclastic illustration is offered: widely accepted explanations of German society as culturally unmodern and antidemocratic are historically and analytically inaccurate. The underlying theory assumes that economic and social modernization and political democracy all come in the same package. I argue instead there are four distinct dimensions of modernization. Once these are recognized, Germany turns out to have led modernization on several key dimensions (notably religious secularization and organizational bureaucratization) on which Britain and the United States lagged. Further, when we disaggregate the dimension of democracy into subcomponents of collegially shared power and extent of the franchise, Germany's path of political change does not differ so widely from that of other leading modernizers. A disturbing implication is that an explanation for the Nazis and the Holocaust cannot be found in a cultural antimodernization unique to Germany, but must be attributed to processes that under other names can affect us all.

The essays up to this point focus on the state-centered theory of change and its ramifications. The last two essays, Chapters 6 and 7, concern the macrohistory of economic change in world perspective. Together, the two groups of essays depict the two master causes of macrohistorical change: geopolitics and markets. Obviously, these are not the only causes of change operating in a multicausal world, but they are key analytical organizing devices around which much of the rest is shaped.

If you like, Chapter 6, "Market Dynamics as the Engine of Historical

Change," can be treated as a *jeu d'esprit*, an intellectual parlor game. The game is to see just how much of today's historical sociology can fill in the blanks in the Marx-Engels theory of history as a series of developments and crises in modes of production. Here I argue that the leading sector is not production per se but market structures, and that market dynamics have driven societal growth and crises through a series of political-economic systems: first, kinship markets that exchanged sexual property for political alliances; second, slave markets in which military slave-takers were the main producers of "goods"; third, agrarian-coercive markets; most recently, modern capitalist markets, which is to say, omnipenetrating market dynamics characterized by pyramiding superordinate markets trading on the means of exchange. In Chapter 7 I reduce the four types to three by subsuming the Marxian slave economy into the larger category of agrarian-coercive markets.

If Chapter 6 is an effort to salvage what is left of Marx, Chapter 7, "An Asian Route to Capitalism," attempts the same for Weber's theory of the religious origins of capitalism. It focuses on the transition from agrarian-coercive economies to the self-sustaining dynamic of modern capitalist growth. My argument is that the institutional breakout from agrarian-coercive structures took place in a small sector of which the key component was a religious economy led by the entrepreneurship of monastic corporations. Here I build on Weberian argument but shift the emphasis from religious cultures to the institutional ingredients of capitalism. In this chapter I also part company with Weber's view that capitalism originated only in the Judeo-Christian West. It took a parallel pathway through Buddhist institutions, adumbrated in medieval China and breaking through in the transition to the Tokugawa era in Japan.

There are two appendices. Appendix A is designed to show that the gap is not so wide between abstract theoretical principles and the endless complexities of real history. Using a computer simulation of some simple points of the neo-Weberian theory of the state, it shows that when abstract processes are allowed to cumulate and feed back upon themselves, many different patterns of long-term history can be generated by the same theoretical assumptions. What varies are only quantitative differences at the starting points. As chaos theorists say, with a little exaggeration, a butterfly in the Bermuda Triangle can lead to tidal waves in India—not because there are no abstract causal processes but precisely because of the working out of these processes. In some sense, this illustrates the old Marxian theme of the "transformation of quantity into quality." Appendix B summarizes a long-buried work by Franz Borkenau on what might be called the geopolitics of languages, bolstering my argument in Chapter 3.

My one apology for this book is the omission of historical maps. Given the importance of geopolitics for so many parts of my argument on causality "from the outside in," it would be highly desirable to see in graphic form what is written about here. Much of my initial formulation of these essays came from poring over historical atlases until a gestalt crystallized otherwise messy fluctuations into a new way of theorizing the very units of sociological analysis. I have reluctantly left out illustrative maps here because black-and-white reproductions convey more of the messy detail than the crisp new gestalt. The ideal publication on macrohistory would contain lavish, full-color historical maps keyed to highlight the dimensions of social structure across the landscape. I urge the reader to read this book while keeping at hand a good historical atlas, such as the series by McEvedy, the *Anchor Atlas of World History*, or the large volume by Barraclough.

Let Fernand Braudel have the last word on the relation between the deeper currents of abstract theory charted by macrohistory and the details that fill the eyes of contemporaries in the form of

l'histoire événementielle, the history of events: surface disturbances, crests of foam that the tides of history carry on their strong backs. A history of brief, rapid, nervous fluctuations, by definition ultra-sensitive; the least tremor sets all the antennae quivering. But as such it is the most exciting of all, the richest in human interest, and also the most dangerous. We must learn to distrust this history with its still burning passions, as it was felt, described, and lived by contemporaries whose lives were as short and as short-sighted as ours. . . . A dangerous world, but one whose spells and enchantments we shall have exorcised by making sure first to chart those underlying currents, often noiseless, whose direction can only be discerned over long periods of time. Resounding events are often only momentary outbursts, surface manifestations of these larger movements and explicable only in terms of them. (Braudel 1972: 21, Preface to the first ed.)

Deeper currents, for today's sociological macrohistorians, are analytically deep, not merely descriptively broad. Metaphor should not lead us to conclude that they are far beneath the surface, but rather that they mesh together to generate the endless array of patterns that are what we mean by the surface of events.

CHAPTER I

Maturation of the State-Centered Theory of Revolution and Ideology

ONCE UPON A TIME we had a theory of revolution and ideology. The basic outlines of the theory were set by Marx and Engels, but the general frame of analysis was widely accepted. Revolutions were class conflicts. A privileged class faced increasing pressure from a discontented rising class. The revolutionary transfer of power eventually broke through the blockage from above, setting off a period of social change. The process was synchronized with a succession of ideological hegemonies. The ruling ideas were those of the ruling elite; as class challengers emerged, their different consciousness acted as a barometer as well as a mobilizer for the coming revolution.

For Marxists, the class actors in the drama were the owners of the means of production versus the suppliers of labor power and the owners of rival means of production. Non-Marxists also made use of the scheme. The English and French revolutions were typically attributed to the "rise of the bourgeoisie," or sometimes to the "rise of the gentry." The wave of nineteenth-century European revolutions and many of the "modernizing" revolutions of the twentieth century were also described as "bourgeois revolutions," and the resulting institutions and ideologies were typically referred to as "bourgeois" or "middle-class" democracy.

The general model of rising and falling classes came loose from an economic basis while preserving its structural features. In U.S. sociology since the time of Pitirim Sorokin in the 1920s, the emphasis shifted to the mobility of individuals. Revolutions were attributed to the blockage of mobility by persons of talent and ambition, while open mobility according to merit was regarded as the safety valve that relieved pressure and prevented revolutionary conditions from occurring. The study of social mobility (later called "status attainment") that dominated sociological research up through the 1960s was in large part the result of accepting the underlying model that the blockage of "rising social classes" causes revolutions, together with a preference for piecemeal and gradual reform that mobility was believed to represent.

The theory of ideology too was modified but stayed within the framework of the original Marxian/Hegelian model. There was nothing explicitly Marxist about Crane Brinton's (1938) natural history of the great revolutions, but the ideological desertion of the old regime by the intellectuals was taken as the first harbinger of upheaval. Karl Mannheim's famous theory of ideology was an extension of the Marxian model that incorporated the utopian ideology of the revolutionaries themselves. Mannheim aimed to step outside of the historical process by locating a free-floating group of intellectuals who could play the role of liberal social engineers; these in turn needed a social base—if outside the class structure—and Mannheim's later work turned to the sociology of education and the sociology of intellectual communities themselves. C. Wright Mills's work in the 1950s and Alvin Gouldner's work on ideology in the 1970s followed a Mannheimian line. In Gouldner's (1976) studies on what he called "the dark side of the dialectic," Marxism was tagged as the ideology of the intellectuals that surreptitiously exalted their indispensability in the processes of revolution and postrevolutionary rule. Gouldner made explicit what was implicitly claimed by the student-based "New Left" of the 1960s: that education and the mass media rather than old class conflicts were the route to power; in short, that the ideology-producing institutions were the center of the political dynamic.

Against this theme, mainstream Marxians continued to see the ideological thrust of revolutions as hinging on class culture. Dispute went on between the line descending from Antonio Gramsci and that descending from Georg Lukacs. The Gramscian line was that the rulers hold ideological hegemony and their control of the media of culture prevents revolutionary mobilization. The Lukacians, in contrast, stressed the autonomous class culture of the working class (as in E. P. Thompson's famous work on the English working class) and thus argued for at least a potential basis for revolt. This view was undermined when Craig Calhoun (1982) demonstrated that the rebellious English workers in Marx's day were not from the factories but from the dying traditional handcrafts and that their ideology was a conservative return to the past. The postmodernism popular today is in effect the triumph of an extremely pessimistic version of the Gramscian line: that the hyperactive cultural marketplace of late capitalism makes revolution and its ideology not only impossible but meaningless.

In recent decades, the old class-conflict paradigm of revolution has broken down, although vestiges of it remain in current thinking about ideology, rather like a flywheel spinning after the drive shaft has broken off. Meanwhile a new theory of revolution has developed based on the wealth of historical data now available. We know a great deal more than our predecessors about the actual participation of social classes in revolutionary politics, and we have a picture of state finance, military structures, economic development, and population patterns that was unavailable in the time of Marx or even of Mannheim and Brinton. And in becoming much less Europe-centered we pay attention to the crises of China, Japan, and Turkey and to what they had in common with Western revolutions as well as what was distinctive. This maturation of comparative historical sociology is the key to our increasing sophistication in the theory of revolution.

The turning point was Barrington Moore's *Social Origins of Dictatorship and Democracy* (1966). In some ways this work might be regarded as the last shot of the old theory, since Moore emphasizes class conflict as a driving force; but now it is the conflicts that emerge from the property systems of capitalist agriculture rather than from industry. Peasant revolts become more central, and so do the interests of government bureaucrats. From here it is only a step to Theda Skocpol's *States and Social Revolutions* (1979). Skocpol represents the full-fledged revolution in the theory of revolutions: for now the state, with its military and fiscal interests, is seen as the central actor and the location of crisis.

By the turn of the 1990s, the new state-centered theory of revolutions was visibly maturing. Jack Goldstone's *Revolution and Rebellion in the Early Modern World* (1991) is an intellectual descendant of Skocpol's theory; Goldstone is a former student of Skocpol's, just as Skocpol in turn was a student of Moore's. Goldstone's work is the state of the art; in the sophistication of its model and in the thorough use of historical materials and comparisons it is surely the best work on revolutions yet produced. This is no idiosyncratic development, for the state-centered theory has been advancing on a broad front. Robert Wuthnow's *Communities of Discourse* (1989) makes an excellent companion to Goldstone, for it too is the state of the art, the best book yet written on the theory of ideology. Wuthnow too draws on the richness of historical materials and the strategy of comparisons to isolate causes; and he too is an heir to the Skocpolian theoretical revolution. Examining these works together, we can see how far we have come.

Goldstone and the Theory of State Breakdown

The original title of Goldstone's manuscript was "State Breakdown in the Early Modern World," which captured the main theme of the new theory better than the published title. Revolutions happen because there is a breakdown from above, not because of insurgence from below. No matter how deprived popular groups are, they are unable to overthrow the state as long as the elites and their military apparatus of repression hold together. Other variants on the social psychology of rebellion are equally impotent in the absence of state breakdown; rising expectations will not do the job either. This point has become one of the solidest findings of the social sciences; it is bolstered for instance by Tilly's (1978) research, which shows that rebellious mobilization will go as far intra-elite conflict and the demobilization of the repressive resources of the state let it.

Goldstone describes three components of state breakdown: (1) fiscal strain, the inability of the state to pay its own functionaries and above all its soldiers; (2) elite conflict, internecine warfare that splits the rulers and paralyzes their ability to act; and (3) popular revolt, which coincides with the other two processes and leads to the destruction of the state and the formation of new centers of power. All three must be present for a full-scale state breakdown and thus for a successful revolution.

This model brings together processes that have been researched separately. One cannot say that popular grievances have nothing to do with revolution; they are one of the factors that flow into popular revolts, along with the conditions spelled out in resource mobilization theory. Similarly, conflicts within the elite have been noted since Marx's *Eighteenth Brumaire*. Much of the revisionist research of the past few decades, documenting the high degree of internal splits within the elites (for instance in the English and French revolutions) has concluded that class conflict had nothing to do with revolutions, since the same classes were represented on both sides. Goldstone transforms this weakness of the old class-conflict theory into a feature of the breakdown theory: a situation becomes revolutionary precisely because structural conditions split the elite into warring factions. Goldstone further shows that the old "pressure-cooker" theory of blocked mobility is wrong; it is precisely in periods of high social mobility that intra-elite conflict is highest.

The core of Goldstone's model is essentially the core of Skocpol's theory. Skocpol too presented a theory of state breakdown based on a combination of fiscal/administrative crisis of the state, conflicts within the ruling elite, and popular revolt. Skocpol specified the antecedents and character of these three components somewhat differently than Goldstone. According to her theory, the source of fiscal/administrative crisis was military strain resulting from geopolitical conditions. The pattern jumps out from her cases, the French revolution following on the war debts of the American wars, and the Russian and Chinese revolutions in the aftermath of the world wars of the twentieth century. Following Barrington Moore, Skocpol's prime example of an intra-elite conflict was that between rural landowners and state bureaucrats, essentially a battle over who was to be taxed to pay the expenses of the state. Skocpol's popular revolts were those of peasants; here again she follows Moore, arguing that the patterns of class relations within capitalist agriculture determine how the peasantry are mobilized and how the elites respond.

Goldstone changes not the core of the theory but the antecedents of the three components of crisis. Goldstone demonstrates that in the early modern period population growth was responsible for all three aspects of breakdown. (1) In a predominantly agricultural economy, when population grows faster than cultivation the price of food and most other staple goods increases. This price increase puts great pressures on state budgets, above all because the state needs to feed its army; this fiscal strain is typically exacerbated because the size of armies jumps enormously (the so-called "military revolution") as population growth makes available more soldiers for contemporary arms races. The fiscal crisis hits full bore if the state has tied its taxation policies to agricultural output, since it is taxing the sector where relative resources are shrinking in real terms.

(2) Population growth generates conflict within the elite, again via several mutually reinforcing pathways. Rising prices make it more expensive for elites to support themselves and their dependents. At the same time, elite families are bigger, and there are more daughters to be dowried and married off, more sons seeking preferment in military or government posts. And rising prices create profits for some families situated in the most advantageous positions in production or trade, so there are more families aspiring to enter the elite; their successful mobility intensifies the competition among those already there.

(3) Population growth means there are more peasants dividing the soil, hence increasing the numbers driven into poverty or into the nonagricultural labor force. The wages of urban workers drop because there is a labor glut. Their real income drops still further because of rising prices. Thus real grievances mount and with them the incidence of popular revolt. Notice, incidentally, that Goldstone finds a real immiseration of the workers that Marx projected for the final crisis of capitalism. Only Goldstone finds it earlier, in the previous round of revolution and in the workers' movements of the 1820s that Marx knew from his youth.

Skocpol and Goldstone provide variants on the same model although disagree on some points. Goldstone criticizes Skocpol's military emphasis as a misinterpretation of the evidence. He points out that the breakdown of the French state in 1789 came six years after the American Revolutionary War against England, a war in which France was victorious. The six years of war, 1778–83, were preceded by a period of peace dating back to 1763; moreover the war was much less expensive than the Seven Years War of 1756–63. The French state had been in a far worse fiscal situation as the result of the continuous wars under Louis XIV during the period 1689–1714, yet there was no breakdown and no revolution. The difference, Goldstone argues, is that Louis XIV and his successors benefited from a period in which population pressure had ceased, allowing the state's real income to catch up and the war debts to be liquidated. After 1750, though, population surged to new heights; and the resulting concatenation of problems is what made the smaller military burden into the catalyst of state breakdown. Goldstone makes a similar critique of the place of the Scottish war in 1637–39 in precipitating England's state crisis and leading to the civil war.

Goldstone's population-driven model and the geopolitical strain model need not be construed as opposites, however. As Goldstone himself stresses, the key factor in breakdown is a strained structural relationship between state obligations and state resources, not population growth per se. To portray Goldstone's model as merely neo-Malthusian would be to caricature it. Goldstone notes that the 1868 Meiji Restoration in Japan was a full-fledged state breakdown, with revolutionary consequences for the structure of Japanese society. But the Japanese population had been stable for a century previous; how then did the Japanese state get into the fiscal crisis that led to the breakdown? In this case, the Japanese elites drew their income in kind rather than in cash; hence the falling price of rice with productivity growth and population stability had similar effects as in the European crises: government budgetary crisis, elite distress and infighting, pressures leading to popular rebellions. It is the structural relationships that matter, not population growth per se.

By the same logic, the key is the balance between military costs and government resource-extracting capability rather than the absolute level of either. In the case of late-eighteenth-century France, war debts, together with costs of the standing army, had been building up for 40 years. By the 1780s the treasury was spending most of its income merely to service the debts of earlier wars (Goldstone 1991: 211). The American war, though not particularly costly, came at just the wrong time. One could show a similar pattern of cumulative military debts owed by the English crown in the early 1600s, and indeed in the accumulation of military debts in the crises of the Ottomans and of various Chinese dynasties. Given that the largest portion of state budgets for premodern states everywhere was devoted to current or past military expenses (documented in Mann 1986), the size of military expenses would always determine one side of Goldstone's balance between state obligations and resources.

There are also more extreme cases in which the state collapses, not merely from long-term military expenditure but because the military apparatus breaks apart by defeat in war. Here we find the several Russian and Chinese revolutions of the twentieth century and also the Turkish revolution of 1920–22. Goldstone makes a pathbreaking analysis of the recurrent state breakdowns of the Ottoman Empire between 1590 and 1660 during periods of strain resulting from population growth and the Ottoman recovery after 1660 when population leveled off. Because of where he stops the story, he leaves out the long-term decline in Ottoman territory under geopolitical pressures culminating at the turn of the twentieth century. Kemal Ataturk's nationalist revolution was a direct result of the Ottoman defeat in World War I, at the end of a series of severe territorial losses. With the British army holding the sultan as a puppet in Constantinople and Greek armies invading the coast of Asia Minor, the army command revolted in the Anatolian interior, threw off the delegitimated Muslim rule, and carried out a secularizing revolution. Revolutions of this sort fit the model of geopolitical strain directly; so does the 1989–91 collapse of the Soviet Empire amid the strains of an expensive arms race under conditions of geopolitical disadvantage (see Chapter 2).

The point is not that we have two rival theories of revolution, but that there is a core model of state breakdown—fiscal/administrative strain, elite conflict, popular revolt—plus a number of pathways leading toward crisis conditions in these factors. Population growth can sometimes play a very large role in building up crisis; at other times geopolitical conditions can have overwhelming effects. In many cases, population and geopolitics interact. This is especially likely in premodern states, where the state budget is overwhelmingly military, population is vulnerable to shifts in mortality from disease, and the economy is not very flexible in its ability to absorb population growth.

This gives us another reason to view Goldstone's work as an extension of a core model of state breakdown that can be activated in various ways. If we insist on the population/resource strain dynamic, Goldstone's model is limited to a particular historical period. The "early modern state" is an in-between kind in which there is a widespread market economy for agricultural products, so that cash prices can affect state budgets; at the same time the early modern state has a weak central bureaucracy, big enough to be expensive but too inefficient to be able to extract what it needs without giving in to the interests of the landed elites. In addition, mortality drives large population swings when diseases are spread through long-distance social networks that do not have the medical technology to control them. What happens as the state and economy further modernize? Goldstone himself makes the point that the population/resource dynamic ended when states entered a strongly growing capitalist economy. England in the 1820s was still struggling with the multiplying effects of population growth, but by the 1830s the institutions of a growing capitalism were able to absorb an even more rapidly swelling population.

If we construe it strictly, under Goldstone's model revolutions are possible only in those parts of the world where capitalist growth has not yet taken off. Surely this claim is unrealistic; and that does not seem to be Goldstone's point. It is more valuable to treat Goldstone's argument as a sophisticated statement of the core theory of state breakdown, and as an application of this model to conditions under which population is the driving force among the background variables. But even when the effects of population are mitigated, a state breakdown can still be activated if geopolitical strains are serious enough. I doubt that the age of revolutions is now over, even for the industrial-capitalist world with all its ability to control or absorb population growth. Geopolitical strain is possible for any state as long as it builds its legitimation around the organization of force upon a territory; some political power-holders will always be tempted to expand their legitimation through military exploits and run the risk of becoming militarily overmatched, outpositioned, or overextended. The theory of state breakdowns will not become a relic of the past; we will no doubt see its application again.

COUNTERING THE CRITICISM OF SAMPLING ON THE DEPENDENT VARIABLE

A great merit of Goldstone's work is that it resolves a criticism leveled against the entire field of historical sociology: sampling on the dependent variable (DV). The argument, expressed most sharply by King, Keohane, and Verba (1994), holds that work like Skocpol's on revolutions is invalid or at least indeterminate. Skocpol chooses cases of societies that have undergone great revolutions and works backward to show the conditions they had in common. The trouble is that her sample is limited to cases where revolutions occurred and omits those where revolutions did not occur. Hence we do not know whether her theory of antecedent causes applies in all cases because she has chosen only those in which they do. The only way to solve this problem would be to sample all societies that go through the alleged causal sequence: to sample on the independent variable (IV). The implication of King et al.'s argument is that all such historical theories are invalid—that because a huge number of states undergoing fiscal strains did not break down, macrohistorical sociology is a vacuous enterprise.

The criticism, taken as a methodological canon for doing historical sociology, is restrictively formalistic. The methodologist, armed with such a criterion but without insight into the cases of interest—here, those where revolutions did occur—would search forever for independent variables to examine. There is also a good deal of macrohistorical sociology that does not fit this mechanical conception of the task. In studying a world system, for example, it is not simply a matter of examining independent variables but of looking at processes that mesh to constitute a system. The IV/DV model presumes that units already exist as fixed entities; but in many areas of macrohistory it is the shape of the units that is shifting. The inappropriateness of the IV/DV scheme is seen even more clearly in geopolitical analysis, where the size and structure of states is not fixed, but shifts according to relationships among clusterings of military force. As we do geopolitical analysis, it dawns upon us that these power clusterings or centers are emergent, not fixed, entities; they are nodes in a network of relations that crystallize at certain moments and in certain configurations, only to be merged at other moments into larger units or fragmented into smaller ones.[1]

The method of IV and DV belongs to a conceptual universe of discrete units that might be called essentialist positivism. The macrohistorical vision of causality (which is developed in Chapters 2–4) is akin to the methods of network analysis. In Harrison White's (1992) classic formulation, identities, social units of any kind, are regions within networks of relations. Such identities are fluidly emergent, temporarily fixed, and transitory. The process of interaction in the network of relations eventually dissolves all such structures back into the relational soup from which they came, to emerge again in different configurations.[2]

Given this line of counterattack, we could stop here, dismissing the sampling-on-the-DV criticism as counterproductive. Goldstone however goes on to meet the criticism on its home ground. Let us idealize the situation and assume that states do have a fixed structure, at least temporarily over a given length of time. The process of constructing state borders cannot be handled within this frame—because it is the frame that is being constructed—but we can examine processes internal to this unit of analysis. Here Goldstone picks up the gauntlet and meets the sampling-on-the-DV criticism straight on. Skocpol could not have done so because she was formulating the model in the first place; she had to sample on the DV and work backward. Goldstone provides a later generation of the state-breakdown theory, and he examines the independent variable across long periods of time, both periods when revolution was occurring and those when it was not.

In Goldstone's model, state breakdown (which he calls "pressure for crisis") is brought about by the interaction of state fiscal distress, competition within the elite, and the potential for mass mobilization from below. He produces quantitative indicators for each of these three components: for England, they are displayed for the years 1500–1750; for France, for the years 1680–1847 (Goldstone 1991: 143, 282, 312).[3] The pattern is reproduced here in Figure 1. Here we see a relative degree of peaking of each of the three components of pressure for crisis in the mid-1600s. When the three components are put together, as called for in the interactive model (since none of them in isolation can bring a state to breakdown), we have the pattern shown in Figure 2. There is a dramatic peak in revolutionary potential, building up from the late 1500s and reaching its height in the 1640s: precisely the time of the civil war and parliamentary overthrow of the monarchy. In France, similarly, the composite index accelerates upward in the 1760s and peaks just before 1789.

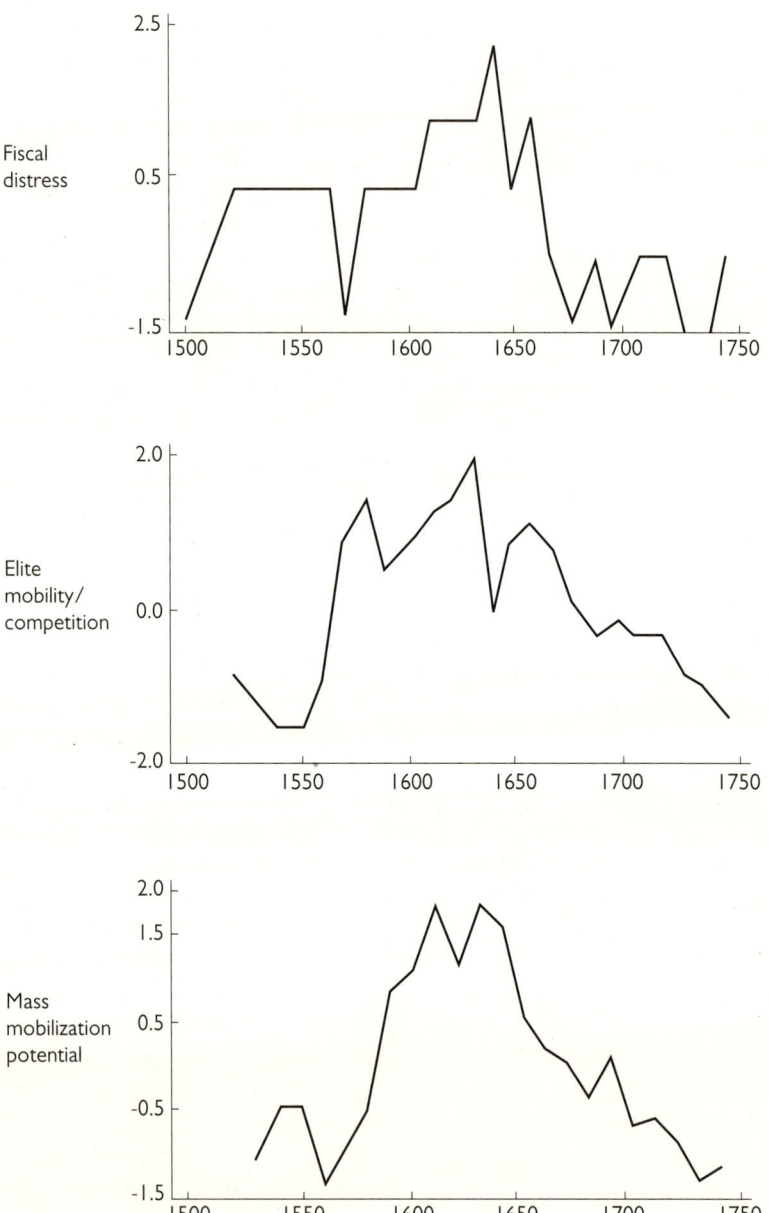

FIGURE 1. Fiscal distress, elite competition, and mass mobilization potential in England, 1500–1750. Reprinted from Goldstone 1991:143.

FIGURE 2. Pressures for crisis (*psi*) in England, 1520–1749. Reprinted from Goldstone 1991:144.

Goldstone's chapters on England and France, which demonstrate not only the causes of revolution but also when revolutions do and do not occur, are from a technical viewpoint perhaps the most impressive pieces of macro-historical sociology ever written. Truly here sociology has come of age.

THE AFTERMATH OF STATE BREAKDOWN AND THE QUESTION OF CULTURE

Goldstone explicitly overturns Marxian theory at a number of points. Some continuity with it remains insofar as state breakdown theory is materialist and structural. In fact one might describe the whole line of theory as "political materialism"; economics is still very important, but most important of all as the fiscal economics of the state. Geopolitical conditions affect the task of coordinating the physical resources of threat and destruction. He shows the rise of the state itself as hinging upon the several ways of extracting economic resources to support the growing and centralizing military machinery; Tilly's *Coercion, Capital, and European States* (1990) reaps another harvest of comparative history in showing how the fates of different state structures depended on which flows of resources they were built upon.

Goldstone is very much a "political materialist" up through the point at which states break down. In analyzing what happens next, he begins to waffle. One part of his analysis here remains ruthlessly materialist. He says that states will be able to pull themselves back together provided they can regain a favorable flow of resources. This may happen because they are lucky enough to enter an era in which population declines (such as France, England, and the Ottoman Empire in the late 1600s). Alternatively, the struggles of the breakdown period may themselves kill off enough population so that pressure is relieved. Goldstone believes this is what happened in the stabilizing transition from the Ming to the Qing (Ch'ing) dynasty in China.

Goldstone also considers why state breakdowns have such different structural results. England, and on a slower pace France, was bailed out of the population pressure dynamic by the takeoff of capitalism; but Spain merely stagnated, as did the Ottomans and China. Goldstone finds Meiji Japan especially puzzling because it carried out extensive reforms that led to rapid economic growth and expanding military power, although under an ideology that claimed to be restoring old traditions. Now Goldstone suggests that material conditions determine state breakdowns but that ideology becomes an independent factor in determining where the society goes from there. That is, ideology plays quite different roles in the three phases of a revolution. First, in the prerevolutionary phase leading to state breakdown, there is a chaos of rival groups pressing all manner of complaints; their ideas are typically conservative and bear little relation to the radical changes that ensue. Second comes the period of struggle over the new revolutionary state; now control tends to drift from the moderate reformers to groups, such as the Jacobins in the French Revolution, whose goals become increasingly extreme and their tactics increasingly violent. Third is the postrevolutionary period when authority stabilizes and a new social structure may be institutionalized. It is in the second and third periods, Goldstone argues, that ideology becomes decisive. Nevertheless, in the second phase of revolutionary struggle, what is going on is really the dynamics of conflict escalation and counterescalation. In Goldstone's own account, the drift toward increasing radicalism is explained by the tactics of small but well-organized networks of political activists, who hit upon themes like national crisis and counterrevolutionary threat in order to whip up popular support against their rivals. In phase two, ideology remains a dependent variable, which Goldstone explains by the process of political organizing in a situation of competition over a new apparatus of state coercion.

It is in the third phase that Goldstone's argument for the independent causal power of ideology comes into its own. He suggests that the European states, because they inherited a religious eschatology of linear progress, were able to consciously innovate and thus arrived at modern democracy and capitalism. Asian societies, on the other hand, were dominated by a cultural imagery of eternal cycles. The result was conservative movements following state breakdowns; and these, although often innovative in their immediate response to crisis, put in place conformist societies that cut off future possibilities of structural change. But here too there is a structural condition: eschatological ideology has transformative effects only when it operates in conjunction with marginal elites. These are persons with upper-class education and access to political circles who are excluded from the highest power because they are not members of the hereditary aristocracy (as in France) or are excluded on religious grounds (as the Puritans were in England). In a situation of state breakdown, such elites attack the entire traditional order, because they have been excluded from power on the basis of a structural principle. Goldstone notes that eschatological ideology has no transformative effect when it lacks elite leadership, as in the popular millenarian movements of the European Middle Ages or the Mahdist uprisings of the Islamic world. Unfortunately, this additional factor undermines Goldstone's emphasis on ideology. For the breakdowns of the Ottoman and Chinese states differed from the European cases precisely on this second factor. Both had relatively bureaucratic forms of recruitment of state elites. Hence second-rank elites formulated their grievances as the corruption or incompetence of existing officials; state reconstruction was a matter of restoring proper order, not creating a new one.

Once again, Goldstone succeeds in explaining the ideological propensities of political groups by their structural positions. Why, then, do we need recourse to an additional factor, an eschatological tradition? Moreover, the historical comparisons do not clearly support the contrast he wishes to draw between the eschatological West and the cyclical culture of the East. Buddhism had plenty of eschatological elements, beliefs in savior-gods and crisis periods of sacred history, and these figured in numerous millenial movements and political revolts in China and Japan. The Ottoman Empire was Muslim; and Islam is just as eschatological as Christianity, complete with a creator God and a Last Judgment. I would suggest that the mixtures of ideological resources accumulated in all the major civilizations were really quite comparable (see Collins 1998), so that social actors in crisis periods could always find something that could be built upon for ideological justification, no matter which direction they turned in. To understand what determined the directions in which they actually did turn, we need to focus on social structure and the dynamics of social action, rather than invoke the blueprints of culture. We are back to the theory of ideology. And for this, we have an excellent counterpoint in Wuthnow's work.

WUTHNOW AND THE POLITICAL MEANS
OF IDEOLOGICAL PRODUCTION

Like Goldstone's, Wuthnow's book is not well described by its title. *Communities of Discourse* was no doubt chosen to appeal to the concern with the inner dynamics of culture. But it gives a misleading impression by conjuring the image of warm, fuzzy discussion groups. Make no mistake; Wuthnow's is a book about social conflicts, and its underlying argument reminds me of Marx and Engels in *The German Ideology* transmuted into the terms of the state-centered theory of today. The theme of the book comes across more clearly in its subtitle: *Ideology and Social Structure in the Reformation, the Enlightenment, and European Socialism.* These are the ideologies of the three great waves of modern revolutions; the first included the English revolution; the second the French and American revolutions and most of the nineteenth-century revolutions; the third the revolutionary wave of the twentieth century up to about 1965. This is such a book as Engels's ghost might have written in collaboration with the ghost of Georg Simmel.

In keeping with today's scholarship, Wuthnow overturns the traditional class-actor dynamic. Nevertheless a version of class conflicts is important in his model. This is the conflict of economic interests emphasized by Moore and Skocpol: the conflict of government officials with landowners over revenues. Wuthnow's is a conflict theory of coalitions. During all three of the revolutionary periods he addresses, new political and economic resources strengthened the state sector; then if there was a stalemate or a prolonged balance of power between the state actors and the major property-owning conservatives, room was opened up for a "third party" of cultural entrepreneurs who eventually benefited from the struggle, *tertius gaudens*. In the Reformation, the stalemate was between the landed aristocrats and the urban/trade-based state structures; in the Enlightenment, it was between the central bureaucracy and independent representative bodies dominated by the aristocracy; in the socialist movements of the nineteenth century, it was between the landowning and bourgeois parties. Class interests continued to operate but they did not directly determine ideology; and the most important class actors were on the reactionary side.

Within the context of these conflicts, Wuthnow documents the shifting material bases of cultural production. During the Reformation, there was a split over what might be called the "ritual economy" of the church. In the rural parishes, everyday life was organized by a calendrical round of religious assemblies that put the local aristocrats in the center of ceremonial attention. It is small wonder that the country landowners were the bulwarks of traditional Catholicism, since they directly patronized its priests and received in return an emotional and symbolic legitimation of their status. Protestantism, in pruning away rituals and substituting sermons and vernacular books, attacked the social as well as the religious status order.

Protestant reforms grew for a variety of reasons; Wuthnow does not focus on these but concentrates instead on the period 1519–59, during which the states of Europe decided whether to adopt the reforms. One could no doubt go back to the schisms in church government in the 1300s, the failure of the conciliar movement in the 1400s (which would have turned the centralized papacy into a republic of bishops), and the crisis in papal finances that led to Luther's repudiation of the revenue-raising sale of indulgences. Here one senses another complementarity between Wuthnow's and Goldstone's concerns, for the medieval papacy underwent a variant of state breakdown. Wuthnow concentrates on the aftermath—analytically, the phase in which Goldstone is weakest. In Wuthnow's model, the Reformation was successful in those places where the state was able to tap new sources of revenue resulting from the growth of trade. These states—above all the free cities and independent principalities of Germany, Switzerland, and the Netherlands, and to a lesser degree Scandinavia and England—were able to build up their own staffs of officials without depending upon the rural economy, the province of the aristocracy. The superior resource mobilization of these states enabled them to challenge the aristocracy for control of the church, its property and its revenues. Religious reformers proliferated in the midst of this struggle; some were selected and institutionalized where the balance of resources most favored the state. Where these conditions were lacking— Spain, France, eastern Europe—the Reformation failed.

The outburst of secularizing intellectuals that comprised the Enlightenment was produced by another shift in the means of cultural production. Here the state was even more important, for the new printing industries depended heavily on government licensing as well as on government-sponsored publications. Intellectuals acquired a new basis for careers as publicists for political factions in parliamentary regimes like England and in the salons that sprang up around burgeoning governmental centers such as Paris. In the background the state underwent a further round of expansion in tandem with the expansion of the capitalist economy; the fusion of these two provided a patronage base for the new intellectuals that was independent of the older intellectual base in the church. For the intellectuals to embark on a round of creativity in their own right, a second ingredient had to be present: a division of authority, so that the central bureaucracy was challenged by an independent judiciary, parliaments, or plural religious institutions. These gave multiple bases for patronage that was partly autonomous from the crown. Intellectuals enjoyed a favorable market and could choose among rival patrons. It appears to follow, although Wuthnow does not develop the point explicitly, that the Enlightenment concern for the supremacy of "reason" was the ideology of intellectuals' autonomy, a reflection of the intellectuals upon a new situation in which they had become the cultural mediators in a political balance of power.

Wuthnow's third case is the rise of socialist ideologies from 1864 to 1914. Here the most favorable circumstance was the strong intervention of a centralized state to shape economic growth. The archetypal example is the industrialization of Bismarck's Germany, which became the site of the strongest and intellectually most active socialist movement in Europe. The shape of political coalitions was crucial. Where an authoritarian state was highly interventionist, the party of the conservative landowners was forced into alliance with the industrial bourgeoisie; the working class, excluded from power, was pushed to the left. In contrast, where bourgeois republicans had won political victories against the conservatives (as in England, France, Italy, and Spain), there was a tendency for all the parties of the left to ally against right-wing resurgence. Bourgeois liberals gave some support to working-class interests, thereby giving reformist politics a moderate character, and socialist ideology was weak.

The immediate material bases for socialist intellectuals were editorial positions with the mass-distributed newspapers and magazines sponsored by their political parties. This base was strongest in Germany, where trade unions and parliamentary politicians formed a virtual state within the state. Not surprisingly, this is where socialist ideas were elaborated most professionally, under the leadership of Engels (publishing Marx's manuscripts in the 1880s and 1890s), August Bebel, Karl Kautsky, Eduard Bernstein, Rudolf Hilferding, Rosa Luxemburg, and others. Foreign revolutionaries like Lenin looked to Germany as the center of the world socialist movement. Russia, which Wuthnow omits from his comparisons, also appears to fit the underlying structural pattern of class coalitions, although the material resources there for socialist intellectuals were more scarce.

Looking back over Wuthnow's comparisons, the continuity with Moore, Skocpol, and Goldstone is remarkably strong. In some respects Wuthnow agrees most strongly with Moore that although history is no longer the old Marxian scheme of rising social classes, class conflicts provide the balance of forces into which intellectuals then move with their own creativity. And the expansion of capitalism plays a causal role throughout, although farther back in the chain. No one has yet made a grand synthesis of all the parts of the picture, but there is considerable coherence around the fateful consequences of the commercialization of agriculture (see Moore), the material economy of the state (Skocpol, Goldstone, Wuthnow, Tilly), the patterns of intra-elite conflict generated by the foregoing (all of these theorists), and the provision of an autonomous space for intellectuals (Wuthnow).

In Wuthnow's treatment of the Reformation, a key factor is the ability of states to tap sources of revenue that do not put them into competition with possessors of landed wealth. It is the failure to do just this that Goldstone shows to be one of the main paths leading to state breakdown in England in 1640 and in France in 1789. In France the Reformation failed because of the dependence of the state on the aristocracy. For geopolitical reasons, this was particularly acute during the Reformation period, when the French king was defeated in war and had to be ransomed by the nobles in 1525. In England, Wuthnow notes in rather Goldstonean fashion, rising agricultural prices in the late 1500s brought a resurgence of the landed aristocracy and an attempt to reestablish Catholicism (1989: 154). The nominal Protestantism of the Church of England was thus caught in the middle of a long conflict between religious traditionalists and sectarian Protestants. The ideological mobilization that Wuthnow explains thus fills in much of the discourse that surrounded Goldstone's state breakdowns.

Wuthnow's analysis of the conditions under which socialist movements were prevalent meshes with Barrington Moore's model of coalition patterns. Moore pointed out that where landowners sell their agricultural products directly to the market and control rural labor using traditional methods of coercion, the aristocratic interest becomes tied to that of the authoritarian state. Subsequently, when industrialization from above promotes the class alliance of landowners and industrial bourgeoisie in a "marriage of iron and rye," the workers have nowhere to go but into revolutionary opposition. If Germany is at one pole, the United States is at the other, although Wuthnow does not go into the latter case. As Moore argued, in the United States the disappearance of the conservative labor-coercing landowners with the abolition of the slave plantations eliminated the aristocracy as a faction in class coalitions. The bourgeoisie (including the small commercial farmers) dominated American politics; without an authoritarian class, for a long period there was no party in favor of a strongly centralized state. Since state patronage, directly or indirectly, is the basis of politicized intellectual movements, the absence of both a strong working-class party and a centralized state accounts for the privatized condition of American intellectuals.

Wuthnow's analysis is concerned with the material bases of cultural production and with the political and economic configurations that give intellectuals breathing space. He does not do much with the content of their ideas themselves. His emphasis, especially in the case of the Reformation, is on the process by which ideas are selected and institutionalized. Some reviewers have regarded this as a weakness, a failure to give ideas their autonomous significance. But before we are swept to conclusions by the force of contemporary rhetoric, let us consider what Wuthnow shows. When material and structural conditions are favorable, there is an outpouring of intellectual productivity. With this proliferation of ideas comes a wide range of disagreement. For creative intellectuals to be in unanimity is almost a contradiction in terms; they make their marks by saying something different than the others. For this reason intellectuals as a group cannot produce structural change because they disagree too much about what direction to move in.

As Goldstone recognizes well enough at points, a proliferation of critical ideologies adds to the atmosphere of state breakdown. But some selection among those ideas must be made if they are to be given any coherence in the period of postrevolutionary reconstruction. This is apparent in the huge range of critical stances on Catholic dogma and practice at the end of the Middle Ages. After 1300 there existed all manner of mystics, occultists, Platonists, scripturalists, pietists, ascetics, and others, not to mention many specific plans for reform of church organization. Luther became central not because his doctrine was somehow more penetrating than that of any of the others, but because his rebellion in the patchwork of German states began a series of political upheavals that finally succeeded in unraveling the central- ized authority of the Pope. Similar patterns seem to hold for other revolu- tions. Whether we like it or not, the creativity of intellectuals is selectively highlighted by upheavals in political structures; it does not in itself determine the direction in which structures change.

This still leaves the question of how to explain the content of ideas in their own right. There is an important sense in which culture is au- tonomous, but that does not mean that it is socially undetermined. Wuth- now makes the point that cultural production expands creatively when the political/economic structure gives it breathing space, a well-supported but competitive market for ideas. The historically constructed autonomy of that space constitutes the autonomy of culture. That is not to say that sociologists can say nothing about the internal organization of the competitive space among intellectuals; the history of creative ideas is the history of the succes- sive rearrangements of the networks of intellectuals and their alliances and conflicts with each other. But it is another story pursued elsewhere (Collins 1998); it is not the driving force of political or economic history.

Sociology After the Fall

Yes, there is a macrosociology after the fall of the traditional Marxist para- digm. The state-centered revolution in the theory of political and ideolog- ical change has given us a coherent model capable of explaining the many variants that make up the richness of modern history. Of course, there are contentions over points of emphasis, loose ends left dangling, gaps and fron- tiers where speculation runs ahead of solid analysis. There may also turn out to be some serious flaws in the state-centered model. But the points of over- lap and coherence among the work of Moore, Skocpol, Goldstone, and Wuthnow, as well as that of Tilly, Calhoun, Mann, geopolitical theorists, and others, strongly implies that something solid has been accomplished at the core of a general theory.

CHAPTER 2

The Geopolitical Basis of Revolution: The Prediction of the Soviet Collapse

A Personal History of a Theory-Based Prediction

IN 1978 I PUBLISHED a theory explaining changes in the territorial power of states (Collins 1978). Extending conflict theory, I decided to take seriously Max Weber's definition of the state as the monopolization of legitimate force upon a territory. Turning this into an explanatory theory meant treating everything in it as a variable. The result was a theory of the conditions that determine geopolitical rises and falls in territorial power, together with the consequences that flow from them. A corollary of the theory is that the legitimacy of rulers varies with the external power-prestige of their state. At the extreme, this entailed an explanation of revolution as the loss of legitimacy and of control over the means of coercion. The geopolitical (GP) theory thus meshed with Skocpol's state-resource-breakdown theory of revolution, which was published about the same time (1979). The convergence between the two theories seemed to me additional evidence that the model was on the right track.

In the presidential election year 1980, Ronald Reagan's major campaign issue was the so-called "window of vulnerability": the claim that the United States had fallen dangerously behind the USSR in nuclear armaments and needed a massive arms buildup to catch up. The early 1980s was the height of the period of nuclear terror, when the antinuclear arms movement mobilized under the image of "five minutes to midnight." I decided to see what my GP theory predicted about our current situation. I honestly had no preconception of what the results might be. The GP theory comprised five principles of causal processes, which were interconnected by a cumulative dynamic. To my surprise, all five of the major principles in the theory indicated that the USSR had passed the peak of its power and predicted that it would decline. The result was not symmetrical; most of these principles predicted that the power of the United States would remain roughly stable.

Only one principle of the five held out the possibility that the United States would also decline, since nuclear war fit within one of the more general categories of events by which state power is destroyed. My optimistic assessment was that the other four principles would take effect before the fifth and that the USSR would disintegrate before the start of a nuclear war. The policy implication was that the nuclear arms race could be safely scaled back without undermining the power of the United States.

In the spring of 1980, I presented this analysis at several places, including Yale and Columbia Universities (Collins 1980). The response was uniformly negative. Russia specialists, who attended some of these talks, were usually conservative émigrés whose dominant feelings were hatred and fear of Soviet power. Their image was of a terrifyingly powerful USSR that must be combated by an equally powerful United States. This stance is not surprising from the point of view of Simmelian conflict theory, that an external threat brings ideological polarization and a cycle of escalation and counterescalation. The response of the liberals was a little more surprising. Some members of the nuclear disarmament movement reacted with hostility. During one talk, an activist accused me of sounding "just like the Joint Chiefs of Staff," apparently expressing the feeling that disarmament had to be justified as a moral crusade, not as an application of *realpolitik*. Perhaps more fundamental was the liberal position that the world was facing mutual assured destruction (MAD), with its implication that both the United States and the USSR were equally powerful and equally in need of de-escalation.

Eventually I published the paper under the title "The Future Decline of the Russian Empire" (Collins 1980). There the prediction rested on the shelf. At any rate, I was not surprised when the strains of the war in Afghanistan brought the disgrace of the war faction in the USSR and their replacement by a reform movement around Mikhail Gorbachev; or when reform turned out to be a slippery slope toward disintegration of the empire.

The incident raises a number of general issues. To what extent is sociological prediction possible? How can we differentiate valid prediction from lucky guesses and from post facto special pleading? How much precision is possible in prediction; and does prediction have inherent limits? What obstacles prevent us from making predictions on the basis of intellectual resources already available? And what are the future prospects for prediction as a tool of applied sociology? Since one key to assessing a theory's predictive validity is its coherence with a wide-ranging and explanatorily integrated body of research, I will review how GP theory has developed and how it meshes with the trend toward a state-centered and military-resource-oriented model of macropolitical change.

Development of the Geopolitical Theory of State Power

GP theory originated in the period when a distinctive line of conflict theory was first developed, in Germany at the turn of the twentieth century. Gustav Ratzenhofer and Ludwig Gumplowicz stressed the military origins of the state. Friedrich Ratzel's political geography discussed the propensity of large states to expand into continental empires. Weber's treatment of the development of the state was formulated in this context; for Weber, the dynamics of legitimacy as well as the formation of ethnic identification and nationalism were connected to military struggles among states and to the organizational mode by which varying proportions of the population were mobilized and equipped for fighting (1968: 901–26). For decades this aspect of Weber's theory lay dormant while emphasis was placed upon functionalist and cultural interpretations of Weber. GP thinking was in bad odor politically, associated with militaristic national policies advocated by early thinkers including Mackinder in England, Mahan in the United States, and Haushofer in Germany.

With the revival of conflict theory in the 1960s came the expansion of comparative-historical research and renewed interest in the autonomous dynamics of the state. Geopolitics was rediscovered, separated from particularistic formulations, and pursued in a more analytical fashion (for overviews of the literature see Enggass 1986; Hepple 1986). In political science, classic GP is generally regarded as foreshadowing the realist school of international relations. Let us consider the various contributions to modern sociological GP theory as they enter into the summary model that I constructed in 1978.[1] The principles are stated as conditions for the expansion and contraction of the territorial power of states.[2]

1. *Size and resource advantage favors territorial expansion.* Other things being approximately equal, bigger, more populous, and resource-rich states expand militarily at the expense of smaller, less populous, and resource-poor states. This principle is often stated in the literature on victory and defeat in war (Liddell-Hart 1970; Andreski 1971; Gilpin 1981; Modelski and Thompson 1988; W. Thompson 1988). Singer finds that the advantage is relatively small but that it is cumulative over time insofar as marginally resource-dominant states add resources from their victims while the latter grow cumulatively weaker (Singer 1979; Singer and Diehl 1990).[3] This may occur by direct acquisition and administration of territory. Resource-dominant states also expand by peaceful or quasi-peaceful means: by demanding that smaller

client states contribute supplies or troops to joint alliances under central leadership, and by adjudicating external and sometimes internal relations of weaker states. Through these mechanisms, the extent of de facto and often de jure military control over territory tends to grow.

2. *Geopositional or "marchland" advantage favors territorial expansion.* States with enemies on fewer fronts expand at the expense of states with enemies on more borders. Here geography enters in two ways: natural barriers in the form of mountains, wide seas, and uninhabitable territories give some states a "back wall" that enables them to concentrate their forces in fewer directions. Against that, large territories without natural barriers can sustain a multitude of states, especially if they have fertile agricultural land capable of supporting large populations. World historians frequently note the pattern of marchland conquerors from the periphery of the great population areas (see McNeill 1963). A high proportion of large-scale conquest states began in the marchland position. All seven of the unifiers of China following periods of multistate fragmentation came from marchlands in the northern regions where population resources were greater than in other marchlands. These cases point up the interplay between marchland and resource advantages. If there is an array of potential contenders situated in marchland positions, the one that will expand the farthest is the one that starts with the best local resource advantage and parlays that advantage into a cumulative growth in resources as it expands against centrally located enemies.

3. *Fragmentation of interior states.* Over time, states in the middle of a geographic region tend to break up into smaller units. This principle is an extension of the previous one. One reason that marchland states expand is that interior states are blocked, over the long run, from cumulative growth in their resource bases. Interior states have potential enemies and allies on many fronts; these circumstances foster balance-of-power diplomacy in which a defensive coalition forms against any momentarily dominant state (Morgenthau 1948; Gilpin 1981). Conflicts among interior states tend to become stalemated and consequently eat up military resources without productive gain. Since such interior states are frequently located on good arable land, they often rank high in military resources, but they are structurally blocked because their expansion possibilities are randomized; only marchland states can enter into long-term cumulative expansion. Earlier comparative historians commonly misattributed this empirical pattern to the greater vigor of barbarians from the periphery against the decadence of advanced civilization. When geopositional advantages are not at issue, however, civilized high-resource states invariably win over resource-poor "barbarian" or tribal areas. The advantage of the periphery is not cultural but structural.

Further, there is visible in the historical atlases a pattern that goes beyond the mere advantage of marchland over center. Over time, in the absence of marchland conquest, internal areas tend to fragment into an increasing multiplicity of states: this happened in China during several interdynastic periods, in Kievan Russia, in the Balkans after the decline of the Ottoman and Austrian Empires, and when the medieval Holy Roman Empire fragmented into the *Kleinstaaterei* of Germany and Italy. Fragmentation occurs because interior states become militarily weakened states incapable of controlling secessions. Unstable and overlapping patterns of conquest and alliance divide administrative authority and make the culture of political identification increasingly localistic.

4. *Cumulative processes bring periodic long-term simplification, with massive arms races and showdown wars between a few contenders.* Principles 1, 2, and 3 are cumulative. Big states swallow up smaller ones or force them into alliances, and marchland states expand into the fragmented middle. The consequence is that over long periods of time (on the order of several centuries) the GP situation is drastically simplified.

This may happen in a number of different ways. Historically, one pattern is for a single marchland conqueror to undergo accelerating growth by conquering interior states. This is characteristic of geographically simple regions with only one major population zone, such as China, or Mesopotamia in the period when it was an isolated region of agriculture. A second pattern, more characteristic of geographically differentiated western Eurasia after the diffusion of agricultural populations, is for two rival marchland states to expand into a stalemated central region from opposite directions. A third variant is for a region to consolidate into two huge power blocks, one of them more centrally located, the other more peripheral.[4]

Each situation fosters a period of high GP tension: at minimum an intense arms race and diplomatic polarization, often culminating in a showdown war (in the terminology of international relations, a hegemonic war; see Gilpin 1981: 186–200). In the first pattern mentioned above, the single large state effectively conquers its world region. When there is a showdown between two large states or blocs, more possibilities hinge on their conflict. One state may destroy the other, opening the way to regional world conquest (as, e.g., Rome conquered Carthage in the western Mediterranean, opening the way to the victor's easy expansion). A historically common alternative is a stalemate between the two contenders that leads to the disintegration of both; this can happen because both sides suffer massive material losses in war, or because resources are strained by lengthy arms races. In such circumstances a bystander state has the opportunity to expand rapidly into the resulting power vacuum.[5]

Corollary 4a. *Showdown wars generate the highest level of ferociousness.* Wars fought where world-regional conquest was in the balance have resulted in the largest massacres of armies, including captives, and have been the most likely to exterminate civilian populations. The level of deliberate destruction rose in the wars of the Ch'in (first unifier of China after the prolonged Warring States period), the Assyrians (first unifier of Mesopotamia), the Romans in their war with Carthage, and the Mongols (first to attempt conquering the entire Eurasian landmass); there are analogues in the dramatic escalation of civilian casualties in the world wars of the twentieth century. Gilpin notes the greater violence of the hegemonic wars of Europe since the seventeenth century (1981: 200–101). Conversely, periods of balance-of-power diplomacy in regions of GP fragmentation have usually been characterized by codes of honor that restrict combat and limit its damages. The mechanism that connects GP conditions with the intensity of violence is the high level of emotional and ideological polarization in situations where extreme structural consequences hinge upon the outcome of battle. In contrast, where the fragmented structure of power among states is little affected by particular wars, and where balance-of-power negotiations lead to frequent switching of alliances, emotional polarization is low.[6]

5. *Overextension brings resource strain and state disintegration.* The further that military power is projected from the home base, the higher the costs. At a calculable point, most resources are used up in meeting these costs; the results are increasing strain on resources at home and vulnerability to military defeat, both of which raise the probability that military power will rapidly unravel.

The principle of overextension through logistical loads has been widely noted in the theoretical and empirical literature. Both Stinchcombe and Boulding proposed formal models for the decrease in military resources deliverable at increasing distances (see Stinchcombe 1968: 218–30; Boulding 1962: 227–76). Collins (1978) found that decline in virtually every case of the centralized Chinese dynasties was initiated by logistical strain and related defeats on distant frontiers. Luttwak (1976) showed the successive reductions in military resources that accompanied Roman commitments on distant frontiers. Kennedy (1987) documented the overextension strains in the decline of the major European empires from the fifteenth to the twentieth century. These case studies also show that the negative effects of overextension operate much more rapidly than the processes of cumulative growth in the resources that fueled expansion. Within a few years, empires that reach the overextension point tend to lose control over military organization and political authority. The result is generally regime downfall or state fragmentation.

Much (but not all) of the evidence for the overextension dynamic was

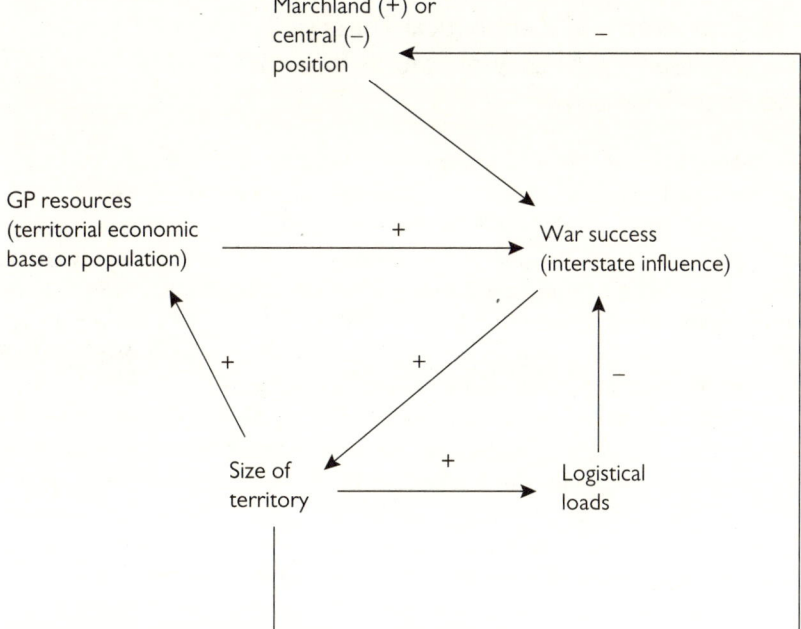

FIGURE 3. Geopolitical model.

based on historical comparisons among agrarian states. The same is true of principles 1–4. To settle the objection that principles based on these historical periods would be outdated under conditions of modern military and transportation technology, I examined the GP stability of modern seaborne empires and the military effectiveness of air power (Collins 1981). The logistical costs and vulnerabilities of these technologies offset their hypothetical increase in range,[7] and accordingly the basic GP principles have remained valid.

The preceding is the theoretical base from which I made a prediction about the future of Russian state power. In the empirical and theoretical literature, the principles of resource advantage, marchland advantage, and overextension are well documented. There were abundant historical materials about showdown wars, but no general theoretical formulation. The cumulative nature of some of these processes had been noted. The theoretical contribution of Collins 1978 was to sharpen the formulation of the fragmentation of the middle (as the converse of the marchland advantage) and to connect the entire package of principles as a dynamic of mutually reinforcing processes, leading periodically to long-term GP simplifications and turning points.[8] These feedback loops are illustrated in Figure 3.

The Connection of Geopolitical Theory with the General Theory of State Formation and State Breakdown

GP theory has long been only a minor interest in sociology; its importance has risen as the theory of the state has become more central. One trend in macrosociology since the 1960s has been to emphasize the external relations among social units. World-system theory has focused on the dynamics among zones of the world economy (Wallerstein 1974, 1980, 1989; Chase-Dunn 1989). Since hegemony in the world system is based on mutually reinforcing economic and military dominance, autonomous GP conditions need to be inserted in the world-system model to account for shifts in hegemony and the rise and fall of states within the world system. In another externally oriented approach, Bendix (1967) formulated the process of modernization, not as parallel and indigenously driven developments, but as a chain of emulation among successive "leader" and "follower" states. Bendix's model includes some Weberian inspiration, since the basis of emulation is the power-prestige of states in the interstate arena, and this may be construed as primarily GP dominance. Bendix's external starting point for internal state changes was adopted and extended by Skocpol (1979) in her theory of revolutions initiated by military costs.

By the 1980s, there was a full-scale movement throughout the social sciences for "bringing the state back in" (Evans, Rueschemeyer, and Skocpol 1985). The agenda was to formulate a theory of the autonomous dynamics of the state, which can of course interact with economic, cultural, and other dynamics but is not reducible to them. The general issue may be conceived of as formulating the dynamics that determine state growth and state decline. Each of these directions of change contains subdimensions. States grow intensively (in their internal organizational size and capacity of control) and extensively (in territory); they go into crisis or break down in a number of ways (again, there is organizational breakdown and loss of extractive capability on one hand, as well as territorial contraction and disintegration on the other). In this context, the theory of revolutions has received the most attention; but we should keep in mind that revolution is one segment of the continuum of state breakdown, and breakdown in turn is the obverse of the more general question of state formation. Viewed in overarching perspective, what we are concerned with are the conditions that move states in various directions along these continuums.

Tilly (1990) provides a recent summary of the upward pathways of state formation. The core of the state is its military organization, together with the administrative apparatus for extracting economic resources to support it.

Once this apparatus existed, it could be used for other purposes as well (including economic regulation and infrastructure, welfare, and cultural dissemination); this part of state organization became relatively large in most instances only very recently, building upon the core of organization servicing the military. Throughout most of history, the state's expenses were primarily its current military forces plus debts incurred in previous warfare (Mann 1986: 416–46). The "military revolution" of 1500–1800 escalated the size of military forces, along with their equipment costs, their permanence, and the centralization of their control (Parker 1988). So far, we have a military dynamic driving the intensive growth of internal state organization over time.

Tilly (1990) shows that variations in the forms of state organization are explained by conditions affecting the kinds of resources that states can draw upon to support military expansion. Depending on whether concentrated sources of capital (mainly urban/trade-based economies) or dispersed economic resources (agricultural land) were more available within their territories, states followed different trajectories of organizational/military growth. At one extreme, rulers rented short-term military force in collaboration with capitalists, thereby fostering shared power in urban oligarchies and federations and laying down structural bases for republics. At the other extreme, extensive landed conquest was the route to the growth of states dominated by military aristocracies. Tilly finds that the mixed form that combined both resource bases was the pathway to the centralized nation-state, which eventually forced the alternative state structures to emulate it because of its superior capacities for military mobilization and administrative control. An important variation among state structures is brought out by Downing (1992), who analyzes the effects of the "military revolution" on democracy. The collegial structures of power-sharing in medieval states were eroded by the rise of centrally provisioned armies. The states most vulnerable to this erosion became autocracies, whereas those that most delayed the administrative structures of the military revolution developed the strongest parliamentary-representative institutions.

THE MECHANISMS OF STATE BREAKDOWN

Schematically, the structure of military resources has been the key to internal forms of state organization. Connecting this fact to GP theory are feedback loops between the two spheres. GP power is in part the result of internal resource extraction (via principle 1); in turn, the rise or fall in overall GP position (as the result of all principles, 1–5) feeds back into the amount of territorial resources available and the rate at which those resources are eaten up in war preparations and violent destruction (see Figure 4).

Consider now the negative end of the state-formation continuum. In re-

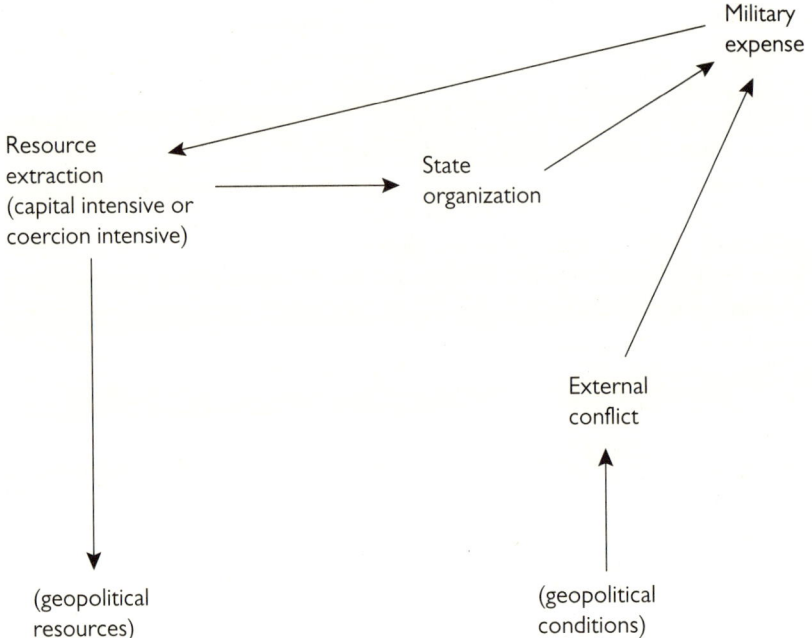

FIGURE 4. State growth model according to Tilly.

cent decades of research, state-centered models have become prevalent in the theory of state breakdown and revolution. A key is the vulnerability of states and their rulers to crises of resource extraction relative to state costs. Skocpol's (1979) pioneering formulation might be called the material economy of the state: the state itself is an economic entity, which forms class interests in its own right. Primary among these are the state administrative class, whose economic (as well as power and prestige) interests favor the expansion of extractive capability. The principal class of opponents is the propertied elite (in agrarian societies, the landowning nobles) whose interests are in evading extraction from their own resources. Insofar as these two classes are intertwined socially and politically, under conditions of state budgetary crisis, conflicts break out within the elite. These conflicts, together with the financial aspect of the crisis itself that paralyzes or alienates the military forces, culminate in full-scale breakdown of the state at the top; this breakdown opens the way to revolutionary forces from below.[9]

The outstanding test and theoretical elaboration of the model of state breakdown was conducted by Goldstone (1991); he built lengthy time-series of empirical indicators of the several aspects of state strain, showing that the composite index of pressures for crisis corresponds with historical ups and downs of state crisis. According to both Skocpol and Goldstone, state breakdown results from the combination of (1) state fiscal strain, (2) intra-elite conflict that paralyzes the government, and (3) popular revolt. Skocpol stresses military strain as the prime source of state fiscal/administrative crisis; the sources of military strain, farther along the causal chain, are specified by GP theory. Goldstone adds causal paths to all three aspects of state crisis, focusing on the ways in which population pressures, mediated by prices, inflation, and taxation, affect conditions 1–3. Goldstone argues against the Skocpolian emphasis on military sources of state fiscal strain, but the two causal chains are not mutually exclusive. In his own model, the key to state breakdown is not population pressure per se but the relative balance between state obligations and state resources (see Figures 5 and 6).[10] In cases where military expenditure and past military debt constitute the bulk of the state budget, GP strain should generate strong pressures for state breakdown, whether or not it is the exclusive source of such pressures. In more extreme circumstances, state breakdown has been precipitated directly by disintegration of the military apparatus in war.

Disputes over the emphasis given to particular parts of the causal chain should not obscure the cumulative achievement of this series of studies. We have good evidence for a core model of state breakdown—fiscal/administrative strain, elite conflict, popular revolt—as well as several pathways toward crisis conditions in these factors. Sometimes, population growth can play a very large role in building up crisis; at other times, GP conditions have overwhelming effects. Often, population and geopolitics interact. For theoretical utility, we would not want to narrow the application of the core model to historical periods when population growth was a major driving force in the background variables. The advance of theory is just such a development of a core model, with ancillary models that make it applicable to a variety of historical conditions.

Our understanding of the relation between state breakdown and revolution theory is now becoming clarified (see Figure 7). As Goldstone shows, not all state breakdowns are followed by revolutions in the specific sense of wholesale transformation of the ruling elite accompanied by political and economic restructuring. More specific theories of revolution (and other postbreakdown paths) are needed if we are to understand and predict these kinds of consequences. It should be noted that my analysis of Soviet decline predicted breakdown; it did not offer a theoretical basis for predicting what kind of regime would follow. As of the late 1990s, it remains undecided whether the former USSR will indeed undergo revolution in the full sense of the term.

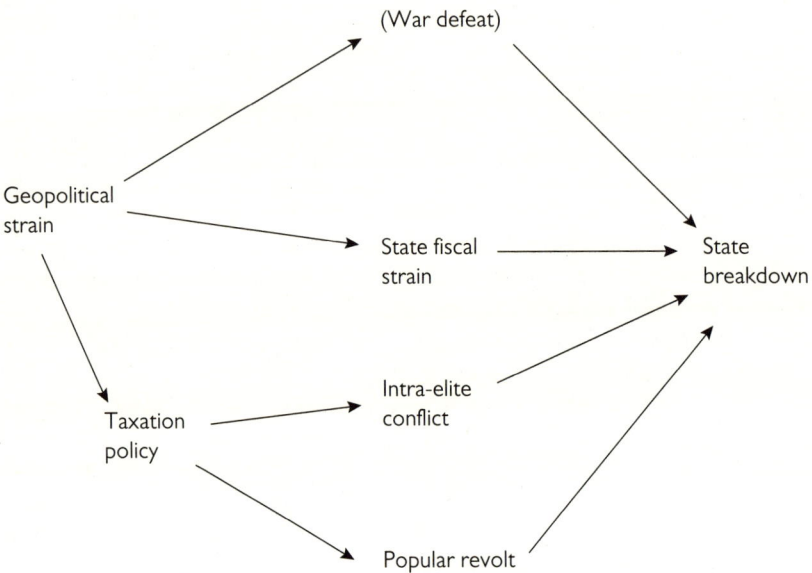

FIGURE 5. State breakdown model according to Skocpol.

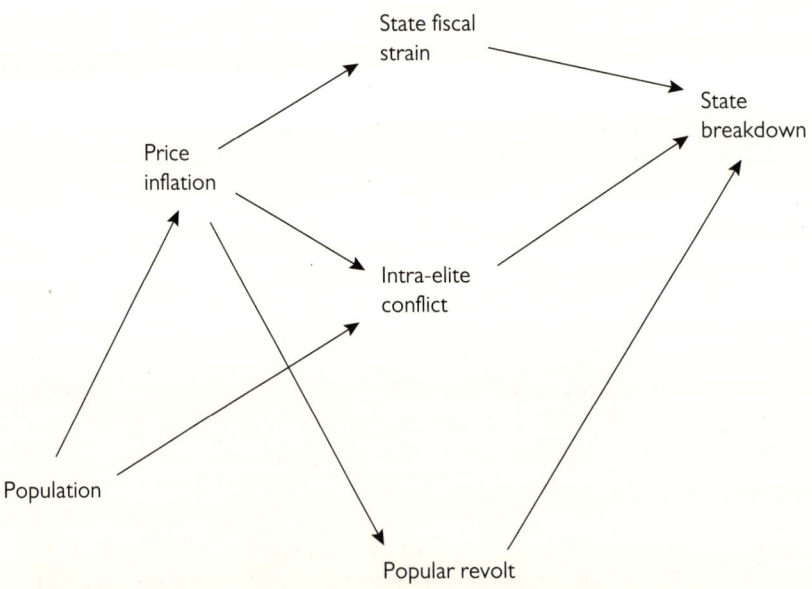

FIGURE 6. State breakdown model according to Goldstone.

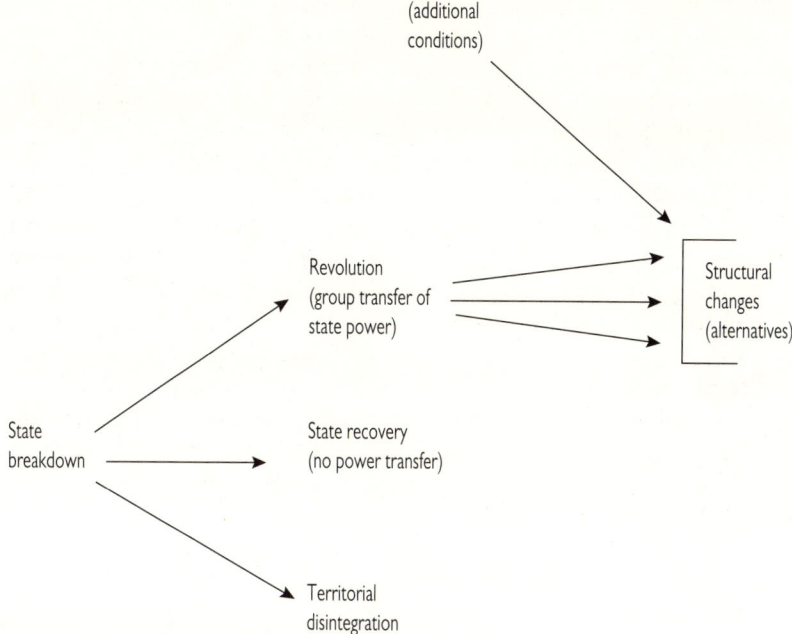

FIGURE 7. State breakdown and revolution.

LEGITIMACY AS A VARIABLE AFFECTED
BY GEOPOLITICAL POWER-PRESTIGE

My own version of the tie-in between GP principles and state breakdown stresses the factor of legitimacy. This is not to slight the Skocpol/Goldstone model of administrative crisis through fiscal strain, intra-elite conflict, and popular dissidence but to add to them a processual dynamic that ties directly into the emotional level of political maneuvering. It should be stressed that legitimacy is not something to be viewed as an abstract and constant property of the political system. On the micro- and mesolevel of social interaction, legitimacy is directly connected with solidarity and loyalty among political groups and the enthusiasm or acquiescence of the masses. Conversely, delegitimation is an emotional and cognitive condition that prevails when elite political activists are divided and uncertain and when masses move from alienated disaffection to acts of opposition. Weber's legacy has misled us here; so much attention has been placed upon the typology of traditional, rational-legal, and charismatic legitimacy as a static classification device that the processual aspects of legitimation are slighted.

Legitimacy is a variable on two levels. There is considerable evidence, from opinion polls in modern times and bolstered by historical accounts for earlier periods, that political leaders' popularity is most strongly affected by periods of military conflict (Ostrom and Simon 1985; Norpoth 1987; Bueno de Mesquite, Siverson, and Woller 1992; Gallup polls cited in Hanneman, Collins, and Mordt 1995). On this level, we have evidence of the link between the military power-prestige of the state and the legitimacy of its rulers. Militarily successful rulers, favored by GP circumstances, make their own legitimacy when they impose their power at home, even if they may have started as coercive and illegitimate usurpers. And war-defeated leaders, however legitimate they may have been, are at higher risk of being ousted. Furthermore, GP conditions determine not only the degree of personal legitimacy of rulers but also the legitimacy of the entire institutional order. Empirically, there is a continuum that extends low to high personal popularity and from delegitimation to legitimation of the political structure. Extremely popular individuals (who would be called charismatic) are able to extend the aura of emotional mobilization to legitimating an entirely new state. At the low end, beyond intensely negative levels of rulers' personal popularity, comes the delegitimation of the entire state.[11]

The argument does not hinge on the popularity of individual rulers per se (although popularity is a convenient piece of evidence connecting legitimacy and geopolitics). Individuals are caught up in larger processes. It is above all the swings of interstate power-prestige that bring about rapid shifts in the legitimacy of rulers. Moreover, a geopolitically induced condition of state administrative crisis, together with intra-elite conflict, tends to bring about the rapid succession of leaders in office. If infighting and chaotic turnovers reach a sufficiently high level, not only do particular leaders lose respect but the very institution of leadership appears ineffectual as well. It is through these channels that macroprocesses of geopolitics become translated into the specific events and personalities that lead to state crisis and breakdown.

Geopolitical Theory's Prediction of the Russian Empire Breakdown

Consider now the specific predictors of the Soviet collapse and how they worked out in fact.

Size and resource advantage had been building up since the expansion of the original small state of Muscovy in the 1390s. By the late 1700s, Russia could field the largest armies in Europe.[12] By the mid-twentieth century this advantage was reversed: Russia (in the guise of the Soviet Union) and its allies had become outweighed by their enemies in total population by a ratio of 3.5 to 1, in total economic resources 4.6 to 1. In troop numbers, the two blocs were much closer: Soviet enemies led by 1.7 to 1 in active troops, and by only 1.1 to 1 when reserves are included. Thus the population of the Soviet bloc was 3.5 times as heavily mobilized as its enemies in ratio of troops to population base. Correspondingly, the USSR spent a disproportionate amount on its military budget (as much as 20 percent of GNP), at the expense of civilian expenditure. It is this strain that Gorbachev addressed early in his period of reform, from 1985 onward announcing and to some extent implementing plans to scale back military forces and convert to civilian production (Becker 1986, 1987; Bernstein 1989; Gelman 1989).

The *marchland advantage* and *fragmentation of the interior* had worked to Russia's advantage during its period of expansion. Muscovy originally expanded from the "back wall" of the sparsely populated northern forest zone into the fragmented states of the central Russian planes and the disintegrated Mongol Empire. A three-sided attack on the interior state of Poland and its subsequent fragmentation gave Russia a stable frontier in Europe, until the defeat of the German central power in World War II in another multifront war allowed Russia to further expand its territorial control in the form of its satellite empire of Eastern Europe. Russian expansion into Siberia in the 1600s had taken place against sparse tribal populations. In south and central Asia and the Caucasus, expansion went on into the late 1800s against petty states left by the disintegration of a succession of empires based in Anatolia and Iran. These GP conditions were reversed to an increasing degree after 1900 (i.e., the negative feedback loops shown in Figure 3 began to dominate the positive loops). Expansion to the Far East brought Russia up against Japan and defeat in the war of 1904–5 (thereby setting off an abortive revolution at home). With the reconsolidation of a Chinese state after 1949, fighting again took place against China in 1969 (following battles in 1929 and 1945), and a heavy troop presence was maintained on the borders between China and the Soviet Union. In the south and west, the former buffer zones of small states were eaten up and Russian troops were maintained in forward positions directly confronting the forces of the NATO alliance. By the 1950s, the Russian Empire defended a land frontier of 58,000 kilometers.

My prediction was that the coincidence of crises on several frontiers at once would precipitate the unraveling of the empire. The logic is similar to that which Perrow (1984) refers to as "normal accidents" in complex organizational systems; in such structures, local breakdowns that can be remedied in isolation ramify into a systemwide crisis when they occur simultaneously. Such events occur on a probabilistic basis, increasing with the number of components. In 1953, 1956, and 1968, Russia had faced a series of uprisings in its Eastern European satellites that had been put down with the aid of loyal Warsaw Pact troops. But the ability to command loyalty depends upon perceptions of overall coercive capability and thus is subject to a "tipping phenomenon" when an atmosphere of crisis makes sanctions for noncompliance seem unlikely (Schelling 1962: 51–118). My projection was that the interaction of geopositional disadvantage with overextension and with the enemy's local resource advantage (such as existed in the USSR's military interventions to prop up client states like Afghanistan) would bring a combination of failures in far-flung regions and would eventually reach a tipping point.[13]

What happened in fact was stalemate and growing domestic disgruntlement over the Afghanistan intervention that began in 1979 and led to the withdrawal of Soviet troops beginning in 1988. The military-expansionist regime that had prevailed up to the time of Leonid Brezhnev (d. 1982) and his successors Yuri Andropov and Konstantin Chernenko was replaced in 1985 by a reform faction under Gorbachev (an Andropov protégé). Nationalist agitation within the USSR began almost immediately in 1986 and continued thereafter. In the outer periphery of the Caucasian and central Asian republics (including Uzbekistan, adjacent to the Afghanistan guerrilla war) interethnic violence broke out in 1988 and 1989. Meanwhile, in the western Soviet bloc, mobilization of dissidence suddenly went unchecked. Dissidence in Poland based on trade union organization that developed in 1980 had been repressed by martial law later that year, following the previous pattern of rebellion and defeat in the East European satellites. In the context of the unfolding GP crisis, however, in 1988 officials of the Baltic republics of the USSR backed proposals for complete autonomy. In Poland in 1988 the Solidarity union strikes led to reform concessions and to free elections in June 1989. The victorious Solidarity candidates were invited by the Communist regime to form a coalition government in August. Simultaneously in Hungary, a split within the ruling Communist Party transformed the unified autocracy into a government of shared rule in June 1989.

Ethnic population movements across borders were initiated under Gorbachev with the policy of allowing Jewish emigration to Israel. Beginning with small numbers in 1986, Jewish emigration increased to 20,000 in 1988 and to 60,000 in 1989. That new openness let loose pressures for ethnic migrations across the Soviet bloc. Within the Russian Federation itself, people who had been displaced during the Stalin years now sought to return to their ethnic homelands. In 1987, when Hungary began to grant asylum to ethnic Hungarians fleeing Romania, Romania temporarily sealed its shared border with Hungary, then reopened it under pressure in 1989. In the same year, Turkey sealed its border with Bulgaria to stem the flow of some 300,000 Bulgarians into Turkey. These developments encouraged East Germans to seek exit visas, and many left through Hungary to Western Europe in the late summer and fall of 1989. It was this movement that proved the tipping point: when Czechoslovakia's borders, under pressure of mass movement agitation, were reopened on November 1, 1989, the flood of refugees turned to open opposition to the regime, and protesters mounted an attack on the symbolic border, the Berlin Wall.

In the two weeks from November 9 to 24, 1989, confrontations with regime forces in East Germany and Czechoslovakia suddenly produced concessions, as Gorbachev refused to commit Soviet Warsaw Pact forces to controlling dissidents, in effect overruling the use of repressive force. The mutual threat that had held together discipline within the Eastern European armed forces disintegrated; two months later uprisings and transfers of power erupted across the Eastern European bloc. These events at the outermost periphery of satellites accelerated the disintegration of the next tier of the Russian Empire. In March 1991, Gorbachev's plans for liberalization of the USSR into a looser federation were upstaged by the withdrawal of six of the republics on the nation's westernmost periphery (the Baltic republics), plus Moldavia, Armenia, and Georgia. Following the breakdown of authority in August 1991 with the failed coup attempt against Gorbachev, the entire Soviet Union formally disintegrated. The pattern, as predicted, was a coincidence of crises on multiple fronts, interacting and accelerating past a tipping point into a generalized breakdown of territorial authority.

Showdown through massive arms races and wars and *an atmosphere of military ferociousness* had been in evidence since midcentury. The world GP situation had been simplifying dramatically during the twentieth century. The Nazi empire and its opposing coalition marked one approach to all-out confrontation of opposing blocs; the Soviet/NATO confrontation absorbed and divided the resources of the defeated party. In this light, the nuclear arms race, with its potential for the most massive destruction of civilian population in world history, does not appear such an anomaly. It fits the pattern of the highest level of military ferociousness, associated with showdown wars when the cumulation of GP resources reaches the point of maximal simplification and polarization. This part of GP theory also supported the prediction of the loss of Russian power, although it left two subpaths, mutual resource exhaustion through an arms race or open war.[14]

The historical outcome was that Gorbachev's reform government, soon after taking office, began to unilaterally reduce nuclear armaments. Gorbachev also began negotiating bilateral reductions after a 1987 summit meeting with President Reagan. From the point of view of GP prediction, resource exhaustion by showdown confrontation had taken effect. The cost of the nuclear arms race had become exorbitant during the early 1980s. The proximate cause was the arms buildup in the United States during the Reagan administration. From the point of view of conflict theory, this escalation in the emotional tone of confrontation followed from a series of threats exchanged by the United States and the USSR after the late 1940s. At some point the mutual escalation must issue either in outbreak of nuclear war or in exhaustion and de-escalation. The cost of nuclear armaments combined with Russia's other military expenses to produce the resource crisis of the 1980s that brought the Gorbachev faction to power. Gorbachev acquired his initial public charisma by reversing the nuclear escalation; in the period 1986–88 he had enormous prestige, especially in Western Europe, on the basis of this policy. This popularity of Gorbachev in turn first broadcast his image as a liberalizing reformer, and his travels abroad on behalf of de-escalation encouraged Eastern European dissidents.

Here too the several processes leading to state breakdown interacted. The threat of immediate use of nuclear weapons by NATO was a policy adopted to countervail the threat of Warsaw Pact forces close to the population centers of Western Europe. In return, the Soviet rationale for maintaining those forces in Eastern Europe was to deter a nuclear strike. At the same time, the presence of Warsaw Pact forces served to bolster satellite regimes. Hence the commencement of nuclear disarmament carried the expectation of troop withdrawals, and this in turn undermined the mutually monitoring coercive coalitions that constituted the authority of the satellite regimes.

Overextension had plagued Russia's GP position in East Asia since the beginning of the twentieth century. In the western part of the Soviet bloc, the acquisition of the satellite empire after 1945 added overextension in another direction, as did intervention in Afghanistan on the central Asian frontier. There are two aspects of overextension: logistical costs that eat up increasing proportions of military resources in transportation; and ideological/cultural resistance, which is manifested in ethnic hostility. The logistical overextension involved a combination of distant military commitments: the USSR frontier itself; the additional effort, at its height in the early 1980s, to build world naval power with the creation of a massive carrier fleet for Pacific, Arctic/North Atlantic, and Black Sea/Mediterranean ports; and military aid transported over long distances to allies in Cuba, Vietnam, the Middle East, and Africa.

The second aspect of overextension, ethnic hostility, results when far-flung conquest produces multiethnic empires. In a wide range of historical instances, ethnic hostility to foreign rule increased when an empire controlled two or more layers of ethnically distinct territories beyond the home ethnic heartland (its inner zone of relative ethnic homogeneity) (Collins 1978). In this respect, Russian overextension approached highly dangerous levels in the period after 1945. In the satellite zone of Eastern Europe, Soviet troops upheld power in territories two and three ethnic layers distant from the Russian homeland. In Afghanistan, and in the Caucasus where Russian troops were stationed against Turkish and Iranian forces, force was again projected beyond a tier of non-Russian ethnic territories. The dissidence mobilized in these regions, both in the period 1953–68 and with greater effect in the breakup of 1988–91, drew primarily upon ethnic identities and hostility toward locally stationed Russian personnel.

I will address below the extent to which primordial ethnic identifications were responsible for the Soviet breakdown. Here I want to stress that ethnic hostility is differentially mobilized and occurs first and most intensely in regions that are geopolitically vulnerable to breakaway. The outer tier of the Russian Empire, the satellite states, was less strongly integrated organizationally; national government structures were left in place along with local-language dominance. Movements that were mobilized to take advantage of Russian GP weakness undercut local Communist authorities oriented toward the Russian alliance. Consequently, satellite breakaways tended to have regime revolutions. Within the USSR itself, mobilization of the movements that led to formal breakup was facilitated by the fact that the component republics were already organized as nominally sovereign ethnic groups (Waller 1992). This organization was the result of the fact that the Russian Empire and its successor, the USSR, were multiethnic conquest states. Multiple ethnicity was embodied in the structure during both its growing and its declining phases; thus ethnicity cannot be considered a primary cause of the Soviet breakdown but is rather the organizational medium through which GP overextension worked itself out.

State breakdown and accelerating legitimacy crisis unfolded along the lines of GP theory. The cumulation of GP strains brought the USSR in the mid-1980s to the point of *state fiscal crisis*. Political breakdown was first manifested in *intra-elite conflict*. The power-prestige of the military-expansion faction was reduced by its failure to keep up with U.S. armaments and by the debacle in Afghanistan. Gorbachev's reform faction came to power and became embroiled in conflicts with the faction based in the Soviet military-industrial complex. This split is structurally analogous to the splitting of elites into factions depicted in the Skocpol-Goldstone model: a faction concerned with state fiscal health (pure state-class interest) versus a faction of "aristocrats" whose material property is upheld by the state and who shunt the burden of extraction onto other classes. Gorbachev threatened to cut subsidies to the military-industrial sector, hitherto the strongest part of the Soviet economy. The result was the equivalent of an aristocratic "tax revolt" as the military-industrial sector sabotaged economic reforms in the direction of conversion to a civilian economy. As a further result, the reform period became one of worsening economic crisis. Gorbachev was in the unenviable transitional position along the slippery slope of reform during incipient breakdown conditions, analogous to the experience of the Necker ministry in France of the 1780s. The worsening geopolitical, economic, and political situations mutually reinforced one another. Gorbachev's reform faction was unable to muster resources to bolster its own power. Ultimately, the continuing intra-elite conflict, which came to a head in the attempted coup by the military-industrial faction in 1991, broke apart state authority and opened the way to revolution, in a fashion that paralleled the aristocratic revolt that precipitated the downfall of the French monarchy in 1789.[15]

The third component of the state breakdown model is the mobilization of oppositional class forces from below (*popular revolt*). The greatest variability in the general theory is at this level. In place of the peasant revolts in agrarian-capitalist societies, we find dissidents centered initially on the nominally ethnic organizations in the peripheral republics who were joined at the height of the disturbance by the educated populace in the main urban centers (Bessinger 1990; Sedaitis and Butterfield 1991; Roeder 1991). Again there was a cumulation and acceleration of the conditions of breakdown and mobilization of dissident movements.

Gorbachev's faction, in its efforts to generate support in the intra-elite conflict against the military-industrial faction, carried out a series of political liberalizations. Early maneuverings were directed at undercutting the power of officials from the Brezhnev era by attacking state bureaucracy and the Soviet Communist Party itself through calls for self-management and accelerated economic development. The idea of *perestroika* introduced in April 1986 can be interpreted as an effort to broaden the base of Gorbachev's support for redirecting state activities from military mobilization to economic development. Political dissidents were released from prison or freed from internal exile in 1986 and 1987, and popular assemblies were developed to undercut existing Communist Party organization. A series of reforms in the electoral process beginning in 1988 created openings in the union republics and culminated in the first openly elected USSR Congress of People's Deputies in 1989. The growth of these alternative structures—what Leon Trotsky in his theory of revolution called "dual sovereignty"—provided an organizational base upon which the legitimacy of the entire institutional order could be called into question. Initially, the mass mobilization encouraged by Gorbachev transformed him into a charismatic figure—the speechmaker amidst the admiring crowds—and shifted legitimacy onto him personally. But personal legitimacy is a two-edged sword, above all in a situation of volatile and shifting resource bases. With the deepening of structural crisis and Gorbachev's failure in intra-elite conflict, he was suddenly delegitimated; along with his personal fall came the delegitimation of the entire regime.

What Counts as a Valid Prediction?

Can successful historical predictions be made? Obviously they can. But it is important to distinguish between a sociological prediction and a guess or wishful thinking. A valid prediction requires two things. First, the prediction must be based on a theory that explains the conditions under which various things happen or do not happen—that is, a model that culminates in if-then statements. This is a more stringent standard of theory than what sociologists generally mean by the term. It is not a category scheme, or a metatheory, or even a process model, which lacks observable if-then consequences. Second, there must be empirical information about the starting points, the conditions at the beginning of the if-then statement. My prediction of the Soviet collapse was based on the principles of GP theory plus empirical data about the condition of the USSR and its enemies as of the 1970s.

A good deal of confusion in the debate over whether prediction is possible has come from failure to distinguish the two components. In the absence of a theory, prediction is merely empirical extrapolation. In making a short-term extrapolation, all one does is make assumptions about a process that is already under way, without understanding what might cause it to change direction. Long-run empirical extrapolation is notoriously unreliable. Much of the prediction that sociologists do is of this sort. For instance, we hear predictions that by the middle of the twenty-first century more than half of American children will be minorities. In the absence of a theory of what determines ethnic identities this sort of prediction is questionable, for it assumes that there will be no ethnic assimilation or change in the social categories of ethnicity. The most famous failure in sociological prediction was a trend extrapolation, when demographers in 1940, lacking any theory that could have encompassed a baby boom, made population projections that turned out to be 100 million short.

Theoretical principles plus empirical data are necessary for predictions in which we can have some confidence, predictions that are more than guesses. The theory must also be validated. The validity of a macrosociological theory is never an all-or-nothing matter. In dealing with complex processual models that take into account feedback among both internal processes and external relations among states, there is never simple and clear-cut statistical acceptance or rejection of an overall model. That is not to say that particular components of the model cannot be falsified by data; but resisting falsification in piecemeal analysis is not the primary way in which the plausibility of a macrodynamic model is built up. The success of my Russian Empire prediction adds to our assessment of its validity, although if the theory had no other basis than this case our confidence in its further applicability would remain tentative. Overall coherence among all the sources of evidence is central to our judgments of validity, and that coherence is displayed to the degree that the theoretical statements summarizing various cases can be made logically consistent with one another. The coherence among GP theory, the military resource theory of state formation, and state-breakdown theory is a source of mutual validation for all of them. In the foregoing review of these models, I have cited a body of research, some of which was produced since 1980, when I put forward the GP prediction of Soviet collapse. Research and theory-development along these lines continues today. For validating the overall model and thereby showing that the basis for prediction was systematic rather than ad hoc, the time at which such research is done is irrelevant. In this sense, the validity of the GP prediction continues to be strengthened (or may conceivably be undermined) by the ongoing cumulation of macropolitical theory.

Theories on the Collapse of the Soviet Empire

With the preceding points in mind, let us consider some of the other predictions and postdictions that have been made about the collapse of the Soviet Empire.[16]

ETHNIC REVOLT

The most notable prediction with which I was familiar in 1980 was made by Helene d'Encausse in 1979 and was based on an empirical extrapolation. D'Encausse calculated population trends for Russians and other ethnicities of the USSR and concluded that the empire would disintegrate in the twenty-first century as non-Russian nationalities became the majority. Was this a valid basis for prediction? Can we extract a theoretical principle from d'Encausse's ethnic population trends? It would seem to be that the sheer size of ethnic groups determines relative political strength and implicitly that multiethnic states tend toward rebellion and disintegration. What is missing is a broader theory of the conditions under which ethnic groups assimilate, remain distinct, or for that matter fragment into still smaller subethnicities. But trends in ethnic boundaries are highly variable, and the major determinant seems to be geopolitical (see Chapter 3). That is, when the core state is geopolitically strong, the prestige of its dominant ethnic group is high and it becomes the target for ethnic assimilation. It is when GP disintegration is already under way that ethnic separatist movements are mobilized as vehicles for the decentralization of power. The conclusion follows that in the absence of the package of GP conditions predictions of the relative size of ethnic populations would not have been a valid prediction of Soviet collapse.[17]

It is important not to raise these issues merely in the spirit of who should get credit for making the right prediction. Prediction is not a one-shot deal, picking out the lucky hits from a series of misses; it is useful only if we know that we have a reliable instrument, a tool we can use repeatedly and in varying circumstances. It was a crucial question, for instance, for Eastern Europe

and Central Asia in the 1990s, and doubtless will be in the twenty-first century, whether ethnic population size alone drives state dissolution or
whether overall GP conditions determine the direction of ethnic assimilation or disassimilation. Only on the basis of a good general theory can we
offer predictive insight.[18]

In this spirit, let us consider the post facto claims that were made after the
1989–90 revolution and especially after the summer of 1991. Most of the arguments took one of the following forms: (a) that oppressive states like the
Soviet regimes were bound to be thrown off by their people; or (b) that a
centralized (and a fortiori socialist) economy inevitably loses out in competition with the higher productivity of free-market capitalism. Leave aside the
fact that virtually everyone before the late 1980s, including most social scientists, regarded Soviet socialist regimes as essentially permanent. How do
the two popular retrospective claims stand up as theories?

OVERTHROW OF OPPRESSION

The theory that the fall of oppressive states is inevitable is clearly wrong. It
was a battle cry of exultation at the moment when the statues were toppling.
In the absence of state breakdown at the top and conditions for resource
mobilization from below, the oppressiveness of a state has been a very poor
predictor of its vulnerability to popular revolution (see evidence cited in
Tilly 1978 and Skocpol 1979).

CAPITALISM VERSUS SOCIALISM

The theory that free markets will always triumph should make us wary,
since it is obviously a form of ideological gloating. But it has a certain plausibility, even for GP theory, since if it is correct it would heavily influence
the resource levels feeding into the military power of states (i.e., it would be
a noncumulative aspect of principle 1, size and resource advantages). To
guard against post hoc imposition of theory on a selected case, we should
consider what general principles are being assumed. One is that economic
productivity in consumer goods is the prime determinant of political revolutions. As a comparative-historical generalization this is plainly untrue.

A second weakness is that the capitalism-is-more-productive-than-
socialism theory is vague with respect to timing. Its current application to
the Soviet downturn of the 1980s is narrow and ad hoc. In an earlier period
(through the 1950s and 1960s until about 1975), Soviet socialist economies
grew more rapidly than most of their capitalist counterparts (Kennedy 1987:
429–31, 490–96). Szelenyi and Szelenyi (1994) argue on these grounds that
the socialist economies may only have been in a medium-run cyclical phase
of downturn in the 1980s and that the political downfall was due to factors
that are fortuitous from the point of view of an economically driven theory.

There is little to conclude from this either way, since there is no well-developed body of theory of long-term patterns of socialist economic change. Unfortunately, the same must be said about long-term patterns of capitalist economies; there is considerable evidence of cyclical processes and crises, but there are no general principles to indicate when and why capitalist economies might be in a cyclical crisis while socialist economies are growing (as in the 1930s) or the reverse (conceivably the case in the 1980s). In the future, social science may improve its understanding and its predictive capabilities regarding such macroeconomic patterns. But the balance of the evidence and the coherence of theory development at this time suggest that even when we understand economic cycles better they will not prove to independently determine state expansion or state breakdown. At best, they will add causal loops that feed into the core model of state resource extraction and its strains.

We also have available a crucial empirical comparison that allows us to test the relative merits of GP and capitalist-productive-superiority theories: temporal patterns in state power of the USSR and China. This comparison would argue against the capitalist-superiority model of state collapse. Li (1993) shows that the vicissitudes of Chinese Communist forces in the twentieth century follow from GP theory, and he predicts, on the basis of China's relative GP advantages at the turn of the twenty-first century, that internal revolution is not to be expected. In other words: socialism per se does not account for variations in state weakness or strength, whereas GP conditions do.[19]

The foregoing does not depend upon denying economic weakness within socialism but only on whether it is possible in terms of general theory to derive from this an adequate explanation of the Soviet breakdown. There exists a well-developed body of analysis of the inefficiencies of a centrally planned economy of state enterprises (Kornai 1992). Moreover, as Walder (1994) and Nee and Lian (1994) show, attempting to bring about reform by introducing market structures within such systems weakens and splits the ruling elite. It undermines the incentive structure for officials, decreases their dependence on central hierarchic controls, and promotes the opportunistic seeking of personal economic gain. Market reforms cannot be the prime explanation of communist regime collapse, however. Market reforms were little developed in the USSR, the linchpin of communist control in Eastern Europe, and most advanced in the China of the 1980s, where the state remained strongest. In Hungary and Poland, where extensive market reforms occurred, two kinds of processes meshed. Market reform generated internal pressures for political change, but these pressures led to full-scale state revolution only in the context of the USSR's geopolitical crisis, which broke down from above.

It may well be true, as Walder and Nee/Lian argue, that market reform will eventually undermine socialism in China. This implies neither a state breakdown nor a democratic revolution. Indeed, insofar as economic growth through market reform further strengthens China's GP position, one would expect a strong state, even as it evolves into some form of political economy other than pure socialism.[20]

PERSONALITY

Another factor retrospectively put forward to account for the Soviet overthrow is the influence of individual personalities. The underlying argument is an antitheoretical one: unique characters such as Gorbachev, who spring up unpredictably, can create crucial turning points in world history. This line of analysis is easily disposed of. Such world-historical personalities do not appear at random; they may have world-historical significance only if they are structurally located in positions where their actions have major consequences. Such positions exist only when there are highly centralized structures of power and when power coalitions around that point are fragmented and in flux. In short, the conditions for the emergence of socially significant personalities are those formulated in state-breakdown theory and its cognates, the theories of state formation and social movement mobilization. The sociological way to put the question is to ask what the requisite conditions are for the rise and fall of individual charisma. The Gorbachev reform movement gives a particularly clear example of how charisma depends on surrounding social dynamics. Gorbachev was an obscure figure, connected through Andropov with the secret police, until he became Communist Party chief in 1985. It was when he embarked upon the reform path, in response to structural crisis, that he became a charismatic figure. In greater microdetail, we can trace his new public personality to the mass meetings and tours that surrounded him with emotional fervor and made him an emblem for liberalizing (and peaceful) hopes.[21] This halo of charisma began to crumble as the crowds he had mobilized went beyond him and the coercive power of his regime was undermined, leaving him as the representative of a weakening state authority. Charismatic leaders—great personalities—rise and fall. The more general sociological lesson is to attend to the conditions under which we can expect such personalities to brighten and dim.

IDEOLOGY

The Soviet collapse is sometimes cited as an instance of the overriding role of ideology. The downfall is variously attributed to the irrepressible idea of ethnic nationalism, the spreading ideas of freedom, or the capitalist market (or more specifically its consumerist ethic). There is no reason to doubt the existence of these beliefs. The question is, did they determine the Soviet transition? And does ideology provide a basis for prediction generally, or for concluding that prediction is impossible?

The structural conditions for the mobilization of ethnic ideologies have been discussed above. The potential for ethnic nationalism always exists; but whether it goes in the direction of assimilation to larger national units (a dominant trend in recent centuries) or toward local particularism is highly variable (see Tilly 1993: 246–47). It is tautological to conclude that the autonomous strength of ethnic ideology per se determines which way it will go. The same can be said about the ideological appeal of capitalism. Procapitalist ideology does not have uniform appeal, even on a decade-by-decade basis in the twentieth century, and there have been a number of reversals in the popularity of pro- and anticommunist ideologies. When and where these variations occur has not been systematically theorized. If we limit the capitalist-ideology thesis to the spread of Western consumerism, it is striking that the contemporary ideology among Western intellectuals and mass-entertainment culture, far from celebrating consumerism, constitutes a "postmodernist" attack upon it. Thus the ideology of antisocialist dissidents has been out of phase with the alleged transmitters of ideology in the West.

More theoretically, the role of ideology in state breakdown and revolution has been addressed by the cumulating body of research that I have drawn upon here. Ideologies associated with the directions that revolutions take have been quite variable, and theoretical explanation has not been well developed. Goldstone argues, like Skocpol, that ideologies are not a significant part of the explanation of state breakdown (Goldstone 1992: 416–48). That is, ideology is a proximate, not a basic, part of the causal chain; it comes into play only once intra-elite conflict and state fiscal crisis are well advanced (compare the formulation of Moaddel 1992). For Goldstone, ideology is a better predictor of what follows once breakdown takes place. Nevertheless, we lack a systematic theory of what ideology will emerge as dominant in particular kinds of cases. There is considerable evidence that ideological movements "march backward into the future." For instance, the major outburst of class conflict in the early industrial revolution in England was mobilized under a reactionary ideology of workers attempting to turn back the clock to artisan production, but it succeeded only in laying the basis for the regulation of factory production (Calhoun 1982).

My prediction for the Russian Empire included the theoretical argument that ideology follows geopolitics. For the parts of the USSR that fell within the geopolitical orbit of nearby Islamic states, I proposed that the spread of Islam would be the vehicle for revolt. The prestige of an ideology rises and falls with the state power of its most visible adherents; thus the success of the Iranian revolution under the auspices of Islamic fundamentalism led to the rapid upsurge of Islamic fundamentalism in adjacent areas, including

Afghanistan. For the bulk of the USSR, my suggestion was that state break-down and regime transition might well occur under the ideology of a dissi-dent form of Communism. This turned out to be how Gorbachev's reform Communism got started, but I did not anticipate that the breakdown would rapidly turn in a procapitalist direction. Here I might have made better use of the general principle that ideologies, like rulers, are delegitimated by de-clines in the power-prestige of the regime that carries them. Just as defeat in World War I undermined the ideological prestige of the capitalist modern-izers who controlled the Russian government and set the stage for a rebound into anticapitalist ideology, the geopolitically based failure of the USSR (and the continuing downward slope of power-prestige for Gorbachev's reform Communists) led to a rebound toward anticommunist and procapitalist ideology.[22]

State breakdowns thus would tend to bring about shifts from one of a pair of ideological rivals to another. Since ideologies are not usually limited to two alternatives, the generality of this principle does not go very far. We need a better theory about the conditions that produce ideologies and ele-vate one or another of them to prominence.[23] Ideology can no doubt be in-corporated into a general, predictive theory of state breakdowns. But instead of making it a free-floating unmoved mover, we need to establish the con-ditions for its variants and the place they hold in the causal chain.

In sum, the rival explanations of Soviet breakdown reviewed here have been ad hoc. They do not rest on general principles consistent with expla-nation across a broad range of cases. GP theory, in contrast, has been based on comparative data from the outset. GP theory of state change is still far from being highly refined and has not been subjected to stringent empirical testing. Nevertheless, it makes roughly accurate predictions and postdictions. It meshes well with the major lines of theory and research on the develop-ment of the state and on state breakdown and revolution. The details of how the Soviet breakdown actually took place are consistent with the processes expected from these models. It is reasonable to conclude that GP theory is a building block from which further prediction-generating work can be mounted.

How Much Predictive Precision Is Possible?

Current GP theory is not very precise. Using historical atlases, one can gen-eralize that the conditions that determine GP advantage and disadvantage change slowly, over hundreds of years (Collins 1978). Since the state con-trols military force within a territory, the lineup of resources among adjacent states pays off in much shorter periods during wartime and related acute pe-riods of resource strains. Major wars typically take two to five years, rarely more than ten. This gives us two different time-orders: (1) the long slow latent buildup or build-down of resources punctuated by (2) the quick depletion of resources during wartime and during overt changes in territorial power. The conditions that determine when wars actually break out, or correspondingly when wars are avoided, include a great many other factors;[24] but these are apparently randomized over the long run, as we can infer because the long-term direction of resource availability eventually leads to corresponding state expansion or contraction. When we apply GP theory to actual predictions, then, we are left with some inherent imprecision.[25] From historical atlases, I estimated that GP resources provide predictability down to units of about 30–50 years; within such periods, it is impossible to know (at least from GP information alone) when the crucial military-driven crises will occur. From the evidence available in 1980, I predicted that the USSR would disintegrate within 30 to 50 years. Frankly, I was surprised that it happened so soon, but it certainly was within the scope of my prediction.[26]

Because of factors on this intermediate or mesolevel of causality, it has sometimes been argued, much more sweepingly, that GP resources are inherently incapable of generating predictions of state power changes because diplomatic alliances can always offset any particular strength or weakness. Mann (1989) argues against Kennedy's (1987) formulation of GP theory, that any such model is invalidated by the unpredictability of diplomatic alliances. But is it in fact the case that diplomacy is a realm of free-floating choices? There has been as yet no systematic confrontation of the literature on diplomacy with that of GP theory, but it is reasonable to expect that diplomacy follows geopolitics. I propose two hypotheses: (a) Geopolitically strong states impose alliances on weaker states adjacent to their immediate zone of military extension. Conversely, weak states seek the protection of adjacent strong states or give in to the imposition of alliances. (b) Where balance-of-power situations obtain (i.e., in zones where multiple states impinge upon each other's borders, the interior zones subject to GP principle 3 stated above), states make alliances on the principle that their enemy's enemies are their friends. This leads to a geopolitical checkerboard pattern and the fragmented interior region predicted by principle 3. These middle or interior regions exist only as long as marchland states are not strong. When power resources cumulatively build up on the opposite edges of such a middle region, alliances shift to bipolar blocs dictated by the largest states. Historical cases ranging from the Roman expansion to the Soviet and U.S. alliances of the twentieth century suggest that, far from offsetting GP principles, diplomacy is geopolitics by other means.

There is a third order of time, much shorter than either of the above. This is social movement time. At its heart are the two or three days during which the state hangs in the balance, the crowds are mobilized in the streets, and waves of enthusiasm or fear forge massive social networks, not least of which are soldiers who waver from one center of power to another. Around this microfocus of time when the state power transition actually occurs—the revolutionary days of popular fame—there is a penumbra of semi-intense mobilization that lasts a few weeks. This period may stretch into months if movement enthusiasm diffuses among a series of state power centers, such as the capitals of Eastern Europe in the fall and winter of 1989–90 or the regional republics of the USSR from 1990 onward.[27]

This microfocus of mobilization time is so emotionally intense and so capable of forging symbols that it tends to obliterate the other two time processes that made it possible (long slow shifts over decades or centuries in relative state resources, and the several years of strain caused by war). It was a journalistic cliche, especially in the summer of 1991, to remark how amazing it was that change could occur in the Soviet regime so rapidly. It would have been *sociologically* amazing, however, if the change in state control had *not* occurred rapidly. At the core of the state (the monopoly of organized military force) is a coercive coalition, enforcers who discipline one another by armed threat. When such a coalition breaks apart and is replaced by another coalition, it must rapidly pass through the tipping point, since it is extremely dangerous for an individual enforcer to stay outside the winning coalition. These tipping points generate extreme and contagious emotions, and they give the sense that everything hangs in the balance, that there is a moment of freedom and choice. This is what generates the ideology that revolutions are uncausable and unpredictable.[28]

Nevertheless, the passage through such tipping points is itself highly structured by the two prior time processes that we have discussed. Just when this tipping point comes to pass is unpredictable, at least from a macro-standpoint; but that such tipping points will occur within a larger time frame is predictable when the macro-orders of causality have moved beyond a particular degree.

Nested Levels of Macro-to-Micro Prediction

What we have been considering here is a macro/micro problem. The different orders of causal and predictive precision highlight the character of the macro/micro relationship. The circumstances that lead to state breakdown occur along a continuum, not in a dichotomy. On the macro end are those patterns of causal connection that are biggest in time and space; on the micro end are the patterns of social organization that can be discerned in successively smaller slices of time and space. Thus the relationship between what is more macro and what is more micro is one of nested levels. The macrogeopolitical level consists in causal patterns that cover periods of decades up through centuries, as well as variability in the degree of connectedness among social organizations in different regions of space.

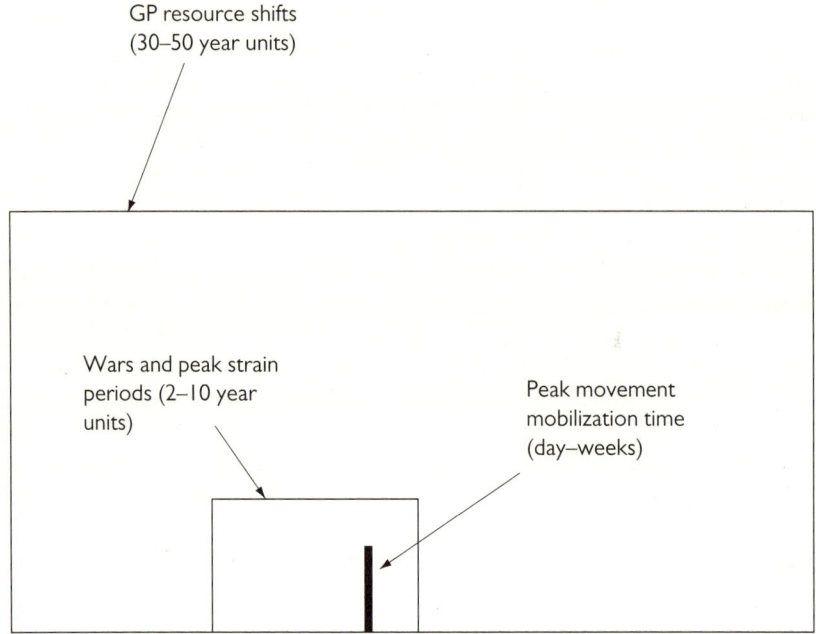

FIGURE 8. Nested macro-micro levels of predictability in state breakdown.

Predictive generalizations at this level can at best issue in statements about the direction of change in GP advantage and disadvantage and point to shifts that take place within a range of 30 to 50 years (see Figure 8).

Nested inside such time periods are moderately large-scale processes such as war and state breakdown. (Given the imprecision of our vocabulary for such matters, we might refer to them as *lower-macro* or *upper-meso*; they link thousands or millions of mutually unseen actors in chains of relationships that may unfold over a period of years.) The problem of predictive imprecision on this upper-mesolevel applies primarily to the initiation of a conflict or breakdown, which may be inherently random insofar as it depends upon the concatenation of smaller crises into what Perrow calls "normal accidents" (Perrow 1984). However, once a breakdown process is under way it displays a great deal of *theoretical* order, in the sense that abstract properties of the unraveling of coercive coalitions and their replacement by others are widely, even universally, found. Recall, however, that successful prediction requires a combination of valid general theory together with empirical knowledge of relevant starting points. Prediction is often not feasible in the heat of unfolding events because information on these empirical conditions is not available.

Focusing in still further, we reach the *lower-mesolevel* of movement mobilization time, and nested within it the heady hours of peak collective behavior time.[29] Implicitly, these lower-meso events are selected from wider but similar time-periods in which routine prevails and nothing apparently happens that is worth analyzing. Once again, we see that the crucial predictive imprecision has to do with the timing of particular kinds of activity in this period. Kuran (1995) provides a stronger reason why the exact timing of the tipping points is socially unpredictable by the participants themselves. This is a theory of unpredictability on the third level of the nested macro-micro continuum that deals with the initiation point for the outbreak of oppositional social movements. The misrepresentation of preferences by individual persons, which is the normal condition within a mutually enforced coercive coalition, can only break down under special conditions (which ultimately derive from the nested macrolevel of processes on the level of state-breakdown). Once the tipping point is passed, however, the social-movement dynamics and the peak periods of collective behavior follow highly structured patterns. Crowds, even at the height of emotional enthusiasm, do not behave randomly but exhibit considerable social coordination down to the level of truly micro patterns (McPhail 1991: 158–84). Such tipping points may also be characterized as points that mark the passage through conditions of critical mass; this occurs under network conditions specified by Marwell and Oliver (1993).

In short, the problem of predictive imprecision occurs at just those points where we shift from the macroanalytic level to a level of social interaction nested within it. The nesting refers us directly to a shift in time orders, which is what the imprecision is about. This is a way of saying that from considerations of factors that work themselves out over a given stretch of time (e.g., a half-century), it is impossible to predict with any greater precision the onset of processes that work themselves out in three to ten years; and these in turn do not allow predicting the precise onset of processes nested within them in even narrower periods of time.

Obstacles to Successful Sociological Prediction

There are a number of reasons why sociologists do not make more good predictions. Briefly listed, these include the failure to distinguish empirical extrapolation from theory-based prediction and the failure to collect adequate data about empirical starting points from which predictions may proceed. In addition, there are competing theories in many areas, and relatively little attention is given to which lines of theory have the highest level of validity (according to the criteria discussed above). Moreover, a great deal of metatheoretical discussion in sociology is concerned not with any particular substantive explanations but with abstract reasons why substantive explanation of human action (and a fortiori prediction) is impossible and perhaps also immoral. Without entering into lengthy debates over historicism, interpretivism, and humanism, I would only note that the impossibility of prediction is refuted in the present case and that in numerous other areas of sociology an appropriate focus upon the best-validated explanatory theory, together with sufficient information about empirical starting points, can yield other successful predictions.[30]

The foregoing obstacles to prediction are internal to the community of social scientists. Some external conditions are also likely to be obstacles to macrosociological prediction of politically significant events. One such influence is the political ideology of the surrounding society, in which we are also participants. I have already noted that, through most of the 1980s, both liberals and conservatives were locked into a stereotyped image of Soviet power. By the late 1980s, Gorbachev's liberalizing reforms were well under way, but U.S. newspapers relegated them to the inside pages. During the 1988 presidential campaign, the presidential candidate Michael Dukakis ignored foreign-policy initiatives toward military de-escalation, even though polls showed that Gorbachev was more popular in the United States than any American politician. Through the early summer of 1989, only months before the overt breakdown began in Eastern Europe, President George Bush and his administration took the line that the reforms were only a ruse and that continued military buildup was necessary (*Facts on File* 1986–89).

Can we extract a sociological lesson about the dynamics of ideology from the behavior of American politicians during the late 1980s? It appears that ideologies forged during previous conflicts are slow to change even when underlying structural conditions change. Only when there is a highly dramatized, overt change in surface relationships does a new set of ideological symbols come to the fore. Before 1989, the dominant perspectives worldwide saw the communist states as permanent and powerful. Within a few years, it became equally common belief that they were doomed to failure. Neither view was (or is) based upon a well-grounded theoretical understanding of the bases of state power. Social scientists are capable of contributing to such understanding to the degree that they can insulate themselves, at least in a portion of their lives, from popular political ideologies.

That this is difficult to do is illustrated by the work of Paul Kennedy. In 1987, Kennedy published a general treatment of rise and decline in state power with an application to all the major states of the contemporary world. He independently formulated several of the major principles of GP theory that I have listed above, basing his analysis on the principles of resource advantage (1) and overextension (4). Nevertheless, he did not predict the decline of Soviet power because his main concern was the danger of U.S. decline, above all as a result of overextension of U.S. military power around the globe. The influence of ideological commitment is visible here. Kennedy expressed the viewpoint of American liberals, who wanted to avoid repeating the mistakes of the Vietnam war; his theory encompassed this concern under the principle of overextension of military power to distant regions that would result in power decline by the attrition of resources. Kennedy's theoretical principles and the historical comparisons behind them are correct as far as they go. His failure in prediction was due to ideological commitments: he focused his attention on the state that he most wished to warn—his own—while losing perspective on the one in which GP strains were greatest.

There are also more routine reasons why we do not develop or use the predictive power of explanatory sociology. Ordinary discourse and the rituals of social interaction tend to reify social institutions, so that they appear permanent and immutable. Ethnomethodological investigations of everyday reasoning show that social actors prefer to take for granted a constant background of normalcy. When some incident forces a breach in normal expectations, we try to mend the breach by reimposing a normal form upon it as soon as possible. This is one reason why ordinary social actors perceive the macrostructures of the world through the lens of ideologies, even though these do little more than impose an arbitrary sense of order upon the world. Nevertheless, the routine of sociological researchers and theorists is not the same as the routine of lay actors. We have built up intellectual resources that enable us to make a routine out of piecing together coherent and empirically validated models of social processes, whose categories need not be the same as those of the taken-for-granted categories of everyday life. It is demonstrable that sociological theory may be used to make valid predictions that go beyond the "unaided eye." It is this which gives a possibility for sociology to make a distinctive contribution.

Future Prospects for Predictive Sociology

The ability of sociology to make valid predictions is a sign of the maturity of the discipline. Valid prediction is not a one-shot enterprise; it rests upon the cumulative development of theory and research. The trying out of promising leads and blind alleys, the accumulation of data and the discovery of distinctions and interrelations, the grasping of complexity and strategic simplification of core models—all this takes generations. But it would be surprising if no progress had been made during the 100 years of sociology's institutional existence. The macrodynamics of political change is one of the longest-standing research interests in sociology. The passion and energy it has attracted over the years have given it a core of theory that can provide increasingly good service as more refined theory is elaborated in the future.

CHAPTER 3

"Balkanization" or "Americanization": A Geopolitical Theory of Ethnic Change

ANALYTICAL UNDERSTANDING of ethnicity is one of the weak spots in the social sciences. A great deal has been written about it, but much of what is said has an ephemeral quality. In the past century, there have been waves of enthusiasm for and against various kinds of ethnic and nationalist movements. The discussions have been heated, caught up in contemporary political moods. Since the late twentieth century, the prestige of ethnic autonomy has been high, and discourse in the social sciences has been replete with morally charged concepts such as multiculturalism, the right to one's culture, and cultural genocide. This is a very different mood than prevailed in the early twentieth century and before, when the liberal ideal was often an inclusive nationalism that would overcome petty regionalisms and local animosities in the name of one people cooperating toward a shared goal. In Shakespeare's *Henry V*, the king's rallying of Cornishmen, Welshmen, Irishmen, and Scotsmen into battle as Englishmen applies the same archetype found in American films of World War II vintage, which conventionally featured a platoon containing a WASP farmboy, an Italian, a Swede, and a Jew who learn to put aside their differences in the common cause. Historically there have been still other variants besides ethnic preservationism and the ethnic melting pot, such as the cosmopolitan eighteenth-century Enlightenment, when a widespread ideal was a superior culture rising above and cutting across the local and the particular.

Analysis has suffered from being unidimensional. We have too easily assumed that everything flows in the same direction, that the world as a whole is on an evolutionary path or has reached a postmodern condition, that there are "ages of nationalism" or ages of political correctness. Consider the polar visions of the twenty-first- (or twenty-second-) century future that are implied in these alternative models: Will it be a future in which every ethnic group will be free and independent, even possessing its own state? Or the continuation of a long-term trend from a heterogeneity of small local groups amalgamating into larger national blocs and thence into a single world culture and comprising, by intermarriage, a single world race? These are the optimistic ideals; their negative counterparts are a world of multiethnic hostility, a coming century of pogroms, genocide, and terrorism legitimated by the aspirations of still-oppressed ethnicities, or a century of bland uniformity, with world hegemony of the English language and American popular culture. Putting the argument in these terms should make us suspect that the future belongs exclusively to none of the above. History has always been more of a mixed bag than such one-sided models depict.

The analytical basis must be dug more deeply. No single process affects the entire world, or even entire regions of it. We need to model the range of variants in ethnic arrangements and state the conditions that move a region in one direction or the other. A region can move toward greater ethnic pluralism or toward greater ethnic uniformity, toward what I have labeled, somewhat tendentiously, "Balkanization" or "Americanization." My argument is that the heart of these variations is the strength of the state: how the military state mobilizes its population and penetrates it with civilian tentacles. On this baseline lie the geopolitical fortunes of states. I present here a state-centered theory of ethnicity to accompany the state-centered theory of revolution laid out in the previous chapters.

Constructing such a theory is a matter of putting things in their context. Researchers have been acutely concerned with ethnicity and its semantic neighbors, race, nationalism, and citizenship; and they have posited numerous causal conditions and processes. My argument is that these causal conditions are indeterminate when we try to generalize them. What works for ethnic assimilation in the United States in the 1950s does not work for the Soviet Union in the 1980s because the geopolitical context is different. Any comprehensive theory of ethnicity must be a multicausal theory. But in a jumble of causes, some are more fateful than others. I argue again that geopolitical relations among states are the switch that shifts the causal track in different directions within each state.

What Determines How Many Ethnic Groups Exist?

For all the research that has been done on ethnicity in the United States, this is not a good place to begin analytical theorizing. Sociological research has concentrated on processes of discrimination; in more optimistic or self-satisfied eras it has focused on processes of assimilation. But these investigations beg the question: why are there ethnic groups in the first place? We have been concerned mainly with why ethnic groups persist or when they disappear. We have not dealt systematically enough with the question of what creates ethnic groups. In part this is because certain ideological assumptions underlie most research. If one is an assimilationist, one tends not to think of the dominant ethnic group as ethnic at all but simply as the mainstream culture of that society. If one is a radical critic, one may recognize and denounce this approach, pointing out that Anglo-conformity or WASP dominance is the privileged status of one ethnic group among others. Either way, insight is lost by taking for granted the cultural categories of what is, after all, a very particular historical condition. Assimilation is reduction in the number of ethnic groups, at the extreme, to one ethnicity per state. The tendency to think of the hegemonic ethnic group as the target of assimilation reveals a general process: some ethnic groups have legitimacy, just as political rule can have legitimacy. The number of ethnic groups varies along a continuum, and the legitimacy of a dominant ethnicity varies as well. The question for an analytically comprehensive theory of ethnicity is, what moves a region in one direction or another?

Or take the question from the point of view of an ethnic liberationist. The rhetoric of one's position naturally assumes that one's ethnic group exists; it has a history, roots, an identity reaching back into the past. The political task is to mobilize this identity still more, so that its members will fight for its preservation and autonomy and ethnic others will be made to recognize the justice of one's claims. The stance of mobilized participants in ethnic conflict is primordialist. This too is data for the detached viewpoint of an analytical theory. It also means that the activist-eye view is not sufficient grounds for a theory, or indeed for very adequate historical accounts. The primordialist makes history a blinkered search into the past, a deceptively clear channel marked by whatever can be construed as one's historical roots. Italians in the United States at the turn of the twentieth century were in the process of acquiring an Italian identity, while their home-land identities had been Sicilian, Calabrian, Neapolitan, Genoan, and so on; and those regional ethnicities themselves were the product of assimilation among previously fragmented villages or clans. The same is true of "Chicanos," the result of assimilation among Indios, mestizos, Spaniards, and other ethnicities. The category-in-formation "Hispanics" is even further along the continuum. Ethnic groups not only reproduce or disappear; they are also created. The process of political mobilizing reduces the number of places where boundaries can be drawn for collective action; conflict creates the framework that is projected backward into a primordial past.[1]

An ethnic group is not merely, or even primarily, a community that shares a common culture and identity. Its identity is constituted by dividing lines, by contrast with others. The key questions are: how many ethnic groups are socially perceived to exist at a time and place? And analytically more important: what determines whether the number of ethnic groups, and therefore also the number of inter-ethnic divisions, increases or decreases? The easy answer to be avoided comes from treating the first question in a matter-of-fact way. By common discourse we know what ethnic groups exist in the United States, or in Bosnia, and with that information in hand we can examine what would seem to be the more important questions of conflict, domination, or harmonization. These kinds of answers, based on research in the short run of the present, are inconsistent from case to case. We need the long-run, macrohistorical viewpoint in order to give the short-run processes their trajectories.

Social Construction of Ethnicity in the Long Run

An ethnicity is best described as a metacommunity, a framework for a community of communities. All members of an ethnic group do not know one another; neither are they linked in a network. Many ethnic groups, such as Germans and Chinese, number in the millions. Ethnicities are often described as cultural units, characterized by distinctive cuisine, clothing styles, and ways of life. These units are socially constructed by two related processes: the social action, originally without self-consciousness, that built these local peculiarities; and the cultural labeling of group boundaries when their distinctive characteristics became recognized as markers by group outsiders, and then, reflexively, by the group itself. Here I focus on two markers that are analytically more revealing, that bring to light the social process that both constructs naive protoethnicity and mobilizes ethnonationalism. These are somatotypes and languages.

SOCIAL CONSTRUCTION OF SOMATOTYPES

People who belong to an ethnic group tend to look alike—or at least group members possess certain physical characteristics frequently enough that it is socially recognized what a "typical" ethnic member is supposed to look like. Scandinavians are expected, with above-average frequency, to be blonde, blue-eyed, and fair skinned; Italians to be dark-haired and olive-skinned; and so on. Physical anthropologists have added a modicum of precision, charting relative prevalence of facial bone structures and skeletal dimensions, of dental patterns and blood types. Mentioning such things can be rather bad form today, insofar as it invokes old discredited theories that imputed distinct historic destinies to "broad-headed" and "narrow-headed stock" or looked for criminal propensities or hereditary pauperism among southern or eastern European ancestries. Very likely there are no important correlations between physical appearance and intelligence, behavior, or culture. I bring in ethnic somatotypes nevertheless, in order to make two analytical points.[2]

First, there is no deep and analytically important distinction between "race" and "ethnicity." Conventionally, races are regarded as physically distinctive (e.g., by skin color), while ethnic groups are merely culturally distinctive. But ethnic groups also have somatotypical differences (hair, skin color, facial structure, and the like), which people commonly seize upon when consciousness of ethnic divisions is high. A sociological distinction between ethnicity and race is analytically pernicious because it obscures the social processes that determine the extent to which divisions are made along the continuum of somatotypical gradations. Race is a folk concept, a popular mythology that elevates particular ethnic distinctions into a sharp break. As sociologists, our analytical challenge is to show what causes placements along the continuum. The racialization of ethnicity is just one extreme of that process. The geopolitical (GP) theory of ethnicity proposed here is, by definition, also a theory of race.[3]

Second, the degree of somatic distinctiveness is socially constructed. Social interaction controls biology. Somatic differences, like everything else, range along a continuum. What determines the degree of similarity or difference in ethnic somatotypes is how separate the breeding pools have been. Peoples who live in areas of the globe remote from one another are likely to have evolved somatotypes that are very different. These geographically separate breeding pools have created the somatotypes of Scandinavians, Celts, Mediterraneans, sub-Saharan Africans, Chinese, Ainu, and all the other somatic variants of the human race. Conversely, where breeding pools are geographically and socially closer, the somatotypes become more similar. At complete social and territorial propinquity, they merge.

Somatotypes are an index of global history; they are geopolitical markers inscribed on the bodies of human beings. Somatic differences among people who currently live near one another reflect past patterns of conquest and migration, including the forced migration of slavery. Where somatic differences are very marked (e.g., by very light or very dark skin), the causal process must have been migration from remote areas of the world, where the breeding pools had been separate for a long period of time. If the somatotypes continue to remain distinct once the groups are in geographical propinquity, it is because social processes continue to keep the breeding pools separate. Ethnosomatic distinctiveness is socially constructed, first in the form of protoethnic somatotypes (black Africans and Celts looked physically different in C.E. 500 because they had never been near each other), later in the form of ethnonational somatotypes upheld by social barriers to interfertilization (e.g., in 1970, when both black Africans and Celts lived in Britain and America).

It is not the color of the skin (or other physical features) per se that determines the social relationship. In nineteenth- and twentieth-century Sweden, extremely blonde, blue-eyed, fair-skinned Finns tend to be looked down upon; they were regarded as slatternly and characteristic of the servant class. The extremely fair somatotype of the Finns is a marker of a geopolitical history in which Finland was a conquest possession of the Swedish state from the sixteenth through the eighteenth century and Finns were peasant workers and servants for Swedish landlords. In the ancient Mediterranean, Greeks and later Arabs acquired light-skinned slaves from eastern Europe, Russia, and the Asian steppe, as well as black slaves from Africa; there both extremely dark and extremely light skins were taken as marks of social inferiority. Geopolitical separation creates protoethnic somatotypes. Geopolitical dominance gives specific meanings to these markers as signs of social superiority or inferiority.

Skin-color racism is a product, not a cause. It is not the case that black Africans were singled out for slavery by Europeans because they were black. The sugar and cotton planters of the Caribbean and the American South initially attempted to work their crops with native American tribal peoples and with white European indentured servants (in effect, slaves for a limited number of years) but were unsuccessful in reproducing these sources of labor. Planters turned to Africa because a supply of slaves became available from the region (Williams 1966). Slavery created racism more than racism created slavery. Africa was vulnerable to slave-trading, in turn, because slavery already existed in Africa, and slaves were readily supplied to coastal ports. Also, the tribal societies of Africa were horticultural and thus much weaker in geopolitical resources than the agrarian states of the Arabs and later the protocapitalist states of the Europeans, who organized the long-distance slave trade.

A comprehensive macrohistorical sociology of the long run would specify, by comparisons and by drawing on the appropriate archeology and paleontology, how many generations of group separation produce what degrees of somatic distinctiveness.[4] The time-process is asymmetrical; differences that may have taken thousands of years to produce can become obliterated within a few generations if extensive interbreeding takes place. Once groups move from protoethnicity in mutually oblivious separation into the situation of mobilization within an ethnonationalist arena, the somatic differences will continue only if they are continually reconstructed. This can happen in two ways: either the carryover from older geopolitical differences into contemporary stratification keeps the breeding pools socially separate; or interbreeding does occur, but the offspring are socially defined as belonging to one group rather than the other, or to a third, mixed, group. If the groups are white Europeans and black Africans, the possible outcomes could be that all offspring are socially classified as black, as white, or as a third category, such as "creole"; a fourth alternative is that the distinction between black and white could simply disappear over a period of generations to be replaced by some other ethnonationalist category (such as

"American"). This outcome would not be strictly a matter of the range of skin colors in such a society, but of what distinctions were singled out or not singled out. Somatic distinctions once taken as significant markers of group identity have disappeared in the past. For instance, the distinction between Romans of the ancient empire and Visigothic barbarians who overran the peninsula in the 400s was eventually forgotten as a social marker, even though the mixture of somatic traits found in modern Italy can be traced to this history.

In the world's future, there will surely be further variations in ethnic divisions. The number of ethnic groups is changed by shifting patterns of breeding pools, which may cause long-standing ethnic groups to disappear and new ethnic categories to be created. The transition period during which ethnic somatotypes are amalgamated may involve heightened ethnic consciousness. In Bosnia, some of the worst atrocities during the ethnic war of the 1990s took place in regions with a high degree of ethnic intermarriage. Such conflicts are possible only where, first, not everyone intermarries, so that there is a pool of "purists" who can put pressure upon the intermarriers, and second, the number of generations of interbreeding is not very deep, so that an intermarried family can be socially identified as exactly that. The contrast becomes clear if one considers ethnic intermarriage in the United States among groups that migrated in the nineteenth century. There are many families, for instance, that have been interbred from Anglo, German, and Scandinavian ethnics; although their descendants at the turn of the twenty-first century may be aware of their family trees, there are few or no live ethnic identifications with any of their antecedents (Waters 1990). Ethnic cleansing would be virtually impossible under these conditions. Three generations of intermarriage probably obliterate prior ethnic lines of distinction, provided that the proportion of the population as a whole that intermarries is large enough. A small minority of intermarriers is always in danger of being defined merely as yet an additional mixed category. A reduction in the number of recognized ethnic divisions is a move along the continuum in one direction. A move in the opposite direction, increasing the number of somatotypes within a region, would require new sources of migration or new barriers to interbreeding.

SOCIAL CONSTRUCTION OF ETHNOLINGUISTIC GROUPS

Let us turn now to the other macrohistorical dimension of ethnic formation. The most readily available, commonsense distinction between ethnic groups is linguistic. Germans are those who speak German or who migrated from a German-speaking area; Poles are those who speak Polish or whose families once did. Ethnicity as language group is a metacommunity even more deeply taken for granted than Benedict Anderson's "imagined communities" of those who read the same newspapers or follow the same broadcasts (Anderson 1983). Confronting those who cannot speak one's language is as sharp a marker in everyday social life as one can experience.

Ethnicity is a process of constructing social cleavages on what appear to be primordial grounds: both language lines and somatic inheritance are outside the control of the individual, deriving from a communal past far enough back that it seems immemorial. In fact, socially constructed memory is short and deliberately biased. It is our business as sociologists to ask macrohistorical questions about the contours in time that produce various kinds of group distinctions. Having attempted this for somatotypes, we may now ask what determines how many ethnolinguistic groups exist? What does it take to create a distinct language—or what is socially recognized as a language, since borders within the continuum of language variation are not clear cut. It is useful to focus on this side of the problem because we have more evidence for the history of languages than we do for the history of somatic types, breeding pools, or customs.

In historical linguistics, a popular model is the pool of language speakers, which is analogous to the biological breeding pool. Socially distinct language pools undergo "linguistic drift," accumulated random changes in one language that create another, as Icelandic was created by drifting away from other Scandinavian languages. Conversely, language groups that come into contact at a stable border interbreed to produce hybrid languages or "creoles." This biological analogy is what I wish to challenge, or at least supplement. The key determinants of language change, those that most dramatically affect ethnolinguistic divisions, have typically been geopolitical.

Although states and ethnolinguistic connections move to different rhythms, there is an affinity between them: strong states foster linguistic uniformity, and highly mobilized linguistic ethnicities strive for an autonomous state. Because this striving toward congruence between state and language is but one factor among several, the congruence is approached only on certain occasions, although analytically fateful ones. The existence of regional dialects within a language does not gainsay the basic effect but does add complexities. Ethnolinguistic identities are layered. The very concept of a dialect, as distinct from a separate language, indicates that some language variation is accepted as normal within a larger overriding identity. From a macrohistorical viewpoint, the sharp distinction between dialect and language is artificial; the two are points on the language continuum, and, for example, Dutch may be regarded as a dialect of Plattdeutsch (so-called Low German, the German of the northern coasts) (Sperber and Fleischhauer 1963: 79). But the analytical disparity between the continuums found in historical reality and the sharp-edged categories social actors use to draw ethnolinguistic boundaries are very much the point of my argument. Ethnicity is constructed. It is a real-life ideal type, constructed not by scholars but by people in ordinary life; and the process of constructing ethnic identities is done with varying degrees of inclusiveness or separation. A GP theory of variations along that continuum will give us the outline of a theory of language change.

PROTOETHNICITY AND ETHNONATIONALISM

Envision an analytical space. At one extreme is the ideal type of a completely isolated community, both for speaking and for childbearing. But such a community represents only protoethnicity, since completely isolated communities have no awareness that they differ from others. Self-conscious ethnic identity, which is strongest at the level of ethnonationalism, comes from entering the arena of states in geopolitical relationship with one another. Ethnicity is an intrinsically messy topic because the historical processes that produce it are intrinsically messy. Our analytical problems stem from the fact that ethnicity is always a distorted concept, an attempt to impose a pure category on a social reality that is not at all pure.

Ethnicity is a construction from combinations of markers: somatotypes, languages, family names that serve as reminders of ancestral differences that may no longer exist, as well as other differences in culture and lifestyle. These may coincide in distinctive, closely integrated local communities. The paradox of ethnicity is that the more locally anchored such patterns are in practice, the less likely they are to be important for social action. It is the larger, looser metacommunities that group strangers into categories for political action, as well as for acts of discrimination and hostility or sympathy and support. In these larger ethnic metacommunities, the generalized notion of ethnicity becomes a social reality in itself in its shaping of macrodivisions in society. It is distinctiveness, however marked, that is operative, not any particular kind of distinction. If one marker is strong enough, other markers are superfluous. For black Americans, the principal socially recognized marker is skin color; language and names are irrelevant. For Jews, the marker of genealogy is imperfectly conveyed by names, together with religiously anchored culture. For Irish Americans, somatic and linguistic markers are too vague or too far in the past to be operative; there remain names of fading significance, together with special-purpose organizations designed expressly to keep alive ethnic heritage. But such deliberately contrived organizations have an artificial quality and are a sign that the stronger social bases of this ethnic division are largely gone.

What would constitute a general theory of the social construction of ethnicity? The degree to which palpable borders are constructed is a variable on a continuum. Primordial protoethnicity would be at one end of the continuum, at which a group is completely isolated: completely homogeneous as a breeding pool, a language community, and in every other respect. At that end, where groups are never in contact, there is no sense of difference and hence no ethnic mobilization. This picture is imaginary, because real communities have probably always had some awareness of the neighbors from whom they differed. The ideal type at the other extreme, complete assimilation, would be a utopia that coincides with primordial protoethnicity, a heavenly goal at the end of history that is the same as the Garden of Eden at the beginning. Complete assimilation is mythical, because it assumes that there is no interaction with the region outside the unit in which assimilation finally occurs. It would be a state without foreign relations. Ethnicity is meaningful only by contrast: there can never be one ethnic group, but always two or more. Assimilation, in practice, means moving toward smaller numbers of ethnic cleavages but never reaching the end point.

The degree of mobilization ranges from protoethnicity, or a minimal sense of distinction from other groups, through increasing group consciousness of and action toward other groups. The boundaries of what is mobilized are variable; the size and extent of the group is constructed simultaneously with its mobilization into political action. Increasing participation in a political arena defines each group membership in relation to other groups that are being defined at the same moment.

The highest degree of ethnic mobilization may be called ethnonationalism. This is ethnicity oriented to using the state as its instrument. Ethnicity is not identical to nationalism, since some ethnic groups mobilize against the state or against dominance by the favored, nationally legitimate ethnic group. Antinational, state-resisting ethnic mobilization too is conditioned by the state, both in its internal penetrative capacity and its external GP position in relation to other states. Ethnicity grows up with the state. Full-scale ethnic mobilization carries in its train aspirations to state autonomy. In practice, whether it succeeds depends upon the GP strength of the state. If the goal of autonomy is politically unrealistic, ethnic groups may settle for local or de facto regions of autonomy, including freedom from being interfered with by the state in matters of language, education, and other means of perpetuating the ethnic distinction. Even less mobilized ethnic groups, the archetypal sedentary farms in remote mountain valleys, lie toward the protoethnic end of the continuum and have little effect on the ethnic process of the society at large until they enter the arena of struggling for position in the queue for national recognition.[5]

A theory of nationalism is a subtype of the theory of ethnicity.[6] The same processes affect both. Nationalism is near one end of the continuum; ethnicity as conventionally defined is at the middle. By the same token, discussions of citizenship belong to the theoretical problem of the ethnonational continuum, whether one is concerned with constructing a highly uniform participatory citizenship ethos (in effect, strong ethnonationalist citizenship) or multicultural or tolerant citizenship, backing off from the ethnonationalist endpoint and attempting to institutionalize a coalition of ethnic identities sharing in legitimacy. A theory of nationalism provides a clue to a theory of ethnicity.

Power-Prestige and Ethnic Legitimacy

In discussing the phenomenon of nationalism, Max Weber noted that the boundaries of a state do not originally or necessarily coincide with linguistic, religious, or ethnic divisions (Weber 1968: 901–40). National identity, he argued, is what is constructed through the political experience of people with their state. Nationalism is not primordial; it waxes and wanes. The most important of these collective experiences, in Weber's view, is all-out military mobilization. French nationalism was forged above all in the *levée en masse* of the Napoleonic wars; German nationalism, which overcame the regionalism of the *Kleinstaaterei*, was molded in the war of liberation against Napoleonic conquest (which not incidentally destroyed many of the minor states and left Prussia, the leader of the liberation war, as the center of national identity). Weber's argument resonates with a neo-Durkheimian mechanism of emotional identification around symbols forged in the heat of collective participation. As Weber puts it, military participation bonds not only soldiers into a "community of fate," but to the extent that warfare is fateful for conquest, migration, or extermination, it bonds their families and other noncombatants as well. The more widespread the popular participation in the military, the more thoroughly national sentiments are spread.[7] Hence the strongest forms of national feeling arise either in the mass armies of tribal coalitions and migrations or in modern states that deeply penetrate their populations. The weakest national feeling occurs in states organized as thin layers of aristocrats monopolizing arms above a mass of disarmed commoners. In either of the highly mobilized forms of military action, Weber suggests, national feeling can be constructed quite rapidly. In the *Völkerwanderung* of early German history or the recruitment of Viking bands, and (perhaps by extrapolation) in other tribal migrations as well, ad hoc coalitions may attract fighting men from many solidarities who take on a new identity, especially if their migration is long distance and their conquest successful. The same volatility of national sentiments, I would argue, characterizes the shifting national loyalties around modern states.

Weber's argument is about nationalism, but it can be extended to ethnicity in general. Put another way, nationalism is the form that ethnicity takes when the gradient of movement is toward expanding ethnic boundaries so that they coincide with state boundaries. The classic statements of "assimilation" come from the period of expanding nationalism and implicitly assumed that the target boundary was that of the state. Weber's argument takes us onto the terrain of geopolitics. Ultimately the core of the state is its capacity to wield military power to control a territory. Neither the boundaries of states nor their power in relation to each other is static; geopolitics provides the principles that determine the increases and decreases in external state power.

I would add the following corollary: the power-prestige of the state in the external arena affects the legitimacy of its rulers in the internal arena. There are of course other domestic sources of legitimacy, but in the dynamics of long-term change the most important factor affecting legitimacy is external power-prestige. (For elaboration, see Collins 1986: 145–66.) The strongest evidence for this connection is revolution: revolution depends almost always on delegitimation of rulers and on splits within the elite, and these in turn reach the necessary extreme proportions typically as the result of geopolitical defeat or the accumulated effects of geopolitical strain. Conversely, the prestige of state rulers rises with military success; even in the absence of war, the ability of a strong state to dominate other states in diplomacy reinforces the legitimacy of its rulers. In short, external geopolitics affects internal legitimacy.

This argument can be extended from the legitimacy of rulers to the legitimacy of dominant ethnic groups. Schematically, when a state is geopolitically strong, the prestige of its dominant ethnic group is also high. Conversely, a geopolitically weak state lowers its dominant ethnic prestige. Combined with the process of state organization and penetration into its own population, these principles enable us to predict the main variations in ethnic structure and long-term dynamics.

1. *State formation and inward penetration constructs the highly mobilized forms of ethnicity.* Under these conditions the protoethnicity of isolated local communities moves toward the end of the continuum at which there is stronger consciousness of and availability for concerted action. The formation of any state at all is the first step toward ethnic mobilization insofar as there is a call to participate collectively as a fighting unit. The degree to which ethnic mobilization moves up this continuum varies by the extent of state penetration.

(i) At one end there is minimal state penetration: the "layer state" of imperial conquest that extracts tribute from indigenous protoethnic or religious communities. Even here, ethnic unity and awareness may be moved up a notch by the imposition from above of collective responsibility for taxation and internal order. Although Greeks, Kurds, and Armenians under the Ottoman Empire might seem like primordial identities, it is likely that the empire's administrative practices in the *millet* system of collective responsibility and religious self-government formed these into larger units than had previously existed or kept them from fragmenting or drifting into different lines of division (Mardin 1997).

(ii) Further up the continuum is the structure of feudal aristocracy in agrarian coercive societies. The volatility of feudal alliance and warfare and the long-distance ties of dynastic marriage politics militate against strong ethnonational identification around the state unit. These antinationalist influences, which are countered in some degree by the vertical demands of lords upon vassals and of the aristocracy generally upon their servants, retainers, and peasants, create some degree of identification with regional ethnicities. Although peasants and servants had little direct political participation under medieval French feudalism, the consolidation of a network of feudal loyalties around the king, branching out from the Ile de France, was a magnetic pole in the space of ethnic identification.

(iii) A highly mobilized, long-lasting military alliance can create ethnic solidarity among its participants even if the state structure is minimal. The ancient Greek city-states mobilized local identities as fighting units that transcended the familism of the clans. Their larger war coalitions, such as those organized against the Persians, expanded the scope of ethnic identification.[8] The war coalitions of the Germanic tribes in the geopolitical vacuum of the falling Roman Empire, ad hoc assemblies of men willing to migrate long distances, who cut family connections and took alien wives along the way, very likely forged new ethnic identities. Among the evidence of this are the new features of the German languages that emerged during these war migrations (Borkenau 1981). These examples warn us that there is no straight evolutionary development from protoethnicity to modern ethnonationalism. Periods of strong ethnic identification around a polity can occur in the absence of anything resembling bureaucratic penetration of society, provided that widespread military participation keeps people busy at war for long periods of time. Once peace comes, or substantial portions of the populace are demobilized by becoming a peasantry subject to a military aristocracy, the large-scale ethnonational identification may disintegrate or move back toward lower levels of mobilization.

(iv) Finally, there is the modern process of state penetration. The bureaucratic expansion of the state, especially from the nineteenth century onward, promoted public education, economic regulation, and welfare, along with physical infrastructure of transportation and communications.

Individuals became public citizens, their names inscribed in records of eligibility for military conscription, taxation, compulsory schooling, health and pension coverage, passports, and work permits. National cultures were created among those integrated into the state, reaching down even to the bedroom. Watkins (1991) shows that after 1870 such patterns as marital fertility, illegitimacy, and the propensity to marry became increasingly similar among local regions within European states. Where previously the biggest diversity had been within states, now sexual behaviors diverged at the state borders. State penetration established ties to the center that cut across local households, neighborhoods, and workplaces. An unanticipated consequence was to make people available for mobilization in social movements and political action on an unprecedented scale. The result of state penetration was to unleash a series of movements and to shape identities that had previously been latent or nonexistent: class conflict, ethnic consciousness, nationalism, and eventually feminism and a host of special issue movements (Mann 1993; Tilly 1995).

A strong move toward sharply drawing ethnolinguistic boundaries to the outside, while homogenizing within, is the creation of a standard national language. At the turn of the nineteenth century, some 40 percent of French subjects spoke a regional language or dialect other than French as spoken in the Paris region. This diversity fell off sharply by 1920 as the result of deliberate government policies, the spread of schooling, and the integration through national transport, communications, and commercial networks (E. Weber 1976; Watkins 1991: 162–63). This is a typical process of state-centered construction of an ideal type ethnonational identity, a movement along the continuum from a larger to a smaller number of ethnolinguistic groups. It is simultaneously a refocusing of salient boundaries, a strengthening of the boundaries between a group defined as "French" and all non-French, a form of ethnonational mobilization. The degree of ethnolinguistic uniformity and the strength of an ethnonational identity come from the power of a state to penetrate its population and draw it into a single national arena.

Even at its most extreme, state penetration does not automatically succeed in forming a single ethnonational identity within the bounds of each modern state. It may instead provide an arena in which ethnic groups are mobilized to struggle with each other over which cultural identity will become the legitimate core of the nation; or for institutionalized set-asides, pieces of the national pie; or for local autonomies; or even for rebellion and separation from the existing state. And the state does not necessarily remain territorially stable. Even states with high degrees of internal penetration may become amalgamated or divided by geopolitical processes. Alongside the process of state penetration, we must also consider three geopolitical patterns.

2. *Geopolitical ascendancy of the state in the external arena elevates the power-prestige of the dominant ethnic group within.* The greater the geopolitical power-prestige, the more successfully the state penetrates its own population when the institutions of national political participation and cultural communication are introduced. A geopolitically ascendant state is better able to assimilate regional and other protoethnicities into a national language, educational standard, and other aspects of uniform public culture.[9] Our prime examples of the creation of national culture such as nineteenth-century Britain are cases in which not only were a national economic market and institutions of transportation and communication being formed, but the geopolitical power-prestige of the state was high. Lacking this power-prestige, national-level institutions become an arena for ethnic conflict more than for ethnic unification.[10]

A weaker version of the same process may be seen in ancient and medieval states. These had little of the capacity of modern bureaucratic states to penetrate society; nevertheless, linguistic uniformity of some degree was imposed over time. The process is similar, but the bureaucratic state is faster. What the Romans did to the Etruscans in perhaps six generations,[11] was done by the postrevolutionary French state to the Bretons in three. Better to speak of this as linguistic ascendancy, a process in which the language of the core region and the ruling class within that region becomes the legitimately dominant language and a defining marker of full membership in the community (de Swaan 1988). Italy was a region of multiple languages until 270 BCE (although of these we know only Latin and Etruscan well). The ascendancy of the Roman state brought the extirpation of Etruscan, although people of Etruscan ancestry survived physically and were absorbed into the marriage pool (Stolz and Debrunner 1966). In Greek settlements of the Aegean, Dorians, Achaeans, Aeolians, and others were recognized as socially separate ethnolinguistic groups. The spread of Greek colonies from the Black Sea to Magna Graecea during 700–500 BCE must have produced considerable mixing and melding of borders with other ethnicities. This was reversed when a political coalition against the Persians polarized "Greeks" and non-Greeks ("barbarians," those whose language sounded like "bar-bar"). The ensuing ascendancy of Athens as military hegemon and cultural metropolis created a standard or ideal Greek in the form of Attic, the dialect of the Athens region. Greek ethnolinguistic identity was politicized and spread still further with the Macedonian conquests of the Near East and the politics of the Hellenistic states staffed by colonists in Greek-style cities throughout the region of conquest. Cultural-linguistic identity became established politically, whether the inhabitants of these cities were somatically Greek in descent or not. Indeed Macedonians themselves were regarded as only dubiously Greek or semibarbarian until their period of military ascendancy.

Such has been a principal dynamic by which large language regions were established on different parts of the globe. In China, writing scripts were standardized by the first large-scale dynasty, the Han, which brought to an end the period of conquest among a large number of warring states (Fung 1952). High-status language was likely standardized at this time too. It is revealing that the Chinese term for themselves as an ethnic group is Han, the name of the first dynasty to establish overlordship in the main population regions between the Gobi desert and the South China Sea.[12]

Since ethnicities can overlap the boundaries of states, geopolitical power-prestige also affects the tendencies for identification in megapolitical groupings. The result is a drive or tension to incorporate members of a common, high-prestige ethnicity into a single political community. This is the source of panethnic movements for amalgamation within the largest possible ethnic boundary. Pan-Slavism was based on the accelerating power-prestige of the Russian Empire during the nineteenth century. The Russian state by that point had amassed population and territorial resources that made its armies incomparably stronger than its immediate neighbors. With the concomitant loss of geopolitical power by the Austrian and Turkish Empires to the southwest, there was a sense that further Russian expansion was geopolitically inevitable.[13] Pan-Slavism provided an ideology for this sphere of influence; it gave legitimation for Russians to continue their advance and for other Slavic nationalities to attach themselves to the prestige of Russian might, redefining it as their own. Pan-Slavism also figured in internal debate within Russia, the counterpart to the Westernizers whose prime concern was the internal modernization of Russia along the lines of European role models. Westernizers were the ideological movement that accompanied the effort for modern state penetration within Russian society; Pan-Slavists opposed the insult to national prestige implied in this dependence on outside models. We should avoid looking at Pan-Slavism through the eyes of Westernizers, who saw it as a reactive romanticization of the Slavic folk and a rejection of modernization. Pan-Slavism was a movement in keeping with contemporary circumstances, the arrival of Russia at Great Power status in the world arena. Pan-Slavism was an ideology that not only asserted Russian cultural independence and superiority but also legitimated further geopolitical expansion of the Russian state and provided the weak states of the Slavic zone with a rationale to join it.

Pan-Germanism was similarly geopolitical. This movement for heightened ethnic consciousness among all Germans was oriented expressly toward those living outside the bounds of the empire established under Prussian leadership in the wars of 1864–71. The Pan-Germanist movement was at its height in the 1890s, as Germany threw itself into the international arms race and belatedly began gathering overseas colonies. That is to say, the ideology coincides with the period when Germany became a full-fledged participant in the competitions that defined prestige among the Great Powers. Pan-Germanism is not a primordial sentiment; it did not exist in the long period of regional disintegration of the parts of the medieval Reich. It built up gradually with the consolidation of a strong German state, Prussia, in the eighteenth century. The cultural definition of a unique *Volk* in the writings of Herder in the 1770s and 1780s occurred in and around the Prussian zone of northern Germany and in conjunction with the development of a culture-consuming public. German ethnonationalism grew from the coincidence of two key processes, the beginnings of the first strong institutional penetration of the state into society and the growing geopolitical power-prestige of one German state after a long period of fragmentation and weakness that had kept German cultural prestige low. Prussia was the center of German nationalism, not because German culture was intrinsically militaristic and "Prussian," but because Prussia was the geopolitical core around which a large unified state was constructed.

The contrast with Austria is instructive. Austria was the geopolitical star among German-speaking states from the sixteenth through the eighteenth century, but two circumstances distinguished it from Prussia: it was strongly identified as a multicultural empire; and by the nineteenth century its geopolitical position was weakening. Initially, Austria had come to prominence as a branch of the dynastic Habsburg Empire riding on the prestige of Spanish power; later Austria explicitly incorporated the ethnic identity of its Hungarian aristocratic allies into its official structure.[14] Although both Prussia/Germany and Austria incorporated non-German speakers through their history of conquests—notably Polish Slavs and *shtetl* Jews in the former, as well as these and a great many other Slavic and Balkan ethnicities in Austria—Prussia's geopolitical expansion was primarily into a zone of German speakers. Prussian expansion also coincided with the mobilization of elite culture-producing institutions: the spread of public elementary and secondary schooling, which had begun in northern Germany in the 1700s, and above all the emulation of academic reforms among German-speaking universities after 1810, which constituted a unified market for academic careers.[15] The institutions of state cultural penetration and the prestige of geopolitical expansion both worked to create a strong ethnonationalism in Prussian-led Germany. Austria, in contrast, had expanded largely into zones of non-German speakers and faced the more formidable task of inward state penetration at the same time that it underwent a series of geopolitical shocks: defeat by the Piedmont/French alliance in 1859 and by Prussia in 1866, resulting in the loss of Lombardy and Venetia to nationally consolidating Italy; and the threat of Russian expansion in the East, which provided support for ethnic dissidence in the Balkans. This GP weakness was not sufficiently offset by the acquisition of Bosnia from the sagging Ottoman Empire after its defeat by Russia in 1877–78 and subsequent partition of its Balkan territories (McEvedy 1982: 34). The two sources of state weakness spiraled back upon one another. The weaker Austrian apparatus of state penetration extracted fewer resources for military action, undermining its geopolitical position and encouraging still further local resistance to central state penetration.

The Pan-Germanism of the 1890s was an ideology based on the momentum of German state expansion. German speakers living in the non-German states of central Europe were encouraged in the hope of becoming unified into a prestigious state sharing in the top rank of world power. Their hopes were heightened as alternative state sovereignty crumbled, first with the concessions made by Austria-Hungary to local autonomies, which put many pockets of German speakers under local control of non-German ethnic institutions, and then in the early twentieth century, with the dismemberment of the Austro-Hungarian Empire into a series of weak states. The virulent ethnonationalism of Nazi foreign policy took Pan-Germanism to its extreme. To regard this as a primordial German cultural stance would be to adopt the content of the ideology as the basis for analyzing it.[16] The ideology of Pan-Germanism exemplifies a universal process: geopolitical ascendancy creates an ideology of ethnic prestige; a track record of successes generates an expectation of more of the same, thereby encouraging both militaristic policies and a widening definition of the ethnic community toward which the expanding state is heading.

3. *Geopolitical weakness of the state reduces the prestige of the dominant ethnicity identified with it.* If geopolitical strains are severe, the breakup of the state leaves in its wake the destruction of ethnonational identity. The breakup of the Roman Empire created the separate ethnolinguistic blocks of southern and western Europe, just as the breakup of the Carolingian Empire paved the way for distinctions among French, German, and Italian identities. The revival of militant ethnonational identities out of the component pieces of the USSR and of Yugoslavia in the 1990s fits the general pattern. Ethnic strife on the local level is not to be explained as the continuation of age-old ethnic hatreds. Ethnic consciousness is volatile because geopolitics is prone to abrupt transitions. It is volatile both upward and downward on the scale of particularistic mobilization. A geopolitically strong state demobilizes fragmentary ethnic identifications within it, and it is the reversal of geopolitical fortunes that is responsible for the surge of fragmentizers.

If the unification of states produces language uniformity, the breakup of states produces language differentiation. The romance languages date from the fragmentation of the Roman Empire. Aside from Italian of the home territories,[17] Spanish, French, Romanian, and a number of others are languages of regions that had been colonized by Latin speakers (some of them ethnosomatically Italian, others not). Conquest by German tribal coalitions brought sharp changes to what are recognizable versions of the present national languages. Changes occurred not only in phonology but most strikingly in syntax. The grammar of the Romance languages displaced the densely packed-in inflections and complex word formation that give Latin its peculiar pungency and freedom of word order. These traits were replaced with reduced inflection and more analytical and word-separating forms (Kroeber 1963: 50–51; Sapir 1921: 144–46). Vocabulary, however, retained many elements of Latin words. It is a challenge for macrohistorical sociology of language to explain why syntax, the deep structural framework of language, is amenable to abrupt changes, while drift works mainly on continuous small gradations in phonology and vocabulary (Aitchison 1991). It appears that drift is more conservative and continuous, whereas language change by abrupt geopolitical crisis also produces radical linguistic discontinuities.[18]

A clue is found in the related process of language differentiation, which develops from stable lines of conflict or from resistance to geopolitical amalgamation that is sustained for a long period of time. The regions of greatest linguistic diversity in the world are generally considered to include the interior of New Guinea, tribal North America, the Amazon basin, and the Sahel belt between Saharan Africa and the Bantu-speaking lands to the south (Kroeber 1963: 22–24; Whitney 1979: 242–45, 256–58). These languages show extreme diversity in structure, even though some argue on evidence of phonetic roots that numerous groups within these areas have common origins (Greenberg 1987). The Caucasus Mountains also have a great variety of languages in a relatively small area. What is it about conditions in these territories that apparently caused languages to move away from each other, especially in the structural characteristics of grammar?

The explanation is at least partly geopolitical. The greatest language diversity has occurred in areas with a high degree of warfare or intertribal hostility, which nevertheless did not give rise to large and stable conquest states (which would have reduced language diversity). In stateless societies, the primary factor that constitutes a tribe as a distinct identity (as opposed to more specific kinship, religious, or political groups within the tribe) is its language (Elkin 1979: 56–58). Here language difference is simultaneously an assertion of group identity and its boundaries. The New Guinea highlands, a territory characterized by what Kroeber has called "astounding speech diversity" (Kroeber 1963: 23), was also one of the main areas of cannibalism and head-hunting expeditions, where exclusion was so extreme that enemies were treated as virtually nonhuman species. The same was true in the Amazon basin. In North America during the tribal period, similarly, an "honorific" form of ritual violence maintained interlocking chains of hostilities without taking territory or eliminating rival groups. The Caucasus also fits this geopolitical pattern, in that historically its rugged mountain geography and its interstitial position between rival lowland empires kept it a fragmented buffer zone.

Languages of enemies, by this hypothesis, are structured by each other—not by direct imitation and borrowing but by opposition. Each constitutes itself by evolving structural forms that differ from the enemy's. The hypothesis is supported by what is known about the effects of external contact between alien languages (Kroeber 1963: 42). Such contact areas have fostered especially rapid language change, but the change does not occur by imitating or borrowing from the external contact language. Among sets of genetically related languages, it is those on the territorial borders, in contact with the most divergent language groups, that change the most. Kroeber suggested that becoming aware of the existence of different forms of grammar catalyzes change in one's own language. The result is not drift across contact boundaries, although the contact group does move further away from its own language relatives who are not near the contact frontier. These changes take off in new directions. This would explain why inhabitants of the Sahel, the border zone between Hamitic and Semitic languages to the north and Bantu tongues to the south, would develop a great diversity of languages of their own, distinguished from those of outside groups and from each other.

Language speakers act in a way that differentiates themselves as sharply as possible from those who are perceived as their enemies. The process is not found only in tribal societies and archaic periods. Labov and Harris (1986) have produced evidence that in the most alienated parts of the black ghetto in large American cities black English has diverged from standard English. That this divergence has taken place in syntax, not merely in pronunciation and vocabulary, suggests the depth of the social conflict and resulting alienation. Residential segregation and poverty, compounded by self-enhancing feedback loops, create an ever more deeply ingrained cultural distinctiveness on racial lines (what I would call the extreme end of the ethnic distinctiveness continuum) (Massey and Denton, 1993). Labov interprets these instances as displaying a general mechanism of language change (Labov 1972; see also Aitchison 1991).[19] It may be this mechanism, operating between Gothic conquerors and once domineering Romans, that produced the sharp change in syntax between Latin and the Romance languages.

Let us consider some possible exceptions to the general principle. Why didn't Italian ethnic identity disappear during its long period of disunity? By hypothesis, the major city-states should have created separate ethnic identities, with their "Italian" cultures diverging from one another, perhaps building on Etruscan (Tuscan), Lombard, Venetian, and other cultural identities. I suggest that two processes militated against this happening, one cultural, the other geopolitical. In the Renaissance and for centuries thereafter, a unitary Italian identity was upheld by the Europe-wide prestige of culture-producing institutions common throughout the peninsula. Italian city-states provided a basis for innovative movements in painting and other arts. The relatively small size of local cities meant that a patronage market for artists had to cut across them as a unitary network. The most visible, high-prestige, culture-producing institutions were identified as "Italian" because the most famous Italians were the artists who moved between commissions in Florence, Milan, Rome, and other cities.[20]

In addition, Italian geopolitics provided niches for ethnic identity. The possibility of Italian ethnic identity was kept alive because of Italy's position as a buffer zone between the big empires. The shifting pattern of unstable conquests and spheres of influence in Italy by France and Spain, and to some extent Austria, kept Italian identity alive; the geopolitical handwriting must have been on the wall that the intruder states would cancel each other out. In addition, the papacy acted not only as the highest-prestige patron of the artistic network but also as a geopolitical magnet for Italian ethnicity. City-state elites, like the Medicis in Florence, expanded their sphere of influence by becoming cardinals and popes, using the church as a substitute for the territorial expansion that was blocked by the gridlock of local powers and the weight of French and Spanish interference. If the Italian peninsula had not been home to the papacy, Italian cultural identity would likely not have survived to be built up into full-scale ethnonationalism in the nineteenth century.[21]

Another apparent exception, the survival of ethnic identity after the disappearance of the state, exemplifies the same corollary to the general principle. A Polish identity was kept alive even though the Polish state disappeared between 1772 and 1795 in a series of divisions among Russia, Germany, and Austria, to be revived four generations later in 1919. The lesson is not that ethnolinguistic identities are indestructible, but rather that they are subject to macrohistorical contours in time. The division of Poles among several different national states (including the overseas diaspora of Poles in the United States and elsewhere) probably slowed the process of linguistic assimilation. Differing rates of language repression or assimilation in the different states allowed a core set of ethnic identity-preservers to survive. On the GP hypothesis, Polish ethnicity would have disappeared more quickly if Poland had been absorbed into only one state rather than several.

"Balkanization" is a handy label for movement on the continuum away from ethnonationalism around an existing state and toward ethnic separatism. The abruptness and militancy of movement along this continuum coincides with the degree of geopolitical strain. A full-scale geopolitical shock, the breakup of an empire, opens the door to full-scale ethnic splits, even creating multiple new ethnicities where a single one had existed before. Lesser degrees of GP weakness encourage corresponding degrees of ethnic consciousness and rebellion. The Ottoman and to a degree the Austrian Empires were the "sick men of Europe" for more than a century, and everyone knew it. Hence these were the regions in which local proto-ethnicities became dissidents. In zones that were weakly controlled by the empire, ethnic nationalists sought their own state. Other regions, still firmly under military control, experienced the mobilization of movements for political autonomy, or failing these, for ethnonationalist control of cultural institutions such as official language and education. The latter movements meshed with the growth of institutions of state penetration at this time, but in this case the penetration not only did not strengthen the central state but weakened it by providing an arena for mobilizing dissident ethnicities.

4. *Geopolitical balance of power fosters cosmopolitanism.* On occasion, the geopolitical situation is stable over a long period of time, with power split among a number of states of approximately equal power. Alliances and diplomacy become oriented toward preventing any one state from outclassing the others in military strength. In these circumstances, the power-prestige of states is stabilized but also denatured. Wars tend to be fought under rules of "gentlemanly" or "chivalrous" combat: large conquests of territory are not expected, and casualties are usually limited. In these instances, ethnonationalism is devalued. Several processes contribute to this result. War is regarded as a game of the elite, with relatively little participation from the mass of the population and relatively little effect on their lives. Changes in rulership are not dramatic, and the military state acts like a thin layer upon society rather than penetrating it. The emotional mobilization caused by mass participation or bloody conquest is missing, eliminating this route toward ethnonational identification. In addition, the practice of shifting alliances to maintain the balance of power keeps ethnic identities vague and superficial, in keeping with the principle that ethnicities are constructed by division and contrast with those whom they exclude. When one's military enemies and allies change every few years, one has a much weaker sense of place in the ethnic order of the world than when long-term geopolitical rivalries frame the ethnonational cosmos.

Among the state elites, especially the military, diplomatic, and political ruling groups, the most salient feature of everyday life is cosmopolitan contact with ethnic outsiders. The situation fosters a lingua franca as a tool of diplomatic discourse. A cosmopolitan language of this kind differs from the pidgin language that grows up to facilitate commerce in trading zones. Whereas those crude languages are simplified for utilitarian practicality and have low social prestige, a cosmopolitan language has high prestige and conveys social superiority. During the balance-of-power wars of the late seventeenth and eighteenth centuries, French culture and language became the mark of good breeding across Europe. Possession of the ideals of the Enlightenment, politeness and rationality, connoted membership in an elite capable of sophisticated interaction in the world of international connections. In cosmopolitan circles, local customs were looked down upon as provincial, and ethnic identities such as Russian or German were deliberately downplayed. Ironically, this cosmopolitanism occurred at just the time when state bureaucracies were beginning to penetrate the cultural life of their respective national societies. The juxtaposition of cosmopolitanism and bureaucratic penetration suggests that geopolitics is the master variable, overriding or at least strongly influencing the character of state penetration.

Self-reinforcing processes were set in motion. The prevalence of diplomatic negotiation and interstate alliance made it necessary for elite personnel to travel a good deal and even to circulate into the administrations of allied states. Some individuals from the cosmopolitan class became almost stateless, moving about and taking positions in the armies or governments of states in which they were national aliens. Belonging to this class were prominent ministers such as Law and Necker in France and Scharnhorst and vom Stein in Prussia. Generals were on loan to foreign governments from the time of Lafayette and Steuben in the American Revolution to "Chinese" Gordon in the Taiping Rebellion, not to mention side-switching opportunists like Condé in seventeenth-century France and Spain. In sharp contrast to the situation of the highly mobilized ethnonational identities of twentieth-century states, national citizenship was not a requisite for government service, even at the top layer.

This cosmopolitanism should not be attributed simply to the lack of deep state penetration into society and a corresponding sense of national identity, but above all to the geopolitical situation. Transethnic cosmopolitanism existed in a range of historical circumstances that varied in degree of state penetration but in which the common denominator was the geopolitical balance of power. Latin cosmopolitanism dominated in the High Middle Ages, giving way to national languages when strong states began to consolidate in England, France, and Spain, above all by effective nationalization of church property and thus of the means of cultural production. French Enlightenment culture held its prestige during the negotiation of alliances after the end of the religious wars, when the balance of power became an explicit ideal. In India, as regional languages grew up among the fragmented

kingdoms after the disappearance of the few relatively wide empires of ancient times (the Mauryas and Guptas), the very weakness of states encouraged an elite layer of high-culture bearers who upheld Sanskrit and its literature as transcenders of local particularities.

Transethnic cosmopolitanism is a permanent analytical possibility, and
cosmopolitan periods may recur in the future. Suppose we enter into a period (or are already in it) in which no state is capable of much geopolitical
aggrandizement. Instead loosely knit alliances and international networks are
the focus of elite action. By hypothesis, the very idea of ethnonationalism
becomes repugnant, at least among the elite, who bend over backward to
avoid extolling the superiority of their own cultures. In the conclusion to
this chapter, I suggest that late-twentieth-century "multiculturalism" and
"political correctness" may be a contemporary version of transethnic cosmopolitanism mixed with peculiar circumstances of geopolitical weakening
and ethnic mobilization at the level of nonelite.

THE AMERICAN QUESTION: ASSIMILATION OR ETHNIC STASIS?

American research on ethnicity has concentrated on the question of assimilation, at one time favorably, more recently negatively. Ethnic relations, once
considered an inevitable process of change in the direction of assimilation, are
now widely regarded as fundamentally static. Ethnic reproduction and class
reproduction have become the favored (and at least in the case of the former,
the morally privileged) sociological position. What we have done is truncate
the conceptual continuum of ethnic change. A theory of assimilation is an
explanation of how ethnic boundaries widen; anti-assimilation theories are
content to show how ethnic boundaries are stuck. Left out is the larger context, which determines whether there is movement in either direction along
the continuum of ethnic divisions between a high and low number of cleavages. Here I review this assimilation and anti-assimilation material cursorily,
with an eye to showing how it fits into the larger geopolitical dynamic. My
main theme is that the mesodynamics of ethnic reproduction and conflict are
short term and of variable strength; they are reinforced by particular geopolitical configurations, overridden by others.

In classic assimilation theories, the baseline was preexisting ethnic groups,
taken as if primordial, which had not yet started the process of assimilation
because of geographic regionalization. This was the situation in prestate and
agrarian-coercive (feudal/extractive) societies. The evolutionary model
posited the stages of contact, transitory conflict, accommodation, and assimilation; change was driven by the development of a market economy, the
division of labor, and urbanization, all of which break down regional distinctions and set in motion a process of assimilation to some larger-sized
group. There is a good deal of evidence that this process occurs often (for

the recent period, see Waldinger 1996; for the turn of the twentieth century, see Lieberson 1980). However, as the experience of agrarian conquest states shows, it is possible for market structures to develop while leaving narrower ethnic boundaries in place, or at least while producing no more than small-scale movements along the continuum of assimilation into larger groups. The Parsees in India, the "king's Jews" in medieval Europe, and the Hanseatic Germans in the Baltic are only a few examples out of many of ethnic enclaves situated precisely in the centers of trade and administration. Even a complex division of labor and exchange in industrial societies can reinforce ethnic distinctiveness. Rural or premigration regional bases of ethnic division can be reproduced by business location and residential segregation. Ethnic groups can establish specialty enclaves within the division of labor, a tendency of which the Indian caste system is only the most extreme example. At one time sociological theorists assumed that the ethnic division of labor was characteristic only of preindustrial and prebureaucratic societies, but there is ample evidence from contemporary societies that it can continue to exist in every form of economy yet known. The split labor market of high- and low-wage sectors and the protection of particular markets by unionization, by ethnically based credit associations, by monopolization through privileged ethnic groups, or by "racial" discrimination are some of the structures through which the ethnic division of labor operates (Bonacich 1972; Hechter 1974; Portes 1994; Light and Karageorgis 1994; Olzak 1992).

Our aim should not be merely to draw up a scorecard of how much ethnic segregation happens to be structured into the division of labor in each particular case, but to explain why patterns vary. Any existing historical situation is the result of a balance between opposing tendencies of differing strengths. The division of labor and the structures of administrative centralization can have opposite effects on the continuum of ethnic boundaries. In one direction, any kind of contact and coparticipation among distinct ethnic groups has the potential to produce assimilation across ethnic boundaries. As long as people come together, there is always the prospect of forming a common culture, developing a new language or *patois*, making friendships and intermarriages, and forming a united front in conflict against more remote parties. Whether this potential for assimilation is realized or whether on the contrary contact merely heightens the sense of boundaries depends on whether tendencies to assimilate across the boundary are stronger than tendencies to quarrel. These tendencies are determined by how much prestige is associated with participating in a common culture legitimated by the state.

The effects of stratification are similar. We are most familiar with the processes by which stratification reinforces ethnic segregation. Differences in class cultures add to (and sometimes also create) differences in ethnic cultures, and vice versa. Sociologists have described many such self-reinforcing loops: in the contemporary United States, the material contrasts between the suburbs and the inner city reinforce family, educational, and attitudinal patterns, which in turn reinforce the distinctiveness between black "street" culture and middle-class white culture; the circle is closed by occupational stratification and the perpetuation of material inequality. Bourdieu's *habitus* theorizes self-reproducing arrangements generally. The pathos of such self-perpetuating models has become American sociologists' stock in trade.

Nevertheless, from an analytical vantage point stratification does not necessarily result in static ethnic boundaries. Stratification can also set up tendencies toward cultural assimilation. Stratification gives prestige to the culture of the dominant class, which has often spread to middle and subordinate classes by the processes of imitation, trickle-down, and imposition by culture-producing institutions. If class stratification is correlated with ethnic stratification, such processes can bring about assimilation of ethnic cultures. In addition, stratification can foster motivation for upward mobility. Insofar as subordinated ethnic groups move up in the class structure or laterally into the centralized organizations of the economy and state, there is a tendency for ethnic groups to be assimilated through structural amalgamation of group boundaries.[22] Conversely, we may expect that the tendency to assimilate is weakest where contiguous ethnic groups are equal in class position and prestige. The issue is which tendency is stronger—the tendency of stratification to reinforce ethnic boundaries or the opposite tendency to motivate assimilation. This again depends on the geopolitically given power-prestige of the state and hence of the ethnic culture of its rulers.

An additional loop between economic interests and ethnic antagonism has received much attention. The mobilization of ethnic antagonism has often been attributed to underlying economic conflicts. Insofar as ethnic groups form enclaves in the division of labor and the lineup of classes, any change in the economic standing of these groups mobilizes class conflict, which surfaces most easily in the form of ethnic antagonism. For example, anti-Semitism, rare in Christian Europe before the eleventh century, arose in violent attacks on Jews, initially in the Rhineland during the 1100s and subsequently in Eastern Europe. This anti-Semitism has been attributed to the spread of a mercantile economy, of which Jews were the spearheads, often in alliance with centralized rulers, making anti-Semitism a convenient rallying point for the traditionalist classes, the peasantry and the nobility (Murray 1978: 69). Similar structural patterns are found in the solidarity of Georgian Jews and other ethnic groups of the Caucasus that sustained their own informal economies within Soviet communism (Portes 1994). Ethnic antagonisms based on enclaves within the division of labor are not uniformly mobilized throughout world history; in many instances they were not mobilized at all. Tendencies to engage in ethnic conflict are just one of several causal forces, which can be overridden by stronger ones. The most central causal condition, along with the degree of state penetration, is the geopolitically based power-prestige of the state's rulers.

"AMERICANIZATION" VERSUS "BALKANIZATION"

Short-run processes within the division of labor, ethnoclass stratification, and cultural mobilization have indeterminate effects: they can either promote ethnic distinctiveness and conflict or foster motivation toward assimilation—above all culturally, but also associationally and somatotypically. Which of these happens depends upon contextual conditions, above all the geopolitical trajectory of the state. We may label two polar types. In the "Americanization model" the state has an expanding geopolitical position. Accordingly, the prestige of the dominant ethnic group is high, and the prevailing motivation is toward assimilation. In the "Balkanization model" the geopolitical trajectory is downhill: the state is crumbling; the prestige of the dominant ethnic group is low; the direction of mobilization is toward ethnic separatism rather than assimilation. In the "Balkanization model" the dominant ethnic group not only lacks attraction; it also becomes a *negative* reference point. So, for example, anti-Austrian and anti-Turkish sentiments became major mobilizing points for political and social action. In the same way, Russian ethnic identity at the time when their Russian-controlled Soviet Empire fell apart became a negative reference point for non-Russians.

The United States was a geopolitically expanding power beginning in the early 1800s and reached a standing of major world power by the time of World War I. The United States from 1800 to 1960, a prime example of the assimilation ("Americanization") dynamic of expanding ethnic boundaries, expanded into the territory of North America against minimal local opposition. By the late 1800s, the size and economic-resource advantage of the United States was formidable on the world scale. In the twentieth century the United States was in the position to pick up the pieces of the costly showdown wars among the major European powers. After 1960, the United States experienced mild geopolitical decline due to a costly arms race (a "cold showdown war") against the USSR, the marchland state on the other side of the old European battle zone. Further strains resulted from logistical overextension against populous enemies in Korea and Vietnam. This explains the high ethnic prestige of Anglo-American culture as a target for assimilation for a century and a half, with some falling off in prestige after 1960.

I have perhaps loaded the dice with the "Americanization model." The United States has not only been a rising geopolitical power, but has also acquired a territory rich in economic resources, and perhaps it was this wealth rather than its power-prestige that attracted large numbers of immigrants.

We may be tempted to modify the theoretical principles to add the following: both geopolitical prestige and economic opportunities increase the legitimacy and prestige of ruling elites and ethnic groups; conversely, both GP weakness and economic decline reduce ruling ethnic prestige. There are grounds, however, for giving geopolitics primacy in affecting ethnic prestige. The prestige of Anglo-assimilation in the United States was high from the early 1800s until the 1950s. If it has been challenged since that time, the correlation is not with economic decline but with geopolitical setbacks: above all the Vietnam War (1963–75), but more generally the Korean stalemate (1950–53), the Iranian/Islamic challenge (1979), and the emergence of a polycentric world. This underscores the point that geopolitical prestige is a matter of trajectory rather than absolute standing; "what have you done lately?" is more important than the absolute level of GP resources of a state and its elite.

GEOPOLITICAL PRESTIGE AND STRUGGLE
OVER THE MEANS OF CULTURAL PRODUCTION

This discussion of mesolevel conditions that affect ethnic boundaries has omitted the cultural media, such as education and language. These have important middle-range effects on both ethnic assimilation and ethnic struggle. As with all such meso conditions, the question is, which effect happens when? Thus in one (assimilation-oriented) model, mass education produces a common culture; the mass media spread a common language; expanding access to these media eventually eliminates all ethnic enclaves except a few residual traditionalists. In the other model (assimilation-resistance or ethnic fragmentation), the opposite occurs—the spread of literacy, newspapers, television, and the like provides the bases for mobilization of cultural separatists; "modernization" does not promote universalism but provides the instruments for reinforced particularisms. In this vein, education operates in a damned-if-you-do, damned-if-you-don't fashion. If the state attempts to impose cultural uniformity through the educational system, the result is resentment by aggrieved ethnic groups. Here we find Lithuanian, Ukrainian, and Armenian nationalists keeping their culture alive under a Russian-imposed education system, ready to burst out when the opportunity arrives. On the other hand, if the state allows cultural pluralization (as Soviet reformers did increasingly in the 1980s), it hands the weapons of group mobilization to its opponents (Waller 1992).

The key to which scenario takes place is not the structure of the education system (or the mass media) but the geopolitical conditions that set the overarching gradient of ethnic prestige. A culturally unified education system and an imposed linguistic monopoly on the means of dissemination will fail if the prestige of the dominant ethnic group is low. At least this will be the case over the time period (apparently several generations under modern conditions) during which state weakness eventually leads to a crumbling of central controls. We should not dwell too strongly on the image of a strong, vibrant current of cultural separatism, meeting in basements and waiting for the time when it can come into the open air. Rebellious ethnic nationalisms are to a large extent constructed, and sudden shifts in the political wind can bring about enthusiasm for an ethnic culture of separatism that was carried for a long time by only a few diehards. The "Balkanization" process can be long and slow, with state control visibly crumbling for decades or centuries; in this case (in the nineteenth- and early-twentieth-century Balkans) overt cultural resistance and mobilization are continuous. Or "Balkanization" can emerge rather rapidly, as in the weakening of central control in the USSR from the mid-1980s onward; in this case whatever twists occur in the rulers' cultural line all feed the same direction of resistance.

On the other hand, the "Americanization model" of cultural hegemony can operate without much more than market processes. Although some Anglos made overt efforts to impose their culture on migrants in the U.S. public schools of the late nineteenth and early twentieth centuries, the pres-tige of Anglo culture seems to have been the dominant factor in bringing about linguistic and educational assimilation. There was never any national control over education, and a good deal of local initiative existed. Variant forms of education were tried: a huge Catholic school system staffed mainly by non-Anglos; a multiplicity of religious colleges; and foreign-language schools, of which only the Hebrew academies have had much staying power. The variant forms of education soon lost their distinctiveness as all began to emulate the high-prestige model: the sequence of grades leading up to the traditional Anglo-Protestant college (Jencks and Riesman 1968). Not that multiethnic competition within the United States had no effect on the educational marketplace; but its effect was to heighten competition over a common currency of educational credentials and to produce the broadest expansion of schooling at all levels in any society in world history (Collins 1979). The result was inflation of a common educational currency, not frag-mentation into separate ethnic enclaves.[23] In the same way, separate ethnic-language newspapers and other cultural media have not flourished in the United States in competition with the Anglo-American mass culture. No state restrictions were significant in bringing about this result; the prestige of the Anglo culture merely outcompeted that of the ethnic separatists.

Problematic Cases

Does geopolitical ascendancy under conditions of modern state penetration always bring ethnonationalism? If we interpret this to mean that the domi-

nant ethnic group comes to define national culture and all other protoethnicities or migrated ethnicities disappear, there are some problematic cases.
What if dominated ethnicities fight back and achieve a permanent enclave
or even a separate state? The best example of this swimming against the
geopolitical tide is Ireland at the height of the British Empire. What if the
dominant ethnicity refuses to allow minorities to assimilate? This is the
problematic case of blacks in the United States.

IRELAND AND IMPERIAL BRITAIN

The legitimacy of a dominant ethnic group does not mean other ethnic
groups necessarily become absorbed into it. Its legitimacy may be defined in
contrast to a culturally subordinate and culturally illegitimate group. The
case of Ireland shows that the administration of conquered territory can institutionalize structures that turn regional protoethnicity into rebellious
ethnonationalism. English overlords of the sixteenth and seventeenth centuries treated Ireland as territory for colonial plantations, like those in overseas colonies; the "wild Irish" were regarded as little different from the
Indian tribes of North America (MacLeod 1967). The class distinction between colonial Anglo-Irish overlords and native Irish was solidified as a political distinction because of the way the English state was formed as a parliamentary regime. Rebellion and civil war had been ideologically promoted
to repulse foreign and Catholic ties believed to be encroaching on national
sovereignty. Parliamentary franchise was strictly limited to adherents of the
national Anglican Church and expressly prohibited to the defeated Catholics
as loyalists of the nonnational king. Oliver Cromwell had carried out an especially ferocious military policy in Ireland in the aftermath of the civil war;
and in the agitation of the 1680s over the feared restoration of Catholicism
by the monarchy, Ireland was the recruiting center for a Catholic loyalist
army. The power-prestige of the Anglo-Protestant ruling class made the division between Catholics and Protestants in eighteenth-century Ireland into
a division between the permanently disenfranchised and the political class in
a classic Marxian sense.

Geopolitics repeatedly reinforced the foreign, non-English identity of
Ireland. The Catholicism of the Irish was a conscious consideration for
diplomatic and military alliances from the time of the Spanish armada
through the landing of Jesuit agents and French support for rebellions,
Catholic legitimists, and royal pretenders in the seventeenth and eighteenth
centuries. The English sense of the otherness of Ireland was reinforced by
worries that it would become an ally of the Continental powers on their
back doorstep. Conversely, Irish nationalism was anchored by the possibility of receiving support from England's enemies. During the American revolutionary war, Irish sentiment was strongly on the American side, and the

English held back large bodies of troops for fear that the French would invade Ireland. During the French Revolution of the 1790s, Irish rebels took asylum in France, and French military expeditions actually landed (Foster 1989: 152). During World War I, Irish nationalists attempted to import arms from Germany. In the nineteenth and early twentieth centuries, Irish immigrants or sojourners in the United States (which of course had fought several wars against England) became the major base of support for Irish insurrectionists, as well as a counterbalance to the cultural tendency toward assimilation in England.

Irish ethnonationalism became increasingly crystallized from the early nineteenth century onward; it was built up by the process of state penetration, which provided the means for mobilizing social movements of all kinds directed against the English state, in England as well as in Ireland. The 1820s in Ireland was a period of mass meetings, marches, and symbolic agitation; that these occurred largely in agricultural and small-town settings shows even more strikingly than comparable movements in England that the basis of mobilization was not so much the spread of industry as the facilitating penetration of the state. The political battles throughout the century in England for extension of the franchise must have brought a sharper sense of alienation to the Irish immigrants, who filled a considerable portion of the industrial jobs in England but were not allowed to vote. The special status of colonial overlordship in Ireland continued through the series of British parliamentary franchise reforms; liberalization was generally more restricted for the Irish than for the English because Irish Catholics had the stigma of a double lack of legitimacy: as colonial subjects and as persons disloyal to the parliamentary regime. The "Irish question" became a bone of contention in English politics as humanitarian issues arising from rural famine in the 1840s meshed with the rights of property and the issue of the franchise. Marginal tenant farmers, the most visible Irish group, were pushed off their lands in each bad harvest by Anglo-Irish (and other) landlords who converted the land to more profitable grazing. Although indigenous Irish Catholics came to constitute an increasing portion of the landowning class, the historical anchoring of class division in ethnoreligious identities increasingly dominated public consciousness as enmities escalated with the rent strikes and assassinations of midcentury.

Political reforms by the English elite, rather than reducing Irish discontent, tended to provoke further conflict. In 1800 the Irish House of Commons, emblematic of the colonial regime, was abolished. The prevailing mood combined fear of Irish disloyalty during war with revolutionary France with concessions over what was increasingly regarded in England as blatant discrimination against Catholics. The English state became caught in a situation of being damned if you do, damned if you don't. Each move was trapped in a three-way conflict (Foster 1989: 148–211). One faction was the landed Anglo-Protestant elite, which opposed land and other reforms but was gradually squeezed out of dominance. A second faction began with the Catholic peasantry and rested increasingly upon a growing middle class, which was gradually enfranchised and eventually came to dominate parliamentary representation. During the transitional period of expanding franchise, Irish members of Parliament were typically Protestant gentry who sought popularity and votes by representing Catholic constituencies, thus redefining class and religious conflicts as matters of Irish national sovereignty.[24] As the magnet of Irish ethnic identity grew stronger than British ethnonationalism, a portion of the Anglo-Irish elite went over to Irish ethnonationalism. The Irish elite now had a choice of identities; segregation and discrimination against the Irish popular classes provided an unassimilated identity on which the Irish elite could anchor. Political opportunities in the English state arena reinforced and compounded the sense of Irish distinctiveness, as Irish members of Parliament became infamous for their obstreperous tactics but also sought-after as wielders of coalition-making power between the English parties.

The third faction comprised Irish Protestants of the dissenting denominations, who originally had also been excluded from the Anglican parliamentary political settlement. These Irish Protestants were concentrated especially in northern Ireland, where they comprised an increasingly prosperous industrial business class. In this zone, the Protestant working class dealt with unemployment pressures and other economic crises by forcibly excluding Catholic workers; class mobilization was superseded by narrowly exclusionary labor tactics on ethnoreligious lines. Irish Protestants (which I designate thus to contrast them with Anglican Anglo-Protestants) became increasingly hostile to English concessions to Catholics. As English politicians, whether from sympathy or weariness of strife, became increasingly favorable to settling the Irish problem by turning Ireland over to home rule by the Catholic majority, Irish Protestant opposition became increasingly militant. Popular confrontation between Irish Protestants and Catholics escalated into military mobilization on both sides and reached a peak in 1913–14 just before the outbreak of World War I. As a result, the limited form of local self-government generally envisioned, under British control of finance and foreign policy, was increasingly replaced by the goal of complete national autonomy.

The turning point coincided with geopolitical strains of the widely extended British Empire. Geopolitical strength is not indexed merely by the size of territory held, but by the logistical costs of defending the territory. The financial cost of the Boer war, a hot issue in Parliament, highlighted the strain of the empire. Irish sentiment favored the Boers, and British military difficulties brought a dawning sense that the overextension of the British Empire provided an opening for independence. The Irish brought their military struggle for independence to a head in 1916, deliberately taking advantage of British commitments in World War I. Although initially most of the Irish population was moderate on the question of home rule (and indeed a sizable Irish force had volunteered for the British army in Europe), the uprising by the radical nationalist faction led to polarization. In the atmosphere of wartime British authorities treated not only the rebels but also moderate Irish nationalists as traitors; the result was that Irish popular opinion swung sharply to the anti-British side. A similar scenario took place in the guerrilla war of 1919–21, as the cycle of atrocities on both sides eventually led to exhaustion and substantial Irish independence in 1922 (Foster 1989: 196–209). British military superiority was stymied by war-weariness following the enormous expense of the World War and by the Irish nationalists' appeal for international support. The United States in particular, as a rising military hegemon, helped dismantle the empires not only of the defeated Great Powers but of the British as well. Over the long historical view, Irish nationalism was promoted by its geopolitical connections to enemies of its English conquerors and came to fruition when the English were geopolitically strained.

WHITE RESISTANCE TO BLACK ASSIMILATION IN THE UNITED STATES

On an analytical level, there are striking parallels between the unassimilable Irish in Britain and black African Americans in the United States. Both began as subjugated populations in colonial plantation regimes, in which political rights were reserved for the legitimated ethnonational group. In Ireland, it was Catholicism that structurally marked and perpetuated the colonial hierarchy; in the United States it was skin color. The South formulated the miscegenation laws that became institutionalized in the custom of treating all persons of mixed parentage as black. American race relations are sometimes described as a caste system, but the analogy to India is weak. Indian castes are part of a hierarchy of numerous gradations, continuously expanding over time; in the United States the line between black and white is the single overriding division. Indian castes were created by a process of emulating Brahman ritual purity as a kind of lingua franca of high social status, in a society where states were weak and legal controls were based on an extension of kinship relationships (Collins 1998: 208–12); U.S. black/white racialism was formulated by the state and enforced by law in many places until the 1960s.

The stronger analogy is between Catholic Irish in the British polity and blacks in the legally segregated United States. Many black Americans came to live not in the officially segregated states of the South but in the industrial North, where they had much the same position as Irish workers in England. In both cases, class distinctions reinforced the culturally imposed dividing line; in both cases, an institutional anchor of state law kept the ethnic distinction salient. Even those who were outside the worst zones of overt state discrimination (black Americans in the North; the Anglo-Irish elite in Ireland, and Irish workers in England) found themselves identified in public reputation by the core category of their ethnic group. There are a number of parallels in the process by which ethnic rebellion mobilized in both places. The 1916 uprising of Irish nationalists in the midst of World War I was a more militant version of the first national political action taken by American blacks, the threatened strike by black Pullman porters during World War II that led to the government's overturning military segregation policies. The British geopolitical strains that led to Irish independence are paralleled, again with less militant outcomes, by the mobilization of black civil rights and black power movements in the aftermath of U.S. geopolitical strains in the Korean and Vietnam wars. The three-way factional fight within Ireland was paralleled by conflicts in the postslavery American South: Irish Catholics and southern blacks were both objects of oppression and also of onlooker sympathy as subordinated rural classes. The conservative planters' elite operated in both places, a portion of which became a "white liberal" faction favoring the cause of the oppressed. And in both Ireland and the United States the lower-middle and working classes (Irish Protestants, paralleled by the middle and lower classes of white southerners) became the most militant opponents of equality and desegregation.

The key difference between the Irish in Britain and blacks in the United States is the geopolitical context. For Britain, Ireland was always a worrisome piece of territory to hold in the balance-of-power politics among its Continental neighbors. In the United States the black population was integral to its territory. Even the Civil War, in which the none-too-long-established federation broke apart into separate states, did not deeply threaten this connection, although it would have done so if the Confederacy had won the war. Black southerners were implicit allies of the Unionists, and it was their white southern overlords who for two or three generations after the Civil War nursed a separate identity based on military memories. The growing geopolitical power-prestige of the federal United States of America on the world scene in the twentieth century was a strong magnet for national identification, beginning with victories in the Spanish-American War and World War I and culminating in the all-out military mobilization of World War II. It was in the context of that war and the ensuing wars of the United States as world-policing hegemon (the Korean and Vietnam wars) that the movement was mobilized for black integration and the destruction of state-enforced legal discrimination. On the whole, assimilation was the aim of the movement at that time, a goal that was welcomed and reinforced by the white elites most identified with the inclusive ethnonationalism of the successful twentieth-century American state. It is this circumstance that provided the sense in the 1960s that racial integration was an idea whose time had come.

As the GP hypothesis predicts, U.S. global power-prestige produced American ethnonationalism. What the GP theory does not directly explain is the source of white resistance to black assimilation. Here we could invoke a number of well-studied processes by which ethnic stratification reproduces itself. I have nothing new to add except the GP context in which this resistance to assimilation went from legitimate to illegitimate. The World Wars, and especially the catapulting of the United States into the front rank of world power-prestige at midcentury, made American integration a strong theme for all ethnic groups.[25] These circumstances also led to GP strains of overextension, above all the embarrassing defeats of the Vietnam War. The black movement in the United States involved elements both of liberalizing ethnonationalism and of separatism. Ethnonationalism came from the strong upward trajectory of American power-prestige, which brought the black integration movement institutional support from the mass media and the discourse of public officials, as well as fervent moral support by the cosmopolitan social classes of the white population.[26] A string of geopolitical setbacks caused the mood of delegitimation of the dominant ethnic group, which in turn fed black nationalism and separatism. The U.S. defeat in the Vietnam War was the equivalent of the breakup of the European colonial empires through the strains of World War II. In both cases, the ethnonationalism of once-invincible states was battered. Declining states face moral onslaughts on the legitimacy of their rule, and these are echoed by their own elites in their loss of self-confidence, a mixture of humiliation and guilt. It is this atmosphere that has encouraged a rebellious nationalism of unassimilated and oppressed populations.

In the United States, rebellious ethnonationalism has not gone very far because the GP strength of the state is still relatively high. With the collapse of the USSR in the 1990s, the GP position of the United States has climbed again by default. For all the rhetoric carried over from the upheaval period of the 1960s and 1970s, black, Hispanic, and Asian ethnic militancies take the form of struggles over the content of schooling in urban neighborhoods and relatively minor issues of deference to cultural symbols, not claims for transferring even fragments of territorial power to autonomous ethnic control. The power-prestige of the state remains strong; we can expect that the prestige of ethnonationalism will remain paramount as long as the geopolitical situation remains the same. The long-run trend, in that case, is toward assimilation.

By this time, the target standard is no longer simply the cultural dominance of white Anglo culture and somatotypes. Pressures for the assimilation of European ethnicities, which reached their peak in the New Deal and the mobilization of World War II, had already produced a hybrid culture (which might well be called "American creole") by the mid-twentieth century. The hybrid nature of that culture will doubtless continue to change, with the incorporation of Asian and Hispanic elements. In many respects, black American culture has already made its mark on American national culture, and vice versa. The differences that remain are largely matters of class culture, plus one distinctive marker: skin color. On this point, the GP hypothesis suggests an optimistic future for assimilationists, a pessimistic one for separatists.

The key to the racialization of the continuum of ethnic distinctions is the cultural definition of the offspring of mixed couples as belonging exclusively to the nonlegitimate category. That cultural definition appears to be dissolving at the turn of the twenty-first century. In the 1990s there was growing recognition of a category of mixed race. The effect of such a change in categorical boundaries would be far-reaching. In the absence of further differentiation of ranked degrees of racial purity such as have existed in Brazil and elsewhere, the breaking up of the rigid distinction between black and white has potential for the entire category scheme to lose its centrality as a marker. We may be seeing the beginning of a racially de-dichotomized America, even though assimilation of all groups of the population may not occur for a long time. A distinctive black racial identity may well continue, anchored in a sizable black lower class segregated by mutual reinforcing feedbacks of class and racial hostility and legitimated by criminalization. The existence of a culturally distinct and hypersegregated black underclass makes black skin a reference point for everyone and keeps the category alive even as applied to blacks of higher social classes. Counterbalancing this racial dichotomy is the potential for an amorphous mixed-race category to deracialize American ethnonational identity. A mixed-race category is not emerging through interbreeding between blacks and whites, as in the scenario of classic expectations and fears. It has come about instead from the blurring of racial identities among some Asians, Hispanics, Amerindians, and others into a transracial category into which white Euro-Americans and African-Americans have also been blending, at different edges. Blacks and whites may not blend together in the foreseeable future, but it is conceivable that both will blend into a larger, culturally dominant category.

If high geopolitical power-prestige elevates the prestige of a unitary ethnonational identity and full mobilization of all its people into the armed forces puts emotional energy into this identification,[27] we might expect that the United States as world hegemon will see the cultural definition of race dissolve in the coming generations. The geopolitical prominence of the United

States of America attracts worldwide immigration, promoting the tendency toward a transracial identity amalgamating a wide variety of world ethic origins. Within this context, a class-based black/white distinction may well continue, but increasingly as a sidelight to the shifting center of American ethnonational identity. The blended Asian-Euro-Hispanic American would be the category into which all else dissolves. All this depends, however, on how long the GP ascendancy of the United States lasts.

THE FUTURE OF ETHNICITY

Ethnic divisions will be both created and dissolved, probably for the entire future of human existence.[28] Their pattern will follow geopolitical dynamics. These may be illustrated in a few immediate possibilities.

The largest geopolitical change at the turn of the twenty-first century is the potential emergence of two huge and powerful states on the world scene: the European Union and China. We can expect both to produce an expansive, newly defined ethnonational consciousness. Already in the 1980s we have seen an attempt to define a pan-Chinese cultural orbit in the guise of Confucian cultural tradition whose leading spokesman has been the Singapore politician, Lee Kuan Yew. Its aim is to transcend the now geopolitically discredited ideology of communism and to put China in the center of ethnonational loyalties that resemble pan-Slavism or pan-Germanism at the time of the expansive Russian and German spheres of influence. How much further this ideology will go depends upon geopolitical variables that may bring China military conflicts and strains as well as regions of direct or indirect control.

The European Union (EU), since it is organized as a federation that transcends national states, is ideologically transnationalist. At the same time, the institutional arrangements and cultural networks of the EU will doubtless foster a European cultural identity. How strongly this moves in the direction of a European ethnonationalism will depend upon the power-prestige of the EU in the world arena. As yet, the federation has been hesitant about mobilizing its military force. If this step were taken, it would likely exert considerable power over its immediate neighbors. Even without using military force to any great extent, the power vacuum nearby in Central Europe and to the southeast invites a sphere of influence. In this respect its main geopolitical competitors are the United States and the United Nations, although the latter appears too inchoate to generate much of a world ethnonationalist universalism.[29]

Consider in closing what light the GP theory casts on two phenomena. One is the seeming paradox that regional ethnonationalisms inside the old European nation-states have been mobilizing at just the time that the EU has become an overarching umbrella: Catalan nationalism in Spain, Scottish and

Welsh nationalism in Britain, Lombard nationalism in Italy, and others. Is this a contradiction? I suggest that they follow from GP principles. The EU has been taking power from its component states, first of all in their autonomy of military action. Since the dramatic experience of military participation is the strongest source of power-prestige, the loss of independent militaries has delegitimated them in some degree as states, and along with that has delegitimated their ethnonational identities. The regional nationalisms that have emerged under this umbrella arise according to the principle that loss of GP power-prestige by a state fosters ethnic revolt. These revolts are mild because the nation states have not broken down by fragmenting territorial force; instead the monopoly of that force has been shifting upward to the EU. The regional autonomy movements do not attempt to reinstate their own monopolies of force, but aspire to act only as semistates under an umbrella of force organized higher up. Such regional restructurings are possible at this time, reversing the trend of rising ethnonationalism that occurred when states consolidated power in the earlier part of the century, because geopolitical power at the level of the nation-state has been superseded in Europe. These regional movements may be phenomena of the transition during which the old nation-states are delegitimated but the full-scale European state has not yet come into existence.

GP theory makes a blunt if not particularly welcome projection of the conditions under which the EU would become the emotional magnet for a new Euronational loyalty and the basis for a pan-European ethnicity: the EU would have to become a full-fledged state in the Weberian sense, mobilizing its population through collective military experience. It is possible, of course, that this may never happen. European reaction against militarism in the later twentieth century may intertwine with existing ethnic fragmentation so as to prevent sufficient buildup of collective sentiment to operate a European armed force. Given the long historical record of state exercise of force and the relative ephemerality of political moods, especially those based in reacting against a previous situation, it is doubtful that European pacificism will remain dominant forever. For as long as it does last, GP theory implies a structural consequence: the EU will not become an object of emotionally compelling loyalty, although it may grow into a comfortable framework of cultural and economic connections.

The GP theory of ethnonationalism also offers a diagnosis of the horrific ethnic violence in the fragments of Yugoslavia. A once coherent state has broken down and experienced the rise of ethnic nationalisms at their most extreme. Yugoslavia's distinctive identity had been as a buffer state, an intermediate zone between communist and anticommunist blocs. The disintegration of the Soviet Empire and the ideological delegitimation of communism left Yugoslavia without identity and without a geopolitical role. As a small state, its position in the lineup of world power-prestige had been that of a broker that gained prestige beyond its resources by facilitating bargains between the power blocs. Cold war Yugoslavia was the archetypical neutral state, the pioneering leader of the neutral bloc. Yugoslavia had no legitimating resource except this niche, which it lost with the downfall of the Soviet bloc. Uncertainties about where new state power might be established led to local arms races and a cycle of atrocities that quickly constructed latent ethnic identities into primordial animosities.[30]

In these circumstances GP theory offers a prognosis as well. The key to ending ethnic strife is to reestablish the power-prestige of the state—not necessarily the Yugoslav state, which is badly delegitimated, but any effective state. The most obvious solution would be for the EU to offer to incorporate all the fragments of ex-Yugoslavia into itself. At the same time, the EU would have to act like a strong state, brooking no opposition to its monopoly over legitimate force on its territory. The EU could effectively disarm the former Yugoslavia, but only by transferring primary emotional loyalty to itself. Serbians, Bosnians, Croatians, and others could again become peaceful citizens on a par with typical citizens in any other strong modern state. Whether this is likely to happen is another story. Since the EU is moving very slowly and cautiously in transforming itself into a full-fledged state, it is questionable whether the EU will be able to offer this kind of solution in the near future.

At the turn of the twenty-first century, the predominant mood in much of the West, including both Europe and the United States, favors multiculturalism, which is characterized by antagonism toward ethnonationalism at the state level and sympathy to ethnic perpetuation in niches below the state level. Is this one of history's pendulum swings, overestimated once again in the short-sightedness of the present, or a long-term structural change? The only way to answer this question is on the basis of a firm macrohistorical theory of the long run, and that is what is only just now coming into being. Nevertheless I will suggest a diagnosis.

The geopolitical core of the state never disappears, but geopolitical situations can take many forms. The structural situation in the 1990s resembles a balance of power, not so much by the strong military mobilization of a half-dozen Great Powers acting deliberately to keep alliances even, but by an inchoate linkage of international networks. Trade, migration, offshore manufacturing, and financial speculation, as well as a jumble of international organizations, do not necessarily make it impossible for states to take action militarily—to do so would be costly, but wars have always been costly, and their economic irrationality has never been much of a deterrent in view of their emotional appeal. What today's transnational networks do is to foster a cosmopolitan elite not unlike the diplomats, mercenaries, and cultural exporters who spanned Europe during the eighteenth-century Enlightenment.

Along with balance-of-power geopolitics goes cosmopolitanism, which looks down on the local and the particular as retrograde and morally inferior. The language of multiculturalism, I suggest, is the lingua franca of today, as French was during the Enlightenment. There is an ironic multi-layeredness to the new lingua franca, for multiculturalism (or "political correctness") is scornful of ethnic nationalism (provided that it is one's own nationalism that is scorned), while it praises the primordialist ideologies of newly liberated ethnicities. Since all ethnicities are constructed and none primordial, this seems inconsistent. So is the notion of tolerance that includes being tolerant of intolerances, or rather, tolerant of certain privileged intolerances. But these concepts are based on a deeper macrohistorical logic. The ethnic particularisms that are delegitimated are those of the nation-state; those that are promoted are those that were never raised to the level of the privileged national ethnic group. It commonly happens that as soon as an oppressed or otherwise downgraded ethnic movement gets close to state power, or mobilizes the arms that put state power within reach, it starts performing the same kinds of offenses against ethnic outsiders that are characteristic of any ethnonationalism. The lingua franca of multiculturalism harbors a romanticism not unlike the Enlightenment's ideal of the noble savage or the state of nature. It idealizes nonstate ethnicities while trying to ignore the state configurations that make ethnicities possible and that draw them toward the state like filings to a magnet. To be socially effective, a lingua franca does not have to speak sense; it only needs to be a shared medium of communication. It is structurally fitting in the balance-of-power situation that prevails, at least among Western societies, at this juncture in world history.

CHAPTER 4

Democratization from the Outside In: A Geopolitical Theory of Collegial Power

THEORIES OF DEMOCRACY are usually written with a particular history in mind, a narrative that drags along the burden of taken-for-granted theoretical assumptions. The archetypal narrative is the history of England, the exemplar of what we mean by democracy. Along with this go several counternarratives or archetypes of what is not democracy—above all Germany, with its culmination in Nazism; Russia, made increasingly poignant by its current battle to throw off a long counterdemocratic heritage; and secondarily France, which falls somewhere in the middle, damned to the limbo of betwixt and between. Much narrative history, and all too often comparative theorizing as well, treats the polar cases as teleological (see, e.g., Greenfeld 1993). We know that England became a full-fledged democracy by following a series of steps on the democratic path. Germany, in contrast, was intrinsically nondemocratic. The pathway leading to Germany's archetypical fate was displayed in eighteenth-century Pietism, the militarism of Frederick the Great, and the failure to effect a bourgeois revolution in 1848; its essence emerged in full bloom with the Nazi regime. German historiography is written in Hitler's shadow, Russian historiography in Stalin's.

Teleology begs the question of turning points. By all standard criteria, the German Federal Republic since 1949 has been a stable democracy; the same has been true of Japan since 1946–52. Does this period of half a century count for nothing in comparative analysis? It is convenient to ignore it, if one wishes to categorize these cases as showing their true colors in the regimes of the 1930s. More systematically, one may dismiss the post-1945 regimes on the grounds that they were externally imposed by conquering armies. Is the principle implied here a valid explanation? It would hold that forced imposition of a political regime is the primary determinant of the long-term character of that regime. As a general principle, there is abundant comparative evidence that it is false. The Soviet-style regimes imposed in Eastern Europe are just one set of negative examples; the repeated failure of north Asian tribal conquest states to extirpate Chinese dynastic institutions are another. It is also false to assume that democratic institutions in Germany and Japan started from zero in 1945. There was a full-scale democracy in Germany from 1919 to 1933, not imposed from outside, and its parliamentary institutions went back even further. In Japan, parliamentary institutions existed from 1889, with universal male suffrage since 1925 and multiple parties until 1940 (Kinder and Hilgemann 1968: 451). Such structural patterns need to be taken into account in any serious effort to explain the existence of democracy in particular times and places.

Teleology enters explicit theory in the guise of "culture." Germany and Japan lack a democratic culture. Conversely, England and the United States were built upon such a culture. Culture comprises that which is handed along from the past; we do things a certain way because it is tradition, because we have done such before, from time out of memory or at least sufficiently far back so that we no longer care how the traditions started. Historians make free use of the concept of culture and its cognates; among sociologists, explicit theorizing defends the concept of culture; in today's metatheoretical polemics, culture is upheld as the bulwark of human dignity, of autonomy from material and structural conditions, or as guarantee of freedom from the deterministic constraints of causal-explanatory theory. In fact, determination by cultural tradition is a particularly rigid and conservative form of determinism. Cultural explanation comes dangerously close to pretending that a label for the pattern at hand is more than a reified description of what is to be explained. Explanation by national character is an old-fashioned version of the same fallacy.

Once it is admitted that a tradition is influenced by conditions at a starting point, it becomes consistent to ask why conditions at some other point in time cannot also change the tradition, perhaps even radically. We need a theory of events and structures; even a theory that gives weight to cultural tradition needs underpinnings to explain when and how this weight may exist. Let us assume that England acquired a democratic culture at some point in time (say 1640 or 1689, if not 1215 or 1832); before that it was on the same footing as twentieth-century Germany or Russia. If there are conditions that give rise to a democratic culture, those same conditions are crucial in formulating an explanatory theory. By the same token, there must be conditions that can modify a democratic culture, that enhance or diminish it or perhaps eliminate it entirely. It cannot be asserted that England will forevermore be a democracy, or even that between, say, 1689 and the present no event or structural transformation could have changed that culture.

And if this is true for England, it must also be true for Germany or Japan or Russia. We know that Germany had such conditions at least twice—in 1919 and again in 1949. And Russia, however ill-fated by its history, has had at least a version of democracy since 1991, so there should be some conditions, generally specifiable, that would make it possible for Russian democracy to prosper. By the same logic, the turn of Germany to the extreme anti-democracy of the Nazi regime has causes in certain types of events and structures. If England can have its turning points, so can Germany, for better or ill. Germany was not necessarily doomed by its cultural essence to become a Nazi state. The fact that this happened between 1933 and 1945 is related to specific causes, which may well be highly proximate ones.

Teleology, Culture, and Unidimensional Causality

The most serious drawback of the teleological analysis of democracy is that it crams a multidimensional process into a single concept: there is a democratic culture that some societies have and others do not. Comparative analysis is then set in motion to show the conditions associated with the relative strength of democracy. Consider, however, where the unidimensional concept of "democratization" came from. The term "democracy" did not become popular until the nineteenth century, but its cognates go back to ancient Greece and Rome. "Liberty" and "freedom" have long been concepts of scholars and political orators; they have been associated with the emotional peaks of political mobilization—popular slogans of defense against enemy invaders, and again of movements of resistance and revolt. Of less antiquity as terms for the political good are "the people" (which seventeenth-century Britons used to refer to the collective aristocracy and gentry vis-à-vis the crown) and "equality." Another concept is "rights," assimilated to one or more of the above. In the heat of political discourse, these terms have often been used more or less interchangeably. They make up a family of rhetoric that by the twentieth century had come to be known by the omnibus term "democracy."

All these terms invoke polarities: freedom versus slavery, democracy versus despotism, rights versus the abrogation of rights. They are polarities with a high degree of emotionality that are invoked with the urgency of all-or-nothing, "liberty or death!" These are battle slogans, and their unidimensionality is characteristic of the polarization of opposing sides that simplifies any intense conflict down to two factions at the moment of highest mobilization. This is one reason why the theory and history of democracy have had such heavy going analytically. Their concepts are inherited from the moments of greatest emotional uplift in political life, and the scholar vicariously participates in invoking these slogans as the focal point of his or her work. The theory of democracy is among the most ideologically trammeled at the heart of its conceptual apparatus.

Analyzed more neutrally, "liberty," "rights," "equality," and the rest are highly ambiguous concepts. Liberty for one group can just as well be oppression of another; the rights of the feudal aristocracy acceded in the Magna Carta 1215 were far from rights from the point of view of the peasantry; and it is notorious that equality in certain respects can undergird inequality in other respects. If we confine ourselves to "democracy," with explicit attention to the structural arrangements so designated, there is again considerable ambiguity as to for whom a given arrangement is democratic and for whom it is counterdemocratic. The Venetian republic, dating from around 1170, was at least a protodemocracy; it was intricately structured to avoid the despotic rule of a single individual or family. On the other hand, its series of electoral bodies were built upon a base of patrician families that from the point of view of those outside their ranks would be regarded as an undemocratic oligarchy. Venetians nevertheless had a tradition and a rhetoric of defending their rights and liberties; and this tradition in at least some respects continues in traditions that have become those of modern democracy.

In the Anglocentric narrative, it has become traditional to accept the Magna Carta as a stepping-stone along the teleological pathway to modern democracy. In the case of Venice, we see nothing but an oligarchy. In the case of the German "free cities" from the period of the medieval Empire to the nineteenth century, it is conventional to concentrate on the negative side; since Germany represents the essence of counterdemocracy, its limited forms of democracy are classified merely as oligarchies. The Dutch revolt against Spain and the formation of the Dutch Republic (1568–84) was the starting point for the popular slogans of liberty, which gained currency in the English revolutions of the following century; because the Anglocentric viewpoint adopts the biases of the English who fought the Dutch repeatedly during 1650–74, the Dutch are not included in the canon of modern revolutions and do not generally count as instances of the democratic pathway. To be sure, the Dutch Republic was an oligarchy, with numerous despotic features from the point of view of those who were not in the ruling religious and class factions; but the same was true in contemporary England for a long time too.

Here idealization, teleology, and unidimensionality reinforce one another. Democracy is supposed to be an unmitigated good; that it may be more of a good for some than for others and may even appear in the guise of oppression in some quarters, are circumstances on which the selective focus of teleological history enables us to close our eyes.

Democratization on Multiple Dimensions: Collegial Power-Sharing and Extent of the Participatory Franchise

Because democracy is a multidimensional set of structures, we will need a separate causal theory to explain its separate dimensions. And each dimension is a continuum, not an all-or-nothing condition. The contrary impres-

sion has arisen because so many points on the continuum have been contested using slogans that made the distance between them seem like chasms
between political good and evil. We need to substitute for teleological narratives the explanation of movement—not always in one direction—along
several continuums. In breaking from Anglocentric teleology, we may anticipate that historical movements along these continuums are not necessarily those of conventional accounts, that England is not always at the forefront of every dimension nor Germany always at the rear.

I propose two key dimensions and one subsidiary dimension of democratization. The two major dimensions are *the degree of collegially shared power*,
and *the extent of the participatory franchise*. The subsidiary dimension is *political
rights*. It is subsidiary because it tends to follow in time from movement
along the main dimensions and is largely caused by them. This will be a useful simplification for our purposes, since the description of the several dimensions is already complicated enough and their causal explanation even
more so.[1]

Collegial power is shared by such institutions as councils involved in collective decision-making, electoral bodies, assemblies and legislatures, and independent judiciaries (for an elaborate typology, see Weber 1968: 271–83).
These are structures that disperse power among a number of actors or units.
Federations and coalitions are forms of collegial power-sharing at a higher
level of organizational structure; however, power within units may be structured internally. For simplicity, let us picture the degree of collegial power
arrayed along an abstract continuum. At one extreme, power is concentrated
in the hands of a centralized hierarchy under the arbitrary control of an autocrat. As we move along the continuum, the number of collegial structures
increases, as does their relative power vis-à-vis central hierarchy. A council
or legislature that meets infrequently and has merely consultative powers
comprises less collegial democracy than bodies with budgetary power, and
those in turn are weaker than those that can initiate policies. At the extreme
(rarely found except in some ancient city-states and contemporarily in some
small city councils), the collegial body is involved in the day-to-day exercise
of power.

The *extent of the franchise* is the proportion of the populace allowed to take
part in politics. The franchise is meaningful only in the context of the collegial institutions that determine the structures of power within which participation is exercised, the mold into which varying numbers of participants
can be poured. Hereditary autocracy is the vanishing point at which there is
no franchise at all. A little farther along the continuum, an example of a narrow franchise is the College of Cardinals, which elects the Popes, and whose
membership has ranged from 12 to 87 (Kelley 1986: 191, 272, 321). The opposite extreme has rarely been approached. In practice, even a "universal"

franchise is restricted to adults (variously defined by age), excludes persons of criminal standing, and so forth. Even within these limits, almost everywhere before 1920 more than half the adult population was excluded: women, non–property holders or non–heads of households, servants, slaves, and laborers. It is striking that the historical exclusion of women from the franchise is ignored by virtually all political theorists; at best, it is regarded as a trivial exception that does not affect judgments about democracy. The analytical intuition here would seem to be a tacit recognition that the franchise is not the only dimension of democratization and that collegial power-sharing is more fundamental. Of course the second dimension is hardly a minor one. If one takes a wide (or even a bare majority) franchise as the criterion of a democracy, there were no democracies until very recently.

Political rights comprise, most importantly, freedom of communication and mobilization (speech, press, assembly). These rights, although symbolically central because of their importance in political struggles, nevertheless are analytically subsidiary in several senses. Many political rights are offshoots of institutional patterns on the main dimensions of democratization. Freedom of assembly and the right to petition collectively for redress of grievances are abstract expressions of the activities members of collegial institutions may engage in. Freedom from arbitrary arrest and punishment are related to the existence of an independent judiciary and to the binding power of a legislature over and above the governmental executive hierarchy. Rights are cultural expressions and crystallizations of the struggle that has propelled movement along the two main continuums of democracy. Rights have a certain analytical independence insofar as states are rarely at the extreme ends of democratization. States with collegial institutions or a wide franchise have often produced censorship and intolerance of wider or narrow ranges of political expression. In general, we can understand rights better in the context of explaining the degree of collegial power-sharing and the extent of the franchise than vice versa.[2]

The intersection of the two main dimensions shows that four degrees of democratization may exist (see Figure 9). (1) One extreme is high collegial power-sharing combined with a low extent of the franchise. An example might be an aristocratic state with an absent or extremely weak central monarchy; the sixteenth- and seventeenth-century Polish state with its elected king approached this condition. Another example would be an oligarchic republic such as Venice, in which a small elite does all the voting and officeholding, while alternating leaders in office and respecting constitutional principles.

Descending this continuum on this column, we arrive at the other extreme of (2), high collegial power combined with a wide franchise. This is the ideal type of modern democracy, perhaps rarely realized. On the other

	High collegial power	Low collegial power
Low franchise	Oligarchic republic	Ideal type despotism
High franchise	Ideal type liberal democracy	Plebiscitarian autocracy

FIGURE 9. Fourfold typology of collegial power and franchise.

column, one end point (3) combines the absence of collegial power with a wide franchise. This is plebiscitarian autocracy, in which there is a single autocrat, unlimited by parliament or the balance of powers but chosen by universal participation. At this extreme, the significance of the franchise in the exercise of power is vanishingly small, but this combination does give a distinctive emotional character to the mass mobilization of fascist states. Historically, this extreme is also found in the case of popular kings and was institutionalized in the tribal practice of choosing dictatorial war leaders by acclamation. Laterally across the continuum would be a wide franchise of electors for a weak consultative parliament such as existed in many European states in the early nineteenth century. (4) At the opposite extreme is the absence of collegial power combined with a zero franchise. This is the ideal type of despotism. In practice, given de facto limits on organizational centralization and the existence of court cliques, some degree of collegial power usually mitigated this extreme.

This multidimensional scheme enables us to capture with greater precision the conceptions underlying conventional analyses of democracy. Most modern research has used a definition stressing competitive elections and guarantees of political and individual rights (Lipset 1994). Implicitly, it is assumed that the elections are to offices that hold real power (not only token authority); it is taken for granted that the power of the elected chief executive is collegially shared in some degree. Taken literally as the sole criterion, open and fair election of a lifetime dictator who was unrestrained by any collegial structures would not be considered highly democratic; in the multi-dimensional model, such a government would fall at the extreme edge of the cell of plebiscitarian autocracy. If the Pope were elected not merely by the College of Cardinals but by the entire Church, the result would be just such a structure. This shows the importance of explicitly considering two dimensions: not just the presence of an election, but also the relative frequency of elections to bodies with varying degrees of collegial power and involving participation by varying proportions of the population.

DEGREES OF DEMOCRATIZATION IN SOME MAJOR STATES

None of the Western societies moved consistently and concurrently toward democratization on the several dimensions.

In England, collegial structures existed in the form of feudal councils beginning in the eleventh and twelfth centuries. Following a series of baronial revolts, an enlarged parliament of nobles voting on financial contributions for war developed by 1265; the bicameral structure of the Houses of Lords and Commons developed between 1295 and 1350. An independent judiciary and local administration emerged in the form of legal guilds and justices of the peace drawn from the country gentry in the twelfth to fourteenth centuries. Parliamentary supremacy over the executive was gradually established after 1710; the absolute power of the monarch was finally lost under George III (1760–1820).[3] The House of Lords retained veto power over legislation until 1911, and the higher aristocracy dominated government ministries of both parties until the Labour government of 1905 (Kinder and Hilgemann 1968: 155, 185, 265, 305, 380, 422; CMH 1910, 11: 339–42; 12: 41–42).

The extent of the franchise participating through these institutions was for a long time quite restricted. The medieval parliament consisted of a small number of hereditary lords. The House of Commons was selected by vote of a small number of landholders, and in the cities, of the wealthiest burgesses. Parliamentary democracy of the first great period of party politics, the Whig and Tory ministries of the 1700s and early 1800s, was based upon no more than 8 percent of the adult population. The 1832 reform bill abolished unequal "rotten boroughs" controlled by wealthy aristocrats and instituted a propertied franchise that encompassed 20 percent of the male population in England, 12 percent in Scotland, and 5 percent in Ireland (McEvedy 1982: 10, 30; Mann 1993: 110–14, 617). In 1867 and 1884, when Conservative governments widened the franchise to property-owning heads of households, first in the towns and then in the rural areas, the number of voters was increased to 4 million out of a population of 25 million (in 1867, 33 percent of the adult males, in 1884, 66 percent). Catholics were barred from voting in Ireland until 1793 (under a very restricted property franchise) and in England until 1829, and they were prohibited from holding judicial and high political office until the 1840s. Jews received the right to sit in parliament in 1866. Full manhood suffrage did not come until 1918, when women age 30 and older were also given the vote. Universal suffrage, including women age 21 and older, came in 1928.

In the United States, local assemblies existed in many colonies during the 1700s. The first radical structural change among Western countries came with the U.S. constitution of 1787, with its elective president and legislative assemblies and parallel structures at the level of the component states. The franchise was restricted in several respects, however (Williamson 1960; Mann 1993: 153). Indentured servitude existed until the early nineteenth century; property qualifications for voting existed in many states. Suffrage in the colonial legislatures ranged from 50 to 80 percent of adult white males; the Revolution expanded this to 60–90 percent and abolished religious restrictions; full suffrage for white males was not achieved until the 1840s (after considerable struggle in some places, including an insurrection in Rhode Island). Slavery excluded 15 percent of the populace from voting until 1870. De facto denial of voting rights to blacks extended until the 1960s in many states. The subjugated population of native American Indians was politically excluded until 1924. The national franchise excluded women until 1920.

In France, medieval parliamentary institutions generally lost their influence during the 1600s after the failure of the aristocratic uprising against Richelieu's absolutist rule. In local affairs, parliaments controlled judicial functions and acted as a check on royal absolutism through the 1700s; their membership represented an oligarchy of the wealthy. During the Revolution, the franchise was given in 1791 to property holders, who constituted 60 percent of the male population, and expanded to all males in 1793. With the coup d'etat of 1799 the influence of voters was restricted by a series of indirect elections, culminating in legislatures with powers only to approve laws initiated from above. Napoleon was elected hereditary emperor in 1804 by plebiscite. After the Restoration in 1815, a legislative assembly continued to exist, based on a restricted franchise confined to the wealthiest landowners (one-third of 1 percent of males), together with a chamber of hereditary peers. In the constitutional monarchy of 1830, the chamber of deputies took the right to initiate legislation. Universal manhood suffrage was established in 1848 with the direct election of both legislatures and the president. After the 1851 coup d'etat was confirmed by plebiscite, power of the elected legislature was restricted to approving laws initiated from above. The regime became increasingly constitutional after 1860 because of the financial difficulties of Napoleon III and ensuing bargaining with parliamentary factions. After 1875 the legislature assumed full powers, including indirect election of the senate and president. Female suffrage was not granted until 1946 (Kinder and Hilgemann 1968: 290, 295, 302, 344, 353; CMH 1910, 10: 61–67, 71, 478–87; 11: 472, 490; McEvedy 1982: 10).

In Germany, collegial power structures had extensive medieval roots. Decision-making by assemblies of notables and aristocrats existed in many parts of Germany in the Middle Ages; the *Ständestaat* mixed the privileges of the "estates" and corporations with officeholding in a princely administration (Rosenberg 1958). The emperor was elected by the extremely limited franchise held by the heads of eight states. An imperial Reichstag consisted of a congress of ambassadors of the multiple states of the empire. There were a large number of "free cities" and self-governing towns controlled by oligarchic councils usually drawn from the guild masters. These municipalities generally lost their independence after 1800, but formal structures of local self-government were usually retained (Bendix 1978: 378–84). The larger states that consolidated in the 1600s and 1700s were autocratic monarchies. Assemblies reappeared in the 1820s with token powers of petition and consultation on questions posed by the government, as in Prussia. Some of the other states acquired moderate constitutions on the French model (ibid.: 424–25; Kinder and Hilgemann 1968: 321). With the unification of Germany in 1871, the imperial Reichstag acquired power over the budget and legislation, while the emperor retained the power to name the chancellor. Structurally the situation resembled the British arrangement in which a strong parliamentary leader could rule the executive de facto (a feature stressed by conservative German political thinkers). Bismarck exercised this power, first in Prussia and then in the Reich, from 1861 to 1890; thereafter until 1917, the emperor overruled his chancellors, especially in foreign affairs.

The franchise in Prussia after 1823–24 was restricted to landowners and was roughly similar in other German states (Bendix 1978: 426–28; Schnädelbach 1984: 15–16). The uprisings of 1848 generally instituted universal manhood suffrage, which was modified but not totally eliminated during the following reaction. The Prussian constitution from 1850 to 1916 divided voters into three categories based on level of taxation, the upper two of which (containing 4.5 percent and 12.6 percent of the voters) elected two-thirds of the delegates. The imperial Reichstag after 1871, an umbrella above the states with their own assemblies, was more liberally elected by universal suffrage of males age 25 and older. The 1919 Weimar constitution extended the franchise to all men and women over age 20. The franchise was abolished, along with parliamentary government and the autonomy of federated states, in the 1933 Nazi coup d'etat and was reinstated in 1949.

England, the United States, France, and Germany varied most in the dates at which collegial structures at the national level acquired high degrees of power. The extension of the franchise was more similar. Taking into account the abolition of slavery, universal male suffrage dates from 1848 in France, 1870 in the United States, 1871 in the German Reichstag, and 1918 in England. Full democratization with women's suffrage occurred almost simultaneously in three states around 1920, with France lagging until 1946 (see Figure 10).

The degree of collegial power and the extent of the franchise do not proceed at the same pace. They are not produced by the same causes and do not constitute a single ethos of democratic culture. What has the appearance of such a culture appears in the ideologies surrounding particular struggles, but these can take very different, even antithetical, forms. The "liberty" of British collegial institutions was for a considerable period explicitly hostile—even to the point of warfare—to the "liberté, egalité, fraternité" of the French Revolution, with its impetus toward the mass franchise. German structural development was not so different from the British; both drew heavily on the survival of medieval *Ständestaat* structures that in the eyes of mass-democracy proponents looked like bodies of reactionary privilege. The prominence of collegial structures in Germany, combined with a narrow oligarchic franchise, made them the target for liberal reformers who wished to reduce traditional privilege, often with the aid of the bureaucratic state. In Germany the two dimensions of democratization were often perceived as mutually antithetical, and the struggle gave some structural basis for an ideological tendency in some factions toward plebiscitarian autocracy. Even so, both Germany and Britain took the route toward an increasingly popular franchise, indicating once again that multiple causes were at work below the level of prevalent ideologies.

We can now recognize several stumbling blocks for developing an adequate sociological theory of democratization. There are two quite different things to explain, and their intermeshings at various points in a two-dimensional field of possibilities produce messy and structurally as well as overtly conflictual histories.

EXPLAINING THE EXTENT OF THE FRANCHISE

Widening of the franchise was largely a phenomenon of the nineteenth century. This was also the period in which the ideology of democracy came to the fore, as against the terminology of liberties and rights associated with earlier struggles over collegial powers. Hence the tendency for theories of democratization to focus upon causes prominent in the nineteenth century.

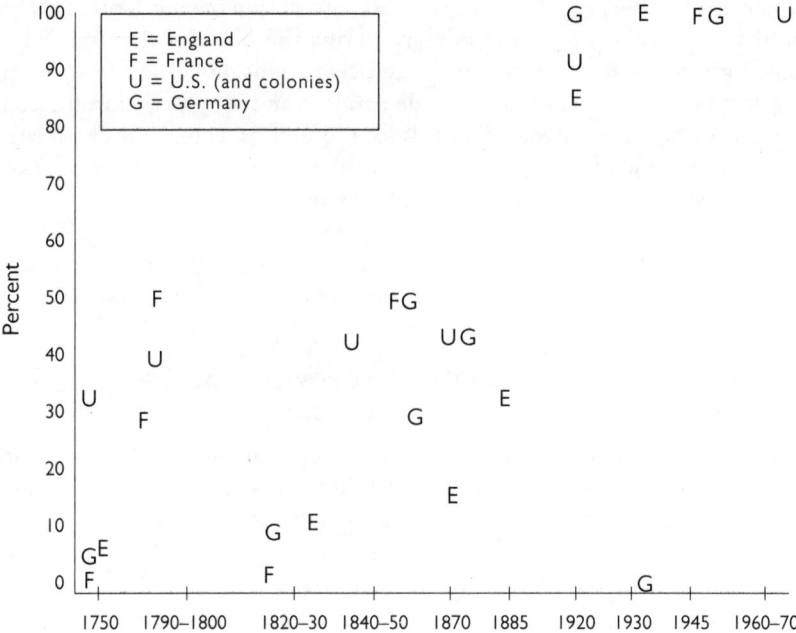

FIGURE 10. Adult population holding franchise, 1750–1970.

Most common is the family of theories that attributes democracy to industrial capitalism and dominance by the bourgeoisie. Lipset (1994) gives a summary of this approach backed by correlations between democracy and economic development in the twentieth century. Marxian theory similarly regards democracy as the expression of the bourgeoisie, the form of government most amenable to its economic interests. But as Rueschemeyer et al. (1992) show, mass suffrage was not produced by the bourgeoisie, which typically favored the extension of the franchise for itself but opposed it for other classes. Instead, it has been working-class movements whose struggles have produced universal male suffrage.

What is valid in the capitalist industrialization model is more limited: industrialization mobilizes the resources that make it possible for all social groups to participate in politics while widening the arena to a national stage (Tilly 1995). Capitalists are mobilized for greater political participation than others by amassing wealth and organizational power; so are, in proportionally growing numbers as the twentieth century has gone on, professionals, workers, ethnic groups, women, and other interest groups. Expansion of the material means of resource mobilization throughout society is the main cause of the widening of the franchise. Mobilization was also induced structurally from above. As Mann (1993) shows, expansion of state activity, above all the leap in the size of the military during the Napoleonic wars, led to much greater penetration of state into society. This mobilized the local interests to make more cosmopolitan demands of and protests against the central government, and hence demands for the right to vote. States with large budgets found it advantageous to spread the franchise because it gave more people a stake in responsibility for its fiscal support.

But widening political participation is democratic only to the extent that there are democratic structures to participate in. The structures of collegial power-sharing have analytical as well as temporal priority.[4] To these we now turn.

CLASSIC APPROACHES TO COLLEGIAL POWER-SHARING: MONTESQUIEU, TOCQUEVILLE, AND WEBER

The collegial dimension of power was emphasized by political theorists with an aristocratic bias, such as Baron de Montesquieu and Alexis de Tocqueville.[5] Both saw centralization of the state as a threat to liberties rooted in the independence of the aristocracy; traditional despotism, Enlightenment absolutism, and the modern Bonapartist dictatorship were put on the same plane. The argument has come down to us as a plea for intermediate institutions between the atomized individual and the all-powerful state. Typically the antidote has been interpreted as a civil society with spheres of autonomy outside the state (such as private property) and assimilated to Aristotle's argument for the middle classes as the basis of democracy. Thus the problem of democracy in post-Soviet states is often interpreted as one of creating a civil society where one had previously not existed.

This sliding away into a theory of civil society loses a crucial point. The state originated as a military organization, acquiring an administrative structure and power of taxation to support the increasing costs of military mobilization. While states take on a broad range of other activities, the coercive and tax-extracting core remains the key without which nothing else is viable. This means that the Montesquieu/Tocqueville argument should be interpreted first and foremost in terms of the state structure itself. Collegial power-sharing means elections, councils, assemblies, and a balance of power among the institutions of political action that control military force and contribute material resources to it. A feudal aristocracy provides one version of balance-of-power institutions. The aristocracy was not a "civil society" outside the state, but the structure of the feudal state itself. This disappeared from view in the era of absolutism, when it was easy to identify the king's administrators with the state, in contrast to aristocrats living upon their "private" domains. Montesquieu and Tocqueville witnessed the French aristocracy in retreat. Our task is to view the matter with greater abstraction, to see the conditions under which collegial power rises and falls. The full flowering of medieval aristocratic institutions of shared power takes us far back into premodern history, into structures in which modern divisions between "public" and "private" had as yet no structural basis; to a time when it was pointless to speak of "civil society," since the patrimonial household of the great lords was simultaneously a military/political unit and a center of production and consumption, workplace and home. Under some configurations, this "parcelization of sovereignty" (in the words of Perry Anderson) produced a collegial structure of shared power (Anderson 1974b). Examining the causes of the rise and fall of aristocratic collegial power will take us down the road to a more general theory.

Weber provided a step toward such an analytical theory by noting the fateful consequences of whether warriors are self-armed or armies are centrally supplied out of the coffers of the state.[6] The former path led to the primitive democracy of tribal war assemblies based on an entire adult male population armed with crude weapons, and it led similarly to the classical Greek polis. When the self-armed warriors were heavily armored knights, the result was feudalism, an aristocratic limitation on the power of the ruler. The other path, centrally supplied armies, which Weber saw as characteristic of Middle Eastern and Asian states, led to the unlimited despotic power of the ruler. Weber's argument casts Montesquieu's aristocratic structures in military terms.

This argument raises two analytical problems. Self-armed forces have disappeared almost everywhere since the "military revolution" of the 1600s, which began to dramatically escalate the size and expense of armies. Medieval collegial institutions, the *Ständestaat*, declined as the military revolution gave impetus to centralized state bureaucracy (Rosenberg 1958). Parliamentary assemblies and councils, once found throughout Europe, were displaced most thoroughly in the militarily modernizing states such as Prussia and Russia. Downing (1992) draws the lesson that states that best evaded or put off the military revolution of centrally provisioned armies (notably Britain, which kept an entrepreneurial structure for raising troops until the 1860s) remained the most democratic. On the dimension of collegial power-sharing, at least, we might conclude that the more medieval the state structure, the more democratic it remains into the modern era. But Weber's (and Downing's) point is historically circumscribed: after a certain time all states had centrally provisioned armies, but contrary to the theoretical implication some of them still had collegial democratic structures. Some even created new collegial structures after they instituted centrally provisioned armies (e.g., Japan created its parliament after the Meiji revolution). The theory of self-armed forces provides us a clue for formulating a model of collegial structures that remains to be stated in sufficiently general form.

The second analytical problem is as follows. Self-armed forces may be the basis for collegial shared power, but this is not their only possible outcome. Autonomously armed forces may simply go their own way, remaining independent of any power-sharing unit. The self-armed knight may become a robber baron, which is to say, a force unto himself, secure in his castle and demanding a share of all property that crosses his borders. The tribal levée en masse of adult warriors does not automatically hold together as a state. Mann (1986) describes how primitive states repeatedly disintegrated as their self-sufficient subjects migrated away from their control. This problem is not confined to primitive economic conditions or to wide-open geographical spaces available for settlement. In geopolitical (GP) theory, the territorial unit of the state is variable. A key question is just where borders will be. The same part of the globe, at different times, may be carved up in many different ways, and into larger or smaller pieces. The territory that constituted the Holy Roman Empire at the time of Charlemagne was later organized into the modern states of France, Germany, Switzerland, Netherlands, and others, and during the intervening centuries into a great many more smaller units, just as at the turn of the twenty-first century it is changing into yet another structure in the European Union. Whether the number of autonomously armed units increases or decreases is a matter to be explained geopolitically. Autonomous powers create a power-sharing structure only in particular configurations, while they act together as a political unit.

The weakness of the Weberian theory of the self-armed forces points us to a way to recast the problem with greater analytical depth. Self-armed forces per se are one condition among several. Under certain circumstances remaining to be specified, such forces enter into coalitions that constitute collegial power-sharing. Under other conditions such forces go their own way, to a greater or lesser degree fragmenting into smaller units. Under still other conditions, the centralizing forces gain sway; coalitions of independent forces become fused into a permanent unit, which reduces the autonomy of its components until they are nothing but a historical memory.

The Ingredients of Collegial Power-Sharing

Collegial institutions derive from a combination of two conditions: independent control by a plurality of actors over political/military resources, and circumstances that motivate these independent resource-holders to form a coalition. Typically, such situations are conflicts with other power-holding units, and their patterns are best seen through GP theory.

European states went through two rounds of maneuvering over collegial structures. In the first round, the independent resources and the circumstances that inspired the formation of coalitions were directly military. Self-armed lords, tribal groups, or other communities constituted whatever political structures existed, and these sometimes entered into coalitions. In this round, whether a coalition was desired, how long it lasted, and whether it fragmented or formed a more centralized structure was determined by the GP advantages and disadvantages in the military struggles of that region.

In the second round, armies were converted into centrally supplied organizations. The independent resources necessary for collegial structures became the organizational structures for extracting wealth and conveying it to the place where it might be converted into military force. Centralizing states became more powerful because they controlled the organized forces directly, but they were also vulnerable, because the costs of military provisions were escalating drastically. Independent resource holders were motivated to form coalitions among themselves in order to resist property exactions by the ruler; leagues of nobles, cities, and parliaments resisted or rebelled against increased royal demands for contributions to war expenses. Again there was a range of outcomes. An aristocratic coalition might be defeated, as the Fronde was during 1648–53, and that defeat brought the eclipse of the Estates General in France and heightened the power of the central state. The aristocracy might triumph and refuse contributions entirely, as happened in Poland after 1572. A segment that refused to pay contributions might withdraw entirely from the existing state structure, as the Swiss cantons did at the time of the Reichstag crisis of the 1490s. Or concessions might be won in the form of greater participation in administrative decisions in return for tax support of the government, the pattern that resulted in the Magna Carta and the 1688 Glorious Revolution. Parliamentary revolutions typically led to an outcome similar to the last, in which the assembly of tax-paying forces wins out entirely, displacing the government. Instead of disintegrating, the victorious coalition is left with the task of taking over centralized military force, thereby committing itself to providing it with material support.

In the second round, as in the first, an increase or decrease in collegial power-sharing results from a combination of conditions: the extent to which independent units control resources needed for military force, whether directly or indirectly; and the extent to which a coalition is held together. Let us concentrate on the last point. A coalition is motivated by a balance between its weaknesses and opportunities. It can fall off the balance in either direction: some forces may pull out of the coalition and go it alone, or some forces may manipulate resources sufficiently to overpower the other partners and reduce them to subordinates. It is a question of organization-building in a situation of multisided conflicts.

THE ANALYTICAL IMPORTANCE OF THE EUROPEAN MIDDLE AGES

If the theory of the expanding franchise is based mainly on the period of industrial capitalism, the theory of collegial democracy finds its testing ground in the Middle Ages. Collegial structures rose and fell during this period. My argument is not one of historical origins, a narrative of the sort that attributes the English democratic tradition to the Magna Carta. Like institutions, traditions wax and wane, and their salience depends upon the existence of contemporary structures that make certain received ideals relevant. Out of many possible origin points, only a few may remain relevant later. My intention is not to engage in retrospective teleology, but to use the Middle Ages as a laboratory for exploring an analytical question: what are the conditions necessary for coalitions to form, to remain balanced, or to slide off in the direction of either fragmentation or usurpation?

For a theory of democracy in two dimensions, the conventional breaking point between "medieval" and "early modern" history is decidedly inconvenient. Generations of historians have imposed narrative order on the period after 1500 in terms of the rise of national states. Some led the way while others floundered, a fateful progression in which latecomers paid the price of weakness and eventually suffered the horrors of recent times. It was easy to weave into this scheme the rise of peoples to democratic consciousness and control. The story of national assemblies and the expansion of the franchise went along with the rise of the centralized state. The discipline of historiography arose as nationalist history-writing, when the profession organized on the basis of national educational systems. The topics of study and the borders of historical specialties have been framed in terms of national units. History is partitioned into the histories of England, France, Germany, Hungary, Greece, and other coevals deemed worthy of writing their own histories—a politically loaded enterprise that goes on today in writing the history of Serbia and Uzbekistan, of Lithuania and Iraq. Whatever came before is subsumed into the prehistory of a national state, or it is put on the other side of the medieval/modern divide, safely irrelevant for the analysis of modern institutions.

The price we have paid for this convenience in historical storytelling is to obscure the analytical conditions for the collegial dimension of democracy. Nationalists, mass-franchise democrats, and state-builders alike tended to view the collegial institutions of the Middle Ages as so much feudal rubbish to be swept away, or worse yet as obstacles to their own ideals. For collegial institutions tended to cut across boundaries to form coalitions as likely to be internationalist as nationalist. They were typically restricted to specific categories of participants, defining their liberties and rights in a manner antagonistic to the simple criterion of mass participation. And they were the chief enemies, in military and fiscal disputes alike, of self-consciously "reformist" and "modernizing" state-builders.

We need to break this gestalt if we are to understand collegial power. Throwing away our familiar historical eyeglasses exposes us to a large swath of history that is not only unfamiliar but also inchoate. A glance through a

historical atlas shows that medieval Europe had extremely messy and shifting boundaries. It is often hard to pick out the states on the map that have
become the dramatis personae of modern nationalist historiography. To
make matters worse, medieval states were not organized in a fashion appropriately designated by solid areas of color inside solid black lines. It is this
nonnational and nonmodern character of medieval states that contains the
conditions for collegial power-sharing.

Medieval state structures took three main forms. In ideal types, and ignoring their combinations and overlaps, they were: (1) centralized regimes
that expanded by military conquest: these had contiguous territory and thus
approximated the geographic structure of the modern nation-state, although some were very small; (2) dynastic marriage alliances: these could
connect far-flung, noncontiguous territories; and (3) federations, or alliances
among political units, which may or may not have been near one another.
From a modern viewpoint, marriage alliances and federations as described
here were not states at all, but this is precisely my theoretical point of entry.
Federations are a type of diplomatic structure. They are "outside" or
"above" the sovereign state. But all these forms are fluid; entering into a
diplomatic alliance makes one less "sovereign" in one's course of action, and
this circumstance encroaches on the core of the state when the course of action negotiated is for mutual military support. Focusing too sharply on the
boundaries of states leads us astray, especially when we wish to understand
the conditions necessary for collegial power-sharing. For it is precisely
through these "diplomatic" structures that autonomous power-holders enter
into coalitions. What we wish to understand are the conditions under which
these coalitions become more permanent or less so, and under which the
coalition increases or decreases the degree of power-sharing within it.
Anticipating the argument, I will attempt to show how geopolitical federations (3) fostered collegial democracy, while conquest states (1) and dynastic alliances (2) tended to undermine it.[7]

To complicate matters, I will introduce yet a fourth structure of medieval
states: (4) the church. Here again we offend against modern distinctions. The
medieval church was not a private institution in the modern sense. It was
much like a contemporary state in its own right. This was particularly so
when abbots and archbishops and the Pope himself were feudal lords, whose
fiefs yielded not only incomes but feudal levées; when monastic orders constituted their own armies of warrior-monks; and when the papacy was a full-
fledged territorial ruler. It is ambiguous whether the church should be called
a state or a set of states. Nominally and to varying extents actually the segments of the church were subunits of the papacy that contributed to its resources and power, which sometimes approached theocratic overlordship
over all Christendom. The segments of the church were also at various times

captives of local aristocrats or adjuncts of secular rulers. My concern is neither to force these variations in church political/military power into one or another side of a rigid definition nor to point to a historical trend; it is to make use of this variation as materials in the laboratory of collegial power-sharing. The church itself has a political history of struggle over its own collegial institutions. We can draw a lesson from the rise and fall of church democracy, which culminated in the breakup of this once overarching coalition in the Reformation. From another point of view, the church is category 4 within a mixture of the other three types, and it is just this overall mixture that is the laboratory of collegial structures on the largest scale. Church units could enter into federations, meddle in dynastic marriages, or ally themselves with or be subordinated to compact conquest states. For all these reasons, the church combined territorial and supraterritorial power. It is a prime example of the cross-cutting structures that are so crucial in the balances of power that determine the fate of collegial institutions.

Medieval history is terribly messy from the point of view of manageable storytelling. This messiness is analytically just what we must come to grips with, for it holds the key to democracy. In essence, democracy is not a "pure" form; it is a balance among many elements and gets its strength precisely because it institutionalizes structural clash. I will illustrate this with three medieval cases: the German Empire; the papacy; and the medieval republics.

Democratic Structures in the Medieval German Empire

The German Empire was full of collegial structures: an elected emperor, a Reichstag and regional assemblies, self-governing free cities, leagues of cities and knights (Barraclough 1963; Bendix 1978; Strauss 1972; Kinder and Hilgemann 1968; McEvedy 1961). The case is instructive because it shows the conditions for the rise and fall of collegial structures and because it included an abortive effort, at the end of the Middle Ages, to turn the empire into a republic. Focusing on medieval Germany is a useful exercise in shifting our Anglocentric gestalt, for the growth of Anglo democracy shows the same structural ingredients, and the crucial differences in the long-term pathways are only in timing and balance.

How did the empire become elective? Early tribal leaders were elected by acclaim by temporary coalitions, which held together only as long as they were engaged in successful conquest. As more permanent states arose, tribal assemblies were generally replaced by feudalism, which was essentially complete by the 1100s. After the split of the Carolingian Empire in the 800s, states began to take on their own character depending on the outcome of local struggles over elective or hereditary rule. In France during the 900s, kings were often elected, and the monarchy became permanently hereditary only after 1223. Kings were elected in Denmark as late as 1370, and in Hungary as late as 1446; Poland vacillated between electoral and hereditary kingship before institutionalizing a weak electoral king subject to an aristocratic parliament, which held sway from 1572 through the foreign conquest of Poland in the 1700s. In Germany, periods of election alternated with hereditary succession. In 982, the emperor was elected by the nobles and clergy; hereditary succession was established in 1024, then blocked by the German princes using electoral power during 1076–1152. The Hohenstaufen family made a strong move in the opposite direction: Frederick Barbarossa (r. 1152–90) established a hereditary monarchy, and Frederick II (r. 1215–50) revived it. In between, a series of child-emperors gave opportunities for foreign powers England and France to intrude with their own candidates. After the death of Frederick II in 1250, the electoral principle was institutionalized, no longer in the hands of the old tribal "nations," but in those of eight electors: the archbishops of Cologne, Trier, and Mainz, plus the rulers of the Rhine Palatinate, Brandenburg, Saxony, Bohemia, and Bavaria.

The electoral structure triumphed for geopolitical reasons. Strong emperors with expanding conquests imposed hereditary succession, strengthening the position of their patrimonial regime. The electoral principle won out just as the empire was beginning to crumble from a combination of geopolitical conditions: military overextension by ambitious emperors leading to financial exhaustion, and competing claims by the emperor and the Pope over the resource base, which divided authority and promoted civil war. In addition, the geopolitical tendency toward fragmentation of the middle took place as stronger kingdoms consolidated in the marchlands (Collins 1978). After 1300, the empire split into fragments. In the 1400s, the lands of the East, once Slavic tribal territories that had been colonized and Christianized by German kings and orders of crusading knights, consolidated into the independent kingdoms of Poland, Bohemia, and Hungary. The French king expanded on the western periphery, intermittently attempting to take over the empire. The English king and the Pope intervened to counterbalance the French. The result was the characteristic dynamic of a fragmenting middle: interference by stronger marchland powers leads to a shifting lineup of factions and clients; the smaller units come to recognize that their autonomy depends upon maintaining a balance of power and playing off one strong contender against another. The electoral structure and the progressive weakening of the empire went hand in hand. By 1350, the position of emperor had become merely a means to enhance the personal prestige of one of the princes. The Golden Bull promulgated at the Reichstag of 1356 institutionalized the semiregal standing of the Electors, including the right to coinage within their own territories.

The scope of the Reichstag grew in the same way. It was a diet of feudal tenants-in-chief divided into three colleges (*curiae*): Electors, princes, and later the free imperial towns. The emperor regarded the diet's main purpose as contributing funds for external wars, but it also became a forum for grievances, an arena for diplomatic negotiations, and both a legitimater and a check on imperial rule. Ambassadors to the diet were delegated no powers and had to continually send home for instructions. To circumvent this unwieldiness, smaller convocations sometimes met in its place. In the 1420s, taking advantage of the emperor's defeats in his dynastic wars, the Electoral College, comprising the six westernmost Electors, claimed to be the successor of the Roman Senate with supervisory powers over the empire. For a time it met yearly, sometimes deposing a weak or incompetent emperor.

A similar dissolution of power went on at a lower level. The struggle of the emperor against his great lords had resulted in concessions to allies a rank below. The emperor granted rights of self-government to "free imperial cities" and gave territorial autonomy to loyal "imperial knights." The proliferation of petty powers resulted in a situation of nearly perpetual local warfare and robbery in the countryside. Local estates rose to oppose taxation by the regional prince. The multiplication of powers built cumulatively upon itself between 1300 and 1450, and eventually reached a degree of local violence that left tiny powers vulnerable to the reimposition of larger states. Between 1450 and 1500 fragmentation began to be reversed, not by a return to a single centralized state but by the growth of mid-sized structures between top and bottom. The princes began to establish central administrations within their territories, as the military revolution in gunpowder destroyed feudal castles and the growth of mercenary armies transformed fiscal costs. The result was a new internal balance of power. The feudal estates that originated in local resistance to higher authority were transformed into representative assemblies operating on principles of majority vote instead of individual veto and private exemption. These Landtags met regularly with the rulers to settle contributions to state finances. In return, they acquired a measure of legal participation in control of the state. For an interval just before the Reformation, German governments approximated constitutional republican structures.

As geopolitical control crumbled among the largest and even the mid-sized states, another form of collegial shared power emerged in the form of leagues among the small players. In the 1200s, clubs or leagues were formed among the imperial knights. In response, leagues of towns were created, which were usually antagonistic to the knights. At their height in the 1300s, the most prominent leagues included the Hanseatic League of trading cities, which spread not only on the seacoast from Holland to the Baltic but inland as far as Saxony; the League of the Rhine; the Swabian League in the south; and the Swiss Federation. Acting as a substitute for a strong state monopolizing force, the leagues constituted diplomatic truces among themselves, provided for collective defense, and attempted to suppress robber barons who threatened trade. The Hanseatic League even won the right to participate in electing the Danish king. Although most of these leagues were later destroyed by the territorial princes, their potential is shown by the fact that at least one of them, the Swiss Federation, eventually became an autonomous republic.

The German Empire began with the same structures that existed throughout much of northern Europe. Why did it elaborate collegial structures during the later medieval period to a much greater extent than other successor states of the old Carolingian empire? The main structural alternatives were the growth of conquest states and the acquisition of territories by dynastic marriage alliances. The former was blocked in the German region by GP weaknesses. Although Germany also had dynastic alliances, typically they existed only among the largest territorial principalities. Leagues tended to be antagonistic toward dynastic principles. The members of German leagues were (1) free cities, which were themselves corporations and hence could not be represented by a ruling family; (2) tiny independent knights, who were unable to build up a critical mass of influence on their own that would enable them to play dynastic politics; and (3) the archbishops, who were celibate priests unable to build overtly hereditary dynasties.

This is not to say that dynastic possessions never built up in Germany. During the 1300s, dynastic alliances began to be consolidated into extensive holdings by the Habsburgs, the Luxembourgs, and the Wittelsbachs. By the 1400s, the Habsburgs had accumulated enough alliances to be able to bargain for marriages connecting some of the largest patrimonies of Europe: Austria, Burgundy, and Spain, along with scattered German holdings. The fate of this empire reveals a structural weakness of the dynastic marriage strategy. Because marriages did not need to be territorially contiguous, state-building in this fashion tended to create patchworks of holdings, with rival or enemy states in between. Even under conditions of feudal levées, there was an advantage in a compact territory. The French kingdom fragmented in the 1300s, largely because of wars with the king of England over dynastic inheritance in France, which encouraged the autonomy of feudal subordinates who played the rival overlords off against each other. Centralized kingships finally began to consolidate in both kingdoms only after the end of the long struggle. When the military revolution began to increase the expense of warfare and the intensity of centralized administration needed to extract supporting resources, the dynastic scatter became a serious geopolitical liability. For this reason, the Spanish Habsburg Empire, although imposing on paper, had extreme geopolitical problems arising from its scatter of holdings, which ranged from the Netherlands to Italy to central Europe. The scatter of dynastic possessions is the equivalent of the GP weakness of the state that has too many frontiers. Normally this is a problem for the state in the middle between marchland states; abstractly the problem is the number of potential enemies to be faced simultaneously. In addition, the dynastic scatter increases the logistical costs of bringing military resources from one detached holding of the state to another.

The upshot is that states built upon dynastic marriages became most powerful where they were able to conquer immediately adjacent territories and to install a compact administration. Gradually they shifted from dynastic/patrimonial to bureaucratic forms of administration.[8] This was the route of the French kingdom, and eventually of the strongest territorial princes within the old German Empire, notably Prussia. In a geopolitical situation where growth through direct conquest was generally blocked, as it was in the fragmented center of Germany, dynastic alliances gave only temporary prestige but added to the GP weakness. Again we see that a phase of GP weakness could contribute to multisided balances of power, which in turn could encourage mixed state structures of shared collegial power. Threatened and ambiguous territorial controls gave rise to new state structures, alliances such as leagues or assemblies, which began to take on military, tax-raising, and leader-selecting activities, thus becoming quasi-states in their own right.

The German leagues, the Reichstag, the Landtags, and the Electoral Colleges were mild forms of collegial democracy. It does not matter for the long run that the internal government of the components of such collegial structures were generally autocratic. An elector himself might be a hereditary ruler in his own domain, and leagues might be formed by unrestrained petty aristocrats. Geopolitical balance and alliance among such autocratic components can lead to larger structures that contain a new principle of democratic power-sharing. Later such structures might be extended downward and inward to encompass greater participation in the franchise. Germany displayed a balance of conflicts and alliances among autocratic persons similar to that found in England. The structures of collegial democracy can grow, seemingly paradoxically, from intermixtures of autocracies; they do not need to arise from an ideology of democracy. The ideals of widespread political rights tend to follow from structures that have institutionalized a balance of power and have thereby neutralized its coerciveness.

THE CONTRIBUTION OF PAPAL/IMPERIAL CONFLICT
TO GEOPOLITICAL BALANCE

Let us add one more structural condition to those that promoted collegial structures in Germany, one that was largely absent in France and elsewhere. In Germany, conflict between church and state was entwined with collegial power struggles. Originally, the power of the German emperor was built in alliance with the church. The emperor promoted conversion and colonization of the pagan regions of the East, endowing monasteries with large land holdings as beachheads of settlement and as sources of military allies. The fact that both emperor and Pope prospered by the establishment of a strong state in the center of Europe, from the northern seas to Italy, eventually made them rivals for its control.

Church organizations, monasteries, and bishoprics alike were the most valuable properties and centers of administration through the High Middle Ages. The investiture controversy was a struggle of organization-building over whether to put these resources into secular or papal hands. Lacking military forces of his own, the Pope played the various kings against one another, using them to enforce edicts of dispossession by excommunication. The battle between Pope and king wavered most evenhandedly in Germany. Repeatedly between 1075 and 1250, the strongest German emperors confronted the strongest Popes, and lost. The result was that in Germany the compromise between secular and church powers leaned to the side of strongly autonomous religious properties. The great archbishops became territorial rulers in their own right. By contrast, in France, the church came under royal control in the late 1200s. By the early 1300s, the French king had forced the removal of the papacy to Avignon, where it became identified with French interests. Thereafter, even when the Pope returned to Rome, the right to tax the clergy was conceded to French kings. The medieval church was never able to operate as an independent force promoting a balance of power within France, as it did in Germany.

During the investiture controversy, the emperor and Pope constantly interfered in each other's elections. The Popes were instrumental in overthrowing Hohenstaufen efforts to establish a strong patrimonial regime based on hereditary succession. The original core of electors, established in 1250 at the death of Frederick II, were the archbishops. The Golden Bull of 1356, which defined the German constitution, was issued at a time when the papacy had been actively deposing and excommunicating German emperors and promoting others. Now a weakened emperor agreed to institutionalize the electoral principle with the consent of the Reichstag in return for excluding papal interference from German political affairs. The compromise weakened the international power of the papacy just as it did that of the emperor, but it increased the local power of the German church. The German archbishops now became largely autonomous rulers. They became the leading exponents of collegial power-sharing in the German Empire and of resistance to unilateral authority of the larger rulers.

FROM MILITARY STALEMATE TO COLLEGIAL ALLIANCES

The lesson of the German case for the expansion of collegial structures is that a particular geopolitical process fosters collegially shared power.

Specifically, a state that occupies a geographically middle position surrounded by other states will suffer geopolitical fragmentation. This fragmentation is reinforced by crosscutting organizational structures, such as the international church, which lay claim to its military and economic resources. Because of this weakness of the central region, stronger states on the marchlands surrounding it intervene in selecting its rulers. Insofar as these "outside" states balance one another off, they prevent each other from extending their territories, preserving the fragmented "inside" as a buffer zone. This GP weakness also prevents the growth of a territorially contiguous conquest state in the interior region itself, obviating its potential threat to centralize power and eliminate collegial structures. And of the great many small states in the fragmented region, most would lack the resources to successfully play dynastic marriage politics. Those few that eventually built up sufficient "marriage capital" tended to accumulate alliances outside the central zone, which generally pulled their interests toward the more compact territories of the periphery and away from the fragmented morass of German territorial politics. These initial processes frequently led to the formation of additional collegial structures: free cities grew stronger as weak emperors made concessions to promote allies against intermediate-sized states. And because the prime military need became more a matter of local defense and providing law and order for travelers than of mounting a full-scale army for big-power campaigns, leagues of small players grew up and organized as collegial bodies in their own right. In short, military stalemate in the fragmented geopolitical zone ruled out major territorial conquests and shifted the emphasis to diplomatic structures, either to interfere in other political units or as defensive alliances with weak executive powers. Insofar as these structures acquired some organizational permanence, they constituted a crosscutting grid of collegial structures of shared and limiting power.

Not just any condition of geopolitical weakness will have this effect. In GP theory (as we saw in Chapter 2), states can be weak because they have fewer military resources than their neighbors, because they are overextended by distant and costly military efforts, or because they hold interior geographic positions with marchland states on the periphery. Generally speaking, weak states per se do not become collegial power-sharing regions because their weakness is usually the reciprocal of the strength of a neighbor, which expands and swallows up the weaker territory. Geopolitical weakness promotes collegial structures only if it remains stable over long periods of time. This happens because the region has sufficient resources to defend itself, because its better-situated enemies on the exterior have geopolitical problems of their own, or because the strong rival states neutralize or manipulate the middle zone because they cannot conquer it for themselves.

Given the conditions that fostered collegial power structures in medieval

Germany, why did these structures not become even stronger? Given the head start, why did Germany not become the first modern democracy instead of less likely regions (on the geopolitical hypothesis) England and France? Our usual teleological pathos might make this seem a question not worth raising, but an attempt to answer it reveals key analytical points. Collegial power-sharing requires not only conditions that restrain or deconstruct centralized power; it also requires that the deconstruction not go too far in the opposite direction, fragmenting power to the point where there is no collective power to share. In fact, Germany at the very end of the Middle Ages made an effort to build the Reichstag into a republic. If this effort had succeeded, Germany could well have been the first large-scale modern democracy. The reasons for its rise and fall provide further clues for a theory of collegial power.

THE FAILURE OF THE REICHSTAG REPUBLIC

Between 1485 and 1520, a movement for collegial power culminated in an attempt to establish strong federal rule (Strauss 1972: 73–161; Angermeier 1984; CHM 1910, 1: 288–328; Cameron 1991). The diet of 1495, led by the archbishop of Mainz, attempted to implement a plan of reform. The Reichstag was made more inclusive by the addition of a college of free cities, and the whole was to meet annually. Expanding on the Electoral College put forward in the 1420s, a permanent Imperial Council was proposed to control the army and approve all acts of the emperor. Taxes were to be levied by all local authorities for the benefit of a central administration and were actually collected in some places in the 1490s. As late as 1522, the Reichstag proposed to establish an imperial customs duty in order to transform the external boundaries of the empire into a single economic unit. Legal issues were to be under the authority of a court independent of the emperor.

Both the emperor and the members of the Reich were willing to consider the proposals because of their mutual needs. On the side of the free cities and the archbishops there was a desire to establish internal peace, protecting the rising tide of commerce against robbers and unruly barons. Among the first legislation in 1495 was a prohibition on knights carrying out private wars. The Reichstag had also become the forum for expressing complaints against papal exploitation of the finances of the German churches. On the other side, the Habsburg emperor, Maximilian I, had been consolidating his dynastic possessions; for the first time in centuries there was an emperor with sufficient personal resources to give prestige to the office. Reformers could hitch their hopes to a reform negotiated from above. The Reichstag, by allying itself with a strong emperor, could become a collegial structure sharing real power.

Through several waves of negotiation during this 30-year period, reforms were attempted that eventually failed. The Habsburg emperor played a delicate balance according to the ups and downs of his military fortunes. Costs were beginning to escalate with the revolution in warmaking. When the emperor's military enterprises in Italy, Burgundy, and the Low Countries hit setbacks, he was especially eager to mobilize the wider resources that the German popular contributions might bring. Too great failure would reduce the imperial prestige and discourage the bandwagon; likewise, too great success would shift his focus to the dynastic expansion that had built the house of Habsburg, making compromise with the German Reichstag unnecessary. In the end, the Habsburgs fell off the balance point in the direction of a purely dynastic state, refusing assent to the strong German federation. Inheriting the Spanish title in 1515 tied its future to the glories and dangers of far-flung dynastic scatter.

On the German side, too, the resolution was fateful. The chance for a federated republic was lost. Failure of political reform was linked to a parallel failure of reform in church governance. In 1512, the last of a series of reforming Reichstags marked a dead end to movement in that direction. Five years later it would be followed by a revolutionary breakup of the church, in which the Habsburg emperor would champion the reactionary side. It will be convenient, before drawing the analytical lessons of the failure of the Reichstag republic, to consider the parallel rise and fall of collegial democracy in the church.

Papal Democracy
and the Failure of the Conciliar Movement

The medieval papacy contained many collegial structures (Southern 1970; Kelley 1986; Oakley 1979; Thomson 1980; Cameron 1991). The Pope was elected by a collegial body; so were abbots by their monasteries, heads of monastic orders by general convocations, and sometimes bishops by cathedral chapters. How did this come about? Initially, the Pope was chosen by acclamation of the "people" (i.e., predominantly the nobles) of Rome. When the papacy grew from a merely ceremonial center into an organization with pan-European powers, the German emperor and the French and English kings began to interfere in the choosing of the Pope. In response, the Pope created the College of Cardinals in 1080 as a device for marshaling supporters against the anti-Pope named by his foreign opponents. The College grew up as an international group of influentials in Rome at the time the papacy was becoming a center of litigation and administration over far-flung church properties. The example shows us there are two ways collegially shared power can be instituted: from below, as subordinates take advantage of a weakness at the top to place limits on a ruler, and from above, as a weak ruler seeks allies against rivals (in this case, against anti–Popes and lay interference). Eventually the game was institutionalized and used by both sides.[9] This second path was also seen in the German Empire, as the emperor himself contributed to autonomous structures by creating free cities and imperial knights as counterbalances to the larger territorial princes.

The cause was again geopolitical. The electoral papacy grew up as an organization crosscutting the states then forming in Europe. By reasserting its organizational autonomy from aristocratic families through the practice of celibacy, and by rationalizing its property holdings and legal-bureaucratic administration, the church began to wield more power resources than secular rulers with their unstable feudal loyalties and dynastic alliances. Growth in church resources posed a challenge to territorial rulers. They could attempt to subordinate church property by tying it to their own families and feudal relationships; the church could assert its autonomy and then go on to subordinate the secular rulers into a military arm for enforcement of theocratic rule; or the secular rulers could borrow from the church the new organizational means of bureaucratic administration, eventually rationalizing their own governing structures and overcoming feudalism with the help of church administrators. The broad sweep of medieval history went from the first, the church as adjunct to the feudal/patrimonial aristocracy in the centuries before 1100; to the second, the rise and eventual defeat of papal theocracy, peaking in the 1200s; to the third, which culminated in the establishment of the secular states of the Reformation. In the second and third periods, conflict between church and state further enhanced the balance of power, over and above the complicated multisided conflicts of feudal/dynastic warfare. During the long period when church and the secular kingdoms were both entwined with and partially autonomous of each other, each interfered in the other's political successions, thereby encouraging collegial structures at the top of their rival hierarchies.

This mutual interference was strongest between the German Empire and the papacy, which had been allies since the time of the Carolingians. The investiture controversy, the struggle over lay appointments and thereby over familial control of church properties, was fought out most extensively between the Pope and the emperor between 1075 and 1122. Since the Pope's main weapon was excommunication and transfer of legal rights to the rival German princes, the result on the German side was to weaken hereditary succession and strengthen the principle of election. Imperial election became firmly institutionalized a century later following the battle between several Popes and Frederick II over the dedication of imperial forces to a crusade instead of to extending Frederick's possessions in Italy. At this moment the papacy came closest to theocratic power. There was an attempt to curtail or eliminate the private use of force in feudal disputes under "God's peace," and the secular arm was to be turned internally to enforcing church edicts of heresy and excommunication and externally to fighting for Christendom as crusading armies. But as the German emperor was vanquished, other regional kingdoms rose in the balance. The height of papal power lasted only about 50 years. The French king emerged victorious from a long struggle to impose the right to tax church property for the sake of military expenses. In 1303 the Pope was taken captive by military force, and in 1309 the curia was moved to Avignon. French power too proved unstable, contested by a long series of wars with England during the 1300s that reinforced feudal fragmentation in France. During the Great Schism of 1378–1417, rival Popes were supported by French and anti-French rulers. This was one of the few periods when a succession of anti-Popes was sustained, and it was a harbinger of the permanent break to come at the Reformation.

The papal attempt at theocracy failed for the same reason the German Empire did: both were brought down by their multisided position at the center of European geopolitics. For different reasons, both were subject to the geopolitical process of fragmentation of the middle—the Germans in the geographic center of Europe were flanked by their own successful marchlands; the papacy located at the administrative center crosscut all the far-flung territorial states and thus faced political (and therefore military) challenges on many fronts. Both the German Empire and the papacy became increasingly collegial control structures, especially in the 250 years between 1250 and 1500. Both tended to support collegial power-sharing institutions within the other. The most powerful archbishops were the core of the German electors, and it was they who made the move to establish Reichstag supremacy in the 1490s.

Conversely, the most extreme effort at church democracy, the conciliar movement, relied heavily on the geopolitical counterbalance of the German emperor. The Council of Constance in 1414–18, which ended the Great Schism, was convened at the initiative of the emperor. The conciliar movement declared that the supremacy of the church assembled was the voice of God, replacing legitimation of the papacy through the charisma of office succession. The "reformers" deposed the rival Popes (there were three of them at the time); a new one was elected by a specially constituted body of 22 cardinals and 30 representatives of the five traditional nations of the Holy Roman Empire. The plan was instituted for regular councils to meet not only at times of papal succession but every five years. Half of all church revenues were to be reserved for the College of Cardinals, and it would have the right to approve all major policies of the Pope.

The conciliar movement continued through the prolonged council of Basel, 1431–49, which attempted to institutionalize conciliar rule. An attempt to depose a recalcitrant Pope and name an anti-Pope failed when the reforming alliance could not hold itself together. The French state, now rapidly consolidating power on its own territories, again wrested separate control of church properties. The German princes eventually bargained particularistic interests for a return to the side of the Pope. Leading church intellectuals like Cusanus grew disillusioned with the ability of the concil- iar structure to bring off church reform and switched their loyalties to the Pope. Another key reformer, Piccolomini, became Pope Pius II and in 1459 declared conciliarism a heresy. The watchword of reform was in the air for a long time before the Protestant Reformation. "Reform" was not a narrow church doctrine or movement but a long-standing slogan express- ing uneasiness over the contradictions between religious ideals and the church's material possessions and political powers. These contradictions made the highest church careers easy spoils for secular and often rapacious politicians, while at the same time church politicians had the means to ma- nipulate the alliances and animosities of the secular rulers and limit their powers. Reform increasingly centered on an attempt to break the uneasy balance of religious and secular powers that hamstrung the political struc- tures at the center of Europe. These were weak collegial power-sharing structures; one direction of reforming movements was the attempt to strengthen them into something like full-scale republics. The calls for church reform manifested in the conciliar movement were paralleled by calls for reforming the empire, which culminated in the reforming Reichstags of 1485–1512.

Failure of the two reform movements led to the Protestant Reformation. Its immediate results were to reduce collegial structures in church and state. The split into more compact national churches strengthened the autocratic states, both on the Protestant side, where churches became an arm of cen- tralized government administration, and in the Catholic realms, where effective control over church property was conceded to the state (Wuthnow 1989). In these states the church hierarchy became more internally auto- cratic; the papacy became less international, more strictly a local territorial principality in central Italy. In the zones where GP power remained most unsettled, however, some pockets of enhanced church democracy were pro- moted. In the fragmented zone of the German Empire, smaller independent units like the burgeoning Swiss Federation and free imperial cities, which were used to mutual self-protection by their leagues, became places where radical self-government was instituted in the form of extreme reforming churches. John Calvin in Geneva, Huldrych Zwingli in Zurich, and other radicals emerged in niches where geopolitical relations left them free to es- tablish congregational forms of rule in territories that were simultaneously city-states and church republics. The Calvinist churches were not only dis- tinctive doctrinally; they were also distinctive organizationally as republics of church members who elected their theocratic leaders, a characteristic that was perhaps even more important for their spread.

STRUCTURAL SHORTCOMINGS OF FAILED MEDIEVAL DEMOCRACY

Consider together the failures of the Reichstag republic and of the conciliar movement. In both cases, a geopolitically shaped structure of decentralized powers balancing weak autocratic heads attempted to institutionalize a hybrid form, a collegial republic. Both coalitions failed because of their ineffectiveness as governing bodies. In the Reichstag, too few of the decentralized powers were willing to give up autonomy and supply enough financial resources to the coalition. On the other side, the "executive" of the coalition, the emperor, was not desperate enough to make concessions of shared power. The Reich members and the emperor were not sufficiently bound together to agree to an institutional compromise. The component units had alternatives: one of the quasi-democratic structures within the Reich, the Swiss confederation, took the opportunity to withdraw entirely and establish its own confederal state, choosing the better-proven route of a small regional republic over a large one. The emperor, too, had the opportunity to "shop around" for alternative sources of financial support. Finally he came down on the side of dynastic marriage connections, which took his attention to territories largely outside of the Reich.

The situation has general significance because its key problem is the same as that which underlay the democratizing revolutions of England and France. The medieval ingredients were much the same. Just as the aristocrats had done in the German Empire, English lords took advantage of geopolitical setbacks and took issue with geopolitically generated military expenses to push claims for collegial representation. Rivalry with papal governments over German territories resulted in German bishops' taking the lead in collegial structures like the Electoral College and Reichstag. A similar case of church interference in limiting secular power was the role that the English archbishop Stephen Langton played in leading the coalition of barons who forced the Magna Carta on the king in 1215. The document began by asserting the independent rights of church property, and it led to the institutionalization of regular parliaments, in which the clergy sat among the most important lords.[10]

Fateful crises occurred in the 1630s in England and the 1780s in France, when kings were forced to deal with power-sharing institutions (parliaments and Estates General) because of the fiscal crisis brought on by the accumulated expenses of past and current geopolitics. The parliaments refused fiscal exactions without receiving major power-sharing concessions in return. The significant point is not so much that the English and French revolutions overthrew the central governments, but that the anticentralizing forces did

not withdraw from central government. The very success of the revolu-
tionists gave them control of the state apparatus. The revolutionary coalitions, in one form or another, stayed together and found themselves forced
by the logic of events to assume responsibility for the state's military forces,
the disposal of the state debt, and the raising of new taxes. In France, the
postrevolutionary government became more strongly centralized than the
old kingship and eliminated many of the old collegial structures. In the case
of the Reichstag republic, there was no revolution, not because the anticentralizing forces were too weak but because they were too strong. The empire was not sufficiently geographically circumscribed. Neither the Reich
members nor the emperor was sufficiently "caged" into a unified structure
that their struggles would end up as an institutional sharing of centrally
effective power. There was not enough of an overarching state for a revolution to be carried out within it. The causes of this state configuration were
geopolitical.

In the case of the conciliar church, the overarching geopolitical unity of
the central authority was not in principle in question, but it had become
questionable de facto as the result of a long period of geopolitical strain. The
issue that brought the conciliarists together was ending the schisms among
rival Popes, with its resulting atmosphere of demoralization. The papacy was
still a quasi-state, the supreme legal authority in the eyes of its supporters and
the source of legitimation for all lesser rulers, who were taken to be its subordinates. The papacy attempted to enforce internal peace within the territory of Christendom, to marshal forces for external war, and to direct the
secular arm in putting down rebellions against its authority. The division of
Popes and anti-Popes was a crisis in the very existence of the overarching
church-state—all the more so because Popes and anti-Popes in actuality relied upon rival strong kings and had increasingly become their puppets. The
conciliar movement arose in the context of a weak papacy, a republic forged
at the moment the central authority needed wide-ranging support to rescue
it from the hands of one or another regional king.

As in the case of the Reichstag republic and the emperor, neither the
coalition nor the central executive was sufficiently dependent on the other.
If the archbishops, bishops, and abbots who took part in the councils could
have forged joint rule over the church, they would have increased their
power over secular rulers, but the unity of interests in conciliar government
was undermined because many of the regional churches were already de facto
national churches (above all in France, Spain, and England, as well as many
of the German principalities), which were unwilling to sacrifice local autonomy. The geopolitics of state-formation had already flowed too far in the direction of consolidating states grasping control of church resources within
their territories. The papacy, too, had an alternative to giving in to concil-

iarism: it could surreptitiously withdraw its claims to state power overarching the component states of Christendom and rely on its direct territorial control of the papal states in central Italy. Taking the latter route, the papacy became in effect another regional power in the Italian "cockpit" and soon was a pawn in the dynastic family politics of the Italian city-states and the nearby conquest states, France and Spain. The papacy after the conciliar movement took a path analogous to that of the Habsburg emperors after the failure of the Reichstag republic. In the case of the papacy, this would seem to have been geopolitically inevitable. What we might call the "greater-papacy policy," maintaining the theocratic claims of the medieval period, had its greatest success in playing off weak European rulers against each other. The rise of strong states around the periphery of Europe, the same condition that made Germany into a fragmented interior zone, left the papacy with no realistic way to maintain GP power but to opt for a "small-papacy solution" in Italy. The Protestant Reformation, following immediately upon the failure of both the Reichstag and the conciliar republics, confirmed and ideologically brought into the open the new geopolitical reality.

The analytical lesson of these failures is that the extension of collegial power is not merely a matter of mobilizing countervailing powers against an autocratic center. There must also be a centripetal force, so to speak, to keep the collegial coalition together at all. For this to happen, geopolitically favorable opportunities for the collegial alliance and for its executive as well must outweigh the opportunities for either side to leave the alliance and go it alone.

Geopolitical Successes Among Medieval Republics

In addition to the abortive collegial power-sharing institutions just reviewed, medieval Europe contained several full-fledged republics. Consider three of the most successful: Venice, the Swiss Federation, and at the end of the Middle Ages the Dutch Republic. All were on the periphery of the German Empire and in the interstices between the larger empires of military conquest. All began as diplomatic structures, alliances among smaller communities that forged a strong collective agency for military action. All illustrate a temporal pattern in the GP theory of democracy: a full-fledged collegial power-sharing state depends not only on initial geopolitical fragmentation, which weakens autocratic rule, but also on subsequent GP advantages, which keep the coalition together.

Venice, initially a fragment of the declining Byzantine Empire, was the only part of Italy outside the German Empire. Its electoral structures crystallized out of local power struggles among rival families of the Venetian littoral. There was no city-state of Venice in the 900s, only a scatter of communities along the island waterways that engaged in family feuds and dynastic alliances to rule over the others (Lane 1973; Kirschner 1995). Geopolitics provided the incentive for unification, the opportunities for military expansion and state-protected trade in the geopolitical vacuum of the Adriatic and eastern Mediterranean. The local balance of power alternated between anarchic conflict and peace imposed by an autocratic doge who headed the communal alliance. The republic emerged as a third alternative, balancing off rival factions and a shared central authority. Doges were elected by acclamation by a general assembly of the community, which is to say, a spontaneous gathering upon the death of the old doge at a central place in the lagoons by the families who wished to continue the alliance. Strong doges attempted to make their rule hereditary, but accession by birthright was blocked from time to time by strong families promoting rival dynasties. In 1032 two permanent counselors were elected to prevent monarchical rule, and in 1070 a Great Council was established to share ongoing control of the state. This structure was elaborated into a hierarchy of smaller and more effective representative bodies, a senate, a ducal council, and a series of elected and rotating magistrates to carry out state business. By the 1200s there was an elaborate system of indirect election by ballots and selection by random lot designed to prevent any manipulation for factional advantage.

Venice was organized by elites as a conservative republic with a restricted franchise. Initially power was shared among some 20–50 major families who together constituted a total of some 500 voters and officeholders out of a population of 100,000. In 1323 membership in the Great Council was made hereditary and a mark of nobility. Flexibility among the elite expanded the number of noble families in the 1300s to some 6–7 percent of the population. For medieval and early modern Europe, Venice was the great exemplar of republican institutions. It created the terms "ballot" and "electoral college," as well as institutions such as the secret ballot, judicial rights, and a public defender to represent poor litigants before the courts. Venetian institutions were a prime source of the doctrine of the separation of powers. Indirectly, Venice provided a model for the constitution of the United States, which was expressly designed by property-holding elites to combine elements of the entire European heritage of conservative power-sharing institutions (Mann 1993). Because the modern period of political mobilization has defined democracy primarily in terms of the extent of the franchise, or alternatively as an Anglo-Saxon development, this Venetian source of modern democratic structures has been largely hidden from view.

Venice was not the only medieval republic to be formed in this way. Similar communal governments were established during the 1100s in Milan, Florence, and elsewhere. Unlike the other northern Italian city-states,

Venice did not fall back into family rule around 1300, after the period of class conflict between guilds and the older propertied aristocracy. The other city-state republics were undermined by the alternation between dynastic dictatorship and mass uprising, with the latter frequently turning into the former. Venice alone was able to keep at the balance point of effective central authority stably shared among rival claimants.

What made this possible? The Venetian republic had the advantage of an especially favorable geopolitical situation. Staying largely clear of the unstable conquests of inland territories and the tangled wars of the German emperor and the Pope, it expanded coastally and by waterways into the fragmenting Byzantine Empire. In the 1170s the doge was prominent enough to act as peacemaker between Pope Alexander III and Emperor Frederick Barbarossa. In 1204, Venice acted as headquarters for the Crusades, which it diverted to capture Byzantium and seize Greek shipping ports. Geopolitical success helped the Venetian citizenry maintain their enthusiasm for collective action. External power-prestige bolstered the legitimacy of the ruling system while providing wealth to keep the popular classes satisfied. Internally, the government structure operated effectively because the doge was the administrative agent for overseas geopolitics. The elaborate checks and balances to prevent tyranny did not hamstring government because the doge was the one permanent official among all the temporary magistrates and counselors. As head of the army and director of foreign policy, he represented the collective enterprise in which all Venetians had a stake. For a long run of centuries, geopolitical success kept the republic alive. On the other side of the Italian peninsula, republics fell into the maw of military conquest states from the north and west.

It is too easy to assume a static formulation that merchant cities with their civic armies promote bourgeois democracy. Over an extended period of time, democracies have frequently fallen prey to inner or outer conflicts. In geographically far-flung coalitions, as we have seen in the cases of the Reichstag and conciliar republics, collective authority was often threatened by the withdrawal of dissident members' support. The smaller city-states tended to cage in their citizens from escape, but could easily hamstring themselves in civil war, especially in class struggle between rich and poor. And even if these problems were avoided, as in the ideal Rousseauist situation of a small egalitarian community, such a state could easily be swallowed up through external conquest by bigger states unless protected by an especially favorable geopolitical situation. Each of these pathways meant that small-scale democracies tended to be brief and temporary structures that were incapable of institutionalizing amidst the larger array of states without a favorable geopolitical position.

The Swiss Federation too developed within a favored geopolitical niche (CMH 1910, 2; Kinder and Hilgemann 1968; Brady 1985). It was one of several leagues that grew out of the fragmenting German Empire and was the only one to prosper and institutionalize as a republic. The Swiss mountain cantons and the surrounding ring of cities below the trade route passes were at the geographical intersection of crosscutting powers. The western cantons were pulled into alliances with France, Burgundy, or Savoy; the eastern cantons were oriented toward the stronger German states. As strong states grew up on several sides, their counterbalancing effects helped this buffer zone to become independent. In the 1200s, the threat of the Habsburg dynastic state expanding from southern Germany led to a defensive confederation of three Teutonic communities, which in 1291 became the Perpetual League of the Forest Cantons. The patriotic tradition of Swiss liberties became established in struggles from the 1270s through the 1290s, elevating William Tell as its heroic symbol. Battle victories in the 1300s over the Habsburgs and then Burgundy started a bandwagon effect. The league was expanded in 1353 to eight cantons through alliances, conquests, and the accession of independent cities (some of them imperial cities and former Austrian allies like Zurich) with their dependent villages. Central Switzerland became a confederation of thirteen cantons. In the early 1400s the federal government made new allies and conquests and was able to form the surrounding leagues into a league of leagues. By 1499, at the height of the Reichstag reform movement, the Swiss Federation felt itself strong enough to pull out of the German Empire by refusing to contribute to the new tax system. It was a choice between a local federation with a record of growing success and the long odds of reforming the weak German Empire into a massive republic.

The Swiss Federation had no government structure except the diet, to which cantons sent delegates. The federal structure promoted republican institutions at a lower level. Externally, it served to keep the cantons and cities from being swallowed up in dynastic conquest states. Internally, it prevented any of the leading members from exercising authoritarian rule over the others. Communal government at the level of cities and rural communes was reinforced. Lacking a local aristocracy, military organization consisted in the mass mobilization of infantry, which bolstered the participatory feeling of democratic solidarity.

Initially, these collegial power-sharing structures developed in a geopolitical vacuum. Favored by its position in the mountainous buffer zone and the tendency for the conquest states around it to cancel one another out, the Swiss Federation enjoyed a string of military victories. Swiss GP strength was the obverse of the GP weakness of the dynastic conquest states around it. This is a general lesson of geopolitics: conditions that penalize one state strengthen its opponents. Where an entire region is stalemated and fragmented, all large conquest states are stymied, and a niche is provided in which a balance of power can become institutionalized in the form of a permanent alliance.

The Dutch Republic crystallized from another interstice of the German Empire ('t Hart, 1993; Tilly 1993: 52–78; CMH 1910, vols. 1–3; Kinder and Hilgemann 1968). When self-governing cities and leagues grew throughout German territory, the Low Countries became one of the regions thickest with Hanseatic cities. As the German Empire fragmented, the Netherlands became a zone of extremely mixed political structures, comprising aristocratic, communal, and confederated rule. When dynastic states consolidated around Europe, the Low Countries were fought over repeatedly and therefore inconclusively, especially by the rival forces of France, Burgundy, and Luxembourg. In the late 1400s they became part of the Habsburg patrimony. One of Emperor Maximilian's projects in the 1490s, for which he negotiated Reichstag financial support, was to gain control of the Netherlands as an inheritance for his son. The "cockpit of Europe" became just such a nexus of intersecting powers that fostered local autonomy. This autonomy was reinforced and ideologically inflamed by the adoption of the republican forms of Protestant church governance. The Dutch Republic was created in the revolt against Spanish Habsburg rule in 1568–84, which also formally ended its inclusion within the German Empire. A collection of *Ständestaat* institutions and defensive leagues were confederated into a States General, made up of deputies from seven republics. Like Switzerland, and later the United States, it was a republic of republics.

Like other successful republics, the Dutch Republic benefited first from the GP weakness of its surroundings and then from its own geopolitical expansion. Its victory over the Spaniards came against a large but overextended enemy, stretched in wars across multiple fronts throughout Europe and overseas, operating at the end of long logistics lines, and reeling from financial strains of its wars. Once established, the Dutch Republic became institutionalized through the power-prestige flowing from its own successes. Its sea-based empire and its commercial wealth came just at the right time to keep the young republic alive, in much the same way that Venice had been undergirded by its geopolitical advantages.

The Dutch revolution was the first of the early modern democratic revolutions, a model for the English revolutions of 1640 and 1688; indeed it supplied both the troops and the constitutional monarch for the latter. Perhaps a better way of looking at it is to avoid the terminology "early modern" and its connotation of breaking from the past. The Dutch Republic was a bridge, like the Swiss Federation, from the medieval republics to the present.

The Contribution of Diplomatic Alliance
to Democracy

Collegial structures arise both to limit and to support a central authority. They are institutionalized only if there exists a balance of centripetal and centrifugal forces. Central power is limited when the center is relatively weak against a balanced plurality of units surrounding it but none of the others is strong enough to replace the central power. This circumstance occurs most often for geopolitical reasons. At the same time, conditions must exist to keep the dispersion of power from going all the way to fragmentation, the parts flying apart. Something must hold the coalition together. Geopolitics is crucial on this side too.

Consider two ways that this balance of coalition-forming and authority-limiting can come about: through diplomatic alliance or internal revolution. Independent units may form a diplomatic alliance: this requires the existence of geopolitical conditions in the larger arena that have allowed them to become independent in the first place and further geopolitical conditions that motivate their coming and staying together. Successful instances of such alliances becoming collegial states include Venice, Switzerland, the Dutch Republic, and as we shall see, the United States of America. Not all alliances make it; without making the full-scale comparisons needed to demonstrate this point, I suggest the major cause is a lack of geopolitical conditions that would support the alliance. Two examples of failed alliances, the Reichstag republic and the conciliar movement, were not pure cases of independent units forging a diplomatic alliance, but attempts to reintegrate once centralized authorities that had fragmented. The opposite case is one in which a centrally controlled state becomes weakened for lack of military and fiscal resources. In its crisis, subordinate units with a modicum of independent powers resist central fiscal demands and end by contributing to the state only if it will institutionalize a shared power structure. This is the route of the democratizing revolutions in England and France; the Reichstag republic and conciliar movements, which fall somewhere along the continuum between the diplomatic alliance structure and the fiscally crippled Great Power, also resemble failures of the internal revolution model. In reality, the internal revolution route to democracy is not a pure case either, since it was the vestiges of older geopolitically determined structures, the patchwork of feudal alliances and dynastic intermarriages, and the heritage of the old international papacy cutting across the territorial states that provided the parliamentary institutions upon which English and French revolutionaries mobilized their takeover of central authority.

Geopolitics influences democracy in two quite distinct phases, which might be described as centrifugal and centripetal processes. It initiates the centrifugal process by constituting a situation of fragmented political units free from the control of a strong conquest state; in the other case it may severely weaken a hitherto successful military state by putting it under intense fiscal strain resulting from its geopolitical ventures and the accumulated costs of its previous conquests. This is a distinctive kind of GP weakness. The formula is not simply that any geopolitically weak state becomes a collegial democracy, for if its weakness is great enough it will simply be swallowed up by stronger neighbors. The GP weakness I am speaking of here is moderate: such a state may be in a fragmented zone relatively immune to conquest or authoritative centralization, or it may be a formerly strong state undergoing fiscal crisis of accumulated geopolitical strains that retains enough geopolitical resources to resist conquest by opportunistic neighbors.

This is only half the story. Centrifugal forces of geopolitics do not result in institutionalized, long-lasting structures of collegial power-sharing unless they are followed by centripetal forces that motivate the coalition to stay together. The first phase, GP weakness resulting in fragmentation or state breakdown, must be followed by a turning of the tide—that is, there must be sufficient GP advantages for the coalition to stay together, not merely to resist central authority but to take command of common activities of their own. The alliance must become an effective state. The cases of the protective leagues within medieval Germany and the Reichstag republic movement show some of the motivations for a coalition to attempt to strengthen its unity in a situation of fragmentation: seeking the advantages of internal peace, putting down brigandage and the disruptions of petty warfare, and protecting trade in a period of economic expansion. The failure of the medieval German collegial structures shows that these motivations in themselves are not sufficient to make the collegial alliance succeed. Both the negative benefits of local peace and the positive benefits of a militarily expansive coalition are important in institutionalizing democracy.

For these reasons, it is flawed methodology to attempt to establish the causes of democracy merely by cross-sectional correlations among a sample of states. Geopolitics is not a condition of a particular state but of an entire region. It is the relationships among areas of strength and weakness across the entire territory of interactants that determines where the very boundaries of the state units will be; the number of states that will exist is a result of geopolitical processes of conquest, alliance, and fragmentation. And geopolitical conditions affect democracy in two phases: first weakening strong military conquest states; then promoting the geopolitical fortunes of collegial coalitions. A theory of democracy resting on cross-sectional correlations among structural conditions will not work here because the key is a pattern of temporal flow: GP weakness followed by alliance followed by geopolitical expansion.

GEOPOLITICAL SOURCES OF THE USA

The interest of a GP theory of collegial structures is not merely antiquarian, a backward look into the now vanished medieval sources of contemporary institutions. A relatively recent state, the United States of America, exemplifies both phases of geopolitics affecting collegial democracy.

The United States formed in much the same way that Switzerland or the Netherlands did. As Li (1996) points out, the independence of the Atlantic coastal colonies originated in the geopolitical strains of the British Empire in a period when it was engaged in conflicts on multiple fronts. Simultaneously, the British were at a disadvantage in logistics costs in long-distance fighting against the settlers of their most populous and resource-rich colonies. The beginning of the struggle resembled the beginning of the revolutions in England and France: demands by the central state to help pay the military costs of the previous conquest of Canada and of the wars with Indian coalitions were resisted by the colonial units with the greatest local autonomy. But in this case the result was not the taking over of a state by a coalition of resistance, but state fragmentation.

Why did the centripetal forces not continue even further? It is difficult for Americans to appreciate the contingency, because we are raised on the ideology of manifest destiny and the habits of retrospective teleology; we assume that the thirteen colonies would naturally have become a single state spreading across the continent.[11] In fact the coalition of rebels did not immediately hold together. As Li (1996) indicates, what institutionalized the federation was at first geopolitical need—settlers' demand to take Indian lands to the west could only be satisfied by the combined army of the federation. The settlers' movement and the concomitant addition of new states to the federation succeeded militarily because external geopolitical conditions turned favorable after 1790. When the French, British, and Spanish forces negated one another in Europe, their support for Indian coalitions blocking USA expansion disappeared, leaving a power vacuum in their North American colonial possessions into which the USA could expand.

An alliance among independent states becomes a collegial power-sharing state in its own right by playing a collective military role. For its first century, the U.S. government performed few activities other than military ones (Mann 1993: 362–73). The United States is an example of how geopolitical power-prestige is a prime source of the legitimacy of a regime: the spectacular geopolitical success of the USA alliance, which spread across the continent and built up its resources to become a world power, both protected and legitimated American democracy. By this route, the originally defensive and ad hoc federation of settler republics became a suprarepublic whose power-prestige and legitimacy eclipsed that of its parts. In a similar way, the legitimacy of parliamentary institutions in Britain was bolstered from the

Glorious Revolution through the early twentieth century by the generally upward track of geopolitical power-prestige during this long period.

CONCLUDING APPLICATIONS:
THE FUTURE OF RUSSIAN DEMOCRACY

Does the GP theory of democracy have contemporary relevance? Numerous democratic state structures have been established around the world by imitating European and American models. These institutions appear to be founded not in geopolitical conditions but in the process of institutional emulation of what Meyer (1987) describes as the legitimate ideal of a modern state. Does the GP argument apply only to an earlier portion of history during which the model was first established? I would argue that it still has relevance. Even as emulation of high-status Western models influences the establishment of democratic structures, the continued viability of such structures may be influenced by the degree to which GP conditions are favorable.

Consider the prospects for democracy in Russia in the period after the anticommunist revolutions of 1989–91.[12] If democracy depends upon a culture of political rights and habits, the prospects are dim; Russia's long nondemocratic tradition augurs nothing but more of the same. Short-term institutional reforms are of little reliability. The mass franchise without a structure of collegial power-sharing has usually been the formula for volatile and short-lived plebiscitarian regimes that slide periodically into autocracy.

The GP theory of democracy, focusing on structures at the level of the organization of military power, offers a different view. The Russian republic itself has the advantage of a federated structure that is held together in some degree by the intersection of ethnic groups across its borders. There are further prospects for federated structures because of the pressures and advantages of diplomatic alliance among the component pieces of the old Soviet Union. If geopolitical conditions favor a federal structure of alliances around a weakened Russian state, this rump federation of the former Soviet bloc could well produce a balance-of-power cognate with the kinds of structures that have promoted collegial power-sharing historically. Such a federation of "greater Russia," if it restricted its sphere of power influences to the nearby fragmented zones of the Caucasus and other weak neighbors, could enjoy a return to at least modest geopolitical power-prestige that would bolster the legitimacy of democratic institutions. The problem for Russian democracy appears to be to recover from its phase of GP weakness sufficiently so that the collegial power-sharing structures of federated governments can be kept in place rather than fragmenting further.

The most optimistic picture of Russian democracy we can construct depends upon future geopolitical configurations. Even if these prove to be

favorable, this is no guarantee that the future of Russia will be internally har-
monious or that a shared "democratic culture" will quickly emerge. But the
culture comes later, following the stalemate of institutional structures that is
the underpinning of democracy. Contemporary societies are not prisoners of
their cultural traditions; it is always contemporary geopolitical structures that
count most.

CHAPTER 5

German-Bashing and the Theory of Democratic Modernization

DEROGATORY NATIONAL stereotypes have become taboo, with one exception. It remains popular and legitimate to depict Germans as authoritarian and militaristic. A staple of American comedy routines is a caricature of the average German as a closet Nazi ready to invade Poland at a moment's notice. Similar anti-German stereotypes are prominent in Britain and elsewhere. The image owes something to wartime memories, but the roots are deeper. Scholarly consensus for several generations has described German culture and society as authoritarian and lacking in democratic institutions and values. Germany is explained as dominated by the Prussian ethos of regimentation and more deeply by the Lutheran ethic of obedience and the Pietist ethic of inwardness and acquiescence, by Romanticism rather than rationality, and by a national identity founded on opposition to the liberal modernism of the West.

These cultural attitudes are usually explained by Germany's position as a late modernizer. Having lagged behind the modernizing revolutions of England and France, Germans arrived on the world scene with a sense of being inferior and needing to catch up. Hence the cultural rejection of the West, together with structural strains of a rapid and externally forced modernization, were manifested in antimodernist movements ranging from nationalism to anti-Semitism and fascism.

The image of Germany as authoritarian is not merely a foreign criticism. It has been shared by German intellectuals since the 1830s and 1840s. The Young Hegelians compared their country unfavorably with France for failing to undergo the political revolutions of 1789 and 1830 (Löwith 1967: 96). The criticism intensified in the 1850s, after the spread of the 1848 French Revolution to the German states failed to establish a constitutional regime and was put down by military force. Germans have regarded themselves as the people who failed to make their own revolution; they have experienced instead revolution "from above" (Moore 1966: 433–42) or by emulating others "from without" (Bendix 1967). The lack of revolutionary will has become a staple of German historiography.[1] The diagnosis is agreed upon by Marxists as well. Germany, having failed to go through the normal sequence of bourgeois revolution, was in a distorted position for undergoing a socialist one; the distortion would come out in the form of fascist counterrevolution.[2]

One incongruity in this account is that Germany, far from being antimodern in the cultural sphere, has been on the forefront of modernist movements. Marxism was the most radically future-oriented movement of the past 150 years, explicitly antitraditionalist and progressive; the reversal that unmasks Marxism as a backward-looking movement is at odds with its surface content. German cultural modernists include Nietzsche, the most radical atheist, and Freud, the most famous sexual liberationist.[3] Virtually all of the radical wings of nineteenth- and twentieth-century philosophy were pioneered by German thinkers: the logical positivists from Ernst Mach to the Vienna Circle; the existentialism of Martin Heidegger and in religion of Martin Buber and Paul Tillich;[4] in theology, the creation of higher criticism and liberal theology, of neo-orthodoxy by Karl Barth and Rudolf Bultmann, and of worldly Christianity by Dietrich Bonhoeffer. Musical modernism was spearheaded by Richard Wagner, Gustav Mahler, and Arnold Schoenberg. In painting, French impressionism of the 1860s was the first modernist movement, but in the following generation the dual centers of abstract art were France and Germany, where abstract expressionism developed around 1905. The self-consciously modernist movement in architecture was led by the Bauhaus school and its expressionist predecessors ca. 1910–30, and in the cinema by the German film industry of the 1920s.

German culture, far from being conservative and conformist, has been in the lead of world movements since 1800. The process of international borrowing and catching up has been largely the reverse of that depicted in the political sociology of modernization. Over the same period England has rarely been a cultural exporter; instead, British intellectuals have usually gone to the Continent in search of modern trends. The Romantics Samuel Taylor Coleridge, Percy Bysshe Shelley, and Lord Byron traveled in Germany in the early 1800s, bringing back the philosophy of German idealism. In the 1840s and 1850s George Eliot began her career, battling theological traditionalism by translating the anthropological humanism and materialism of D. F. Strauss and Ludwig Feuerbach. In the 1890s, Bertrand Russell traveled to Germany to study modern social welfare legislation and wrote his first book, *German Social Democracy* (1896). In this period it was typical for philosophers, mathematicians, and scientists to visit German universities to keep up with advanced ideas. The pattern of borrowing from Germany was even more pronounced in the United States. Transcendentalism in the 1830s was an import of German idealism. American philosophy, science, psychology, and even sociology from 1860 to the early 1900s were largely the products of professors who had gone to study in German universities; an estimated 10,000 American students went to Germany in the late nineteenth century (Berelson 1960: 14). The migration of anti-Nazi refugees from Germany in the 1930s prolonged U.S. cultural dependence upon German academic disciplines through the middle of the twentieth century (Fleming and Bailyn 1969). Paradoxically, Britain and the United States, allegedly the two most modern societies, have been culturally the least modernist and the most dependent on foreign imports.

France has been the other center of world cultural modernism. Foreign pupils flocked to Paris for science and mathematics from the 1760s until about 1840, when momentum in those fields swung to Germany. In literature since Charles Baudelaire and Gustave Flaubert in the 1850s and culminating in Stéphane Mallarmé's symbolist circle of the 1890s, and in art since the impressionists, Paris has been the world mecca of modernism up through the latest "postmodernist" version in the 1980s. Even France responded to the pull of German cultural innovation: there was a cult of German philosophy among the leading French intellectuals of the 1810s and 1820s, popularized by Mme. de Staël and Victor Cousin. In the 1870s and 1880s after defeat in the Franco-Prussian war, a number of French intellectuals, Émile Durkheim among them, sojourned in Germany to learn techniques of educational innovation and the content of the modern disciplines. In the 1920s and 1930s French thinkers imported German phenomenology and existentialism, and through the 1950s Freudianism and Marxism. Even in the most self-consciously avant-garde world center, there has been a periodic tendency to look to Germany for innovation.

How may we explain these contradictory pictures of political versus cultural leadership and lag? Let us disaggregate the phenomenon. Modernity is not a unitary package; it is made of at least four distinct components that respond to different causes and move independently. In the following, I outline the historical experiences of Germany and other leading Western societies in their degrees of (1) bureaucratization, (2) religious secularization, (3) capitalist industrialization, and (4) democratization. Rather than lagging, Germany led in time on several of these dimensions. I will also cast doubt on the extent to which Germany was "behind" in the sequence of political modernization. Such judgments assume a standard of comparison; and this should be based on the actual condition of other countries such as Britain, the United States, and France at specific points in history, rather than an ideal that most societies did not approximate until quite late. If Germany was only haltingly democratic before the end of the nineteenth century, the same was true in varying degrees of every other major society as well.

One outcome of this analysis will be to show that the stereotype of German backwardness and antimodernism is inaccurate, not only in culture but also in most institutional spheres, even the political. My point is not to reverse the stereotype, to celebrate Germany in place of denigrating it. We should seek the analytical lesson: understanding the multidimensional process that makes up social change in the modern era. The negative aspects of modernization, all too obvious in many facets of German history, are the more sobering because they exemplify or exaggerate tendencies that exist in the structure of every modern society.[5]

Four Modernizing Processes

A unidimensional model of modernization implies movement along a single continuum, varying only in speed and the duration of halts and regressions. A multidimensional model better accounts for a variety of sequences. Why focus on these particular four dimensions, bureaucratization, secularization, capitalist industrialization, and democratization? These four components of modernization capture what is valid in the classic unidimensional models while pinning them to appropriate institutional spheres. The polarities of *Gemeinschaft* and *Gesellschaft*, mechanical and organic solidarity, point to the growth of large-scale organization above local and personal relationships, but this happens in two separate ways, by the growth of bureaucratization and of the market. The theory of increasing differentiation is a generalization of increasing division of labor, which points again to a process occurring within the market economy, and in a different way within bureaucratic organization. In a more abstract sense, religious secularization may also be regarded as a form of differentiation of cultural spheres (Parsons 1964); but this rather pallid description fails to capture the vehemence with which the battle was fought between upholders of religious dominance and secularizers or the malaise that has characterized modern culture in just the places where secularization was most extensive. Another proposed master dimension of change, rationalization, is unsatisfactory because of its ambiguity; the term variously connotes efficiency, predictability, or formalization, which do not necessarily go together or occur in every institutional sphere.

An advantage of focusing on concrete institutional changes (bureaucratization, secularization, capitalist industrialization, and democratization) is that these are easier to attach to theories of causes and consequences. The fourth process, democratization, calls for special comment. In comparison with the others, the topic of democratization has undergone the least satisfactory development toward a historically causal theory. Capitalist development has attracted a great deal of refined theorizing and efforts at comparative historical testing. Organizational sociology has focused on bureaucratization, the sociology of religion on secularization. Systematic and comparative work in political sociology, however, has been more concerned with the theory of revolution (and secondarily with state-building) than with a theory of democratic structures, and we are far from agreement on their causal conditions. Evolutionary modernization theories are a stumbling block here, for it is not at all clear that democracy is a specifically modern institution, except in the brute historical sense that the societies conventionally taken as exemplars of modernity—Britain and the United States—have been democracies. The structural features of democracy do not follow from any of the classic unidimensional polarities of social change (*Gesellschaft*, differentiation, rationalization).[6] Historically, democratic structures of various kinds existed long before the other dimensions of modernity: collective assemblies in many hunting-and-gathering bands and in tribal societies; Greek city-states; collegial power-sharing bodies of notables, elective kingship, and independent judiciaries in medieval feudalism. The range of historical comparisons needed has been an obstacle to developing a full causal theory of democracy.

It may well be that democracy is *not* inherently very modern, indeed that it goes against the grain of other features of modern social structure. That may explain why democracy is the characteristic that is most variable and most often undermined, as in the Nazi episode of the early twentieth century. This is a reason why Britain and the United States could be rather *less* modern on many traits, whereas Germany and France have been exemplars of many features of modernity, while at the same time having the rockiest experiences with democracy.

Bureaucratization

Bureaucracy is the basis of many of the most characteristic features of modern life. Bureaucracy displaced the typical premodern organization, the household, where authority was based on kinship and inheritance and subordinates were in the position of servants or personal followers. In its place, bureaucracy separates personal and family identity from organizational position, thereby introducing career criteria of "merit" and "achievement." In its separation of personal from organizational property, it introduces a new ethical standard from the standpoint of which the traditional mingling of spheres is corruption. Bureaucracy is responsible for the impersonality of modern life; by the same token it usually opens a sphere of privacy for the individual apart from public roles. Bureaucracy operates through paperwork, records, and formal rules; these make possible whatever efficiency (and inefficiency) comes from continuity and routine. They also are the instruments by which the individual is separated from the position, and the organization from the family and the personal clique. The expansion of paperwork is now considered a pathology of modern life, but it has been a major civilizing process, expanding the sedentary, nonmanual occupations. It is this group that comprised the original educated stratum in societies in which most people, including the military aristocracy, were illiterate. The growth of organizational paperwork has been responsible for much of the expansion of the middle class, even more than the expansion of business, which originally was carried out largely in small household-based units.

The growth of bureaucracy was not an all-or-nothing transition. Literacy, written communications and records, and general laws were introduced into patrimonial household organization gradually and in varying degrees. The qualitative breaking point came when these instruments were used to overthrow the kinship/personalistic structure and to emphasize the organization over and above the persons within it. Frederick the Great, spending long hours checking reports from subordinates, uttered, "I am the first servant of the State!" This is the recognition of bureaucracy, just as Louis XIV's "L'état, c'est moi" expresses patrimonialism.

Bureaucracy developed gradually over a long period in several parts of Europe. For many centuries, bureaucratic structures intermingled with nonbureaucratic forms in the *Ständestaat* and other mixed organizations. The predominance of relatively pure bureaucracy as the principal form of organization in the modern West was pioneered in the German states, especially Prussia. Prussian governmental administration moved up the continuum of bureaucratization during the 1700s, while many of its features spread to the *Kleinstaaterei*, the smaller principalities.[7] Thereafter Germany acquired a reputation for proliferation of official titles (Chesterfield [1748] 1992: 88), the result of establishing administrative ranks among middle-class officials that gave them public standing independent of the hereditary aristocracy. In Weberian terms, the bureaucrat acquired a status-honor specific to his office.[8]

The key antibureaucratic feature, ownership of governmental office as a source of private revenue, had disappeared in Prussia by 1750. In 1770, an examination was established for employment in the Prussian bureaucracy, thereby placing a premium on university legal training, although nobles were exempted at first. Legally permanent tenure for officials and freedom from arbitrary punishment and dismissal came with the reforms in 1794. In 1804 the educational requirement was strengthened to require three years of study at a Prussian university for all higher offices. The Prussian reform movement of 1806–12 consolidated the bureaucratic structure of government through the abolition of serfdom where it still existed, the establishment of legal equality by abolition of the Estates, the elimination of the aris-

tocratic caste system in the army and state administration, and the elimination of guild restrictions on entry into crafts and industries. With the foundation of the University of Berlin in 1810 and an accompanying series of
official examinations, university legal studies became rigorously required for
government employment. Thus Germany became the first society in the
West to establish anything like the Chinese imperial examination system. At
that point, all features of Weber's ideal type were in existence. It is not surprising that a German would be first to formulate the theory of bureaucracy.

The absolutist state in France made steps along the path of bureaucratization, but less rapidly than Germany. Several features undermined the bureaucratic structures that developed (CMH 1910, 8: 36–52; Goldstone
1991: 225–43; Bendix 1978: 331–38). Venality of office, repeatedly used by
the government to raise funds, contravened the key bureaucratic structures
of centralized control and the separation of personal property from the property of the formal organization. Tax farming was a version of the sale of government offices to private persons, which expressly condoned what in a
bureaucratic context would be considered corruption, making personal
profit from public revenues.[9] The multiplicity of courts and feudal and royal
jurisdictions confused the lines of authority and obscured a clear-cut
bureaucratic hierarchy and division of functions. Laws and procedures regulating taxation, criminal justice, and military service applied not uniformly
but according to distinctions among a large number of categories of persons.
The aristocracy overruled the bureaucracy at many points, exempting themselves from the jurisdiction of officials and claiming many positions by virtue
of their family status, especially in the military command and the judiciary.
In the aftermath of the 1789 Revolution and Napoleonic reforms, office-
owning was abolished in favor of salaried positions. The French bureaucracy
lagged behind the German, in part because of the persistence of a party spoils
system through the many regime changes of the nineteenth century.
Competitive examinations arrived after 1848, and the formal training of
officials in the Grandes Écoles began in 1872 (Mann 1993: 461–63).

England remained relatively unbureaucratic much longer (Gusfield 1958;
H.-E. Mueller 1984; Mann 1993: 454–55, 463–64). During the eighteenth
century, most offices were owned as sources of private revenue; until 1800,
most officials were absentee sinecurists who employed deputies to carry out
their duties at a fraction of their own incomes. The structure stymied any
chain of command or centralized budgetary accounting. Until 1872, army
commissions were sold to officers. The colonel was an entrepreneur who
raised a regiment; his profit depended upon the spread between the funds al-
located by the government and the costs of provision for his troops. The
navy was more centrally administered because of its heavy investment in
ships and equipment, but captains still could engage in private profit-

making by making economies in provisioning and by carrying commercial goods on board (Stinchcombe 1995). The disparity with Germany is all the more striking, since it was the Prussian army reforms of 1733 that developed a standing army under universal conscription and were the opening wedge to bureaucratization. The British judiciary at the local level was staffed by justices of the peace drawn from the resident aristocracy. Aristocratic landowners also provided policing until a centralized police force was organized, beginning in the 1820s in London. Sinecurism and office-owning began to be reformed in the 1790s and were largely abolished by 1832. Appointment by personal patronage persisted until 1853, when a second wave of reform began in the Indian Civil Service. The shift to full-scale bureaucratic criteria in England was not carried out until 1870 with the introduction of formal examinations for administrative positions. The army and university reforms of that period were part of the same package.

In the United States, public administration originally was carried out by political patronage, and at the regional level by local notables.[10] Reform came about because of vehement disputes over political spoils with each change of party dominance, culminating in quarrels among senators and the assassination of the president in 1881 by a disappointed office seeker. Bureaucratization advanced at the federal level with the civil service laws of 1881–95, which introduced competitive examinations and formalized ranks and promotion procedures, insulating careers against political replacement or other dismissal for non-work-related reasons. Because of the decentralization of government to the level of states and their subunits, the movement for bureaucratization of administration—which went under the more appealing name of the Progressive movement or Good Government movement—continued in various regions until 1920 and even later.[11] A unified federal budget did not appear until the 1920s.

To late-twentieth-century ears, the term "bureaucracy" is a negative one, associated with unpleasant features of modern life: impersonality, paperwork, and the disenchantment of world views. Bureaucratization is also responsible for traits that were strongly fought for by reformers and modernizers, above all universalism, the implementation of the rule of law without favoritism. In the sphere of organizational life, bureaucracy means security for employees against arbitrary control and punishment by their superiors. Bureaucratization was the main route out of the brutality that characterized most premodern societies and was widespread in the 1600s. Usually, officials were the first to be exempted from torture and degrading treatment, and it was through the spread of bureaucratic jurisdictions that the inviolability of the human body and the inner self were extended to the entire population.[12] In a society divided between hereditary aristocrats and the common people, whom they almost literally crushed under foot, bureaucracy opened a

sphere that gave dignity to the individual apart from birth and personal connections. Bureaucratization has been one main source of the modern tendency toward social equality, not only of procedural rights but also of personal status in the Weberian sense.

Secularization

Until the twentieth century, the aspect of modernization most vividly in the
consciousness of the persons who underwent it was undoubtedly secularization. The displacement of religion from the center of attention, from the rituals of everyday life, and from the public symbols and pronouncements that
legitimated political power and social rank produced a series of shocks and
controversies. In the eyes of traditional people at any point during the past
300 years, the modernizer is a blasphemer. On the other side, reformers regarded themselves as moving from superstition and oppression to reason and
humane morality.[13]

Premodern European societies were pervaded by the church. In the medieval period, the church virtually monopolized literacy and education, provided the physical setting for most popular culture in its buildings and festi-
vals, owned much of the land, provided much of the economic dynamism
in its monasteries, and shared political rule either by cooperating with secular powers or in its own right. With the Reformation and the growth of the
absolutist states, a number of these features changed. Monasteries lost their
importance, and property passed largely into secular hands. The Reformation strengthened the tie between states and the church. In the Protestant
states, the church usually became nationally established, under direct political patronage and power of appointment. In the Catholic states, generally a
modus vivendi was created by which state supremacy was guaranteed (as evidenced by Gallicanism in France and Spanish dominance of the Counter-
Reformation papacy) (Wuthnow 1989; Cameron 1991). International politics until the late 1600s was commonly carried on in terms of religious wars
and alliances.

Battles and shifts along the continuum of secularization occurred in all the
major European societies at different rates. Germany, led by Prussia and the
other northern states, became the first relatively secular modern society as
the result of a combination of factors. Chief among these were the predominance of state bureaucracy over the church and the reform of the educational system under lay control.

Protestantism in general was far from being a secularizing force. Initially,
it was a revival of religious intensity in everyday life, to some degree in reaction against the tendency to secularism during the Italian Renaissance and
the most worldly period of the papacy. Thus there is no reason to expect

that Protestant England should have led in secularization. Religious feelings were stirred by a series of dynastic conflicts pitting Catholic against Protestant claims to the English throne. The revolutions of the 1640s and 1688–90 were mobilized by religious animosity.

The 1700s in England are often regarded as a period of urbane rationality in which religion was reduced to Deism. The last notable prosecution for blasphemy occurred in 1729–31, when a Cambridge fellow, Woodston, was jailed for publishing pamphlets on the allegorical interpretation of scripture. England remained a society dominated in several respects by coercively enforced religion (Chadwick 1966; CMH 1910, 10: 621–54; 11: 330). Catholics were prohibited from holding military commissions, from entering the legal and teaching professions, from voting, and from sitting in Parliament. Performing or hearing mass was punishable by imprisonment. Sentences were carried out as late as 1782, although enforcement gradually abated. In Ireland, English conquest beginning during the 1500s and culminating during the Protestant Commonwealth of the 1650s had combined with religious confiscations to reduce most Catholics to peasantry under Protestant landlords. In 1793 a restricted property franchise gave the vote to a small number of Irish Catholics. After massive Irish agitation in the 1820s exacerbated by famine, Catholic emancipation was passed in 1829 for both England and Ireland, allowing the vote but to an even more restricted franchise and continuing to bar Catholics from the highest political offices and from the universities and public schools (i.e., the endowed secondary schools). Other penalties and restrictions, including nonrecognition of marriages performed by Catholic priests, were removed in the 1840s. Jews received the right to sit in Parliament only in 1866 (60 years after the emancipation of Jews in Prussia).[14]

In popular as opposed to elite culture, religious fervor grew. The Methodist movement of popular preaching (originally a movement within the Church of England) spread widely from the 1740s through the end of the century; the Salvation Army was founded in 1865. In the early 1800s, the Church of England underwent an activist puritanical revival in the form of the Evangelical movement, which crusaded for total Sabbath observance, including a ban on public transportation and any public nonreligious activity on Sundays. The reputation of Victorian England for extreme prudishness was due in large part to the influence of the Evangelicals. The growth of the industrial working class and the commercial middle class both contributed to making England an intensely religious society for most people until around 1890–1910 (Thompson 1963). Before that time, secularizers in England looked to the Continent for leadership.

Waves of popular revival movements in America paralleled British ones from the mid-1700s onward. At the time of the Revolution the disestablishment of the state churches of the various colonies opened America to vigorous market competition among religious denominations and sect-building entrepreneurs. This religious market continued to flourish through the late twentieth century. The relatively low levels of church membership found among the popular classes and on the frontier in the early 1800s gave way to rising religious membership and participation that continued into the midtwentieth century and even later in some respects (Warner 1993; Finke and Stark 1992). The secularization that gradually pervaded British intellectuals and the educated classes during the early twentieth century met with stronger resistance in the United States. The celebrated Scopes trial in 1925 about whether evolution should be taught in public schools was only one of a long string of battles over religious content in public culture throughout the century. In the pervasiveness of religious belief and church attendance, the United States remains the least secularized of all the major Western societies.

France acquired a reputation for religious wickedness dating from the anticlerical barbs of Voltaire and the philosopher and atheist D'Holbach in the 1760s, and reinforced by the diabolism of the literary avant-garde after Baudelaire in the 1850s. Battles over secularization in France were vehement and highly variable in their outcomes.[15] In the 1680s and 1690s, court ethos was dominated by religious observances and the ostentatious expression of religious sentiment. Rival religious tendencies and orders battled over precedence. Pietist movements within Catholicism such as the Port-Royal movement were banned and suppressed in the 1660s and again in 1710. At other times, the pendulum swung against rationalistic and worldly political movements such as the Jesuits, who were expelled from France in 1765. Active Protestants were hanged, jailed, or sentenced to hard labor in the galleys until the 1760s; a royal decree of toleration finally came in 1787. Jews had no civil privileges until 1789. During the Revolution, the pendulum swung wildly. Christianity was briefly abolished in 1794 and replaced by a Deist state cult of the Supreme Being. In 1801 Napoleon made a concordat with the church that guaranteed state salaries for priests and reestablished the Gallican principle of state appointment of bishops and other propertied posts. Protestant and Jewish congregations were also allowed under state regulation.

The effect of the French Revolution was to polarize religious politics. Reactionary conservatives became Ultramontanists rather than Gallicans, extolling obedience to the Pope instead of national political accommodation. The church was generally allied with monarchists and the propertied upper class, but over time conservative ranks were split by quarrels over the relative precedence of state and church. Catholic claims for autonomy and primacy in cultural matters became all the more intransigent after the Pope declared the doctrine of papal infallibility in 1870. Again polarization emerged from conflict: in this case the Pope was responding to the threat to papal territories around Rome during the movement for Italian unification (which the French emperor supported). Separation of church and state was finally carried out under the Third Republic in 1905.

The church had dominated European culture and public consciousness since the Middle Ages because it encompassed most of the material means of cultural production. Even when an alternative base in the form of a marketplace for books emerged—beginning in the 1500s and first reaching proportions where it could support full-time writers in the mid-1700s—for a long time the biggest sellers were religious books. Sustained production of intellectual culture was based on the university, an institution developed in the Middle Ages under the auspices of the church. The popularity of universities declined in the Renaissance, and after a post-Reformation resurgence declined again in the 1600s and early 1700s. During these times secular intellectuals formed their circles with the support of aristocratic patrons. Nevertheless, the main cultural results of these new social bases, the Humanist revival of classical Greek and Latin literature in the 1400s and 1500s and the emergence of modern research science in the 1600s, were generally absorbed into the universities and legitimated as allies of Christian culture.[16] The main threat to religious culture was the movement during the 1700s known as the Enlightenment, whose social base was government officials and the salon society of the politically active aristocracy. This group typically favored abolishing the universities as reactionary institutions, a course of action that eventually was carried through in revolutionary France (Wuthnow 1989; Collins 1998: 640–42).

The biggest structural impetus to secularization occurred when the university passed from church control. This happened first and most influentially in Germany. The university reform movement of the 1780s and 1790s, which culminated in the foundation of the new-style university of Berlin in 1810, was oriented toward eliminating the dominance of the theological faculty and raising the philosophical faculty, which had previously been a preparatory school for undergraduates, to the level of a graduate faculty (Collins 1998). The subjects of the philosophical faculty—including history, language, and science—were made independent fields of research. Professors were now expected to be researchers and innovators, and the principles of autonomy of teaching and of learning, *Lehrfreiheit* and *Lernfreiheit*, were announced in the constitution of Wilhelm von Humboldt, the Prussian minister of education and religion. The invention of the modern research university spread first to other German states as the result of competition for prestige and a common market for professors. The university soon became the locus for leading research in science, as well as for new

waves of scholarship in the humanities. Previous bases of intellectual production, the private patronage that had sustained scientific research and the
book markets that were the base for innovation in literature, were upstaged
during the early 1800s by the systematic innovation promoted by competition among research professors. In secondary and primary education too, a
series of Prussian reforms in 1763, 1787, and 1812 established universal compulsory schooling to be provided by lay teachers independent of the clergy.
This system of secular schooling spread quickly to the other Protestant states
and after the unification of Germany in 1871 to the Catholic states of the
south (Mueller 1987: 18–26).

The German universities were the principal organizational basis for secularization, and cultural modernization elsewhere followed the importation
or imitation of the German university reforms. By the 1850s, British intellectuals and educators were acutely conscious of the superiority of the
German over the English universities, which were still dominated by the
clergy and teaching a traditional undergraduate-oriented curriculum. In
1854–56 and 1872, British universities were reformed along German lines
by abolishing religious tests that had excluded Catholics, Protestant non-
conformists, and Jews; by secularizing the teaching profession by eliminating the requirement that fellows be in religious orders; by replacing patronage appointments to fellowships with competitive examinations; and by
establishing research-oriented faculty positions.[17] The watershed in
American intellectual life, too, came with university reform along German
lines. The religious colleges that had constituted American higher education
were supplanted, in the space of a generation, by the new-style university
following the foundation of Johns Hopkins University in 1874 and the
University of Chicago in 1892 as German-style research graduate schools;
similar reforms were instituted at Harvard in the same period (Vesey 1965;
Flexner 1930).

In France, secularization was the subject of a lengthy series of battles that
resulted in swings between clerical and anticlerical dominance. For this reason, it was in France that the issue of secularism was debated in most explicit
and intense form, but the actual transformation to a modern base of cultural
production occurred relatively late (CMH 1910, 8: 52, 752; 9: 126–29; 10:
73–93; 11: 23–26, 297; 12: 92–93, 114–18; Weisz 1983; Fabiani 1988).
Before the Revolution, education in France was largely in the hands of the
Catholic clergy or nuns, and all other schools were under clerical supervi-
sion, with the exception of government technical schools for military and
civil engineers. The Revolution abolished the universities, along with the
privileges of the church, also eliminating lawyers and law schools in its attack on the Old Regime. The new educational system built up during the
Napoleonic period left primary schooling to local authorities, and in 1808

after state rapprochement with the church, to Catholic teaching orders. Secondary schools and higher education were centralized under the Imperial University, which monopolized teaching for its degree holders, made all appointments, controlled salaries and curricula, and formed a regular career hierarchy of teachers, inspectors, and governors. The head of this bureaucracy was appointed by the state; under Napoleon, this was a bishop who restored Catholic orthodoxy in education. Unlike the German universities, the professors at the highest schools were not expected to do independent research, which was reserved for members of the central institute under governmental patronage. The old university faculty of philosophy was replaced with faculties of science and literature. Under the new system, innovative research continued in the mathematical sciences, where the École Polytechnique supported many leading scientists, but languished in other fields, where institutional dominance passed to the Germans.

The Restoration intensified clerical control, making all primary and secondary teachers subject to the bishops, multiplying ecclesiastical schools at the expense of those under secular auspices, and dismissing professors such as Cousin from university posts (1822). Struggle between the Ultramontane papal faction and national royalists tended to block the more extreme claims of the former, however, and conservative secularists like Cousin were recalled in 1828. Rigid state control of the church pushed the Catholic conservatives into opposition to the government and thus played a part in the agitation for liberal rights and electoral principles that led to the constitutional monarchies of 1840–48 and 1859–70 and the revolutions of 1848 and 1871. The revolution of 1848 briefly gave security of tenure to professors, although under the dictatorship of Napoleon III tenure was revoked, and liberal professors such as Charles Renouvier were excluded. Degrees in history and philosophy were eliminated in 1854 and the medieval *trivium* and *quadrivium* reinstituted in the university curriculum. In primary education, where secular schools had been the majority in the 1840s, religious schools took the lead in the 1860s. Catholic militancy in turn stiffened the secularizers in the government who defended the supremacy of their own administration. The tendency built up under the Second Empire. Ernest Renan and Hippolyte Taine agitated after 1865 for a secularizing reform to allow France to catch up with Germany in science. The struggle broke out in full force under the Third Republic in the 1870s and culminated in the reforms of 1881, which deliberately imported many aspects of German-style educational structures (Mitchell 1979). Clergy were excluded from university teaching and from the right to confer degrees, and a centralized system of public and compulsory primary schools was established. Not until 1905, however, did lay teachers replace religious orders in elementary schooling, thereby removing education entirely from the hands of the church.

The university revolution is the reason why Germany since 1800 has been the world leader in religious secularization and hence in the creation of modern culture. In Germany, intellectuals acquired a base for cultural production that stressed innovation and the independence of scholarship from outside control. This independence was not absolute. In several episodes politically conservative regimes dismissed professors for political liberalism, and sometimes for religious unorthodoxy.[18] Yet overall, the tendency was for scholars to pursue their own paths. This became explicit by the time of Bismarck's *Kulturkampf* of 1872–86, which resulted from the unification of the Reich and the joining of Catholic territories to the already much more secularized Prussian north and gave rise to a struggle to remove all education from clerical to state control. This period is the explicit triumph of German anticlericalism, but its institutional roots go back much further, and the Prussian state church had long been subject to strong influences from the secularizing ministers and university philosophers.

One area in which German professors were unusually free to innovate was in biblical, historical, and philosophical scholarship, in which German academics produced a series of cutting-edge developments that undermined traditionalist religious doctrine. During the period 1790–1820, the philosophies of German idealism promoted a rationalized pantheism that became a substitute for scriptural Christianity. In the 1830s and 1840s, D. F. Strauss's historical scholarship on the life of Jesus created a sensation that was followed by claims by Feuerbach and the Young Hegelians that humanism or even political liberalism was the modern form of religion. Modern political radicalism, formulated by Mikhail Bakunin and by Marx and Engels, emerged from these circles of young German academics in this period. From the 1820s onward, theologians in Germany developed a liberal wing (Ferdinand Baur and the Tübingen school; later in the century Albrecht Ritschl and Adolf von Harnack) that incorporated historical scholarship and philosophical idealism as tools with which to fashion a religion closer to the modern temper. In the 1880s, Friedrich Nietzsche could declare that modernity had already triumphed and that God was dead; in the early 1900s, another thinker connected to the main German academic networks, Sigmund Freud, could analyze religion as a psychological pathology.

These continuing waves of antireligious cultural innovation, scandalous to traditionalists, developed in Germany because of the independent academic base. Before England and the United States underwent their own university revolutions, their intellectual and religious modernism came from sources outside the country; their secularizing modernist thinkers sojourned in Germany and translated avant-garde works on religion from the German.[19] During the first generation of university reforms, British and American universities remained semireligious, recapitulating the episode of idealist philosophy that Germany had experienced at the turn of the century. A leader of academic reform at Oxford, Benjamin Jowett, was tried for heresy in 1855 for his liberal theological writings, but was acquitted. Full-fledged secularization in the Anglophone world did not take place until the twentieth century. The first publicly outspoken atheists, such as Bertrand Russell, appeared in England around 1910. In the more conservative United States, Russell was banned from teaching at the City College of New York in 1940. Even more modernist movements, grappling with the issue of meaninglessness in a culture where religion was dead, first appeared with the existentialism of the 1920s in Germany and the 1940s in France and surfaced again in the postmodernism of the 1980s. Since the original battle against religion, later twists on the secularization theme have continued to emerge in the Continental centers of cultural modernity and to be imported by the less secularized follower societies of the Anglo-American world.

It is not my intention to replace the conventional interpretation of the German cultural *Geist* as reactionary antimodernism with an equally *geistig* explanation of Germany as modernist. It is a matter of the organizational transformation of the means of cultural production. Above all, this was the creation of the independent research-oriented university. Because it was pioneered in Germany and its imitators around the Western world lagged behind Germany for several generations, Germany was the exporter of cultural modernity virtually until the 1930s (and to some extent beyond, due to emigration of the most modernist German intellectuals). If Germany also suffered from the most vehemently antimodernist movement in the form of the Nazi regime, this was in part because the opposite movement of cultural modernists had gone furthest there.

Capitalist Industrialization

The industrial revolution is conventionally attributed to England during the period 1770–1820, with all other societies following behind. The image of a sudden break in economic development is an exaggeration based on Anglocentric thinking. The spread of mechanized production after 1770 was an episode within the long-term growth of a market economy. Wallerstein and Braudel date it from the mid-1400s (Wallerstein 1974; Braudel [1979] 1984); others discern an initial capitalist takeoff within medieval Europe of the 1100s and 1200s (Gimpel 1976; Collins 1986: 45–58). The institutional bases for earlier capitalism were widely spread over northern and western Europe. Germany was an important part of the market economy during the 1400s and early 1500s, when the main trade networks passed through Augsburg, Nuremberg, Leipzig, Frankfurt, and Cologne. Commercialization of Scandinavia and the Baltic was carried out by the cities of the

Hanseatic League, and German bankers were leaders of European finance. The Netherlands, leader of economic growth in the 1600s, was one of the fragments of the decentralized *Kleinstaaterei* of medieval northern and central Europe, institutionally a continuation of the free cities of the Hanseatic pattern, as the Low Countries had been part of the medieval German Empire until 1345 (Kinder and Hilgemann 1968: 192). In the 1700s England pulled ahead, although the growth of manufactures and agricultural production in France was comparable during much of the period. In considerable part, the transfer of leadership to the English Channel was due to destruction of Germany in the Thirty Years War. Even so, Germany shared in the intensification of production in the 1700s, especially on the cutting edge of industrialization in woolens and metallurgy, in a belt from the North Sea to the upper Rhine, and from the Danube to Saxony (Mann 1993: 262–63; Barraclough 1979: 144–45, 180–81).

England's period of clear-cut economic leadership was relatively brief. Germany played catch-up, but it did not start from institutions alien to the capitalist market. In its network of partially independent cities, it retained much of the bourgeois structure of earlier centuries, freed after 1810 from guild restrictions and supplemented by active economic promotion by the state, plus the innovative impetus of university research laboratories beginning in the 1820s and polytechnic institutes from the 1830s. Major obstacles to German economic development were geopolitical, the multiple customs barriers that were a product of political fragmentation; these were overcome by the Prussian-led customs union after 1834. Thereafter the German rate of growth was rapid, closing to approximate equality with Britain in agricultural productivity by 1900 and about 75 percent of Britain's per capita industrial production by 1913. Only the United States made a comparable run at Britain's early lead, surpassing British agricultural productivity by 1840 and industrial productivity by 1913 (Mann 1993: 262–65).

On the whole, movement along the dimension of economic modernization did not make for large differences among the major Western societies. France, in the eyes of contemporary observers the wealthiest society from the mid-1600s through 1780, lagged thereafter but only relatively so. It continued to move along the economic continuum, but at a slower rate than England, falling behind Germany between 1880 and 1900. The "industrial revolution" in England was not clearly visible in the changing material conditions of life until the 1820s,[20] and its distinctiveness did not last long, as railroads and mechanized factories spread widely on the Continent by the 1850s.[21] It was during this 50-year niche, when England seemed to stand alone on the forefront, that Marx and the other Young Hegelians formulated their ideas of modern history and the image of Germany as a backward society was created. This piece of rhetoric designed for purposes of political agitation has since become a free-floating myth used to account for all that differs between Germany and the other Western societies. It was none too accurate at the time and soon became even less so.

Democratization

The dimension on which England is usually regarded as unequivocally leading and Germany as lagging has been democratization. Both German thinkers themselves and foreign critics tend to ascribe conservatism, traditionalism, and authoritarianism to Germany on the grounds that it failed to carry out a bourgeois revolution, especially in the form of a popular revolution from below. This conventional interpretation considerably overstates the case. Consistent comparisons have not usually been made, but an outline of the pattern of revolutions would show that: (a) Germany has not been lacking in revolutions, ranging from the Protestant Reformation through the 1807–14 reform and liberation movement, the 1848 uprisings, and the successful 1918–19 revolution; (b) most revolutions everywhere are made as much from above as from below; (c) many revolutions—not only those in Germany—fail to end with political democratization, and the comparative evidence does not support the claim that democracy is necessarily produced by revolutions, much less by bourgeois ones (Goldstone 1991: 477–83); (d) the pace of democratization did not vary as widely among Western countries as the conventional picture supposes, when degrees of democratization are taken into account.

The most important analytical point is that democracy is not an all-or-nothing condition but a series of variations along a continuum. There are at least two continuums, two major dimensions of democratization: (1) the extent of *collegially shared power* (through parliaments, councils, and other structures); and (2) the *proportion of the populace that participates in the political franchise*. In the previous chapter, I attempted to marshal the comparative evidence for movement along each dimension of democratization. In brief summary, none of the major Western states moved rapidly, continuously, or synchronously along either dimension of democratization.

Parliamentary institutions and other collegial power-sharing structures existed all over medieval Europe. Many of them survived on the local level in Germany, as much as or more than elsewhere, up through modern times. In England, parliamentary domination over the monarchy began after 1710 and was generally established between 1760 and 1820. The hereditary House of Lords continued to share power until 1911, and the aristocracy dominated government ministries until 1905. In France, after a brief period of control by the revolutionary assembly in the 1790s and again in 1848–51, a token assembly coexisted with autocracy until full parliamentary control emerged in 1875. In Germany, following decades of token parliaments, the imperial Reichstag acquired power over budget and legislation in 1871, while the emperor retained power to name the chancellor. Ministerial responsibility to parliament lagged until 1919. The oldest strongly collegial power structure was the United States, dating from 1787.

On the dimension of the extent of the franchise, in England less than 15 percent of adult males had the franchise before 1832. The percentage expanded to about 33 percent in 1867, to 66 percent in 1884, and to full male suffrage in 1918; universal suffrage for women age 21 and over was granted in 1928. In the United States, colonial legislatures enfranchised 50–80 percent of white males and slightly more during the Revolution; full suffrage for white males was reached in the 1840s and for black former slaves in 1870 (although de facto not until the 1960s); universal adult franchise (including women) arrived in 1920. In France, after a brief episode of full male franchise in the 1790s, there was a tiny franchise; it was expanded again to all adult males in 1848 and to women in 1946. For the German Reichstag, full suffrage for males over age 25 existed after 1871; universal suffrage for men and woman over 20 was granted in 1919. None of these states reached 100 percent adult suffrage until 1919 (Germany was the first).

If we combine relatively effective parliamentary power with a wide male franchise, the United States, France, and Germany all reached this level around the same time, 1870–75, England not until later. To judge England the leader in democratization is either to engage in retrospective teleology or to give overwhelming weight to the early parliamentary regimes, with their aristocratic bias and their very limited franchise.[22] My point is not that Germany has historically been highly democratic, but that its degree of limited democratization is not at all unusual. No states were truly democratic until the twentieth century; if any led the way earlier, it was the United States, although with its severe (if not unusual) blights of slavery and the exclusion of women.

The World Wars and the Nazi Regime: Geopolitical Roots of Modern German-Bashing

On the whole, the image of Germany as uniquely authoritarian and traditional is not justified by the evidence. Germany has been the world leader of modernization on the dimensions of bureaucratic universalism, religious secularization, and postreligious culture. German economic modernization lagged behind that of England and France between 1650 and 1850, but the German economy was by no means static during this period. Thereafter it rapidly narrowed the gap with England and overtook France by 1880. In democratization, German collegial institutions at the national level expanded in the 1800s along lines pioneered in England, although with somewhat weaker powers in relation to those of the autocratic executive. The extension of the franchise was on about an even pace with that in every other major society except the United States. The record of freedom of expression was spotty everywhere, with Germany lagging little if at all in the nineteenth century.

Germany had many elements of conservatism and class deference, but this pattern is not unusual when we compare it, not with an ideal type of egalitarian democracy, but with actually existing societies during the nineteenth and early twentieth centuries. Social conservatism was more pronounced in Germany than in the United States but was quite similar to that in England. Statistical evidence on the concentration of landholdings and distribution of wealth and income shows that around 1900 Britain was by far the most inegalitarian of the major Euro-American societies. France, the United States, and Germany all had approximately the same, moderate level of inequality (Barkin 1987). Ideal typical comparisons are even less justified when we recognize that every society has been divided by conflicts over just these issues. A false perspective is produced by writers such as Peter Gay (*Weimar Culture*, 1968) who concentrate on the conservative and antidemocratic factions while slighting the opposition of German liberals and socialists. Similarly, a false ideal type is created on the other side by those who depict only the English and French traditions of liberal egalitarianism and ignore British and French conservatives. One can make a good case, in fact, that England was the leading conservative power during the period from 1776 to 1914, opposing the American and French revolutions and lagging in mass democracy as late as 1917. It was the success of English aristocracy in resisting modernity that German conservatives before the World War held up as their ideal.

Germany's reputation for antimodernist conservatism in the eyes of the other Western societies dates from World War I and especially from the Nazi regime of 1933–45. Before then, modernizers in Britain, the United States, and even France looked to Germany for the avant-garde path, especially in culture and administrative organization (Mitchell 1979). The reason for the shift in imagery is geopolitical. Britain and the major German states had been allies ever since the War of the Spanish Succession (1701–13), with France their primary enemy through the Napoleonic Wars and beyond. The turning point came in 1904 with the formation of the Entente among Russia, France, and Britain, a reversal of alliances that set up World War I.[23] The United States, which had never had any military relationship with Germany (but plenty of cultural dependence) and a long-standing alliance with the French against Britain, was dragged into the anti-German coalition. Allied propaganda during the war created the popular image of Germans as

medieval barbarians and Prussian power-lackeys. There was nothing structurally inherent about this reversal. If the United States had happened to be
allied with Germany against England, it is easy to imagine that propaganda
could have been created depicting Germany as the land of the beer-drink-
ing common man and England as ruled by haughty and bigoted aristocrats,
deferred to by servile lower classes with cap in hand.

Full-scale democracy during the Weimar Republic did not last long
enough to dampen the wartime anti-German image. The rise of the Nazi
regime and the ideological mobilization that went along with World War II
tarred all German institutions and culture with the same brush. Since 1940
most academic scholarship on Germany has been written in Hitler's shadow,
raking through previous German history and seeing everything possible as a
foreshadowing of the Holocaust to come. Such post hoc explanation, in the
absence of systematic comparison or generalizable theory, has been of little
value. If Germany, by and large, has followed the same paths of institutional
development as the other major Western societies, the roots of the Nazis
must be sought in a more uncomfortable place: in conditions common to us
all. Without attempting to review the voluminous research literature on the
social bases of Nazism, let me suggest that the crucial causal variable is
geopolitical.

It is generally the case that when a state loses a war the party in power at
the time is delegitimated. The same process strengthens its domestic opponents. The Wilhelmine Reich that lost World War I was a regime in which
parliament shared responsibility. All parties, including the Social Democrats,
who held the largest number of seats after the 1912 election, had voted overwhelmingly for war credits. All the political parties as well as parliamentary
power were delegitimated by the war loss. The revolutionary transfer of
power in winter 1918–19 made the new democratic regime responsible for
negotiating the humiliating Versailles peace settlement. The Weimar Republic, under liberal/left control until 1930, did little to restore Germany's international prestige. The popularity of the Nazis was to a considerable extent
based upon its militancy in throwing off war sanctions and resurrecting
Germany as a Great Power. Confined to the international issue alone, there
is nothing here that differed from the common pattern of states seeking national power prestige through military strength. We see this also in the cases
of Britain and France in the imperialist period of the late nineteenth and early
twentieth centuries and in the drive for territorial acquisitions by the United
States from the 1790s through the Spanish-American War. The Weimar
regime, lacking international power-prestige, had its weak legitimacy further
undermined by economic ineffectiveness, both in the inflation of the postwar
years and by the Great Depression.

What was most distinctive about the Nazis was their domestic policy, their attack on democratic institutions, and their rabid antiuniversalism, which led to racial genocide. These were not dominant positions in German culture. The National Socialists took office in 1933 in a coalition government, having won a minority 288 of 647 seats; they took absolute power in a coup d'etat (Kinder and Hilgemann 1968: 470–71). A substantial portion of the German population was attracted to the Nazi program, and others acquiesced in it. Acquiescence to government power, however, is not a uniquely German quality; it exists among the majority of people in every state. The plebiscites held during the 1930s that overwhelmingly ratified Hitler's foreign policies involved the normal sociological processes of crowd enthusiasm, as well as political manipulation, and the enforced nonparticipation of the strongest opponents. In addition, the German population was attracted, in a way that general sociological principles would predict, to the revival of international power-prestige as well as to rapid recovery from the massive unemployment produced by government-directed, essentially Keynesian, economic policies of the Hitler regime.

The portion of the German population that was pro-Nazi has been much more extensively studied than comparable groups in other societies. Survey evidence indicates that anti-Semitism was not the primary attraction of the Nazi movement. Among early converts to Nazism, less than 15 percent were preoccupied with the threat of "Jewish conspiracy," as compared with over 50 percent who were concerned with the threat of communism (Merkl 1975: 449–522). Anti-Semitism was one of two predominant themes in the Nazi movement of the 1920s: blaming the Jews for German defeat and anger over the Versailles treaty; that is to say, Hitler linked an older and relatively weaker movement in Germany, anti-Semitism, with the prevailing mobilizing theme of the period, state delegitimation through military defeat. By the late 1920s, Nazi election campaigns played down anti-Semitism because regional evidence showed that it did not attract voters (Goldscheider and Zuckerman 1984: 144).

A virulent anti-Semitic movement had existed in Germany and Austria since the turn of the century, but to attribute it to uniquely German cultural qualities (e.g., in the argument of Mosse 1964) is to misstate its sources. In the early 1890s, the anti-Semitic People's Party won some electoral victories in Germany, with the result that anti-Semitism spread to the conservative and center parties. These parties lost ground in the late 1890s, and anti-Semitism subsequently declined as a political issue. The center of anti-Semitic movements in the German-speaking states was Austria, dating from the 1880s, and was directly connected with the ethnic rivalries of the multi-ethnic Austro-Hungarian Empire (Schorske 1980: 116–80). Historically, the strongest roots of anti-Semitism were in the eastern part of this zone, in Slavic Eastern Europe. Until the mid-1800s, Jews from the Polish part of

Russia were banned from admission to Russia proper. When barriers were lifted in the 1860s, Jewish migration into the Ukraine and Russia led to the pogroms of the 1880s (CMH 1910, 12: 339–41). Until World War I, the main instances of official government anti-Semitic policies were in tsarist Russia, Poland, and Hungary (Goldscheider and Zuckerman 1984: 139–47). German anti-Semitic activities during the same period are not to be minimized (Jochmann 1988), but in comparison with their extent and above all their violence in Eastern Europe, indigenous German anti-Semitism was derivative and secondary.

Hitler brought this Austrian and East European style of anti-Semitic politics into Germany at the end of World War I, where it became subordinated to more central issues of fascist authoritarianism. The conditions for a truly genocidal mass action emerged later, again because of military-geopolitical events. The mass killings of the Holocaust took place, not immediately following the Nazi coming to power in Germany in 1933, but from 1941 onward, as the German armies moved east into war with Russia. The Slovak and Romanian governments organized their own massacres; in Lithuania, the Ukraine, Poland, and elsewhere in the East local auxiliaries aided the Nazis in exterminating Jews (Fein 1979). It was in those eastern regions that the large majority of Jewish deaths took place (Goldscheider and Zuckerman 1984). The massacre of ghetto Jews in Poland was for the most part carried out by Soviet prisoners of war under the direction of German military police units that were themselves reluctant to commit the actual killings (Browning 1992). Genocide in the context of war hysteria (not unlike that which occurred again in the 1990s in Yugoslavia) was taken to unprecedented levels by the deadly combination of modern German military organization and long-standing antagonism of Slavic peasantries to the segregated *shtetl* communities of eastern Europe.

To concentrate exclusively on German culture as the source of anti-Semitism is to overlook comparable ideological movements, not only in eastern Europe but in all the major democracies as well. In the United States there were anti-immigrant movements, racial supremacists, and anti-Semites; in England imperialists and eugenic purists; in France, anti-Semitism peaked with the Dreyfus Affair at the turn of the century, along with antimodernist and antidemocratic movements such as the *Action Française*, which have been categorized as fascist in the same sense as the Nazis (Nolte 1969).[24] The intensities did not reach such extremes, but they are marks along the same continuum. The most famous ideologists of anti-Semitism and racial purity in the nineteenth century were the Englishman H. S. Chamberlain and the Frenchman Joseph de Gobineau. On the other side, the German opponents of the anti-Semitic movement have not been given as much attention. Nietzsche, popularly regarded as a Nazi precursor, was an explicit enemy of the anti-Semitic movement. Other critics included Max Weber (see Weber 1991: 246–61). German anthropologists and philologists such as Theodor Waitz, Adolf Bastian, and Bastian's pupil Franz Boas were the leading scientific opponents of racial theories because their historical research showed that language groups (e.g., Indo-European, Semitic) should not be confused with biological stocks, that culture is independent of biology. These positions have nothing to do with national character. The autonomy of disciplines within the German research university was responsible for this aspect of German intellectual modernism.[25]

It is a melancholy fact that the horrors of racial genocide were not confined historically to Nazi Germany: the Amerindian population was decimated and subjected to forced population movements by the Spanish and the Anglo-Americans; whole clans of "wild" Scots were hunted to extermination by British armies in the 1620s; the English attempted the forced evacuation of all native Irish, on pain of death, to a reservation on the barren lands of northwestern Ireland in the 1650s. This massive "ethnic cleansing" failed mainly because the English lacked the organizational resources to carry out their plan. Nevertheless, one quarter of the Irish population died, and 80,000 were shipped to the West Indies as slave labor (CMH 1910, 4: 522, 536–37; Foster 1989: 122–23; MacLeod 1967). The difference here from the Holocaust is a matter of numbers and of modern organizational efficiency, not of basic impulse.

The rise of the Nazis to power in Germany was the result of a contingent factor that cut across the processes of modernization. If the reversal of alliances had not taken place, and France instead of Germany had lost World War I and experienced sanctions similar to those imposed by the Versailles treaty, it is plausible that French fascists could have come to power in the 1920s or 1930s. One can imagine the reconstruction of cultural history that would have followed: the Americans and the British would no doubt have extolled the reasonable and moderate path to modernization followed by their German friends and condemned the excesses and lack of an organically growing democratic tradition that led to fascism in France. It is possible to imagine a similar scenario playing itself out today. Suppose the United States were to lose a war and be plunged into an economic crisis. In the fray of political infighting, the government loses control over the legitimate means of violence. A popular movement emerges to restore order by marshaling private armies; as this movement of vigilantes becomes threatening, the faction in control of the government engages in extralegal measures that further break down the habits of democratic government. The hypothetical situation is not fanciful; these were the steps by which the Nazi minority arrived at the position to carry out their coup d'etat against a delegitimated democracy.

In the United States, the ideology of any successful antimodernist movement would of course be tailored to local traditions. A U.S. fascist move-ment would be most successful not by wrapping itself in swastikas but in American flags; its image of the racial enemy would be tailored to current conditions, perhaps singling out Hispanic immigrants or economic-imperi-alist Japanese. There is no reason why an authoritarian racist-nationalist antimodernist movement would have to be anti-Semitic; in fact, the partic-ularistic definition of fascism as anti-Semitic per se keeps us from under-standing the universal dynamic. Fortunately, the basic structural parts of the scenario—defeat in war coupled with economic collapse—are remote. But the theoretical lesson of the German case cannot be dismissed with reference to a particular cultural history. It is structural conditions for democratization and for antidemocratic overthrow, and for modernity and antimodernism as well, with which we must be concerned.

The Moral of the Story

Military victors write the histories. That is one source of distortion about the patterns and causes of modern social change. A deeper problem is the preva-lence of a unidimensional rhetoric that imposes a single line of development on a multidimensional process. We have seen this multidimensionality twice over: in the concept of modernization, which can be decomposed into bureaucratization, secularization, capitalist industrialization, and de-mocratization; and again in the concept of democratization, which has different causal trajectories for collegial power-sharing institutions and for the extent of the franchise. Both popular opinion and scholarly consensus have misperceived the path of Germany in the process of modernization; this means they have also misperceived the paths of most other societies, but in opposite ways. Britain and the United States are much less exemplars of ideal-type modernity than is usually supposed. On important dimensions, they are among the more traditional and nonmodern societies of the past two centuries in the West. France, where extremely modernistic tendencies have cropped up from time to time, has also had severe conflicts with anti-modernist forces. If we insist on a composite, global judgment about the principal historical location for the emergence of modernity, Germany is as good a candidate as any. Its troubles may be an archetype of the difficulties inherent in modern social structures.

CHAPTER 6

Market Dynamics
as the Engine of Historical Change

LET US TRY an exercise in theoretical imagination. Suppose that Marx and Engels were on the right track regarding the main historical types of social structures and their engines of transformation but that their formulation is too crude. Let us assume, however, that there is something workable in their classifications of primitive communism, the slave economy, feudalism, and capitalism. Imagine, though, that the leading sector in each is not a mode of production and accumulation but a particular type of market, and that it is because of market dynamics that each form of social organization undergoes growth, crises, and transformation into another type.

My argument is deliberately unserious in the following respect. I would not suppose that markets, even in imagination, are the only important dynamic in world history. Other agents of change are possible, including geopolitics (which in earlier chapters has taken pride of place), population, and ecological pressures. But let us see how far we can go with an omni-market model.

Some Principles of Market Dynamics

Schematically, let us hypothesize that all markets have the following characteristics:

1. Each form of market exchange is based on a particular kind of property. Something must be appropriated in order to be exchanged; and exchange consists in transfer of the rights of appropriation.

2. Markets vary in their openness. A given market is not necessarily open to all potential buyers and sellers. Full information on the terms of trade is not necessarily or usually widely available. Typically, market participation is stratified, either because of ecological access or because of deliberate politi-

cal controls from above or within. As has been argued by Harrison White and earlier by Max Weber, the ongoing construction of noncompetitive niches or monopolies may be the essence of markets (White 1981; M. Weber 1968: 144–50, 341–43, 638; see also Murphy 1988). Hence there is always some tendency (not necessarily constant) toward unequal exchange and economic inequality.

3. Markets as social structures tend to expand over long periods of time to include more people or goods or relationships, and especially more territory. Expansion in these respects may go on at the same time that participation becomes more restricted, especially for producers and sellers as against laborers and consumers.

4. The structural expansion of markets results in economic and organizational growth by increasing the volume of goods and stimulating innovations in production. The sheer volume of trade has different meanings depending on whether it is *extensive growth* (in the terminology of Eric Jones [1988]) that merely keeps up with population and its geographical spread, or *intensive growth* in per capita production. There can of course be stagnation or downturns in either or both respects (Curtin 1984). What is important is that there are very long periods in which the up side of the dynamic prevails.

5. Markets for a particular item of exchange tend to give rise to superordinate markets that trade on the terms of trade themselves. Future and long-distance exchanges become commodities that can be traded in their own market. Superordinate markets may be pyramided upon one another. Money, debts, mortgages, stock ownership, rights of purchase, licensing, and other media of exchange can become objects of superordinate media traded in yet further markets.

6. Markets tend to reach crisis points over the long term. (This is in addition to short-term cyclical swings, which may also be present.) Such crises include a slowing or reversal of growth of a market's principal form of production; the severe limitation or destruction of its principal form of market exchange; and the transformation of social organization into a structure based on a different form of property.

These propositions leave vague the mechanisms by which these processes occur, especially lateral expansion, growth, and crisis. The dynamics will become clearer when we have examined the major historical types of market systems. Let us consider here the central Marxian issue, why such structures undergo crises. One might say that there is a contradiction between the character of markets as allowing stratified participation structured by protective niches (2) and their tendency to expand laterally (3) and in volume (4). In addition, the rise of superordinate markets (5) helps fuel a crisis.

Braudel characterized two kinds of markets: relatively localized, face-to-face exchanges in which custom and surveillance enforce a "fair price" and keep profits and exploitation low; and long-distance and future-oriented exchanges in which capitalist brokers manipulate conditions to achieve large profits (1977: 51–53, 62). Capitalism exists at the level of superordinate markets, and the tendency of such markets is toward monopolization and exploitation. Schumpeter agrees to the extent that he defines capitalism as "enterprise carried out with borrowed money" and speaks of banks as "the headquarters of the capitalist system" (Schumpeter 1939; 1962: 126). One might argue, then, that market crises occur because superordinate markets become increasingly concentrated and end up restricting the market to the point of strangulation.

But although superordinate markets are stratifying, it does not follow they must produce stagnation or ever-narrowing concentration. Both Schumpeter and Weber viewed superordinate markets as dynamic and, up to a point, as sources of growth and change. For Schumpeter, markets for financial instruments remove resources from the self-reproducing flow of existing exchanges and recombine them into new forms of organization, thereby opening new product markets. Weber noted that the tendency of any given market is toward monopolization (1968: 144–50), but appropriation on one level (e.g., medieval seigneurs monopolizing land or capitalists expropriating workers from their means of production) makes possible a superordinate market with its own dynamics (e.g., loans secured by private property in land; stock certificates). This higher-order market outflanks the original monopolizers by subjecting them to competitive pressures on the means of monopolization, such as inflation of the currency.

Schumpeter argued that monopolies favor economic expansion by protecting profitability in risky ventures, whereas full market competition drives profits down toward zero. But only an optimal level of monopoly formation should have this expansionary consequence. Too little monopolization means lack of profit, and too much means stagnation due to strangulation of demand. As both Arthur Stinchcombe and Jack Goldstone have pointed out (in personal communications with the author), higher-order markets in instruments controlling the terms of trade are futures markets, hedges against uncontrollable contingencies or investments in the long run. If futures markets are inherently risky, this is especially true of those superordinate networks of political power that uphold the fundamental mode of property. Crises in these superordinate structures are capable of bringing down the whole system of exchange.

Politics and warfare are themselves competitive markets for material inputs, stimulating the production of weapons, fortifications, military transportation, and the material means of civil administration. These too are superordinate markets, from which the success of political alliance-making or military expansion feeds back into stimulating lower-level production markets. By the same token, the cost of political and military investment can outrun its returns and set a crisis reverberating throughout the system.

Add to this yet another superordinate market sector, the production and circulation of cultural goods in the form of religion, education, entertainment, and personal display. These can be called status goods, since they become visible emblems of group membership and individual ranking. Here again we sometimes find hotly expanding markets. When production of status-impregnated objects like personal clothing, home decorations, religious icons, or musical instruments expands, it sets in motion a process of adjustment in social relationships. Any new material inputs that expand the sector of church buildings, schools, entertainment, and other symbol-circulating specialties will mobilize concerns about status identities throughout society. Growth in material wealth imparts a marketlike dynamic to interpersonal relationships that are mediated by such symbolic goods, whether this takes the form of competition over religious display or a succession of styles of adornment and consumption. Higher-order markets for social status markers in turn feed back into demand for material goods to support the status–goods sector. Here again we have a superordinate market stimulating material production. But just as political and military sectors, operating in a steamed-up market mode, can increase the level of conflict and even of physical destruction, so too can mobilization of cultural competition absorb more in costs than it puts back into the material economy.

Our general line of approach, then, is that stratifying and cost-accelerating tendencies within markets, particularly in superordinate markets at their most politicized pole, periodically bring market systems into crisis. At their outermost sweep, these crises are the turning points of history that bring an end to one system of property exchange and replace it with another.

KINSHIP MARKETS, SLAVE MARKETS, AGRARIAN-COERCIVE MARKETS, CAPITALIST MARKETS

Here, then, are my candidates for systems of market dynamics in world history. First, in kin-based societies, the central market is the kinship system itself: the market for alliances made through intermarriage. Instead of Marx and Engels's primitive communism characterized by collective property, we have sexual property as the mode of appropriation. One might call this a "Lévi-Straussian" market, which culminated in the "kinship revolution" that destroyed the kinship-based structure and replaced it with the rise of the state.

Second, I will treat slave markets as a dynamic system. The major examples are the same as those described by Marx and Engels, ancient Greece and especially Rome. Here, however, I depart from Marx and Engels in treating slavery not as a form of production but as a form of exchange. In slave markets, slaves were not primarily producers but commodities in this system; the productive class was the military, and structural crisis occurred when military slave production ceased to pay for itself. A variant of this system was the market for slave soldiers that became prominent in medieval Islamic societies.

Third, I treat the market systems of the medieval agrarian societies organized by patrimonial households, "feudalism" in Marxian terms. Market structures here centered on land rent, typically in struggle with another structure, taxation. Perry Anderson has proposed a crisis of feudalism based on the struggle over rent and the expansion of the market for land and its produce. I would add another candidate market here: the rationalized corporate properties of the monasteries, which constituted the leading edge of medieval capitalist development both in Christian Europe and in Buddhist China and Japan. Both property structures, that of the landed military aristocracy and that of religious corporations, were eventually expropriated in the crisis of agrarian-coercive markets.[1]

Finally, I will comment briefly on modern capitalism and its proliferation of superordinate markets, including its capacity for undermining socialist enclaves within a capitalist world system. The final question must be whether omnicapitalism too has a built-in trajectory toward its own structural crisis and transformation.

It will be noticed that my thought-experiment is a Weberianization of Marx. To be sure, all societies are structured by social arrangements of control over the means of production, by which surplus is accumulated. The question is whether such relations have a dynamic that explains the major structural crises and changes across human history. I submit that this has never been shown, and that most efforts to do so slip away in the direction of market relationships. Roemer (1982, 1986), in reformulating Marxism to provide a technically defensible model of class exploitation in each historical mode, abandons the criterion of extraction of surplus labor at the point of production. For Roemer, a class is exploited if it would be better off withdrawing from existing market relations, and it is an exploiter if it would be worse off by withdrawing. Although Roemer's is not a dynamic model of crises and structural change, it underlines the centrality of markets to property relationships. We have no theory showing how crises in modes of production operate as the driving force across kin-based/stateless, ancient/slave-owning, feudal/agrarian, and capitalist societies. Most efforts (such as Marx's own) have dealt with the emergence of early capitalism or the dynamics of mature capitalism. Perry Anderson's *Passages from Antiquity to Feudalism* (1974a) is the most comprehensive effort to date to explain earlier transitions, but it diverges in just the direction of market dynamics that I emphasize here. The same is true of Sahlins's and other efforts to specify a Marxian dynamic of band and tribal economies (see, e.g., Sahlins 1972).

A materialist theory of markets does not stand or fall on the question of class agency, and still less on the issue of class consciousness. It is structures that have dynamics and crises; the expansion of a particular kind of market system, and the difficulties that flow from its crisis, wash over everyone in a society. It is not necessary that the main actors on opposing sides of political struggles be slave owners versus slaves, capitalists versus land-owning aristocrats, or capitalists versus workers. Nor does the lack of explicit class consciousness so often noted (e.g., by Runciman 1983 and Ste. Croix 1984) prevent a market dynamic from taking its course. What is important is that a crisis of a particular kind of market system makes the continuation of that system costly or impossible. Insofar as its political organization needs material inputs, politics too will undergo crisis when the exchange system does. During a shakeup there are inevitably some who seize new political and economic opportunities. What differentiates them is not their class background, but the new class positions they create from the structural possibilities open to them. In this sense, a structural model of world history like that put forward by Marx and Engels may still be our best guide to understanding long-term changes.

CAVEAT: IDEAL TYPES AND EMPIRICAL COMBINATIONS

My thought-experiment is argued in terms of ideal types. I propose simplified models of several types of market dynamics. Any particular society may include several of these forms. Tribal societies may include both the kinship dynamic and a slave dynamic, just as societies dominated by the slave dynamic include some of the dynamic of agrarian-coercive property; and into agrarian-coercive markets may intrude elements of kinship dynamics (as in the Germanic and Scandinavian invasions of medieval Europe) as well as features of capitalism. The overall trajectory of each historical formation results from the combination of its component dynamics.

Any particular society may also include sectors that are not market structures at all. In most societies before modern capitalism, there were major areas of local autarky characterized by subsistence and reproduction of unchanging structures. Such self-reproducing structures may have been quantitatively by far the largest part of that society's activities. Although market sectors may have been small, they were disproportionately important if they alone were the source of dynamism. These minority sectors were likely to be the main source of material resources for the state and other nonproducers, and thus especially fateful for the growth of a superstructure. This is equally true in a kin-based society, where most kinship systems may have operated according to Lévi-Straussian short-cycle exchanges but the growth of political power came from those few "entrepreneurs" who invested their marriages in long-cycle exchanges. The majority of the population in ancient Mediterranean regions stood outside of the market relations of the military/slave economy, and the rationalized religious economies of Cistercian and Buddhist monasteries were only part of the European and Chinese economies of their day. But if markets inherently expand their scope (at least up to the point of crisis), then such leading sectors are where the action is for major structural change.

This is not a theory of a sequence of stages. The kinship revolution does not automatically lead to a slave market economy, and the growth of medieval monastic capitalism (as in China) does not necessarily issue in modern, all-encompassing capitalism. I follow the classic Marx-Engels ordering of types, but largely to remind us that they are the baseline from which my reformulation takes off. It would be more useful to see, between kin-based economies at one end and capitalist economies at the other, several variants within agrarian-coercive economies. In this "middle" segment of world history, the massive slave-market economy of Greece and Rome was an unusual variant, but it was the predecessor of the European social structure that eventually emerged as modern omnicapitalism. The ancient Mediterranean slave market and the Islamic slave-soldier market were special kinds of superordinate markets within the coercive-rent and tax-extraction forms of agrarian society. An additional variant, corporate religious capitalism again emerged within agrarian-coercive societies and gave at least two of them—Europe and China—a special capitalist dynamism.

This brings us into a frontier area of historical sociology. We are only recently coming to appreciate that the West did not have a monopoly on the breakthrough into capitalist markets. (On this point, compare Braudel 1979, 2: 93–112, 519–34; 3: 417–61; Elvin 1973; Jones 1988; Collins 1986: 45–76; Abu-Lughod 1989.) It appears that there were two or possibly three breakthroughs, which ended up competing within the gradually closing world system. The Eastern breakthrough, in T'ang through Sung China, subsequently stagnated in the Ming and Ch'ing dynasties, but it is arguable that it laid the base for the takeoff in Muromachi and Tokugawa Japan, which structurally underlies Japan's surge in the twentieth century. The Islamic societies of the Mediterranean too had a combination of market structures that for a time had considerable dynamism before entering a period of stagnation. Though there is much more to be understood, none of this should in principle be surprising in an explanatory theory of market dynamics. What follows is a sketch of its principal forms.

Kinship Markets

In stateless societies, the principal form of property is sexual property. Rights of sexual access and all that goes with it are appropriated and exchanged. Those rights legitimize the propagation of children and hence inheritance channels, as well as define residence obligations and hence shared household goods and activities. The right of permanent and exclusive sexual access constitutes marriage; the accompanying rights and obligations make up the full-fledged kinship system.

In a society in which the only important organizational structure is kinship, marriage alliances are simultaneously military, political, economic, and religious. Kinship-based societies vary a great deal in their complexity and stratification. These variations are related to the amount of surplus produced by existing technology—hunting and gathering, horticulture, fishing, pastoralism—and by relative environmental abundance or scarcity (Lenski 1966; Johnson and Earle 1987). But any stratification must be organized as a version of kinship, since there are no other organizational forms. As Lévi-Strauss (1969) put it, the appropriation of women by males and their exchange among groups creates alliances; the type of exchange system determines the size and shape of mutual obligations and hence the structure of the society.

Such societies are relatively egalitarian in the sense that there may be little material surplus and little difference in its distribution. Traditional social science glossed over the point by referring to "stratification only by age and sex." But these are the essence of a system of property: in its more extreme forms, males hold property in females, and the aged hold property in the young, whom they dispose of in marriage alliances. A wealthy man or a wealthy family is rich in daughters or perhaps sisters; by investing them, he (and they) can become richer still in sons and allies and in the material gifts and military support they can bring him. "Kinship capitalism" is investment in relatives.

We might say that men and women, as well as the old and the young, are the principal social classes in kinship markets. There are wide variations in their "class" privileges and in the intensity of "class" mobilization and conflict. In some kinship systems women have considerable degrees of power or at least resistance to male domination. But women maneuver within the system of sexual property exchange that makes up the surrounding alliances. Men tend to dominate sexual property because they control the political/military network. Women are relatively autonomous when the alliance structure is weak (as in hunting-and-gathering bands), and they exert the most power when, in certain political and ecological conditions,

sexual property and economic subsistence center on female lineage and residence patterns (Blumberg 1984; Chafetz 1984; Collins 1986: 271–321). The
expansion of the kinship market tends to trap women increasingly into a
male-centered system of sexual property.

There is no accepted theory of the dynamics of kin-based societies. Lévi-
Strauss (1969) proposed that the important differences among kinship systems is the extent of alliances implied in their marriage system. Some systems
of rules produce short cycles, in which two or a few groups constantly in-
termarry, braiding their sons and daughters together across the generations.
These systems create local ties and reproduce a static structure. Other marriage rules produce long-distance alliances: kin-group A marries with group
B, which marries with group C, which marries with group D, and so on.
Eventually a group marries back into group A. Such long-cycle forms
(which Lévi-Strauss calls generalized exchange, in contrast to the restricted
exchange of the short-cycle forms) produce bigger alliance networks; hence
these groups tend to become politically and militarily more powerful.
Successful investors in kinship capital reap increasing numbers of obligatory
ties that bring in wives and produce children. The result is a spiral of increasing resources.

In Lévi-Strauss's model, the split between kinship speculators who follow
the long-cycle route and those who follow the conservative short-cycle
strategy eventuates in a kinship revolution.[2] The one becomes a rich and
cosmopolitan upper class, lording it over a localized and resource-poor
lower class. Eventually the top groups invest directly in military power,
thereby establishing the state and breaking with kinship society entirely.
Lévi-Strauss's model is parallel to that of Marx and Engels on capitalism: the
kinship market leads to class polarization and to a crisis that overturns the
property system and gives rise to a new form of property.

Lévi-Strauss's model, although worked out in detail for some kin-based
societies, is schematic and incomplete. Lévi-Strauss confined himself to systems of rules that positively prescribed particular kinds of marriages (such as
between matrilateral cross-cousins). He did not extend his analysis to bilateral and cognate lineages or to systems in which particular kinds of marriages
are not prescribed but only prohibited. It is reasonable to suppose that there
are within these forms also distinctions between those that tend to localize
or randomize kinship alliances and others that tend to produce increasing returns on kinship investments. Generalizing beyond Lévi-Strauss, we may
expect a dynamic within all kinship societies that is based on the growth of
alliances through certain strategies of marriage politics, and eventual dominance of the "kinship capitalists" over the "kinship proletariat," which fails
to make such investments.

Lévi-Strauss's model has been criticized as overly idealized. The kinship rules may say that a man should marry his mother's brother's daughter. But what if there is no such daughter because she was never born, or has died, or has broken the rule and married someone else? What if there are too many sons or too few daughters, or vice versa? The Lévi-Straussian model proposes that all such contingencies are random and have no structural effects. They slow down the working of the kinship dynamic, but they substitute no alternative dynamic. In the long run, the families that consistently follow an expansionary or a static investment strategy reap the results accordingly. Although demography is full of accidents, demography is also subject to structural pressure. A family that brings in returns of many wives for its sons and thus has favorable opportunities for political expansion will be motivated to have many children. We may hypothesize that the long and short cycles will have different demographic consequences, fostering population growth or stasis, respectively. Thus, for example, kinship markets may eventually cause population to strain ecological resources, with fateful consequences for productive and social organization.

As the market for alliances heats up, groups sometimes leap ahead by creating kinship ties by fiat. As Weber pointed out, a group of armed men may form an organization and legitimate it by inventing fictional common ancestors (Collins 1986: 272–76). This enables these new pseudo-kin to enter the kinship market with existing kin groups and build further marriage alliances. The varieties of kinship systems thus appear to be connected to the level of competition in family geopolitics. Kinship rules are strategies constructed in response to the external pressures and opportunities of the tribal "world system." Lévi-Strauss's distinction between restricted and generalized exchange foreshadows a more basic distinction between conservative kinship market strategies, which reproduce local ties, and aggressively expansive strategies of marital investment. We should recognize here the tendency for kinship markets, like all kinds of markets, to expand laterally to new territory and new relationships. Existing kinship alliances create military power and pose impressive models for others to emulate. There is a tendency for others to jump on the bandwagon by allying themselves with already successful groups. Even those who continue to oppose a successful group may imitate their organizational forms. Searle (1988) describes in this fashion the spread of what she calls "predatory kinship" in Viking Normandy.

Is there any sign of the other patterns I have hypothesized: growth in volume of production, subordinate and superordinate markets spinning off from the primary kinship market? Kinship societies were not totally stagnant in material production. They brought about several of the great economic transformations in world history over a very long time period: the development of horticulture, metallurgy, and animal husbandry, the harnessing of animal power, and eventually the urban revolution. These may have been connected to the expansion of kinship markets, which resulted in population growth and extension of intergroup networks. Marital exchanges were channels for material gifts and countergifts that constituted early forms of trade. In the patrilocal and patrilineal market forms that came to dominate in the protocivilizations of Europe and Asia, women were the primary good that circulated among communities. Material wealth tended to follow. Lévi-Strauss regarded women as the medium of exchange in this system. Women functioned as money in yet another sense, as stores of value, producers of children and hence of the long-term fate of the family.

Women were often the principal workers in material production. In hunting and gathering and in primitive horticulture, women produced most of the food relied on for subsistence. A male kinship-capitalist who was rich in women was thereby rich in whatever material goods existed.[3] As herding, fishing, and heavy plow agriculture developed, primary production was taken over by men, and women became economically important primarily as producers of sons. The growth of production that accompanied the shift from hunting and gathering to horticulture, and again from horticulture to agriculture, appears to have been driven by a concentration of labor forces that became available as some kinship capitalists made good on their investments.

THE KINSHIP REVOLUTION AND THE RISE OF THE STATE

In this Lévi-Straussian model of kinship dynamics, the state emerges because of a revolutionary split between the alliance-rich and the alliance-poor. It is not a Marxian revolt by the "working class" of this system, the women; rather—and this may be more common in historical transformations—a split emerges within the dominant, property-owning class, in this case the males. As evidence, Lévi-Strauss suggested that this is how the protostate was emerging in highland Burma, and he inferred some such development from the data on early kinship in India and China (1969: 234–68). Historical evidence related to this view of the transition from kinship alliance to state structures are available for Heian Japan, for archaic Greece and Italy, and for the early Norman state.[4]

The customary theories of the rise of the state have stressed that some combination of military conquest, technological innovation, and ecological caging gave rise to new organizations—armies, states, priesthoods, cities—that transcend kinship ties. But are these explanations really alternatives to a kinship revolution? In many instances, a militarily organized group (typically pastoral nomads from the periphery of settled cultivation) arrived as conquerors and thus created a two-class system. But the conquerors had to become organized among themselves, and it is likely that at the early core of such military alliances were cosmopolitan, aggressive investments in kinship alliances. Conversely, settled populations most vulnerable to conquest were those whose kinship systems were local and based on a short cycle and provided little power even for defensive alliances.

The same may apply to peaceful transitions to the state through the establishment of temple-based religious or redistributive centers. How was the surplus wealth that could be used for redistribution produced in the first place? Economic transactions in kin-based societies were organized by the circulation of ceremonial objects as protomoney, which facilitated the trade of mundane objects (Mauss 1967, 1969). Some highly competitive exchanges in rich environments constituted superheated potlatch systems, which stimulated production and the accumulation of wealth. Mauss's description invites comparison with capitalism in a kin-based context. Sahlins (1972) argued that the "intensification of production" in this "domestic mode of production" was due to politics, specifically the status competition among "big men." But the dominance of the "big man" is itself produced by a wealth of kinship ties. One might say that kinship investments result in accumulating not only power but also wealth, which is further invested in the politics of status competition. This is the dynamic by which stratification expands within kinship-based societies until it reaches the point at which the kinship structure breaks down.[5]

After this, kinship-alliance markets continue to exist, but they are no longer the leading edge. In state-organized societies, that role goes to slave markets or agrarian systems based on rent and taxation. Such societies retain an element of kinship politics. Their primary unit is the household, whether the small peasant or craftworker's home or the big fortified households and palaces of the lords. This is the structure that Weber called "patrimonial." Each household is the home and property of family, but it also includes nonkin. The number of the latter, including servants, soldiers, retainers, and guests, determines the power of its head. The scale of the economic, military, and political structure in such societies is limited by the fact that the only large-scale organizations are links among households. This structure is thus a mixture of kinship and nonkinship forms. Marriage alliances remain important for maneuvers within the property-owning class, but vertical relations among nonkin classes are the foundation of the larger structure. The Lévi-Straussian dynamic no longer exists; the leading edge of market dynamics is elsewhere. It is not until the triumph of modern capitalism, in conjunction with the bureaucratic form, in which organizational property is separated from family household property, that this vestigial kinship-alliance market is reduced to triviality.

Slave Markets

There have been various forms of slavery in many different kinds of societies. Types of slavery have included incidental bondage in kin-based societies; the debt-slavery of early Greece; military and administrative slavery (especially in Islamic societies); agricultural slavery in conjunction with serf-dom or other peasant exploitation (especially in medieval Korea, also in Russia); slave plantations in full-scale capitalist societies (e.g., the U.S. South); and omnipresent slave labor penetrating all aspects of life, most notably in Rome (Patterson 1982, 1987; Crone 1980; Hellie 1982). But slavery was the leading market dynamic primarily in ancient Greece, Rome, and their Mediterranean counterparts such as Carthage. I will concentrate on this latter, the Marx-Engels "slave mode of production," with a glance at the "slaves on horses" of the Islamic world.

The central form of property in a slave-market system was the slaves themselves. Hence it is a mistake to regard the slaves as the primary producers. It is the military who were the producers of this commodity; their productive labor was the fighting that captured the slaves. In Rome, this military "working class" was very large: under the republic it consisted of half of all citizens, and under the early empire 20 percent of Italian free-born men were in the military (Runciman 1983: 168).

The dynamic of the military/slave system was expansionary. This has several aspects. Inside the core state areas, warfare had a cumulative effect on the production of slaves. A victorious state grew richer in slaves, thereby increasing its internal resources, which in turn increased its military power. The early local power of Sparta was due in part to exploitation of helots, freeing its population for full-time military mobilization (although the helots were closer to serfs than to chattel slaves). Rome is a more impressive example of cumulative military success, especially after the enormous influx of slaves won in the wars with Carthage set in motion a geopolitical juggernaut. Such a cumulative dynamic, if left to itself, would result in the complete concentration of military resources in one state, but additional geopolitical factors affect military expansion as well (see note 12).

The military/slave dynamic expands both internally and geographically. Some wars were directed against barbarians on the periphery of state-organized societies. The immediate cause of hostilities may have been barbarian incursions, but the kinship-based barbarian groups had become organized as large-scale military coalitions in part because of the extension of slave markets outside the boundaries of civilization.[6] Once a market for slaves captured in internecine wars existed inside a civilization, barbarian entrepreneurs had an incentive to supply slaves on their own, usually from the outback (Finley 1982: 103). In this way slaves came into Greece from Thrace and the Scythian steppes, the interior of Asia Minor, and Upper Egypt and Ethiopia. Roman slave networks extended first into Gaul, then Germany and Britain. Slavery appeared in Scandinavia, formerly an external area to the system, when it became incorporated as a periphery of the Roman world system. Scandinavian slavers in turn sent Finnish and Russian slaves to Byzantium.

Slaves were among the earliest and most important commodities flowing through the trade network as external areas successively were drawn into the orbit of historical civilizations. Slavery was not necessarily created by the civilized traders or their tribal contacts on the growing periphery; many kinship-based societies had indigenous forms of slavery, although usually not in the form of a chattel slave market (Patterson 1982). Expansion of the slave market was not without geopolitical cost for the core. The growth of market structures increased political and military organization on the periphery and probably also stimulated population growth, thus bringing on the barbarian threats that eventually turned the military balance against civilization.

If the slave market is the dynamic sector, we should expect it to produce innovations, and it did. Classical antiquity is regarded as a period of technological stagnation, which is often attributed to the disincentives created by slavery. But if we see the military as the productive sector, it makes sense that here is the area in which technological innovation did occur. There was a long series of innovations in military hardware: bronze and then iron weapons and armor; the engineering of fortifications and siege engines; in naval warfare, a full-scale arms race eventuated in development of multitiered galleys mounted with catapult artillery (Foley and Soedel 1981; Adcock 1957: 58–61). These were implements of destruction, but they must have stimulated production by armorers, shipbuilders, and the construction industry. The legionary economy of the Romans spilled over into the civilian sector in the form of road-building and city-founding (Mann 1986: 272–80).

The slave-producing sector was most important as the driver of growth in Roman society. Market growth occurs both laterally, as we have seen, expanding the geographical scope of markets, and qualitatively, as more kinds of activities and goods are brought into market transactions. The slave market shows a strong pattern of pyramiding superordinate upon subordinate markets, a pattern that I have hypothesized occurs in markets generally. Slaves are first of all commodities, but they are also easily mobile and capable of stimulating other economic activities. Slaves were used in agriculture, especially for market production; in mining, large-scale fishing, and forestry; in crafts, especially in their proto-industrial concentrations; and in transport and commerce. As the slave economy spread in Greece and most prounouncedly in Rome, virtually all economic activity became dominated by slaves and ex-slaves (Runciman 1983).[7] Slaves also made up the bulk of the administrative personnel of Rome, at least until A.D. 200. The only important activities not dominated by slaves were military service (which was in the dynamic market sector) and subsistence farming, which was not. Slaves were never the majority of the labor force, comprising even in Roman Italy at its height (the first century B.C.) no more than 30–40 percent of the total population and elsewhere a lesser proportion (Mann 1986: 260). But structurally, slavery was the sector that made the difference.

All of the foregoing areas of production were subordinate markets for which the slave market was superordinate. Hence one might speak of sub-pyramiding markets throughout ancient society as slavery expanded. Superordinate markets also appeared above the level of the slave market. A superordinate market is an investment in long-distance and future activities, a purchase of media of exchange that can eventually be cashed in. This superordinate market emerged first in Roman politics. If the army was the instrument of production, entrepreneurship took the form of investment in military expenditures. After the citizen armies of the Punic wars brought in the first great wealth of slaves, generals and politicians increasingly became investors. Troops were privately paid, with the general recouping his costs from the spoils of victory. Julius Caesar, himself a successful military entrepreneur, was financially backed for large-scale campaigns by wealthy investors (Runciman 1983: 170–71).

In the great expansive period of Roman military power and of the slave economy (notably from 130 B.C. down to the end of the republic), investment in military expeditions was financed by a particular class. Weber commented: "in all antiquity there was but one capitalistic class whose rationalism might be compared with that of modern capitalism, namely the Roman knighthood. . . . The capitalism of this class was entirely relative to state and governmental opportunities, to the leasing of the *ager publicus* or conquered land, and of domain land, or to tax farming and the financing of political adventures and of wars" (Weber 1961: 247).[8] Military campaigns, such as Caesar's in Gaul, may be regarded as the flow of labor and capital to areas of greatest return. In the earlier period of heightened competition among Mediterranean city-states (Greek, Italian, and Phoenician) and subsequently among the Hellenistic empires, mercenaries moved in response to anticipated payoffs, which in turn depended upon booty, mainly slaves.

The military-driven slave market, together with the ancillary inputs of slaves from the entrepreneurs on the periphery drawn into this market, was the main dynamic for the commercialization and commodification of ancient society. To be sure, large sectors of the ancient economy were not commodified. Given the low efficiency of overland transport, the market layer existed primarily as a strip along the coasts and navigable rivers.[9] But in its monetized sector, Rome became perhaps the most commodified society in world history. An unprecedented range of things came to be for sale (Runciman 1983: 157–64): human beings, in the form of slaves; sex, as open prostitution; votes, less legitimately but very widely; even a recognized fee for applause for speeches in the law courts. The Roman state itself, like the army, until the Diocletian bureaucratic reforms after A.D. 285, was largely a set of profit-making enterprises. Government contracts were let for tax collection and army provisioning; licenses were sold for exploitation of forests, mines, and fisheries and for disposal of public lands and war booty. These superordinate markets gave rise to still further pyramiding by private *societates* subtending these contracts. Among the urban poor, tickets of entitlement to the imperial corn dole became heritable and salable. This omnicommodification of the core of Roman society, I contend, was the result of the slave market. Slavery was the cutting edge of the penetration of a money economy. Its spread into subordinate (slave-worked) and superordinate (politically speculative) markets constituted the dynamic of economic growth. Morally, slavery broke symbolic barriers: if people could be bought and sold, so could everything else.

THE CRISIS OF THE SLAVE ECONOMY

The successive changes and crises of ancient society were transformations brought about by the military/slave market. The producers in this system, the soldiers, became alienated labor. The original democracy of the city-states had developed when free peasants found the economic means to arm themselves and participate in collective organization of phalanx-like formations or war galleys (Weber 1961: 237, 240; Bryant 1990). In the Roman republic, the soldiers were eventually alienated from the means of production—in this case, the material means of violence—insofar as they no longer supplied and owned their weapons. Marius's reforms of 108 B.C., which included the recruitment of an army of propertyless proletarians equipped by the general and paid in wages, set the pattern for military entrepreneurs whose civil wars eventually brought down the republic. At the same time, the disappearance of the self-equipped, economically independent soldier undermined the basis of popular citizenship. Another alienation came in parallel. Roman soldiers, conscripted from rural smallholders, often lost their land while absent for long periods of war; this brought about the huge transformation of Roman society from 300 to 100 B.C. (Ste. Croix 1983: 106). These displaced smallholders had no alternative but to become full-time professional soldiers or urban proletariats living on patronage. Moreover, the earlier soldier-landholders were displaced by agricultural slaves working land that had fallen into the hands of the entrepreneurial class who also financed the wars. This transformation has all the earmarks of Marxian alienation: the (military) producing class was subjugated by the products of their own labor (the slaves), now circulating in a commodified system of exchange.[10]

The height of the slave economy was the late republic and early empire, after which the market for slaves dried up. The slave economy coincides with the great expansion of trade, coinage, and other indicators of economic growth after 200 B.C. It leveled off during the first century B.C. and underwent economic contraction after A.D. 200 (Hopkins 1980). The stabilization, or at least the end of *intensive* growth in the early empire, coincided with the end of the military slave-production dynamic. At that time, Rome was already undergoing the structural change that constituted the downfall of its mode of production. In this perspective, the "fall of the Roman Empire" in the conventional military-political sense was not itself the structural revolution. The property and market system had already destructed from its own contradictions, and the military collapse was merely an aftershock in the realm of the superstructure.

Max Weber ([1909] 1976) made the classical form of the argument, and the main points were taken up by Perry Anderson (1974a): as military conquests ceased, the supply of slaves dried up, and with them the economic system based on slavery. Weber (and Anderson) still view the slaves as producers, however, especially in agricultural labor. Hence when the slave supply ceased, agricultural slaves were reorganized into families and eventually into a dependent peasantry.[11] In my reformulation of the slave-economy model, military production of slaves is the fulcrum of investment and commodification and the host of superordinate and subordinate markets. Thus the decline in slave production and exchange resulted in the collapse of the central form of exchange relations. The economy limped along for a while, centered on government extraction of taxes from the richer provinces, to pay for the armies stationed on the frontiers (Hopkins 1977). But this was a circulation without an expansionary dynamism, leaving the system passive as production subsided to the level of local subsistence.

The Weberian model makes geopolitics the ultimate cause of change. The reason the system collapses is theoretically external to the exchange system, although predictable from geopolitical considerations. State expansion always comes up against limits.[12] In my expanded model of military/slave production, increasing geopolitical difficulties are created by the dynamic of the market itself. As we have seen, the expansion of core slave markets turns the "barbarian" external area into a periphery. Here appear native slave traders, military contractors, markets for mercenaries, in short the commodification and political organization of those societies. Such newly incorporated areas of the "world system" turn to exploiting market relations (especially slave markets) with even more remote areas. The area of geopolitical organization expands outward, upgrading external areas into peripheries. In this manner political, economic, and military organization spread to Scandinavia, eastern Europe, and central Asia. The effects of this diffusion, probably including demographic stimulation, were found in the colliding bumper cars of wars and migrations, the *Völkerwanderung* that eventually brought aggressive incursions into the Roman Empire itself. The military/market process created semiperipheral powers (in Wallerstein's sense) out of former peripheries and shifted the geopolitical balance of resources in the ancient world system.

There was a simultaneous transformation of the military/market system at the frontier, outside it, and inside it. Beyond the *limes*, Germans were organizing into pro- and anti-Roman factions, according to their exchange links as mercenaries, slave traders, and allies (Borkenau 1981: 131–288). The border troops themselves had come to consist largely of Germans (a phenomenon not paralleled in the eastern Mediterranean, where the slave market had not displaced the peasantry to the same degree). Those German/Roman legions should be regarded as the mediating portion of the links with the outer mercenary/slave markets, reminding us that geopolitical "borders" are a broad zone of exchanges rather than a sharp ceremonial or legal line.

The invasion of the Germans and the collapsing loyalty of the Roman army were parts of the same process. They represented the revolt of alienated military laborers taking their revenge at last upon the system that subordinated them. More accurately, the Germans were the structural inheritors of the long-since alienated military labor of the Mediterranean, who had now largely become servile proletarians and quasi-serfs. The Roman system of production had become a temptingly soft target for invaders because the entire military-based economy had fallen. It no longer provided incentives for adhering to old structures.

This revolt of "military workers" is equivalent to Marx and Engels's projected revolt of factory workers under the final crisis of industrial capitalism. But although the Roman Empire could be conquered, it could not be taken over structurally except by invaders who fit into its current form as a collapsed market system. Thus although the German conquests of the western Roman Empire brought a renewal of the supply of slaves from A.D. 400 to 600, there was no revival of the slave-market dynamic (Wickham 1984: 31). The slaves were quickly settled on the land as peasant rent- or tax-payers, not resold or circulated in subordinate markets. The structural transformation had already taken place, and a new form of agrarian-coercive relations came to dominate.

ISLAMIC SLAVE-SOLDIER MARKETS

The military slave-production dynamic is a Western pattern, in which must be included not only the European states of the Mediterranean but the Islamic states as well. In Asia, slave markets played no such significant role. In China, India, and elsewhere, for the most part slavery was of relatively small scale, and large-scale chattel slavery linked to military expansion never took hold. This particular market dynamism was absent in the East.

The Islamic military/slave system differed from the Roman in that it bypassed the step of investing slaves in the economy. Slaves were used above all in the military itself and as government administrators. Agriculture remained in peasant rent/tax forms, and crafts and commerce were in the hands of the free classes.[13] Slave armies began after 800 in the disintegrating Abbasid caliphate as princes attempted to avoid losing military power to feudal clients (Crone 1980; Pipes 1981). The pattern expanded in the Ayyubid regimes of Egypt and Syria, as princes vied for power by using slave soldiers who were loyal to them personally (Garcin 1988: 116–20). A revolt of the Mamluk slave-soldiers brought them into power in Egypt during the period 1250–1500. Now former slaves recruited additional slaves, since children of these now dominant soldiers were no longer part of the slave class and were excluded from the system. Successive sultans purchased new slaves to man their personal armies. The development of slave-soldier markets was based on internal conflicts promoted by central power holders struggling against feudal decentralization within the military class.

Unlike the Roman army, the Egyptian army was not in the business of capturing slaves. Slaves were purchased on international markets, since it was desirable that slave-soldiers should come from distant cultures so that they would have no local ties. The Mongols' conquests in the 1200s made large numbers of slaves available, and Christian slave traders, especially Genoese merchants, were instrumental in keeping Islamic slave armies supplied. The market for slave-soldiers gave a strong impetus to the spread of world markets and helped focus the states of the Islamic Mediterranean on international trade described by Abu-Lughod (1989). In order to pay for slave imports, the Egyptian and Syrian military lords became capitalists. State-owned land was assigned to officials for tax farming in order to equip troops. Corvée labor on this land was turned to commercial crops and manufacturing, including textiles, paper, and sugar refining (ibid.: 216–35). The slave market stimulated many other areas of market production and led to the development of credit instruments, accounting, and banking. Successive layers of superordinate markets included the reselling of credits (Goitein 1967; Udovitch 1970). Once again we see a market dynamism that did not depend upon a powerful bourgeoisie: state officials spearheaded market growth and acted both as the major producers and as the biggest customers.

The downfall of Islamic slave-soldier markets brought a decline in market relations throughout the eastern Mediterranean. A slave market depends on military conditions and is vulnerable to geopolitical limits. The Middle East developed its slave economy in part because of its middleman position in world trade patterns, in part because of its access to reservoirs of slave manpower from the nomadic and tribal regions that surrounded it. This same geography put it militarily on the defensive against incursions from all directions. The use of slave armies for internal power struggles added further burdens. The ratio of military to population size in Egypt was two to three times higher than in contemporary France (Garcin 1988: 124–25). When its resource base was undercut by recurrent plagues after 1350, which were themselves a result of closure of world trading networks (McNeill 1976), the system could no longer be sustained. The core of the economy appears to have been caught between increasingly costly slave imports and lower production of export goods with which to pay for them. We should not regard this as an accidental result. A market that depends on geopolitics reaches inevitable reversals as the costs of military power become overextended in relation to the resistance encountered. Who lives by geopolitics dies by geopolitics.

The far-flung slave markets of Western societies may be regarded as the first structural tendency toward capitalism, permeating Roman and then Islamic societies, giving impetus everywhere to widening market structures. Within the military/slave mode, market structures reached their limits and fell back but left a residue of market institutions that could be fateful later on. Not least important was the geographical extension of economic and political structures to the peripheries of the Mediterranean. The slave trade together with the market for mercenary soldiers shaped the rise of German and later of Scandinavian states to the north of the Roman Empire, while in the Islamic orbit the same process was repeated with the rise of coastal slave-trading states in Africa between 1700 and 1850 (Wallerstein 1989: 143–47, 164–66). It is not surprising that, with the upsurge of the modern capitalist world economy, slave-market structures played at least an initial part in its expansion.

Agrarian-Coercive Exchange

I call the generic type of society based on agricultural production and a militarized state "agrarian–coercive exchange." Following Wickham (1984), we can say it has two main subtypes, *rent coercion* and *tax coercion*. In both, the main form of property is land and attached labor. Whether the laborer is a free peasant or a serf, it is the coercive power of landowners that extracts produce. This coerced produce, or its monetary equivalent, circulates in exchange systems of varying compass, some quite localized, others traveling considerable distances. In a system of rent coercion, landlords with their own military means directly appropriate surplus produce and labor services; in a system of tax coercion, agents of a distant state monopolize the means of violence. As Wickham has emphasized, much of the politics of agrarian-coercive societies centers on the conflict between landlords and state officials (sometimes between these different activities of the same individuals).

The agrarian-coercive relation does not fill its contemporary universe. Typically there is also a sector of independent agricultural producers who may be subsistence farmers or petty producers for local markets. This simple commodity mode of production and its direct local exchange is also the most typical form of handicrafts production in agrarian societies. The agrarian-coercive structure has room to expand into the sector of subsistence or the market of petty direct producers, as well as into the external area still organized by kinship exchange (or sometimes by slave markets). Thus in archaic Greece there was a large sector of independent small farmers that was undermined by debts and gradually taken over by a coercive mode of production. In this case, the variant comprising debt-slavery is close to the agrarian-coercive mode rather than what I called the military/slave market; Greek debt-slaves were tied to their land and did not move in a chattel market. We have seen how the corresponding small-farmer class in Rome after the Punic wars was turned into a military proletariat in the expanding slave-market dynamic.

Within agrarian-coercive exchange, it is the rent-coercive form that is expansionary, while tax coercion tends to stifle market dynamics. I will qualify the latter statement shortly, but let us note for the present that rent coercion is the more decentralized form. A landed military class extracts production most immediately for investment in armaments and soldiers. Because their power is local but military conflicts are far-flung, such aristocrats cannot usually commandeer sufficient instruments of force but must buy them on the market. And because multisided military competition is a competition for allies, ambitious lords must continuously compete to impress one another to maintain their status. Decentralized rent-coercion structures, however primitive, involve a good deal of exchange of display goods, ranging from ceremonial gift networks or potlatches of barbarian chiefs to elaborate displays of the lifestyle, hospitality, and culture of the courtly aristocracy. The resulting inflation of both military and display goods drives up the costs of rent coercion and causes market expansion.

Among the superordinate markets that are built up during this process are religious organizations. The material expansion of churches in agrarian-coercive societies depends initially on aristocratic patronage. Here again there is a direct investment in the means of emotional production to promote status display in the supernatural dimension and thereby expand their social alliances. Once established, monasteries, temples, and churches become economic and political units in their own right and play into the expanding market on the material plane as well as the cultural. They add to the decentralized competition among organizations and fuel economic expansion.

This impetus toward market dynamics comes primarily from the decentralized, rent-coercion forms. Against this, the centralized state usually attempts to impose tax coercion directly upon the agricultural producers. To the extent that the state is powerful, it overcomes decentralization and may eliminate the market or bring it to a standstill. Nevertheless, the king or emperor is at times relatively weak, sometimes only a nominal first among equals. When this is the case, the ruler may fuel market competition in much the same way as any other grand aristocrat, investing coerced produce in market transactions to purchase military force and status display, both secular and religious.[14] Thus monasteries were often founded as agents of weakly organized states, receiving land as a means of administering conquered territories without relying on help from feudal lords. Sometimes monasteries were also used as sources of military manpower, especially in early medieval Germany and eastern Europe, as well as in Tibet and Japan. Via this route as well, monasteries can come loose from secular control and become independent actors in the market economy.

THE EXPANSION OF AGRARIAN-COERCIVE MARKETS

The decentralized rent-coercion form has an expansionary dynamic. Perry Anderson (1974a) describes one version of this in his "feudal dynamic" of landed property, which he finds distinctive to Europe. To this I would add the powerful agent of economic transformation that I call "corporate religious capitalism," which played a crucial role in Europe, China, and Japan. Both of these variants of agrarian-coercive economies fit the overall pattern of market dynamics postulated at the beginning of this chapter: a distinctive form of property (in these cases, landed estates structured by military rent coercion and its corporate religious property variant); stratified market participation; lateral expansion and qualitative growth; superordinate markets rising upon the media of exchange; and ultimately long-term crisis. The crisis and downfall of these agrarian-coercive property forms occurs against the background of the rival form, tax coercion by the centralized state. The tax-coercive state may successfully destroy feudal rent coercion and confiscate the monastic economy (both of which happened in China and in Europe). In other instances, the decentralized agrarian property forms may never have been free to develop in the first place.[15] Where the market dynamics of feudal rent coercion and the monastic corporations went the furthest before a crisis occurred, the state prevailed in a form that itself became subject to the market dynamics of modern capitalism.

In Anderson's argument, the expansion of agrarian-coercive relations is driven by the struggle over rent between lords and peasants (1974a: 182–209). The former (which includes the church as rural landlord, as well as whatever central government may exist), press surplus extraction upward. Peasants respond at first by increasing production. This leads to a general round of expansion. Both lords and peasants expand production geographically, by migration or by local forest clearing, swamp draining, and intensified cultivation. When possible, peasants escape to the frontier, but coercive relations catch up with them when landlords expand too, sometimes as religious missionaries (as in northern Europe during the early medieval period) or as military crusaders (as in the Baltic). Both lords and peasants have incentives to promote technological innovation, thereby bringing about productive improvements ci. .u.teristic of this period. Military expansion, both overland and naval, is part of the overall dynamic, since the landlords are, so to speak, a class of direct military producers. The parts of this system interact: military competition among the lords drives up the demand for rent extraction, and this in turn sets processes in motion that result in still further competition for land and in further military confrontations.

For Anderson, the height of this "feudal" expansionary dynamic was the European High Middle Ages, around A.D. 1000–1300. The crisis point was reached after 1300. The supply of land was used up; there were no more easily accessible external territories, and internal reclamation reached its ecological limits. Because expansion had also taken the form of population growth, the crisis was also one of overpopulation. Declining levels of nutrition resulted in vulnerability to plague, itself fostered by closing the geopolitical connection with Asia. Pressure on land drove up prices, whether in kind or in money. Exchange became monetized because the lords increasingly demanded money in order to participate in the more elaborate forms of exchange that had grown up. Higher lords needed money for mercenary armies, which replaced feudal levées of retainers, and for more expensive new weapons: metal armor, heavier war horses, crossbows, and eventually firearms.

I would add that there was also more expenditure for status display. The "civilizing process" involved building more elaborate country houses and replacing crude military fortresses. Clothing, jewelry, cuisine, and works of art and culture became part of the display necessary to cut a figure as a political actor. Since society remained organized around households, political influence was measured by the number of guests, friends, and retainers one could attract to one's circle (Girouard 1978). Increased competition in peaceful politics, as well as in war, drove up aristocrats' costs. For these purposes, nobles needed liquid cash and hence commuted dues in kind and labor services. Thus resulted the monetization of the countryside.

Aristocratic pressure on peasant producers was both direct and indirect. Peasants were subjected to coercion when the lords had sufficient instruments of power, and they also became subject to market forces transmitted through commodity prices and the money supply. The 1300s and 1400s were a time of peasant revolts, which contributed to the dissolution of serfdom and reinforced the tendency set in motion by monetization. Thus the late-medieval aristocracy moved toward further capitalist enterprises, with enclosures of common land, wool production, mining, and other activities for the mass market. The aristocrats became rural capitalists, the peasants a rural proletariat.

Anderson describes his dynamic for medieval Europe, but it also seems to fit China and perhaps other societies (Eberhard 1977: 109–236; Elvin 1973: 54–90, 113–78; Gernet 1982: 129–49, 235–330). In the strong state of the Han dynasty (ca. 200 B.C.–A.D. 200) there was more government tax extraction than rent extraction by independent landlords. An approximation of the rent-coercion mode appeared with the breakdown of the Han, and subsequent strong states, notably the T'ang (ca. A.D. 600–900) struggled to reestablish an omnipresent tax-coercion mode. Across this flux of central state power, there was an increasing expenditure for military and status consumption as armies grew, innovations were made in military and transport technology, and new artistic products were produced. The pattern of geographic expansion was the same as in Europe: to escape both warfare and predatory taxation in the north, peasants colonized southern China (especially ca. A.D. 200–600); later their colonization of the northeastern frontier resulted in the agricultural settlement of Manchuria and the emergence of a state there. Landlords followed a similar peasant expansion to the south, where eventually larger commercial estates produced tea and silk for the market. Like Europe, China was gradually monetized. By the mid-Sung (1000–1200), there was a massive population, monetary inflation based on paper money, large-scale trade, and a full-fledged crisis of government finances.

RELIGIOUS CORPORATE CAPITALISM

Anderson's model focuses on the rent struggle among the classes of landlord and coerced agricultural labor. I suggest that an even more powerful dynamic was driven by a specific organization in the landlord sector, the monasteries. The Buddhist monasteries of China (especially ca. 400–900) and the Christian monasteries of Europe (above all the Cistercian order, ca. 1000–1300), were on the leading edge of economic development in their time. Both developed a form of market production and exchange involving agriculture and even industry. Based originally on the accumulation of agrarian-coercive extraction, the monasteries went on to a form of capitalism that broke through the agrarian-coercive mode. As I have argued elsewhere, these monastic sectors approximated most of Weber's characteristics of rationalized capitalism: the freeing of all factors of production to move to areas of greatest return, supported by an infrastructure of political regulation of exchange and property rights and by a universalistic and disciplined ethic. These conditions, generally lacking in the larger society, existed specifically for resources and personnel within the religious enclaves. The monasteries were centers for the accumulation of wealth; for intensification of production, including technological innovation and quasi-industrial production by mills, ironworks, and factories; for the plowing back of profits in land acquisition, loans, and trade. The spread of crusading and missionary movements, whether Christian or Buddhist, widened the geographic scope of European and Chinese civilization respectively and constituted the leading edge of economic development in the "medieval takeoff" of each (see also Collins 1986: 45–76).

The great advantage of monastic organization over the surrounding society was that it escaped the household organization of production and politics. Monks, because of their celibacy, were outside the system of family inheritance of property and status. Thus they were the first approximation of a freely recruited and mobile labor force within agrarian-coercive society (after the decline of slave markets in the West, which were inferior in motivational incentives). Monasteries acted as corporate enterprises, whose gains could only be plowed back into further production—if they were not used for ostentation or confiscated by secular powers. Buddhist and Christian monasteries moved along a similar trajectory (Southern 1970; Ch'en 1964). The earlier monasteries depended on aristocratic patronage. One might describe them as places where aristocrats invested some of their surplus extraction in religious status display, funding prayers in their own honor, ceremonies for their courts, and sinecures for their superfluous children.

As monastic wealth increased, various reform movements promoted both ideological purification and organizational autonomy from the secular aristocrats. In China the most successful movements were the missionary-oriented Amidaists and later the Ch'an (Zen) sect, which broke with the ritualistic sects of the capital cities and set up rural monasteries using manual labor from novice monks (Ch'en 1964: 350–64; McRae 1986; Dumoulin 1988: 155–265). In Europe, corresponding waves of reform (by Cistercians, Augustinians, and mendicant friars) broke with the ritualism of the earlier Benedictines. The reform monasteries drove the early phase of economic expansion. Eventually the aristocracy began to piggyback on them for purely economic purposes. In T'ang China, landlords escaped government taxation by dedicating their land to monasteries but retaining indirect control. In northern Europe, monasteries remained more independent, but fueled the expansion of the monetary sector and bulk trade that eventually came to engulf the secular economy. Thus Anderson's "feudal dynamic" and the crisis of the rent struggle may be due in considerable part to the leadership of the monastic sector.

This religious capitalism developed strong superordinate markets. One might describe the monastic sector itself as a kind of superordinate market that came loose from the aristocratic investment of agrarian-coercive extraction in religious status display. Monasteries acted as banks, stores of value, and centers of investment; they were also targets for confiscation by governments hungry for cash. The government seized the wealth of Chinese

Buddhist monasteries repeatedly, notably in the years 446, 573, 712, and 845. In Europe, the same fate befell the trade-rich Templars in France in 1307 and in England in 1312. The trajectory led up to the wholesale confiscations of the Protestant Reformation in the sixteenth century. During the height of monastic capitalism, specifically religious currencies also circulated. In China, the government taxed the monasteries by requiring monks to purchase ordination certificates. By the 1100s these certificates circulated as currency and were the subject of yet a further superordinate market in which speculation on their future value took place (Ch'en 1964: 241–44, 391–33).

In Europe, the papacy developed after 1050 as a government within the religious sector, adjudicating property claims among religious organizations and reaping monetary and political rewards for judicial services (Southern 1970). Another superordinate market emerged with the growth of universities, originally to train canon lawyers and theologians for the burgeoning papacy and local administrative centers of the church. This educational market began around 1000 and reached its height with the crisis of church politics after 1300. Educational production acquired its own dynamics as various regions competed to found their own universities and the number of students increased. The flow of educated personnel from the church into secular administration heightened the demand for educational credentials. Expanding educational production resulted in a spiral of credential inflation. The superordinate currency of university degrees became devalued after 1300 as they became widely available, and late medieval universities frequently were in financial crisis (Collins 1981a).

Another superordinate currency was created by the sale of indulgences— that is, certificates of religious merit that were redeemable in time off from Purgatory. In real life, this was equivalent to commuting into money prices the ceremonial penance that the lay devout performed to raise their social status. By the 1400s and 1500s, papal debt-financing depended heavily on selling these cultural tokens. The aggressive salesmanship of papal agents and the inflationary spiral as indulgence-selling campaigns increased were the proximate cause of the rebellion by local religious organizations that set off the Reformation (Southern 1970: 133–69). This might be regarded as the revolutionary destruction of the corporate-religious economy.[16]

THE CRISIS OF AGRARIAN-COERCIVE EXCHANGE

We have two different hypotheses to consider on the crisis of agrarian-coercive exchange. According to Perry Anderson (1974b), the feudal-rent crisis in Europe did not lead directly to capitalism, but to a transitional form: the absolutist state, which propped up the aristocracy in its struggle to maintain coercive control over the peasantry. The internal conflicts within absolutism, between government's taxation of aristocrats and aristocrats' rent extraction from subordinates, had to be resolved by revolution before capitalism could emerge. The feature of European absolutism that distinguishes it from other historical variants of the agrarian tax-coercive state is that it was already heavily permeated with market structures. The pyramiding of superordinate markets noticeable in the religious sector was also a feature of the absolutist state. An example is the sale of public offices, which kings initiated in order to raise money. The government acted as capitalist, manipulating and controlling the market for offices. As in all such structures, despite the fact that the market was highly restricted, the consequences of such sales fed back into the financial situation of the whole economy and drove up the costs of government itself. Thus the venality of office contributed to the long-term spiral of government weakness that eventually brought the downfall of the patrimonial-absolutist state (Goldstone 1991). As Wallerstein has argued, the political transformation of which the French Revolution is an exemplar came about in a society in which capitalist structures had already become dominant (1988: 57–112).

In the religious capitalism model, capitalism is present even earlier; first in the monastic sector, then permeating secular life. The revolutionary transition is the crisis of religious organization. In Europe, this was the Reformation. It not only overthrew the superstructure of religious currencies such as indulgences, but also confiscated corporate religious property and ploughed it directly into the secular economy. For China, the problem has not been much investigated in this light. But it is apparent that the expansionary phase of the Buddhist monastic economy was over by the time of the Sung dynasty. Its revolutionary downfall was a combination of property confiscations together with governmental regulation, as well the stealing of its ideological thunder by the Neo-Confucian religious movement after 1050. Here too the Buddhist equivalent of the Reformation was followed by an expansion of the secular economy. The Sung economy was at least partially permeated by capitalism, having far outgrown the monastic sector. Market growth was apparent in all directions. There was a superordinate structure of currency inflation and speculation, coupled with massive expansion of government employment and the growth of a highly competitive examination system for officeholding credentials (Chaffee 1985).

Fiscal crisis and geopolitical vulnerability in the Sung state eventually led to external conquest. But such conquest is not necessarily equivalent to structural change or downfall. Previous alien conquests repeatedly resulted in assimilation to Chinese institutions, and the Mongols were no exception. The fact is that the crisis of the medieval Chinese economy did not lead on to the modern dynamic of omni-expansive capitalism. China appears to have already outgrown the agrarian-coercive structure as the core of its economy, but was dominated by a strong state attempting to maintain traditional tax-coercive forms. In the later dynasties, especially the Ch'ing, the economy had become a market of petty commodity producers, with a thin layer of tax-collecting state bureaucracy above it. Elvin (1973) refers to this structure as a "high-level equilibrium trap." It is large-scale entrepreneurs who are absent; neither corporate monastic capitalists nor aristocrat-landlords remain to play this role, and bourgeois capitalists do not emerge in their place. This is the turning point, still poorly understood, that constituted the "fall of the East" (Abu-Lughod's phrase [1989]) in comparison to the West.

Yet in larger perspective the East did not fall. At just the time that the market dynamic in China was stagnating, Japan was going through a feudal period in which Buddhist monasteries fueled a monetized market expansion. Both state and Buddhist institutions had been imported into Japan on Chinese models, and we may regard Japan as continuing the Chinese market dynamic. The reimposition of a centralized state by the Tokugawas after 1600 crushed the independence of the monasteries. As in the Protestant Reformation in Europe, this was followed by a large-scale market expansion in the secular economy. Japanese economic development after the Meiji Restoration was not a sudden leap but the further extension of these market structures' long-term growth.

Capitalism

Capitalism has all the dynamics of markets to an especially strong degree. One could describe modern capitalism as the quantitative dominance of market dynamics such that all other structures are reduced to minor roles. The "rise of capitalism" was a long and slow process; just when it occurred is a matter of debate. Its predominance came about because a tipping point was passed. Market dynamics have always been a leading factor of social change, both in growth and in structural collapse. Historically, markets have been the leading edge of change, but large areas of society remained outside, localized and conservatively self-reproducing. Once a certain proportion of market penetration was passed, its dynamics became overwhelming. Differences in quantity turned into differences in quality.

The "takeoff" of modern capitalism is an acceleration of the curve. I have suggested that "rationalized capitalism" in Weber's sense, made an early appearance in the monastic economies of medieval China and Christendom. Abu-Lughod (1989) suggests that market dynamics also existed in the "world system" of long-distance trade in Eurasia around the twelfth and thirteenth centuries. For Wallerstein (1974), a European capitalist world system was expanding, with characteristic cyclical rhythms, by the sixteenth century. If this process seems to accelerate almost into a different dimension, most notably in England by the late eighteenth or early nineteenth century, this is because a quantitative tipping point was being passed. This need not have been, let us say, a shift beyond 50 percent penetration of large-scale markets into local markets and subsistence relations; the "point of no return" may well be on the order of 20 percent penetration. These figures are overly schematic, in that there is not merely one dimension of market penetration—as if it were only a matter of market versus nonmarket relations. Since the growth of capitalism is the pyramiding of superordinate markets, "penetration" is the degree of connection to various levels of the pyramid.

Probably there were several tipping points in Europe: in the thirteenth century, when secular capitalism outgrew monastic capitalism; in the sixteenth century, when Wallerstein's world market capitalism appeared; in the eighteenth, when the growing scale of commercial agriculture and manufacture culminated in the industrial revolution; and perhaps in the late nineteenth century, with the omnipenetration of the institutions of financial pyramiding. With the passage of each point, the curve of some aspects of market penetration turned more sharply upward. In this light, the victory of Europe over North Africa and Asia (especially China, India, and the Islamic Middle East) was not necessarily the victory of dynamism over stagnation but a reaching of higher tipping points first. China became increasingly market penetrated from the eleventh-century Sung dynasty onward, when secular capitalism outgrew monastic capitalism. But this happened at a slow pace, with a predominance of relatively localized and unpyramided markets that made it weak and even stagnant when it came into competition with the more rapidly accelerating European markets.

Capitalism is the strongest example of the proliferation of superordinate markets, and indeed of all the versions of market growth and expansion—laterally in space, in volume, and in qualitative innovation. More and more aspects of the factors of production are drawn into markets. As the complexity of manufacturing and differentiation of products grows, "side-markets" branch out around previously existing ones. Even more significant is "vertical" pyramiding of markets for the media of exchange. Banking expands into new forms of debt and investment. Stock markets pyramid transactions: futures sales, options, selling short, leveraged buyouts. In these metamarkets, profit is divorced from production. Investors with the proper strategy can make money on bull or bear markets, in times of inflation or deflation, in growing or shrinking productivity. Speculation in money markets and international rates of exchange add further layers on top of existing market layers, as does the trading of mortgages and rediscounting of notes. Stratification within the system depends upon being nearest to the center of exchange in these superordinate networks. Insurance funds and pension plans, collected at a lower level to protect individuals or firms against future contingencies, become available as blocks of funds or stocks that themselves are key resources in leveraged buyouts and in plundering the assets of previously successful enterprises. Dynamism here means both an expansion of metamarkets and never-ending struggle within the "topmost" layer.

The "monopoly" phase of capitalism is a misnomer. The era around 1890 saw a relatively simple form of financial pyramiding in the form of trusts. Because this was the first time superordinate financial markets were highly visible, Rudolf Hilferding, Lenin, and others thought their era represented "the highest form of capitalism." But this monopoly capitalism consisted only in control of particular products. More extensive superordinate markets have turned out to be possible: conglomerates can expand across product lines, and the trading of complex financial media has undermined some of the earlier, lower-level monopolies.

Capitalism is an omnimarket society. Over time, it becomes increasingly so, in apparent defiance of zero-order logic. A society that is already thoroughly penetrated by markets can add further superordinate markets through pyramiding. In effect, there is no such thing as market saturation. Omnicapitalism stays dynamic by creating new markets for superordinate goods, including both financial instruments and consumer goods impregnated with social status. The growth of the tertiary sector is like a capitalist tower of Babel, endlessly building toward the sky.

Superordinate markets for cultural products add further complexities to the media of social exchange. Once education becomes connected to opportunities for employment, whether as a state-enforced license or as an informal status emblem, credentials undergo a currency-like inflation as increasing proportions of the population compete for more schooling (Collins 1979). As the market for degrees expands, educational entrepreneurs respond both by creating more schools and by elaborating more advanced and more specialized degrees. This in turn drives up the credential requirements for professions and for bureaucratic employment. Self-reinforcing relations between the supply and the demand sides of education have intensified, especially since 1950, with no end in sight.

It is striking that in modern capitalism everything is commodified except the most central commodities of the previous systems. The elaborate exchanges of sexual property at the center of kinship-exchange systems now are taboo within our own market system. Sexual property survives only in the most truncated form, as bilateral exchanges between two individuals in a marriage (or the equivalent arrangement between unmarried parties). These sexual exchanges are now charged with purely personal emotions (i.e., the modern cult of love) and are considered illegitimate as channels for political alliances between families. Slavery too, once the central commodity of a large-scale system of exchange, is now very strongly prohibited. The same is true of the central property relation of agrarian-coercive exchange, the appropriation of the labor of dependent serfs and peasants by militarized landlords.

Also taboo are the forms of superordinate structure that were typical in agrarian-coercive politics—the venality of office, the sale of military commissions, tax farming, and the like. As if the Hegelian logic of negation applies, the main form of property in previous systems becomes negated and superseded by later forms. Market relations were excluded from the organization of the state in order to create modern bureaucratic government. Eliminating venality of office and tax farming was crucial for gaining central, uniform, and hence rational-legal control over the means of government administration. In effect, "political workers" were expropriated from the means of administration. According to Weberian theory, this helped expand the capitalist economy by creating a governmental regulatory sector for market transactions. Yet soon thereafter, markets came back into bureaucracies on a higher floor, so to speak, with the rise of a superordinate market for educational credentials.

THE FAILURE OF SOCIALIST AUTARKY

The geographic diffusion of capitalism as the omnimarket society has been its most obvious success. Around the world, regions of autarkic subsistence or of purely local markets have steadily eroded. In this respect, capitalism is a much more powerful market than its predecessors. The last pockets of tribal and peasant autarky, still very large (even numerically predominant) under previous market forms, virtually disappeared in the twentieth century. The geographic expansion of capitalism was particularly obvious in the late twentieth century, as it penetrated the communist bloc. Socialism, at least as we have seen it so far, does not appear to be a higher stage of historical development, but a resistance on the part of some relatively powerful agrarian-coercive states—Russia and China—to being pulled into world capitalist markets. State-administered communism is an extension into industrialism of the centralized tax-coercive agrarian structure that was historically antithetical to markets.

Even before the downfall of the European communist regimes in 1989–91, they were being pulled back into the capitalist system, whether explicitly or surreptitiously. Socialism in itself has no dynamic of growth; ideologically, its focus is on equitable distribution, and it lacks the self-propelling forces of expansion and innovation (including the tendency to pyramid superordinate exchanges) found in market societies. Deliberate development managed from above has no direction except insofar as it emulates the external benchmarks of capitalist innovation.

Communist societies have not been able to close their borders to the world system; military rivalry alone, on the level of hardware technology, sees to that. Cultural products too overflow borders easily, and it is by this route that the status-emulation products of Western mass markets have created demand in the East. Once started along the path of integration with Western markets, the communist states become subject to the pressures of world financial and trade structures. As of the late 1980s, market-oriented reforms within communist states were limited to allowing petty commodity production and exchange; what was lacking was the superordinate markets, especially for financial investment, that have fueled capitalist innovation in the West. By opening borders to Western business (a process rampant in China in this period), the East has attempted to reap the benefits of superordinate markets located in the West. The effect will likely be further integration into the capitalist dynamic. Political upheavals within state socialist rule only accelerate a structural shift already in motion.[17] Even those regimes (such as China's) that hold together politically must operate under conditions set by world capitalist markets.

In the medium run, socialism as we know it seems destined to disappear. Will this lead to the triumph of global capitalism? Perhaps. But let us not forget the sixth hypothesis listed at the beginning of this chapter: market systems issue in crises, reversals of growth, and eventually transformation. Kinship markets collapsed when investors in long-term marital alliances consolidated political power and shifted to the new organization of the coercive state. Military slave markets mobilized their own external opposition, which undermined them when they reached their geopolitical limits. Agrarian rent extractors were squeezed out by the rising costs of domination as markets for weapons and status goods expanded. The religious corporations built with earnings from coerced produce became autonomous sectors of protocapitalist growth but were brought down eventually through inflation of their cultural currency and were expropriated.

In each type of market system, the property form upon which it is based eventually disappears and is replaced by another form. What can this be, that transcends the omnimarket and superpyramided property forms of capitalism? It is doubtless too early to say. But it seems certain that history is far from coming to an end. If history is any precedent, the capitalism that is dominant today has plenty of upheavals in its future.

CHAPTER 7

An Asian Route to Capitalism

THERE HAVE BEEN three main types of economic structures in world history: (1) kinship-organized networks lacking a separate state organization and in which economic exchange is shaped by marital alliances and ceremonial gift exchange; (2) agrarian-coercive societies in which a specialized military class appropriates the land and coercively extracts most of the surplus produce; and (3) capitalist market economies with their dynamic of self-transforming growth.[1] Market relations alone are not enough to create major economic change. Markets may exist in other types of societies but remain ancillary and subordinate to the traditional economic structure. What such societies lack is the sustained innovativeness of modern self-transforming capitalism, which expands into mass markets and proliferates market niches and new products.

Historically, self-transforming capitalism (type 3) has gone through three key phases:

3a. a small leading sector within agrarian-coercive societies set the innovative dynamic in motion;

3b. the spread of capitalist market structures dynamicized by agricultural production; and

3c. the industrial revolution of machine production harnessed to inanimate energy sources set off the expansion of nonagricultural production.

Our task is to explain how at least some world regions first passed from type 2 to 3a, and thence to 3b and then 3c. The industrial revolution (3c) could only have occurred upon the basis of 3b, a preexisting agricultural market capitalism (Moore 1966; Wallerstein 1974). Large-scale industrial technology is economically useless if it does not occur within the context of institutions supporting a mass market and the mass provision of the factors of production. Technological innovation, the creation of machines as well as other new techniques of production and distribution, is not the key but only the most visible form of this structural dynamism of capitalism. The most important transformation, the topic of this chapter, is two steps further back: the breakout from an agrarian-coercive structure in a leading sector (3a) that introduces the structures of self-sustaining growth.

Such a leading sector is potentially revolutionary because it is antithetical to the structural conservatism of agrarian-coercive organization. That is not to say that agrarian-coercive societies are stagnant in every respect. Such societies can undergo geopolitical expansion and contraction, population growth and decline, geographical migration and concentration. Long-distance trade routes may develop or atrophy and may even constitute what are sometimes called world-systems (Gills and Frank 1991; Abu-Lughod 1989). The key question is whether such changes merely add quantitative variations within the agrarian-coercive social structure of economic relations. As long as the dominant structure is a military governing class coercing production for its own consumption, wealth concentrates in the palaces and monuments of the capital cities and does not circulate back through investment in a sector where capitalist innovation becomes sustained.

The transition from type 2 to 3a and thence to 3b took place in a leading sector composed of the material economy of religious institutions inside agrarian-coercive society. In this chapter I argue that this occurred in medieval and early modern Japan through Buddhist institutions, paralleling the early economic development of Europe under Christian auspices. The view that Asian capitalism is an adaptation of a Western transplant has recently been challenged by a number of rival interpretations. One argument, focusing on Asian economic growth in the late twentieth century, holds that capitalism is compatible with many aspects of long-standing Asian culture and social structure, even if the capitalist takeoff was not initiated in Asia. A stronger claim is that in Japan, the cultural, economic, and social structures of the Tokugawa period significantly prepared the way for industrial capitalism. Stronger yet are arguments that Japan independently developed capitalism before the European incursion. These revisionist arguments are weakened, however, by their failure to examine ostensible historical causes against a full-scale theoretical model of the transition to capitalism. Particular items of culture such as Confucian values (suggested in McCormack and Sugimoto 1984 and Rozman 1991) or a religious work ethic (Bellah 1957) are not in themselves sufficient to carry through a breakout from agrarian-coercive structures; nor is the existence of merchants or trade (stressed by Sanderson 1994; Hamashita 1994; Kawakatsu 1994; and Howe 1996). Only in the context of a general model of the institutional components of capitalist growth, and of the obstacles to these institutions in agrarian-coercive societies, can we assess whether the conditions for the independent development of capitalism existed in Japan or anywhere else.

We begin, then, with a general institutional model of capitalist development. A previous application of this model showed how the Christian monastic economy during the High Middle Ages (1050–1300) initiated the earliest phase (3a) of capitalist transformation in Europe. The Protestant Reformation of the 1500s and the accompanying confiscation of church property marked the full breakout to the secular economy, the second phase (3b) of structural growth (Collins 1986: chap. 3). Here I will develop the argument in regard to the economic effects of the main popular religion of East Asia, the Buddhism of medieval China and Japan.

The Structural Components of Self-Transforming Capitalism

What conditions make it possible for capitalism to break out of an agrarian-coercive system? The fullest picture of the institutional requirements and their corresponding obstacles in traditional structures remains that provided by Max Weber. Here we must refer not merely to Weber's work on the Protestant ethic, or even to his comparative studies of the economic propensities of the world religions, but to his full institutional model. Weber provided the most comprehensive overview in his lectures, which were compiled as *General Economic History* (Weber 1961); I draw here on the formal model given in Collins 1986. In light of the historical phases of capitalist growth listed above, Weber's theory leaves a good deal unfinished. It does not solve the question of how either capitalist agriculture (3b) or industrial revolution (3c) came about. I suggest that Weber provides the best analytical model for 3a: the obstacles that a leading sector faced in breaking out from agrarian-coercive structures and the social institutions that had to be constructed to overcome those obstacles.

The following scheme, modified from Weber and Schumpeter, gives three sets of conditions, each with its subcomponents (see Figure 11). One or another condition in isolation is insufficient to undermine agrarian-coercive structures; assembling all the ingredients into a package is what results in the takeoff of self-sustaining capitalist growth.

First, there must exist markets for all the factors of production: land, labor, and capital. It is not enough that markets exist for commodities, whether luxury goods or even bulk trade in the staples of life. As long as land itself is not for sale but is controlled by military coercion or political allocation, as long as labor does not move according to market incentives but remains tied to a physical or social location, and as long as capital, in the form

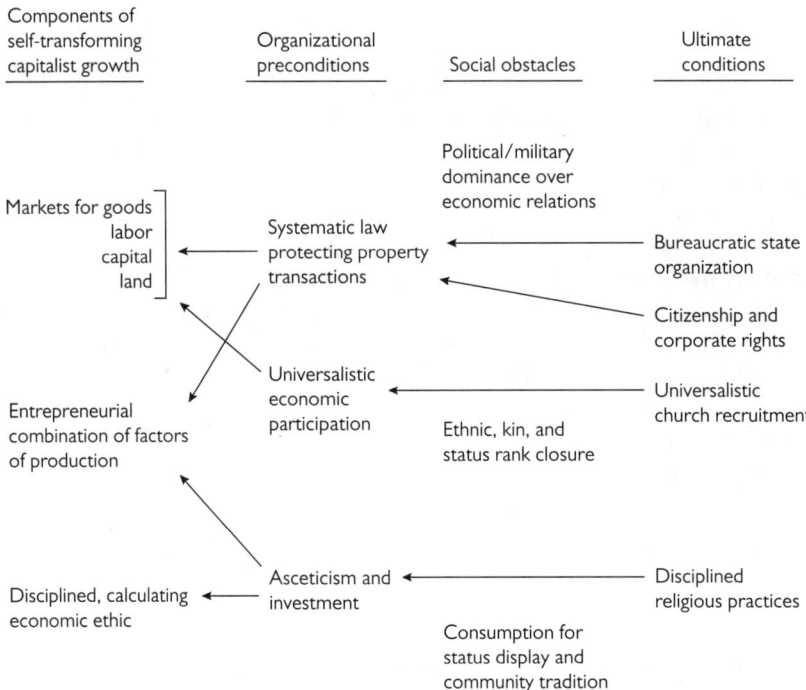

FIGURE 11. Chain of causal conditions for self-transforming capitalist growth.

of both financial instruments and material implements of production, is not readily bought and sold, the factors of production do not move flexibly and rapidly to the areas of greatest return. Neither will there be a competitive process replacing inefficient industries with more productive ones. The existence of commodity trade alone does not guarantee the existence of a competitive capitalist market penetrating and transforming all sectors of society. Modern capitalism is explosive. It tends to dominate the polity and forces all other institutional sectors to accommodate themselves to it. It is this character that is lacking in the commodity markets of agrarian-coercive economies.

The second major condition necessary for capitalist growth is that control of all the factors of production must be combined in the hands of entrepreneurs. Enterprises must exist as organizations that acquire land, capital, and labor according to the needs of production for the market. It is this entrepreneurial organization, as Weber stressed, that makes possible the calculation of opportunities for profit and hence for the directed flow of investment. Connected with this are the characteristics Schumpeter (1961) made central to his definition of capitalism: capitalism as enterprise carried out with borrowed money; capitalism as a market system in which banks act as the headquarters, deciding among rival claims for capital investment according to competitive bids for potential profit. Banks in this sense may emerge only gradually, and banking itself may begin as a side activity of entrepreneurs in trade or in agricultural or finished goods production. The key is that the flow of investment capital should develop in conjunction with enterprises.

As Schumpeter stressed, entrepreneurs make new combinations out of available inputs of labor, land, and capital. In markets for well-established products, competition drives down profits; hence the greatest profitability comes in creating new products, and moving into new market niches. This entrepreneur-driven model has been extended further by the network theory of capitalist markets, which says that mutually monitoring networks of producers seek profitability by creating noncompetitive market niches through innovation and product differention (White 1981). It is this entrepreneurial competition that makes capitalism repeatedly self-transformative. The search for profits under the pressures of competition in all of the factor markets (including the pressures of financial marketplaces) leads to the proliferation of market niches, which contrasts with the relatively static range of products in the controlled markets of agrarian-coercive economies.

A third factor to which Weber gave special prominence is an economic ethic of disciplined work and calculation of productive gains. Ideally this attitude is shared by both laborers and entrepreneurs. An economic ethic involves not only the motivation for hard work, but a self-controlled orientation toward long-term gains. It means both forgoing immediate consumption and restraining greed for rapid gains through sharp practices in favor of regularly accumulating small gains in repeated, reliable business dealings. The Weberian economic ethic is a combination of self-discipline, ethical self-restraint, and calculation of long-run productivity.

SOCIAL OBSTACLES TO CAPITALISM

Historically, there have been obstacles to all of these capitalist institutions. Most factors of production have not moved on markets, and all have been subject to military predators, arbitrary restriction and confiscation by state elites, and the dominance of political structures over economic ones. In most societies there were barriers to full participation by all sectors of the population in the market economy. Certain occupations, such as merchant, might be confined to particular ethnic groups who were treated as outsiders by the host community, while prohibited to the members of the dominant ethnicity. Particular ethnic groups might be allowed to practice certain occupations but be denied other opportunities. The typical form of organization was the patrimonial household based on the kin group, which was surrounded, according to its social rank, by servants and armed guards. This structure limited the market participation of most persons inside the household production and consumption unit. The hierarchy of social status, anchored in the power of military aristocrats and sometimes religious ritualists, formed closed strata of hereditary status groups for whom only certain occupations were honorable.

This is not to say that individuals and families were necessarily immobile. Some aristocrats were killed or their families died out; others fought their way into power. But this process of replacement did not so much undermine hierarchical divisions as reinforce them, above all as a source of social motivation. Merchants were a subordinate group in agrarian-coercive hierarchies, typically dishonored and kept under tight controls. Where possible, successful merchants attempted to convert their wealth into land and officeholding, thereby becoming members of the aristocracy, rather than reinvesting it in innovative production. Lacking such safeguards, whenever merchants' wealth grew large it was threatened with confiscation or its equivalent through forced loans. Under most circumstances, merchants did not revolutionize production within agrarian-coercive structures because their trade reinforced the existing pattern of coercive hierarchy and its preference for traditional social and economic relations.[2] Thus, even highly developed trade relations in some early periods (stressed by Abu Lughod 1989, Chaudhuri 1990, and Gills and Frank 1991), in the absence of the social structures of dynamic capitalism did not imply that a self-sustaining economic transformation was under way.

Entrepreneurial organization, like market relations, was generally inhibited in agrarian-coercive societies by the lack of property institutions to protect market transactions and legal mechanisms for adjudicating contracts and assessing damages. To the contrary, law tended to reinforce the rights and exclusions of a hierarchy. The ruler might claim ownership of all land or distribute it on political conditions to military retainers or tax farmers. Where aristocrats held legal ownership of land, they typically monopolized the right for their status group. Peasants were involved in a variety of land-tenure systems, but even those providing nominal ownership rarely allowed freedom to transfer property on an open market. Control over the factors of land, labor, and capital was structurally dispersed rather than concentrated in entrepreneurial hands.

Finally, the disciplined economic ethic was antithetical to the typical form of status culture in aristocratic-hierarchic societies. An emphasis on consumption as a form of status display and as a means of enhancing one's rank inhibited the asceticism and investment habits of the wealthier classes, while the traditional rituals structuring the seasonal rounds of the year regulated both work and consumption for the laboring classes.[3]

How then were these obstacles overcome? Weber sketched a combination of political and religious causes flowing into the institutional structures of capitalism, represented in the middle and right-hand side of Figure 11.

1. The development of systematic law protecting property and facilitating transactions. Further back in the chain of causes, systematic law arises in connection with the bureaucratization of the state, the replacement of arbitrary personal authority with an administrative structure of written rules. Thus some degree of bureaucracy is a precondition for capitalism. But a counterbalancing factor is necessary, since bureaucracy if left to itself in the context of an economy of coercive extraction generally wields its formal regulations not to protect capitalist property relations but to suppress them, as was the bias of the Confucian bureaucracy in China. For this reason Weber added that citizenship rights must emerge among those classes with the greatest interest in capitalism. It is the combination of citizenship and bureaucracy, and the balance between them, that mitigates the extremes of each one and makes possible a legal system favorable to expansion of the capitalist market and entrepreneurship.

2. Weber stressed the role of universalistic religion of salvation, above all Christianity, which broke through the barriers of ethnicity and kin group. This had the unintended effect of opening up the realm of economic relationships to a unitary ethical standard and paved the way for universal participation in capitalist markets for the factors of production.

3. Weber also theorized that religion is a source of the economic ethic of ascetic self-restraint and calculative rationality directed toward economic productivity. Weber's most famous argument here concerned the Calvinist doctrine of predestination and the psychological tensions it produced. In the historical background is the longer sequence through ancient Judaism and Christianity. In world perspective, Weber stressed the economic importance of a religion oriented toward salvation rather than magical manipulation for immediate material ends or ceremony and ritual, which reinforce rather than break through traditional practices and social strata. Among salvation religions, Weber emphasized the importance of the variant that ties religious standing to ascetic, ethical activity in the world rather than mystical accommodation or transcendence.

REINTERPRETING THE WEBERIAN MODEL
AS AN ECONOMY OF RELIGIOUS ORGANIZATIONS

The Weberian model was a pioneering effort in comparative analysis of world economic and social change. Only partially finished at Weber's death, it sketches the broad range of institutional components that undergirded the breakthrough into capitalist growth. Here I will broaden and reinterpret the argument in several respects. Contrary to what Weber himself argued, we should not assume that the breakthrough was made only in Europe. I will downplay Weber's emphasis on the content of Protestant doctrine because religiously based economic breakthroughs have occurred in conjunction with other doctrinal beliefs: in the Catholic doctrines held by activist monastic movements in the European Middle Ages, and in the Buddhist doctrines of both monastic and popular salvation movements in medieval China and Japan. To abstract and generalize from Weber's point, not only Christianity but all the great world religions break down social barriers and enforce ethical universalism. From a sociological viewpoint, how does this universalism arise? Doctrine is never free-floating but is always embedded in social practices. The universalism of a religion is manifested in practice by its proselytization of everyone: what makes Christianity, Islam, and Buddhism "world religions" is that they recruit potentially the whole world. In an agrarian-coercive society a universalistic religion is the one institution that recruits its members—priests, monks, and devout laity—from all social strata. Furthermore, if the religion is staffed by celibate priests and monks, its positions must be nonhereditary. Its organization does not structurally reinforce the family inheritance of position that is predominant elsewhere in society but introduces a practice of individual religious achievement. In Buddhism as in Christianity, mass proselytization spreads these ethical and motivational structures widely and thus religious movements become vehicles for social transformation.

It is necessary also to revise Weber's position on the significance of monastic religion. From Weber's viewpoint, monasticism siphons off religious motivation. It creates ascetic discipline but turns it to otherworldly ends, preventing an orientation toward transforming the ordinary world and leaving the nonmonastic laity with a religion of ritualistic accommodation to circumstances. In dramatizing the significance of the Protestant Reformation, Weber depicted medieval Catholicism and the monastic religions of Asia as foils, thus obscuring their significance in initiating the earlier breakthrough to economic dynamism within agrarian-coercive societies. Monasticism could play the role of leading sector because it comprised a substantial material sector of the agrarian economy in its own right. Religion initially contributed to capitalism not primarily by inspiring the beliefs and motivations of lay people, but by expanding the religious organization materially. Monasteries, temples, and churches at first formed their own market and property relations, accumulated wealth, and pioneered new economic structures. This made up a substantial sector in medieval economies where religious organizations at times held as much as one-third of the cultivated land and perhaps even more of the portable wealth. Within its own sector, religious organizations broke through the obstacles to economic growth within traditional societies as well: in Schumpeter's terms, monasteries were the first entrepreneurs.

All the institutional paths in Figure 11 were formed initially not in the agrarian-coercive society at large but within the enclave of the religious economy. Catholic Christianity had its disciplined economic ethic based on the ascetic and routinized life of the monks. Weber and others noted the irony that the ascetic Protestant, prohibited by religious scruples from freely spending the rewards of his disciplined labor, ended up growing rich. The process is even more evident in the case of the monasteries, where the fruits of religious discipline became material capital for investment. Since celibate monks could not siphon this off into family consumption, it was the monastic corporation that grew rich.[4]

In the sequence of events leading to breakthrough from agrarian-coercive structures, monastic capitalism was the leading sector (3a). The spillover into a secular economy (3b) occurred first through the spread of proselytizing movements that began in the monastic orders. In Europe, China, and Japan, there were periods of burgeoning movements to found new monasteries, typically by reforming orders tightening monastic discipline (Cistercians in Europe, Ch'an in China, Zen in Japan). As they flourished, the monastic economy expanded geographically while amassing wealth. Organizational growth was accompanied or followed by proselytyzing movements of monastic preachers among the common people (e.g., Augustinian, Franciscan, and Dominican friars; the Pure Land movements in Chinese and Japanese Buddhism). The result was to create hybrid forms of quasi-ascetic lay religiosity. On the material side, these movements also spread market relations and disciplined economic practices in lay society. Still later, full-scale transformation to a secular economy came about by "reformations," political confiscations of the old monastic property holdings whose wealth was transferred into secular channels. Religious motivations for salvation were forced into channels of worldly activities, including economic ones.

In long-term perspective, the leading sector in the initial phase of breakout from agrarian-coercive structures must have involved religious organizations. For the reasons given above, neither merchants nor military aristocrats were likely to be leaders of the first phase of structural change. Religious organizations mobilized resources from all social classes in a way no other institution did. At the top, religious organizations were protected by the rulers, who used them to provide ceremonial legitimation. Religion received an inflow of sons and daughters of the aristocracy, who brought wealth and prestige with them, as well as energy and ambition to expand the influence of their adopted institutions. Religious organizations received land and other material contributions, both from the ruler and from lower aristocrats bent on sheltering their property from state exactions. They also provided careers for middle and even lower classes, thereby mobilizing social energies that would otherwise have remained in circumscribed locations. Religious organizations had an advantage for productive accumulation over other sectors of agrarian-coercive society: the monasteries were the only organization that was not structured as a patrimonial household bound by personal relations. For these reasons, the growth of the universalistic religions at the heart of the status order of agrarian-coercive societies was uniquely suited to reorient material goods and social energies into investing in new forms of production and exchange.

The theory is presented in ideal types. Multiple causes have contributed in varying degrees to the structural transformation of agrarian-coercive societies. Occasional circumstances enabled some merchants to overcome their traditional limitations as auxiliaries to military aristocracies, and some military specialists to shade over from coerced booty capitalism into making innovations in production. The thrust of my argument is that such developments by themselves would have been swallowed up by the dominance of agrarian-coercive relations if the leading sector of religious economy had not unleashed the first relatively large-scale phase of innovations in production, thus mobilizing much larger portions of the subordinated classes than were stimulated by the economic activities of traditional merchants or aristocrats. The religious economy was not the only contributor to dynamic capitalism, but in the initial phase of breakout from agrarian-coercive relations, it constituted the leading sector.

The Long-Term Pattern of East Asian Capitalism

Japanese economic development followed a long-term pattern of economic growth that began as far back as medieval China. Key Japanese political and religious institutions were imported from China in several waves that set Japan on the path toward an expansive market economy. In both China and Japan, the phase of capitalist expansion in the secular economy was preceded by an economic boom within the enclave of religious economy. In Asia, a Buddhist monastic economy laid the foundations of growth: first in early medieval China, resulting in a breakout to secular economic boom in the Sung dynasty, and again in Japan, where imported Chinese Buddhist institutions spearheaded a growing market economy. After a Reformation-like confiscation of Buddhist property on the eve of the Tokugawa regime, secular capitalism took off. In terms of the general scheme given above for transformation of agrarian-coercive structures, I will concentrate here on 3a, the Buddhist religious economy as the leading sector of capitalist expansion, and 3b, the breakout from the religious economy to a wider secular economy of agricultural capitalism.

A neo-Weberian model of the institutional conditions for dynamic capitalism has been applied to explain the economic growth of medieval China (Collins 1986: 58–72). The Buddhist monastic economy expanded in the period of multiple states (ca. A.D. 400–600) following the disintegration of the Han Empire and reached its culmination in the T'ang dynasty (618–900). As in the case of medieval European Christianity, the enclave of the religious economy spilled over and set off a boom in the secular market economy. In both cases, the monastic economy was transcended, outmoded, and plundered in "reformations" that returned the church to small, relatively propertyless organizations purveying a privatized religiosity. It is this second-wave market boom that characterized the Sung dynasty (960–1280). With its massive urbanization, commodity production, and population movements, the Sung was the first protomodern economy (Jones 1988: 73–86). With this change came modern economic woes as well: the Sung economy was the first to have full-scale price inflation, the elaboration of superordinate speculative markets in financial instruments, and along with these, governmental party politics based on interests and ideologies of the market (Eberhard 1977; Gernet 1962; Elvin 1973, 1984). The Sung market economy eventually stagnated. Having broken through to protocapitalism, in subsequent dynasties the market was asphyxiated by governmental regulation, confined to local exchanges that never regained the dynamic of self-generating economic growth. The Sung economy was probably the world's first to sustain a shift in per capita productivity (Jones 1988). Such growth ceased in China after this period; Elvin (1973) describes the post-Sung Chinese economy as a "high level equilibrium trap" in which productivity sustained an unprecedentedly huge and growing population but could not regain the mechanism of qualitatively transformative growth.

Japanese society built on the structural transformation set in motion in China. Japan provides an approximation of what China would have become if it had continued the trajectory of the T'ang and Sung dynasties. It was during those time periods that Japan imported organized structures of state and religion beyond the level of clans. Japan broke free from the direct influx of Chinese culture at just the time that China was turning, institutionally and ideologically, against Buddhism. It is medieval China, Buddhist-dominated China, that Japan continues. The stifling bureaucratic centralization of the Ming (1368–1644) and Ch'ing (1644–1911) dynasties became dominant in China after the independence of the Chinese monasteries had been crushed and their properties confiscated, at just the time that Japan was becoming socially and culturally autonomous. In modern Japanese development we have a laboratory for what a society built upon Buddhist organizational structures could produce.

While Buddhism was declining in China in the period of Neo-Confucian revival, from 1200 to 1500 Chinese Buddhist organizations pro-

liferated throughout Japan in the form of the Pure Land and Zen movements. The making of the dynamic market economy dates from those
centuries: the monasteries and the popular Buddhist movements built up
networks of transactions that by the outset of the Tokugawa unification
put Japan economically on a level with any other part of the world (see
Figure 12).

GROWTH OF THE MEDIEVAL BUDDHIST ECONOMY IN JAPAN

The beginnings of economic growth in medieval Japan can be traced
through several waves of religious movements. (Sources for the following
discussion are Kitagawa 1990, 1987; Dumoulin 1990; Collcutt 1981;
McMullin 1984; Yamamura 1990b; Hall, Nagahara, and Yamamura 1981;
Hall and Toyoda 1977.) The original Japanese society of kin-based clans
was organized in the sixth and seventh centuries into a centralized state, primarily by establishing Buddhism as a state religion. The original Buddhist
temples were modeled on organizational lineages imported from China and
Korea, at just the time when T'ang dynasty Buddhism was wealthiest and
most powerful. In Japan it grew even more dominant than in China, since
the rival power of Confucian bureaucracy that eventually undercut
Buddhism failed to develop in Japan. The great Buddhist temples operated
economically much like the court aristocracy. Located in or near the capital cities, Nara and subsequently Heian (Kyoto), they were nodes of the
agrarian-coercive economy, delivery points for goods from their landed estates. The temples had more organizational dynamism than the aristocratic
estates, establishing branches throughout the countryside, sometimes at
considerable distance, often by incorporating local Shinto shrines under
their jurisdiction. The major Buddhist temples became the leading landholders and centers of the largest extractive networks.

Around 1165, the court-centered government gave way to feudal decentralization, initially to a system of rival courts and in about 1330 to full-scale
breakdown of central authority. This disintegration coincided with the
emergence of two new kinds of Buddhist movements, the popular Pure
Land sects and the more elite Zen. The major Pure Land sects and their
offshoots were movements of wandering evangelists (Jodo, founded in 1175;
Jodo Shinshu or Ikko, founded by Shinran in 1224; Nichiren-shu, founded
in 1253; Ji, founded in 1275). Whereas the great court monasteries recruited
primarily from the upper class and emphasized elaborate ceremonial, the
Pure Land sects simplified the ritual of salvation down to chanting a few sacred prayers or vows (nembutsu). The economic base of these movements
became the collection of alms from the common people. Temples were
built in the small towns as well as in the commercial quarters of the cities.
Encouraging lay participation, some evangelists (above all the Ikko move-

Date	Period	Political organization	Economic organization	Religion
	Archaic	Warrior clans	Kin-based economic networks	Clan cults
700–1185	Nara/Heian	Chinese-style centralized court administration	Agrarian-coercive: estates of court aristocracy and clergy	Court-centered ceremonial Buddhism
1185–1333	Kamakura	Warefare between rival courts	Market economy around temples	Pure Land and Zen movements spread to hinterlands
1333–1460	Muromachi	Feudal decentralization	Geographic spread of market economy	Large Pure Land and Zen temples
1460–1570	Sengoku "Country at war"	Feudal lords: merchant city-states; Buddhist temple-states; peasant *monto* federations	Town-and-country market networks; rapid population growth	Struggle among Buddhist armies
1570–1600	Wars of reunification	Victory of Oda Nobunaga over temple-centered coalition	Secularization of temple properties	Delegitimation of Buddhist dominance
1600–1868	Tokugawa	Absolutist court controlling alliance of feudal lords	Agricultural capitalism; urban mass consumer markets	Religious secularization
1868–1912	Meiji Restoration	Centralized bureaucracy; parliamentary government	Industrial capitalism	Religious secularization

FIGURE 12. Institutional and economic development in Japan.

ment) broke down the lifestyle barrier between monks and laity by allowing priests to marry, in effect creating a "Protestant" form of Buddhism that
paralleled the break from celibacy in European Christianity following
Luther.

Zen began by recruiting from the higher classes, especially the feudal warriors, while retaining contacts with the court aristocracy. Zen too reformed
court Buddhism, in this case by emphasizing meditation over ceremony and
magic. In the 1200s and 1300s, one major branch of Zen, the Rinzai lineage,
built large monasteries with the patronage of both the Kamakura shogun and
the Kyoto aristocracy. By the late 1300s, the great Rinzai temples in the two
capitals, the so-called Five Mountains, presided over a hierarchy of secondary
and provincial temples throughout the country, whose revenues contributed
to the elite temples. Because of its influence on elite culture, Rinzai Zen is

the most famous version of Japanese Buddhism, but other branches of Zen spread more widely around the countryside and probably had more effect on the economic practices of everyday life. A rival branch of Zen, the Soto lineage, expanded into a different niche: small-scale rural monasteries where meditation exercises were made available to the common people. Soto provided the elementary education that promoted widespread literacy among the Japanese population. Like the Pure Land movements, Soto Zen helped break down the barriers within traditional Buddhism between the lifestyle of the monks and that of the laypeople.

Monasteries and religious movements became the dominant Japanese institutions during the Muromachi (1333–1460) and especially the Sengoku era, the time of "the Country at War" (1460–1570), when Japan became de facto a region of multiple states consisting of rival military domains, self-governing cities, and monastic states. The Sengoku period was the equivalent of the political decentralization in Renaissance Europe. From the point of view of orthodox political legitimacy, this was a time of disorder (literally, "Sengoku" was "the country upside down"), but politically it offered structural freedom of action, and economically the market economy first reached a considerable level of wealth during this period. With some twenty major *daimyo* (independent military domains) and dozens of smaller ones, even the nominal authority of the emperor and the shogun were almost completely disregarded. In the core economic regions of central Japan, there were effectively independent city-states governed by merchant councils. Counted among the most powerful daimyo were several of the Buddhist temple headquarters, whose armies rested upon the largest economic bases and often defeated the secular lords.

Both materially and motivationally, the Buddhist organizations, and especially their popular branches, constituted the leading sector of economic growth.[5] Figure 13 reproduces the institutional components of self-sustaining capitalist growth given in Figure 11, substituting the institutional forms developed within the Buddhist economy.

Markets for the Factors of Production

COMMODITY MARKETS

The initial economic effect of the temples was to widen the markets for commodities. The traditional ceremonial temples of the old heartland around Nara and Kyoto acquired bodies of wandering ascetics (*hijiri*); these were in fact itinerant merchants and artisans who established a network of regular market relations in the countryside (McMullin 1984: 44). From the mid-1100s onward, the burgeoning movements of Pure Land and popular Zen introduced market relations into the hinterlands. The old organization

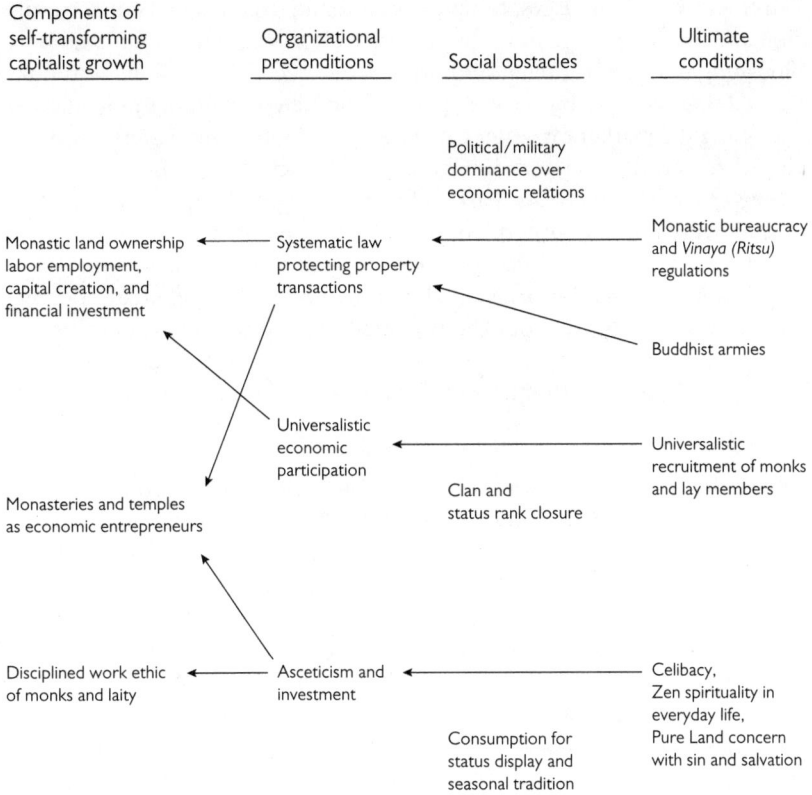

Components of self-transforming capitalist growth	Organizational preconditions	Social obstacles	Ultimate conditions

FIGURE 13. Religious capitalism in Buddhist Japan.

of rural Japanese society, largely restricted to the level of the clans, now acquired universalistic networks of travel and cooperation through religious participation.

All these developments promoted growth. Population expanded from 5 million in the eleventh century to about 10 million in 1300, reaching perhaps 18–22 million, by various estimates, in 1600. Land under cultivation expanded, with the biggest growth occurring between 1450 and 1600 in the Sengoku period of warring states (Jones 1988: 153; McEvedy and Jones 1978: 179–81).[6] Most important, the area of population settlement, originally concentrated in central Honshu, the old heartland around Nara and Kyoto, spread laterally across the Japanese archipelago and became denser in the center as well. The geographic expansion and density of Buddhist temples both promoted and benefited from the population growth.

In the early Middle Ages, temples became the largest centers of accumulation and hence the organizations most capable of engaging in foreign trade. Sojourning in China for religious purposes fostered trade relations, as monks financed their voyages by carrying goods. The Zen monasteries pioneered in developing the market for tea in Japan, just as the Ch'an monasteries had developed tea production and distribution in T'ang China. The monasteries became one of the first mass markets for bulk commodities of everyday life, but they were not of course the only traders. Especially in the 1500s, pirates carried large quantities of goods across the East China Sea. But this illicit trade was just the kind of interstitial commerce found in agrarian-coercive economies generally, without the potential for transforming the economic system that existed in the monastic sector, where trade was combined with the other institutional structures of dynamic capitalism.

LABOR MARKETS AND SOCIAL MOBILITY

Still greater dynamism was introduced as Buddhist temples promoted markets for labor and capital. Monks operated outside the putative fixity of social position. External social rankings tended to translate into rankings within the monasteries as well, and aristocrats monopolized the abbothood of the great monasteries; but farmers, craftsmen, and dispossessed persons could enter lower monastic positions and had opportunities to rise with the expansion of Buddhist institutions. In Kyoto during the 1300s, taking the tonsure was used as a means of freeing oneself from court rankings; such *tonseisha* priests had no formal ties with temples and continued a secular lifestyle (Varley 1977: 186–89). By decreasing the gap between laity and clergy, such individuals tended to delegitimate Buddhist religiosity in the next century by giving monks the reputation of worldliness.

Viewed from another angle, this weakening of the border between the clerical and lay worlds opened the gates for a period of unprecedented social fluidity. Religion was not the only sector in which social mobility became possible. The wars of the Sengoku period broke down the dominance of the older court aristocracy and the shogunal clans; smaller daimyo had their moments in the sun, and the military reorganization into mass armies allowed the rise of commoners like the dictator Hideyoshi. Even here the religious movements tended to initiate these processes.[7] The Sengoku breakdown of central control started with wars among the most powerful monasteries, and the trend toward building mass armies began within the monastic sector. By the late Sengoku period, wealthy merchants from cities like Sakai were participating in the high-status ritual of tea ceremonies on an equal footing with aristocrats. This is one reason the Tokugawa regime began by attempting to reestablish feudal deference relations that had considerably broken down. The social fluidity of the pre-Tokugawa period reflected the increasing interactions between wealthy monasteries, cultivated merchants closely connected with the religious economy, and a new style of military adventurers whose resource base was the burgeoning market structure.

Social mobility at the higher levels of society and the formation of occupations ambiguously placed between aristocrats and commoners are the easiest kinds to document for the premodern period in which common people were largely invisible in records. But it is clear that the occupational mobility that developed within monastic careers also affected peasants and artisans. In the lower ranks of the monasteries, and even more so in the popular Buddhism movements, the bulk of the members would have been from these classes. These religious organizations became the framework within which labor could move to new places and occupational opportunities could expand. The religious economy also overlapped with the surrounding secular economy. Larger labor markets grew up in conjunction with monasteries in the market towns (*jinaimachi*) that formed inside the precincts or around the monastery gates (*monzenmachi*).

FORMATION OF PRODUCTIVE CAPITAL

The development of productive capital was also promoted. The early temples brought new lands into cultivation. Monastic evangelists, from the time of the earliest Pure Land movements down to proselytizers from the humbler branches of Zen in the 1600s, were associated with road- and bridge-building, well-digging, and land-clearing.[8] Temples not only created physical capital in the agrarian economy but also took the lead in organizing industries that converted agricultural produce into finished goods. Once we clear our minds of the preconception that industrial capitalism should first emerge in urban settings, we can see that rural or quasi-rural capitalist production arose in the Japanese monasteries, just as it did in the Cistercian monasteries of medieval Europe. By the 1330s, the main bulk industries such as sake brewing in the Kyoto area were dominated by the Mt. Hiei monasteries overlooking the city. Other products (cotton textiles, salt) were produced by guilds (*za*) initiated under the protection of the temples that borrowed Buddhist organizational forms.[9] In the late 1300s, the *za* shifted from a collective service obligation to lords to a contractual relation with a proprietor. A superordinate circuit of capital was created as members paid fees for the right to enter or leave a *za* (Toyoda and Sugiyama 1977: 137–40). In the Sengoku period (1465–1580), the *za* form was used to create self-governing city councils of elders; for example, the great commercial city Sakai began as a *za* paying dues to temple patrons.

Finance capital also emerged out of the temples. In China, this path had developed in the T'ang dynasty, where monastic agents were charged with annual missions of investing and returning a profit (Ch'en 1964). In Japan, temples received donations from the aristocracy in the form of land, buildings, and precious materials. These gifts were part of the status display of the aristocrats, who raised their religious and social status through the most prominent means of public dramatization available in medieval society. The temples used such materials partly for consumption and display, but also put them into a pool of accumulated resources. The temples converted goods extracted by the leisure aristocracy into capital for wider circulation and productive use. Japanese temples accumulated cash as well as goods and engaged in loans. Moneylending by guilds emerged as temples gave patronage to their favored adherents, extending their legal rights to them and protecting them from political interference. Much of this lending took the form of consumer financing extended to aristocrats and samurai, with the result that the landholding class tended to become debtors of the temples, which until late in the Sengoku period constituted the bulk of the creditor class. Although such lending was not a very productive investment of capital, some of the capital accumulated by the temples was invested internally more profitably in their far-flung networks of economic enterprises.

As the temples became rich, a superordinate market arose in the sale of offices. By the 1380s, abbots and senior monks (especially of the far-flung Rinzai Five Mountains organizations) paid fees for their appointments. Since they often held office for less than a year and dispersed gifts and lavish ceremonies at their accession, it is apparent that these positions were expected to be lucrative and that a great deal of wealth was being extracted from the monastic economy by these officials. The shogun began to rake off part of the wealth in the form of fees for certificates of appointments and in the 1400s was inflating the turnover to maximize its income from the monastic sector.[10] The business atmosphere of these monasteries was so intense that the iconoclastic Zen master Ikkyu described the monks as more like merchants than Buddhist priests.

THE MARKET FOR LAND

The market for land was slower to develop than the markets for goods, labor, and capital. Nevertheless, the temples were the first to pry land loose from military-political control. The temples' acquisition of land by gift, government deed, proselytization, or reclamation put land into a sector where there were formal instruments of accounting and transfer. Struggles among branches and schisms of the Buddhist sects led to early instances of litigation over land rights, which began to create a body of doctrine and practice for civil land transfer. The result was hardly negligible. In the core provinces of central Honshu, the temples held up to 90 percent of the estates.[11] In the mid-Muromachi period the land income of the great Rinzai Zen temples was larger than that of the imperial family. The regions where the Buddhist temples owned the greatest proportion of land were those where the market economy developed most spectacularly by the 1500s (Hauser 1974; Hall, Nagahara, and Yamamura 1981).

MONASTIC ENTREPRENEURS

The temples were the first entrepreneurial organizations in Japan, the first to combine control of the factors of labor, capital, and land so as to allocate them for enhancing production. Not surprisingly, it is in the monasteries (especially the great centralized orders of the Rinzai Five Mountains) that we find the first development of rationalized administration with annual plans and strict accounting practices. By the mid-1400s, there were detailed account books and regulations that required countersigning by oversight committees and heads of subtemples (Akamatsu and Yampolsky 1977: 327–28; Collcutt 1990: 621–22). This structural development helps explain the considerable expansion of agricultural production that began in the mid-1300s (Yamamura 1981: 310). It is reasonable to infer that the prosperity of the monasteries and their methods set the course followed by the regional daimyo during the Sengoku period of the 1470s–1580s. Yamamura (1981) emphasizes the rational practices of the daimyo in land reclamation, water control and irrigation, and mining. These, together with double cropping and the introduction of markets for fertilizer, led to a large increase in agricultural output from 1550 to 1650, the foundation for Tokugawa economic wealth. Now we see the daimyo, in contrast to their previous role as mere extractors of feudal rents, acting as overseers and providers of the factors of production (Nagahara 1990: 342). This role of the overlord as entrepreneur had only one previous model: the monastic proprietors.

The Buddhist Economic Ethic

An ethic of self-discipline and ascetic restraint on consumption, resulting in accumulation and investment, originated in internal reforms within medieval Japanese Buddhism. The earliest temples in the Nara and Heian periods (ca. 700–1200) had carried out an ostentatious aristocratic court display, combining Shingon magic and ceremony with the traditional ritualism of the dominant Japanese clans. The Buddhist movements that proliferated from 1200 onward reacted against this dominance of ceremonial religion, in one direction with Zen reforms in the monasteries, and in another direction with the Pure Land movements of simplified participation among the common people.

Zen introduced disciplined monastic life and attempted to shear away magic and ceremony. Zen meditation practices were oriented not toward producing deep trance but tranquil attentiveness with eyes half-open (especially the *zazen* of the Soto branch). Ch'an monasteries of T'ang China, in breaking away from reliance on aristocratic donations and toward economic self-sufficiency, had made work part of the religious discipline. In Japan, Soto broke from aristocratic patronage more sharply than Rinzai. In the more extreme forms of Zen, the activities of daily life—work among them—were regarded as opportunities for meditative practice. Religious discipline was thereby extended into economic activities in a potentially very thorough way. Accounts of the enlightenment of famous monks included their experiences while performing humble tasks like sweeping. Soto Zen in particular emphasized that the religious ideal was not to escape from the world but to continue the attitude of concentration in normal activities even after enlightenment (Dumoulin 1990). Scholars looking for sources of the Japanese work ethic have pointed to Suzuki Shosan in the early Tokugawa period, a Zen monk independent of the main sects. Suzuki proselytized among the common people, explicitly declared that all work was Buddhist spiritual practice, and formulated an ethic for merchants that stressed the performance of duties without greed for personal gain (Nakamura 1967; Yamamoto 1992).

The evangelical sects began even earlier to promote economic development among the common people. The Nichiren movement gave special emphasis to asceticism and discipline. Radically anticeremonial, it pruned ritual and doctrine down to reciting the name of the Lotus sutra. Nichiren-shu was a movement of emotional evangelism that called for continuous purification in the midst of everyday life. Like the other branches of the Pure Land movement after Shinran's reforms, religion shifted its emphasis from the worldly benefits believed to follow from magic and ritual to ethical concerns with inner sinfulness and otherworldly salvation. For this reason, Shinran is sometimes described as the Martin Luther of Japan. Opponents sometimes derided the Pure Land movement as an easy path to salvation, since it held that one need only recite the *nembutsu* chant in order to be reborn in paradise. But this was to misstate the social and psychological reality of the Pure Land practice. Its missionaries preached that the tortures of Hell awaited human sinners, and there was tremendous emotional pressure not merely to make a first sincere invocation of divine grace but to continuously reaffirm one's commitment in daily life. The Nichiren movement was famous for its vehement attacks on the sinfulness of the dominant social order of aristocrats and grand prelates, and for its intransigence in the face of religious persecution. As its monasteries and lay adherents grew, in the 1400s it became famous for its military contentiousness. Nichiren Buddhism became an activist religious ethic on a par with the crusading orders of medieval Christianity and the Puritan movements of seventeenth-century Protestantism. It is an apt comparison between the Puritan armies of the English revolution and the Nichiren Buddhist armies of the previous centuries.

Nichiren-shu spread primarily among townspeople and was the main urban religion at just the time when Japan was transformed from a land of rural manors into a network of market towns. The rival Ikko movement built on yet another social base, organizing bands of adherents among the peasants. It is the most spectacular example of a religious network penetrating the countryside and linking it to urban centers. Following reforms that centralized the organizational networks during the mid-1400s, Ikko local congregations throughout central Japan passed along regular contributions, not to a regional temple or abbot but directly to the central headquarters (Weinstein 1977). This was the great Ishiyama Honganji at Osaka bay, which became the largest and most powerful temple, indeed the most powerful economic and military unit of any kind, in Japan during the 1500s. It also provides a striking example of how religiously organized economic networks overflowed into the secular economy. Osaka, the city that by the early Tokugawa had become the storehouse of Japan and was soon to become a city of great merchant enterprises like Sumitomo and Mitsui and of a self-conscious merchant ideology, originated as a *jinaimachi*, a market town within the Honganji precincts. The religious economy at its most effective produced the leading point of the secular market in Japan.

The Buddhist Contribution
to Bureaucratic Legalism and Property Rights

Let us now ascend the causal chain to ultimate conditions (see the upper right side of Figure 13). The effects of universalistic recruitment and Buddhist spiritual practices have already been discussed. Special comment is called for on the way in which Japanese Buddhism provided systematic law to protect property transactions. In Europe, Weber ascribed this role to the emergence of state bureaucracy together with the traditions of Greek citizenship and Roman law. In the Confucian institutions imported from China, however, there was no independent profession of the lawyer and no body of law apart from state administrative law, which was decidedly *not* oriented toward protecting private property transactions. Moreover, even the state-bureaucratic aspect of Confucian institutions did not take in Japan, where first the court aristocracy and then the independent feudal warriors dominated government. Tokugawa pacification was not the imposition of a centralized state bureaucracy but a carefully monitored alliance and balance of power among locally armed and administered domains of the daimyo. Some bureaucratic elements eventually grew as the Tokugawa shogunate and regional domains developed internal administration, burdening officials with heavy loads of paperwork, extensive regulations, and recordkeeping (T. Smith 1988a: 138–39).

The structural problem was that the samurai were subject to codes that regulated their behavior toward their lords and within their own status group, but there were no laws regulating their relations with the lower social orders. Merchants and farmers had no rights under samurai law, and the samurai were de jure free to act violently toward these inferiors, especially in punishing personal affronts that violated the code of ritual deference (Henderson 1968; Katsumata and Collcutt 1981; Ikegami 1995). The bulk of law in the daimyo domains, developed during the Sengoku period, consisted of house precepts regulating behavior of the warrior-retainers. Separate regulations were issued for common people, but they focused largely on criminal behavior and disloyalty and did little to regulate property transfers. Civil law and its protection for private property transactions scarcely existed, although the daimyo sometimes adjudicated disputes within their domains. Throughout the medieval period, as in much of Chinese history, governmental policies implemented by shogun and daimyo tended to favor periodic debt cancellation to protect samurai or farmers acting against the interests of creditor merchants and temples. Under these conditions, it is hard to imagine how extensive markets for the factors of production could emerge or entrepreneurial investments could flourish. The economically active parts of the population were unregulated and unprotected by law, while the legally bound and power-holding sector of samurai were prohibited by their code from conducting economically gainful activity.

The conundrum is solved once we put Buddhist organization back into the picture. Buddhism, within its own sphere, had systematic legal regulations that enabled it to expand its own markets for the factors of production and thereby inseminate the surrounding society. Internally, Buddhism had a long-standing legalism, embodied in the *Vinaya* regulations, which covered every aspect of monastic life, including monks' personal possessions and use of collective property. In both the Chinese and Japanese monasteries, a full-scale bureaucratic structure emerged. Monks held specialized positions as scholars, assistants, attendants, workers, lay brothers, guards, and more. The higher administration of a monastery was divided between the Western section, in charge of religious training and practice, and the Eastern section, which took care of the material and financial activities of the organization (Akamatsu and Yampolsky 1977: 325–28). The Eastern section was quite large in the wealthy temples with many branches and property holdings.

The task of administering internal transactions among parts of a temple's corporate properties acted as a wedge that steadily widened the scope of legal regulation of economic transactions. In the formative economic period of the Middle Ages, when the temples were the major holders of *shoen* (estates that extracted rents in kind by officials of the nobility or the temples), temple law was the law of their domain, and outside authority had no legal right of entry (McMullin 1984: 26, 32; Wakita and Hanley 1981: 318–22). After 1300, temples acted as the legal authority and arbitrated disputes between merchants in the temple-gate and precinct towns that grew up around the temples. When in the Sengoku period many of these towns became self-governing, especially those under nominal control of the Ikko and Nichiren sects, the merchant and artisan *za* acquired rights of adjudication in their own spheres.

In principle, under medieval law land could be assigned only by a lord; private transactions in land were illegal. Nevertheless, in self-governing cities such as Sakai, it was possible to buy and sell land. Buddhist-inspired legal structures protected property from debt cancellation. Such property protections spread into the feudal domains as well, as the warring daimyo tried to attract merchants to their domains by guaranteeing similar property protection in the castle towns.

That Buddhist organizations developed an internal legal system would not in itself generate legal rights in the surrounding political order. Moreover, in Japan there was no equivalent of the papacy, which in Europe acted as a governing body and court of appeal for property disputes and transactions among the church bodies and guarded church property against secular power (Southern 1970). The papacy gave a special impetus to European legalism by developing canon law and incorporating law schools into the church-sanctioned universities (Berman 1983). There was no equivalent in Japan, but there was a substitute: the power of the great monasteries based on their monk armies. From the times when the monastery guards (*sohei*) of Mt. Hiei overawed the ruler at Kyoto in the late eleventh century to when the Pure Land sects mustered tens of thousands of troops during the Sengoku period, Buddhist organizations became increasing well equipped to defend their rights. The *sohei* often went into action on behalf of property claims; many of their military incursions into Kyoto were instigated by quarrels between rival sects (or sometimes between sects and secular interests) over properties (see, e.g., McMullin 1984: 22). Japanese historians have always described these incidents in tones of disapproval of the rowdiness and unspirituality of the monks, but from an analytical viewpoint they represent the existence of a political machinery of Buddhism capable of enforcing property rights.

Sociologically we are reminded that Weber pointed to the origins of citizenship in the social organization of armaments, such as the warrior phalanx of the Greek city-state and the self-equipped knight of the European feudal system (1961: 237–40). In both cases the citizenship rights of joint political participation took form through corporate bodies of armed men. In Japan, these corporate bodies originated in the Buddhist orders. The Japanese Buddhist conception of "citizenship" did not stress the rights of the individual monk but rather the collective rights of the *sangha*, the monastic body as a whole; the power of the monastic armies translated this into rights that were effectively, if grudgingly, recognized in practice. In the Sengoku era, the corporate form spread outside the monasteries through the *monto* (peasant confederations) promoted by the Pure Land movements. The era of the Buddhist armies coincided with the transformation of Buddhist temples into economic entrepreneurs and with the rise of indigenous Japanese capitalism. These powers were shorn in the sixteenth century by Oda Nobunaga's and Hideyoshi's conquests, but by that time capitalist dynamism had been transferred to the larger society.

Religious capitalism in Japan, as elsewhere, made its inroads invisibly. Not that contemporaries were unaware of the economic activities of the church, but they perceived those activities as abuses, fallings away from the religious ideal. Criticism of temple moneylending, of commercialization, and of merchants and peasants who did not stay in their places was abundant from Muromachi onward (Collcutt 1990: 607). The great temples were regarded as corrupt, and the political independence and wealth of the Ikko and Nichiren commoner sects were seen as outrages to social rank. In the 1500s the visible strength of the Buddhist economy produced ideological repercussions: widespread sentiment was that Buddhist priests were hypocrites under a cloak of false religiosity, and "priest" became a term of abuse (McMullin 1984: 268). Similar sentiments about the papacy and the Catholic monastic orders on the eve of the Reformation were prevalent in Europe, where the visible wealth of the church and its precedence over spirituality helped to delegitimate these institutions and prepare the way for a military-political purge. But by then religious institutions had done their work. Religious capitalism had inseminated the larger realm, and the resources made available by the growing capitalist economy were available to be mustered by the enemies of the church.

The Breakout to the Secular Economy

In the Muromachi period secular capitalism had begun to be emancipated from temple capitalism. New guilds arose independent of the temples; moneylenders and markets in the *monzenmachi* loosened temple control. By the late 1400s, as the Sengoku period of warfare began, the *shoen* system of land tenure had largely disintegrated as local administrators, warriors, or peasant villages took possession. Although the great temples of the traditional orders were thereby gradually dispossessed, the newer religious organizations of common people played a key role in property transformation.

The peasant uprisings of the 1470s and later, which deprived temples as well as aristocrats of traditional coerced land rents, were successful mainly when organized as peasant confederations (*monto*) under the Ikko Pure Land sect. Economic control shifted from the more traditional temples to the most market-oriented temples. The Ikko headquarters, the Honganji at Osaka bay, led the change to cash contributions. The *monto* exercised self-rule over a large territory of north-central Japan and paid no taxes to the secular lords for a hundred years.

The final shift to a secular economy came with the wars of unification under Oda Nobunaga and Hideyoshi in the 1570s and 1580s. The growth in military organization at this time was made possible by the development of temple capitalism and its overlapping into the secular realm. The organization of large-scale Buddhist armies spurred the shift from feudal levées to the mass disciplined troops of the late Sengoku period (Kitagawa 1990: 122; Sansom 1961: 289). The Negoroji, a huge Shingon temple that ranked with the Honganji as the greatest feudal lords in the economic heartland of central Honshu, was a prime producer of muskets and mortars. Its soldier-monks hired out as mercenaries and allied themselves with Nobunaga in his early campaigns (Hall, Nagahara, and Yamamura 1981: 4; McMullin 1984: 43–55, 155, 237). Nobunaga's famous innovation in breaking with samurai tradition and enlisting armies of musket-armed commoners was the adoption of the monastic lead.

By 1550 the *monto* were mobilizing forces as large as 20,000, including musket corps. Japan became reunified when one of the daimyo took control of enough commercial centers to use their resources for assembling armies larger than those of any opponents. This happened around 1580, when Nobunaga's forces had grown to 137,000.[12] The capacity to mobilize troops depends upon logistics; that such huge forces could be brought to the field is an indication of the market networks in existence at the time. The wars of unification centered on the military alliances for or against the greatest monasteries. The Honganji, which controlled the richest part of central Honshu, was the center of the anti-Nobunaga coalition. Supplied by water and connected to a network of water transport through central and even more remote areas of Japan, it withstood a ten-year siege, and its capitulation was the decisive point of the war.

The unifiers Nobunaga and Hideyoshi carried out a policy of monastic property confiscation similar in many respects to that of the Protestant Reformation in Europe. Guild privileges were undermined by the establishment of free markets; toll barriers (which temples had operated as sources of revenue) were abolished and free movement of merchants within domains allowed. Nobunaga enhanced the attractiveness of his domains to merchants by protecting them from debt cancellation decrees previously promulgated by secular lords. Hideyoshi went further, abolishing the self-governing towns that had emerged under auspices of the temples, abolishing guilds, and exempting merchants and artisans from land rents, in order to free them from the control of both aristocrats and temples. The end result was that the Buddhist capitalism was substantially eliminated. Temples were reduced to tiny, essentially propertyless units. Falling precipitously from their peak in the medieval period, when the temples held at minimum 25 percent of all cultivated land, by the early Tokugawa period their holdings had declined to 2.5 percent (McMullin 1984: 251).

TOKUGAWA DEVELOPMENT OF MASS-MARKET CAPITALISM

The leading sector of Buddhist capitalism had catalyzed a secular capitalism that by the 1500s made central Japan a network of market towns. Accumulated economic resources were available to be reorganized in military and political forms, making possible the new regime of the conquering generals that became the Tokugawa government. The phase of full-fledged agricultural capitalism was entered: commercial relations permeated the countryside, while a new leading sector of nonagricultural goods and services began to move Japan toward yet further phases of capitalist growth.

The Tokugawa was the period of the second-wave economic boom. As secular market capitalism (3b) outgrew religious capitalism (3a), Japan took on the familiar traits of urban wealth of that time. But economic growth in the Tokugawa was not all smooth sailing. After about 1720 the further development of capitalism was rather mixed. But it was not all stagnation. From 1600 onward, Japan's economy was well within the scale of that of Western Europe as a whole. In Europe, too, there were periods of 30–100 years in which one national region or another led or lagged, but within a largely common institutional structure and an interconnected market economy (Mann 1993: 262–63). If England or the United States was ahead in the middle decades of the nineteenth century when Western contact with Japan was resumed, Japan's ups and downs occurred within a similar range of variation as those of other advanced Western economies (e.g., France) of the period after 1700.[13] On most major dimensions the Tokugawa was a substantially modern society. Its troubles were largely those of a market-dominated economy, and the political difficulties of the shogunate were those that beset regimes dependent upon a highly monetized commercial base. Dominance of a capitalist market economy made the government prisoner of its tax base and ruined military aristocrats dependent upon the old agrarian-coercive system of extraction (Goldstone 1991: 402–14). For these reasons, the significance of the Meiji Restoration has been overrated. It was a political revolution within a substantially modern institutional structure, not a sudden deus ex machina that initiated the break with traditionalism and opened the way to a miraculous leap forward into parity with European pacesetters. In this respect, the Meiji revolution resembles the series of French revolutions from 1789 to 1871, which swept away the remaining legal institutions and traditions of aristocratic domination of the old agrarian-coercive regime. In both the European and Japanese cases, the institutional structures of a capitalist market economy had already penetrated the traditional shell.

It is sometimes argued that Tokugawa Japan was not capitalist insofar as it had little technological innovation, especially in the area of industrial machinery. In this respect Japan contrasts sharply with the popular image of the industrial revolution breaking forth with steam engines and factory machinery in England around 1770. Nevertheless, the institutional core of capitalism, laid out in Figure 11, does not involve the technology of mass production per se. As Weber noted, industrial technology is the result of the impulse to rationalize production applied to the specific area of factory production; it is a late component in the causal chain (1961: 133–36). Rationalization in this sense means an application of the economic ethic of calculation and investment directed toward the steady expansion of profits. But rationalization of technique need not involve hardware; in Europe, as in Japan, rationalization was evident in the development of systematic methods of increasing agricultural production (experimenting with crop strains, systematic rotation, fertilizers, etc.), which was a subject of popular handbooks in both places by 1700 (T. Smith 1988a: 173–98). On the Tokaido road between Kyoto and Edo, express shipping companies rationalized their routines to bring down the speed of delivering messages and goods from six days to two between 1650 and 1800—not so different from the stagecoach companies stepping up the speed of communications in England at almost identical dates (Moriya 1990: 107–12; Braudel 1979/1984: 1, 424–28).

Japanese capitalism developed without much innovation in industrial technology because of its particular pattern of market growth. Agricultural production intensified through small enterprises, not large ones, and textiles rather than heavy industry predominated until the 1930s, making labor-intensive technologies most profitable (Rosovsky 1961; T. Smith 1988a: 42–45). It is a mistake to assume that labor-intensive technology cannot be innovative or involve calculation oriented toward rational exploitation of market opportunities. One of the earliest markets in the Tokugawa economic expansion, the silk industry, rationalized production by selectively breeding silkworms to improve quality and local varieties. A division of labor also grew up in markets for producers' goods outside the traditional consumer sector (Morris-Suzuki 1994: 34–39). Here we find capitalist innovation involving neither labor-saving machinery nor large firms but rather the growth of specialization and interchange among many small units. By the late Tokugawa, it is estimated that "industrial" output, consisting of nonagricultural production and services that made household consumer goods available to even the poorest social levels, contributed 40–45 percent of the national income (Howe 1996: 54). In the 1910s and 1920s, after Japan had entered the world market, Japanese enterprises deliberately simplified technologies imported from the West to fit Asian export markets for cheap goods, as well as Japanese patterns of decentralized production organization and maximal conservation of limited raw materials (Morris-Suzuki 1994: 67, 107–8).

The Japanese had early developed a mass-market economy by a route alternative to the machine production of standardized goods. Instead, Japanese capitalism expanded by multiplying market niches for a variety of products across a range of quality. This organization of productive networks is sometimes mistaken for a "handicraft mode of production" believed to be characteristic of feudal or premodern markets. It better fits the niche-seeking market expansion theorized by White (1981) and that became so prominent in the specialized consumer markets of the late twentieth century (Sabel 1994). Even as applied to the West, our view of the industrial revolution is too stereotyped around the iron-and-steam revolution of 1760–1830, which was followed by the "second industrial revolution" of chemical and electrical products around 1880–1940, and the so-called "postindustrial" or "postmodern" economy of electronic communications after 1960. In the scheme of this chapter, these are all phases of (3c). Instead of regarding Japan merely as a latecomer to the industrial revolution, we should consider how it illustrates alternative paths across the phase of mass-market production and technological innovation.

The Significance of Religious Capitalism in World History

Capitalism does not expand into a full-fledged system, penetrating new market niches and generating new products and techniques, until a composite set of social institutions is assembled. Giving the Weberian model a Schumpeterian twist, we may say that all the factors of production (not commodities alone but also land, labor, and capital) must move in response to market opportunities, packaged under the control of entrepreneurs motivated by an economic ethic of future-oriented calculation and investment. The most valuable point in Weber's analysis is that the dominant structures of agrarian-coercive societies were severe obstacles to the institutions of dynamic capitalism. Merchants, monetization, and long-distance trade were by themselves compatible with the continued dominance of agrarian-coercive structures. Breaking out required a set of structural transformations: property relations to free up all the factors of production and provide legal protection to their market transactions, the dissolution of social barriers against full participation of individuals in the market, and the circumvention of status hierarchies in which incentives worked against long-term calculation, ascetic restraint, and investment.

Weber's lead is useful in another respect: religious institutions were the most likely place within agrarian-coercive societies for a leading sector of capitalist institutions to first be assembled. I have suggested that the full set of such institutions could be found within the enclaves of religious economies in three historical instances: medieval Christian Europe, medieval Buddhist China, and pre-Tokugawa Buddhist Japan. In each case the initial breakthrough of the religious leading sector was followed by a church reformation that narrowed the distance between religious specialists and laity and confiscated religious property. Each resulted in a second wave of self-transforming capitalist growth in the secular economy of agricultural capitalism. It remains to be explained why some of these developments moved yet further to an industrial revolution in nonagricultural production, but it seems clear that this could only have occurred against the background of the prior breakout from agrarian-coercive structures.

The logic of the Weber-Schumpeter model is not Eurocentric, even though Weber's own historical application of it was. In broad form, agrarian-coercive structures existed worldwide. The breakout through a religious economy also happened in several parts of the world, and in both Christian and Buddhist forms. Religious capitalism in medieval China laid the foundation for the Sung dynasty's crucial position in the world trading system as depicted by Abu-Lughod (1989), just as religious capitalism in Western Europe helped a remote and barbarous end of the world trading network begin its aggressive expansion. Religious capitalism in late medieval Japan laid the institutional groundwork for a further phase of secular capitalism. This in turn led the general revival of East Asian economic dynamism that surged to such heights in the world trading system of the twentieth century.

How Simulating a Compact Theory Can Reproduce the Tangled Pathways of History

Robert A. Hanneman, Randall Collins, and Gabriele Mordt

ONE REASON WHY sociological theories fit the social world only very loosely is that they often pay little explicit attention to time and history. Theory usually enunciates general tendencies: for example, rulers require legitimacy, conflict produces solidarity, a military-industrial complex promotes war. Each proposition stands alone as a ceteris paribus generalization. Deductions about the behavior of the systems described by such statements are often far from obvious for a variety of reasons. Most important are multiple causes and feedback processes among them. Even in very simple theoretical models, there can be unexpected outcomes. Positive loops accelerate basic processes and bring some of them to ceilings at which they rest; negative feedback provides counteracting forces, which sometimes lead to a stable equilibrium, sometimes to oscillation, and sometimes to chaos.

When a theory is formulated verbally, such as Weber's or Simmel's classic statements about conflict, these alternatives are left open. We do not know what is implied in a theory as long as it is left on the level of separate general principles and is abstracted out of time. One way to overcome this ignorance is to perform experimental research on such theories by means of computer simulation. This activity is a discovery-making process in the sense that one does not really understand what the theory is saying about the world until one has experimented with it as a dynamic model.[1]

Such experiments reveal several things. First, they force us to think through the abstract principles of existing theories and to add mechanisms that make these principles capable of producing realistic outcomes that accumulate in time. The holes in a theory are usually not obvious until one attempts to write a program that specifies what will happen as processes iterate and interact. In this way, computer simulation is a stimulus to theory building.

Dynamic simulation experiments also often reveal how important brute quantitative conditions are in shaping overall patterns of social action. Different quantitative starting points can produce dramatically different outcomes, even within the same theoretical model. It is experimentally demonstrable that quantity does turn into quality. The fact that arbitrary differences in starting points can make such large differences for subsequent pathways, as noted in the "butterfly effect" from the lab lore of chaos theory (Gleick 1987: 9), is related to the following point as well, for the enormous varieties of history appear to be merely quantitative variations produced by a relatively simple underlying generative mechanism.

Computer simulation methods can help to bridge the gap between theory and history. It is often asserted that the infinite variability of history can never be explained by the abstract principles given in sociological theories, and that we can never do more than describe and interpret particular historical sequences. However, a relatively simple dynamic theory does not produce only one outcome, but a pathway of various outcomes through time, and indeed a series of different pathways through time determined by the initial conditions. The instabilities of real history, with its strange branching patterns and sudden turning points, do not prove that a theoretical explanation of history is impossible. On the contrary, just these kinds of patterns are produced by some computer simulations of a simple abstract theory.

Dynamic theory simulation is halfway between quantitative and qualitative sociology. Sociological approaches that put process in the center of their worldviews tend to emphasize unique occurrences or configurations of events and experiences (e.g., symbolic interactionist or other interpretive approaches at the micro/meso level; much of contemporary historical sociology at the macro level). From the point of view of an unsympathetic formal/quantitative sociologist, such qualitative sociology looks like reliance on anecdotal data and on explanations that are plausible at best, but never demonstrable. The qualitative/interpretative sociologist does not disagree but claims that this is the best that one can do and that formal/systematic sociologists do not get even this far.

Practitioners of dynamic theory simulation can very well share the highly processual worldview of qualitative sociologists; there is indeed a huge variety of historical events, pathways can be quite unstable, and many different sequences can happen. Nevertheless, dynamic simulation does not take historical fluidity and particularity as the bedrock of analysis but goes on to investigate how various sequences are generated from a relatively compact underlying model. A key point is that dynamic simulation shows that the degree of instability and particularity are themselves variable: under some conditions, life unfolds in simple repetitions or linear sequences; under other conditions—which can be located by means of simulation experiments—the same causal processes result in much more complex patterns, or even in regions of chaotic unpredictability. The viewpoint of dynamic theory simulation enables us to do justice both to the processual-particularistic aspect of reality and to the generalizing and formal-systematic aspect.

A CONFLICT THEORY OF LEGITIMACY DYNAMICS AND EXTERNAL STATE POWER

To illustrate the process of discovering theoretical implications through computer experiments, we simulate some principles drawn from classic conflict theory: the relationship between external conflict and internal group solidarity enunciated by Simmel (1955) and Coser (1956), and Weber's (1968: 901–26) discussion of the link between the legitimacy of rule and the geopolitically based power-prestige of the state. Since our concern is theory development rather than textual exegesis, we limit ourselves to the general statement of principles that we simulate here.

The Simmel-Coser principle is that conflict with external groups increases internal cohesion. As a corollary, leaders of groups seeking domestic support for their power are motivated to find conflicts with external enemies (Coser 1956: 87, 104). Weber suggests some implications of these principles for international conflict and political power. He ties the legitimacy of rulers and the legal order to the geopolitical power-prestige of the political community. The power and prestige of political communities, in turn, is largely determined by their capacity to dominate others (Weber 1968: 903–4, 911, 925). We infer that there is consequently a variable tendency of political communities to expand and engage in conflict in order to enhance their domestic legitimacy. The legitimacy of state rulers is not a constant but varies over time. Rulers with low legitimacy tend to lose power and to be thrown out of office and replaced by others; extreme losses of legitimacy combined with other factors can result in revolution (Skocpol 1979; Goldstone 1991). Rulers in victorious and expansionary states, however, acquire a halo of legitimation. In this regard, whether legitimacy is traditional, charismatic, or rational-legal is less significant than whether the legitimacy of the ruler, state, and law is high or low.[2]

We propose that politicians are legitimacy seekers. In the long run, they tend to follow policies that maximize their legitimacy. Weber's model implies that the strongest source of legitimacy comes from ruling a state that enjoys high prestige deriving from its power relationships with other states. Winning a conflict with another state is the most dramatic and emotionally compelling source of rulers' legitimacy. There are other sources of legitimacy as well: the current economic conditions of a society affect the ruler's popularity; dramatic incidents, crowd dynamics, and interaction rituals of leadership give officials the halo of emotional impressiveness; and both internal and external conflicts can raise group solidarity around a leader.[3] To explore one theory at a time, we will restrict our attention here to external power-prestige and legitimacy irrespective of these other inputs.

To say that politicians are legitimacy seekers is not to imply that they always calculate their foreign policy moves in order to enhance their domestic legitimacy. No doubt politicians make this sort of calculation in varying degrees. In the short run, both leaders and followers may become caught up in an emotional dynamic when opportunities for international conflict are initiated (such as the widespread enthusiasm over the U.S. military buildup in Arabia after Iraq invaded Kuwait in August 1990). In the long run, rulers whose states aggressively seek out international conflicts (and are successful in them) will benefit from legitimacy gains, which in turn reinforce the aggressive policy. Rulers who do not act to maintain power-prestige tend to be replaced. A state need not be overtly aggressive. The expansion of Rome's empire after 200 B.C., as well as of the U.S. world sphere of influence from the late nineteenth century onward, occurred largely in response to enemy provocations and appeals from allies. What we propose is that, as opportunities for international conflict occur repeatedly over the years, the dynamics of legitimacy seeking determine whether a ruler picks on a particular incident as a grounds for war or lets it go by.

Though we have couched our model in terms of overt warfare, the power-prestige of a state should be taken more broadly. A state acquires high power-prestige not only by winning wars but also by playing a prominent role in international affairs. Its ambassadors and emissaries are policymakers at conferences and on foreign visits, and Great Powers arbitrate the fate of smaller states with actions ranging from economic and military aid to armed intervention. We suggest that the same dynamic holds generally whether a strong state acquires territory by conquest or by economic penetration of trade and finance; whether it directly administers the weaker regions or acts as the leader of a coalition of allies.[4] Success in these ostensibly more peaceful and less intrusive forms of power-prestige usually depends upon a state's ability to win wars, established as past record or as current threat. There is a connection between legitimacy-seeking generally and the ups and downs of military power.

Overt warfare and assertion of domination over other political communities by imperial conquest increases the legitimacy of rule, but not without cost. After examining the basic dynamics of conflict and legitimacy, we will elaborate the theory in two directions. First, we add assumptions about the rates at which material benefits and costs change with the acquisition of empire, following the principles of geopolitical theory (Collins 1986: 145–209).

Second, we consider the consequences of territorial imperialism for the domestic political economy. Weber (1968: 917–19) discusses some dynamics of "imperialist capitalism" that tie the expansionist tendencies of political communities to the degree of dependency of the economy on the state. To the degree that economic production depends upon the capacity of the state to dominate other communities, expansionism and imperialism are promoted. Here Weber's discussion anticipates subsequent treatments of the "military-industrial complex."

POWER-PRESTIGE, LEGITIMACY, AND INTERNATIONAL CONFLICT

It is useful to begin with analytically simplified models of the separate parts of the legitimacy-seeking theory. These are ideal types or pure forms in which only specific processes operate. Taken by themselves, these initial results are historically unrealistic but demonstrate the dynamics inherent in the theory. From this theoretical core we develop these models in three steps of increasing complexity: (a) the dynamics of legitimacy and state conflict; (b) geopolitical and logistical limitations on the processes; and (c) the consequences of state-dependency of the economy and what Weber called "imperialist capitalism." Even the final composite version of the model is highly idealized and does not take into account the full range of historical complexities. Nevertheless, it provides some interesting approximations to historical events, including those of the late twentieth century.

The core of the theory is diagrammed in Figure A.1. The motivation of rulers to initiate external conflict is directly proportional to the difference between their current legitimacy and a goal of maximum legitimacy. For any given level of conflict initiated, the degree of success or failure is determined by the proportional superiority or inferiority of the power of the focal state to that of its enemies. Change in prestige in the status order of political communities is directly proportional to success in conflict, and legitimacy follows, with delay, from prestige.

The dynamics of the inner loop of Figure A.1 are extremely simple. If the focal state is stronger than its enemies, success ensues, followed by increased prestige and legitimacy until the ruler has achieved his or her goal. Where the focal state is weaker than its enemies, conflict is initiated and losses ensue, leading to declining prestige and legitimacy and therefore to increased aggressiveness by the ruler. That is, the ruler is trapped into accelerating unsuccessful conflict, which presumably leads at some point to his or her downfall. These processes are obvious once the theory is formulated as a feedback loop. We suspect, however, that most social scientists who have stated a model of "seeking conflict for seeking solidarity" have not thought in terms of a dynamic system, and hence have missed the implication that conflict, in the long run, can either cease or accelerate.

This first simulation experiment then immediately leads to a theoretical

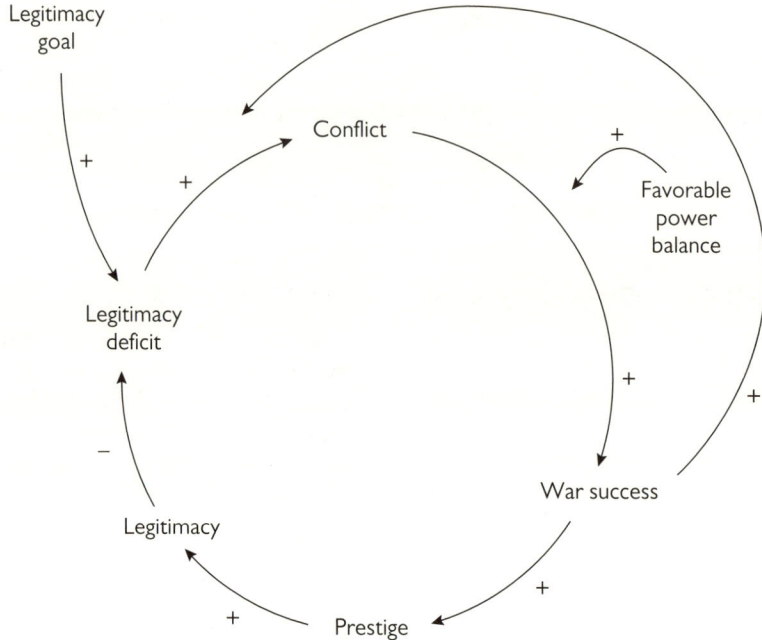

FIGURE A.1. Legitimacy and conflict.

elaboration that was not discussed by Weber. Rulers who are unsuccessful in conflicts will find little benefit in pursuing a self-destructive cycle, while rulers who are successful are likely to pursue even more aggressive policies. This outcome is captured by adding the outer loop of Figure A.1. For any given level of legitimacy deficit, the bellicosity of the ruler is increased if there is a history of successful conflict. If conflict is unsuccessful, however, the ruler's taste for further conflict initiation is reduced, even in the presence of continuing legitimacy problems.

Figure A.2a and A.2b display some of the results of two experiments with a simulation model based on Figure A.1. In both cases we have assumed that the ruler is suffering severe legitimacy difficulties (.25 on a scale from zero to 1.0) and that some history of successful conflict exists (for without it, no conflict would be initiated under this model). In Figure A.2a, we display the trends of conflict and legitimacy for a scenario in which the focal state is stronger than its enemies (by a 6:5 ratio); in Figure A.2b, the focal nation is weaker (by a 5:6 ratio).

In these experiments, conflict with a weaker enemy leads to success, which leads to both increased legitimacy and increased intensity of conflict

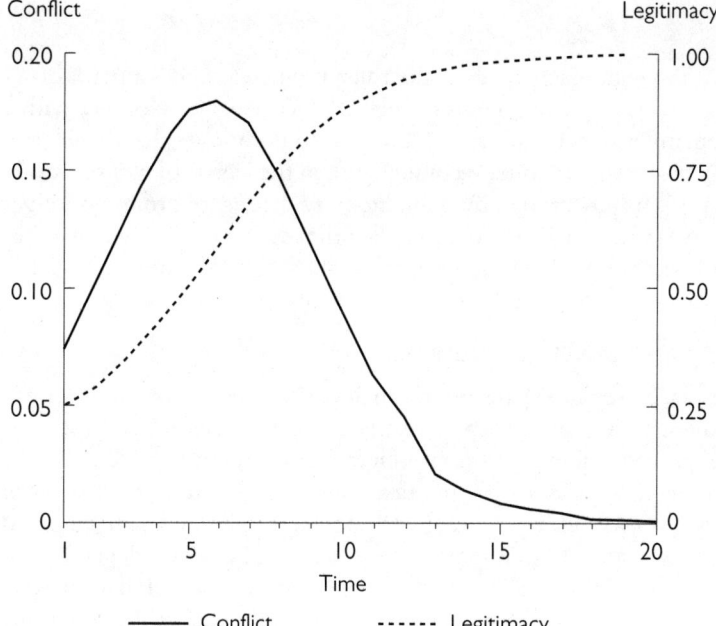

FIGURE A.2a. Legitimacy-seeking with a weaker enemy.

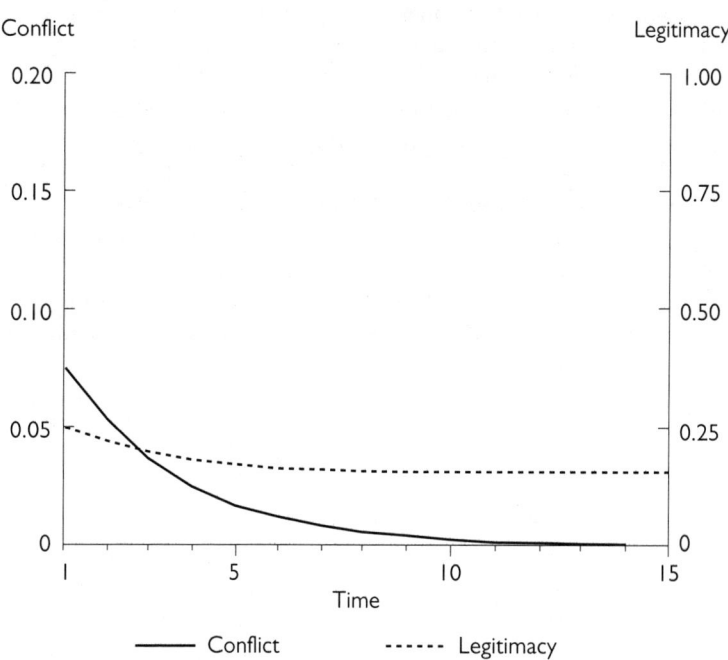

FIGURE A.2b. Legitimacy-seeking with a stronger enemy.

initially. As the legitimacy needs of the ruler are increasingly satisfied, however, the motivation to engage in further conflict declines. Conflict with a stronger enemy results in failure, which leads to both lower legitimacy and a declining propensity to initiate conflict. When the legacy of past success in warfare has been fully eroded by contemporary defeats, the ruler no longer initiates conflict and settles for chronic illegitimacy at a lower level than before the process began. These results are not surprising. We now proceed to elaborate the model to include related theoretical principles.

THE COSTS AND BENEFITS OF EMPIRE

Rulers do not persist in expansionist policies in the presence of more powerful enemies. However, even where there is initial superiority over enemies, the process of expansion produces both benefits and costs. The benefits of empire are not only political but also economic. Possession of dominated territory allows the core to extract surplus through enforced levies, land taxes, and cheap imports. These benefits, however, depend upon the regime's capacity to pacify the dominated territories, maintain internal control, and defend distant boundaries. We next suppose that the economic benefits of empire increase in direct proportion to the size of the empire (i.e., within a homogeneous periphery). However, the costs of maintaining control over empire increase exponentially with the size of the empire by the principle of exertion of force at a distance. At some point, then, expansion by direct territorial domination no longer pays for itself.

Within the space over which domination is exercised, it is useful to distinguish between the "core" (the homeland of the dominant political community) and the "empire" (the homelands of subjugated political communities). Core territories will be assumed to differ from imperial territories in two ways: first, core territories are more productive than imperial territories; second, no resources are expended to maintain internal control within the core. The logic of the model is not affected by this overly schematic assumption. Imperial territories require that coercive force be constantly expended to maintain internal control over them and to protect their boundaries.

The power of the ruler, regarded as a constant in the initial model, is transformed into a variable when the costs and benefits of empire are taken into account. The power of the ruler is equal to the total production of the territory controlled, less expenditures on conflict and on internal control. The expenditure on conflict is a function of the intensity of conflict and a loss rate on the power exerted. This loss rate is assumed to be a nonlinear function of the equality of power of the contestants: where the focal state and its enemies are equal, each unit of conflict is assumed to be very costly; as the focal state's superiority increases, its relative losses decline exponentially. Expenditures on internal control increase exponentially with the ratio

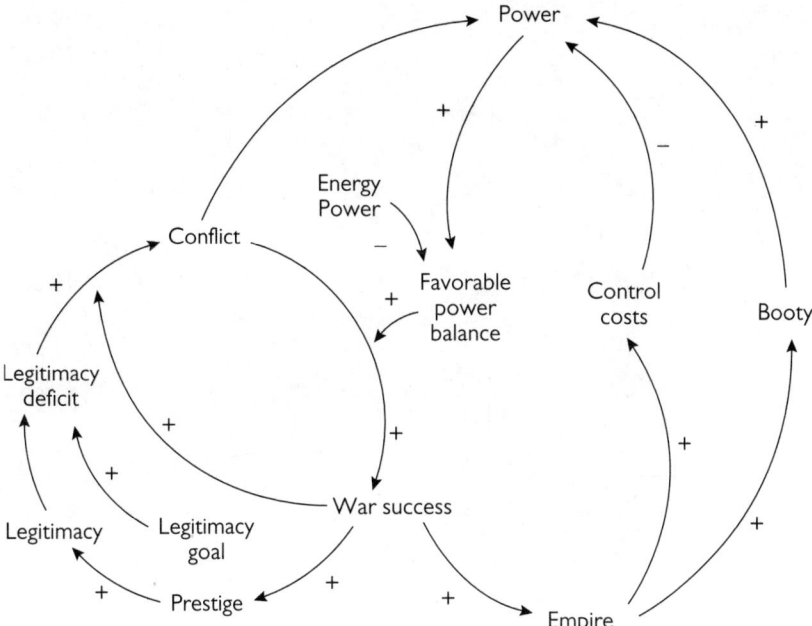

FIGURE A.3. Cost-benefit model of empire.

of the size of the empire to that of the core. At some "tipping point" the costs of controlling the empire exceed the production that can be extracted from it.

The general logic of the costs and benefits of empire are diagrammed in Figure A.3. To provide a sense of the dynamics of this system, specific values for the magnitudes of parameters were selected. These specific values, of course, are arbitrary. They are selected to illustrate the consequences of adding "booty" and "internal control costs" to the basic drive of the ruler for legitimacy through external conflict. To illustrate these dynamics, we have performed several experiments. We will dispense with the case in which the focal state is less powerful than its enemies and focus instead on variations in the initial legitimacy of rulers. These are key experiments because there are now two rather separate sets of processes governing state expansion: the legitimacy needs of rulers and the costs and benefits of empire. In the first model (Fig. A.2a), the ruler always achieved the desired legitimacy by defeating enemies, leading to a pattern of stable, low-level conflict. When constraints of cost and benefit are included, however, rulers may not achieve satisfactory legitimacy, despite military superiority.

Figures A.4a and A.4b show some of the results of two experiments with

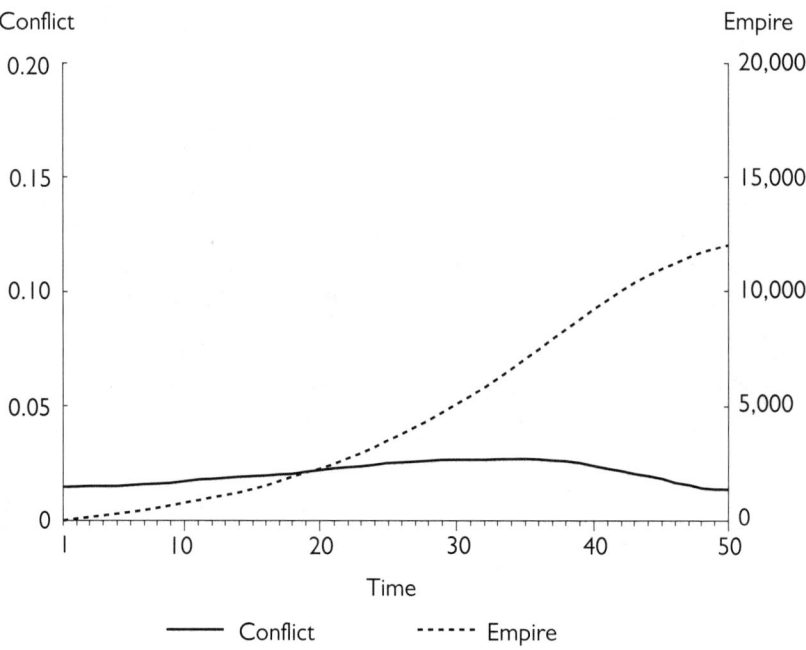

FIGURE A.4a. Cost and benefit experiments with high initial legitimacy.

a model including costs and benefits. In Figure A.4a, the legitimacy of rule is initialized at a relatively high level (.75 of the hypothetical maximum). In this circumstance, the behavior of the model is much the same as when external geopolitical constraints were not considered. Stimulated by a moderate deficiency in legitimacy, the ruler pursues a strategy of slowly accelerating conflict; the empire expands but does not reach overextension because the ruler's needs for legitimacy are satisfied. In Figure A.4b the ruler faces a more difficult task because of an initial lower level of legitimacy (.25 of the hypothetical maximum). In this case, the break-even point of costs and benefits is reached before the ruler has satisfied his or her legitimacy needs. The result is a pattern of episodic efforts to increase legitimacy by external conflict. Each effort is initially successful but results in overexpansion and collapse. Because of delays and nonlinearities, the timing and time-shape of each expansion-collapse episode is unique. This uniqueness is not accidental; it results from the operation of a deterministic system under varying historical conditions.

IMPERIALIST CAPITALISM AND THE MILITARY-INDUSTRIAL COMPLEX

The above discussion of state expansion is tied to the legitimacy-seeking political motives of rulers. In this regard, the theory is congruent with major

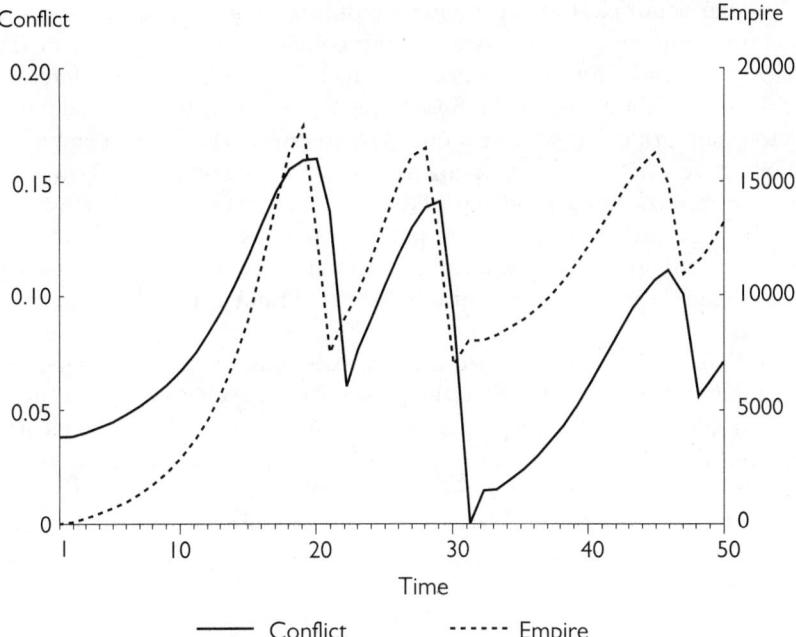

FIGURE A.4b. Cost and benefit experiments with low initial legitimacy.

elements of theories of "predatory rule" (Levi 1988; Tilly 1990). In addition, Weber argues that imperial expansion of core states alters the domestic political economy in several key ways that may escalate the process. Expansion by direct conquest leads to an increasing dependency of economic activity on the state. Increasing dependency ties the interests of economic actors to imperial success and may create pressures for continuing expansion. Weber also notes, in passing, that increasing dependency of the economy on the state may retard the development of independent capitalist forces with more pacific interests in trade and market development (1968: 915). This point has been more fully developed by others as one source of bureaucratic impediment to capitalist-led dynamism in some classical empires (Hall 1986).

In mobilizing for international conflict, the state creates potentially powerful classes with interests in conflict itself: the military, armaments producers, and capitalists who advance funds to the state. Territorial expansion also creates new sources of profit for classes of "imperial capitalists": populations from the core seeking land (settlers), imperial tax farmers and administrators, and entrepreneurs in the imperial territories who organize production for export to the core. These classes also depend on the state to maintain the empire as their source of livelihood, and consequently they promote imperialism.

Weber is not clear about the mechanisms by which the changes in the political economy of the core affect the conflict-seeking behavior of the ruler. One possibility is that rulers, recognizing the sensitivities and interests of the military, armaments and finance capitalists, colonial settlers, administrators, and producers, will be more likely to pursue conflict and empire as an effective mechanism for closing gaps in domestic legitimacy. That is, in the presence of high dependency of the economy on the state, the tendency for the legitimacy-seeking ruler to pursue conflict is accelerated. In the absence of economic dependency on the state, the ruler is less likely to pursue this option so vigorously because it may be unpopular with major constituencies.

In Figure A.5 we have added these connections to the loop-diagram of the model. Conflict gives rise to the proportional development of an "arms industry," including arms producers, the military, and finance capitalists funding the state. The level of the arms industry is treated as responding rapidly to conflict initiation but dissipating only with delay to reductions in conflict (war debts must be repaid, armies demobilized, and manufactories turned to other purposes). The creation of imperial capitalist classes follows from territorial conquest. The "imperial capitalist" portion of the economy is taken to be directly proportional to production in the colonial territory. Together, empire and a large domestic warfare apparatus generate a state-dependent economy.

As shown in Figure A.5, conflict is assumed to be initiated by the ruler in pursuit of a fixed legitimacy goal. According to this model, in the presence of high economic dependency on the state, the ruler directly translates legitimacy deficits into the pursuit of international conflict. In the presence of low economic dependency of the economy on the state, however, the ruler's pursuit of international conflict as a mechanism for legitimacy production is retarded.

The results of several simulation experiments with the imperial capitalism model are presented in Figures A.6a–h. Again, we have restricted our attention to the situations in which the core state has an initial power advantage over its enemies (where there is no power advantage of the focal state, the dynamics follow those shown in Figure A.2b), and in which the enemy's power is regarded as a constant. Since we found that the initial legitimacy of the ruler was critical in determining the nature of the realization in the previous model, we again examine two basic scenarios: one in which the ruler initially has high legitimacy (.75) and one in which the ruler faces severe problems (.25). In each experiment, because the core state initially has no empire the pressures of imperial capitalism are low. Within each legitimacy scenario, however, we examine two alternatives. In one case, the core state has an initial high level of economic dependency on the military-industrial

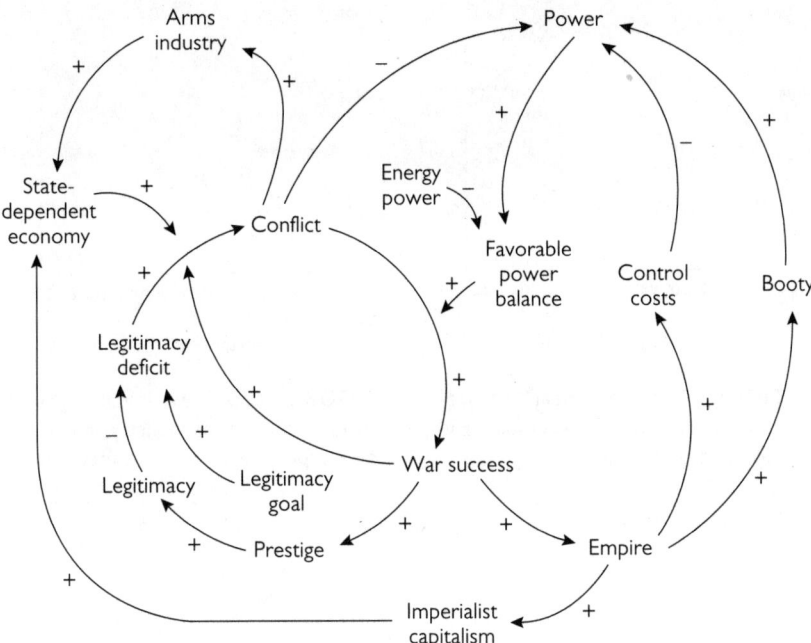

FIGURE A.5. Imperialist capitalism model.

complex (25 percent of all production is initially in the armaments industry); in the other, we initialize the role of the armaments industry in the economy at a low level (2 percent).

The first two sets of results in Figures A.6a–d are scenarios in which the ruler initially faces severe legitimacy problems. In the first set (Figures A.6a and A.6b), the arms industry is initialized at a low level, in the second set (Figures A.6c and A.6d) at a high level (these results are variations on Figure A.4a). In both cases, the ruler pursues a policy of vigorous foreign conflict and expansion that leads to imperial overextension and "chaotic equilibrium" of empire and legitimacy. The pursuit of empire is substantially delayed by initially low levels of imperialist sentiment. In both cases, the maintenance of a substantial empire leads to permanently high levels of imperialist capitalism. The continuous high levels of conflict generate a total "warfare state" in which virtually all of the product of both the empire and core are devoted to military activity.

The last two sets of results (Figures A.6e–f and Figures A.6g–h) suggest a rather different result where the legitimacy of rule is initially high. In both of these scenarios imperialist expansion and the creation of an empire of roughly the same final size occurs, but the process is far slower and achieves

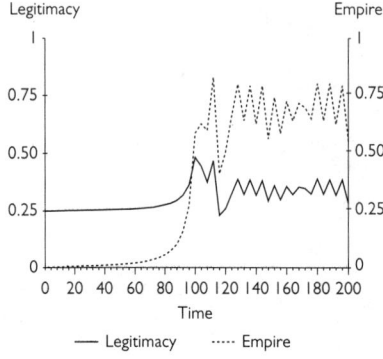

FIGURE A.6a. Low initial legitimacy and low arms industry: empire and legitimacy outcomes.

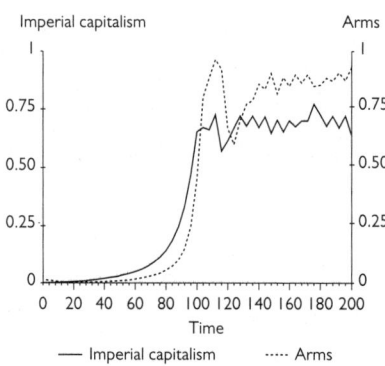

FIGURE A.6b. Low initial legitimacy and low arms industry: imperialist capitalism and arms outcomes.

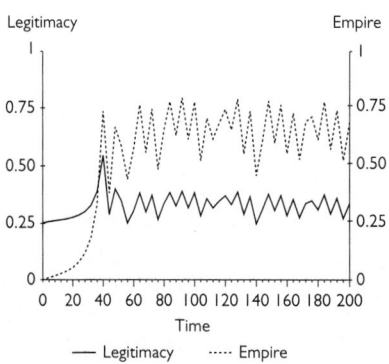

FIGURE A.6c. Low initial legitimacy and high arms industry: empire and legitimacy outcomes.

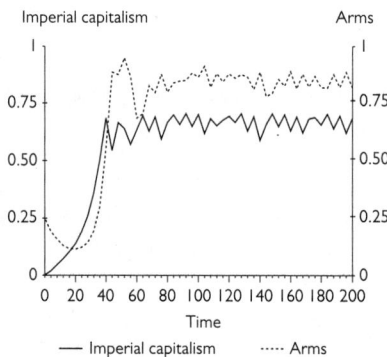

FIGURE A.6d. Low initial legitimacy and high arms industry: imperialist capitalism and arms outcomes.

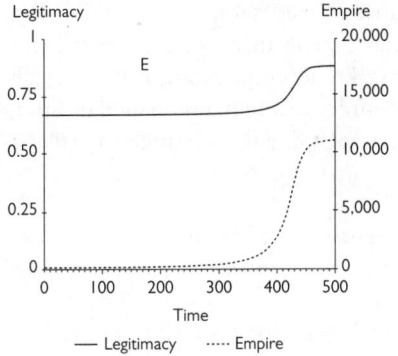

FIGURE A.6e. High initial legitimacy and low arms industry: empire and legitimacy outcomes.

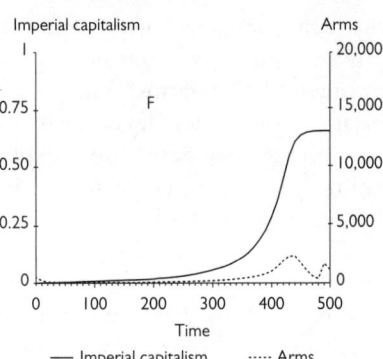

FIGURE A.6f. High initial legitimacy and low arms industry: imperialist capitalism and arms outcomes.

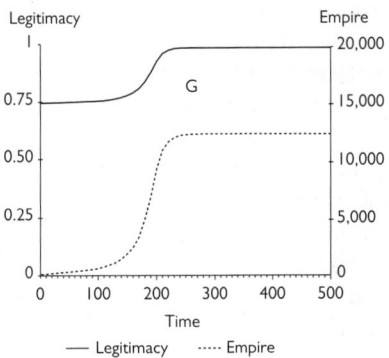

FIGURE A.6g. High initial legitimacy and high arms industry: empire and legitimacy outcomes.

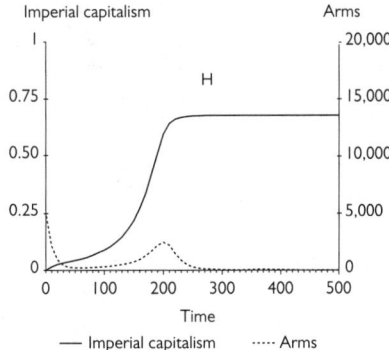

FIGURE A.6h. High initial legitimacy and high arms industry: imperialist capitalism and arms outcomes.

the legitimacy goals of the rulers. Because of this, while the resulting empire's economy is dominated by imperial capitalism, further conflict is not pursued, and the arms industry withers. These empires are not internally pacific because they devote as many resources to the maintenance of internal order as they derive from exploitation of the empire. Since the ruler is satisfied, however, he or she no longer pursues expansionism, despite the sentiment of imperial capitalists.

The most striking results of the current model are the ways in which longer-term dynamics of expansionist states are contingent upon the initial legitimacy of rule. Where legitimacy is high (but not at the level desired by the ruler), expansion occurs slowly with less intense conflict. In the long run, the resulting empire is as large as that of more aggressive rulers but has a quite different character. In these cases, because of the relatively low level of conflict and the reduction of conflict once legitimacy goals are met, the domestic military-industrial complex is of little significance. In contrast, where rulers embark on expansion in the presence of severe legitimacy deficits, the resulting empires are as large but are characterized by chronic instability, continuing (if variable) high levels of conflict, and the creation of a fused economy and state in which virtually all resources are devoted to warfare. The model suggests, then, that expansion by direct territorial conquest always gives rise to capitalist imperialism, but only variably to a "warfare state." Paradoxically, imperialist capitalism flourishes in states that are not highly militarist. Although these results are schematic, they may throw some light on the differences between the degree of militarism in the United States and other types of imperialism in world history.

The final model is too complex and nonlinear to deal with directly by mathematical solution. By means of experiment, however, many of its general properties can be discerned. One of the most interesting of these is illustrated in Figure A.7, which charts the range of long-term outcomes of legitimacy graphed against the initial level of legitimacy. At low levels (below about .08) and high levels (above about .60) the model proceeds more or less smoothly to a single equilibrium. In the intermediate range of initial legitimacy, however, the model generates periodic and then chaotic behavior.

ELABORATIONS AND LIMITS

The theory developed here remains highly idealized and incomplete. Of its numerous limitations, three are critical. In the results reported above, the enemy is regarded as not initiating conflict and as having a constant capacity to resist the imperial pretensions of the core political community. This simplification allows us to understand the dynamics of one community in a "constant" environment. A more realistic approach would lead to a model of multiple political communities, each of which is hypothesized to behave

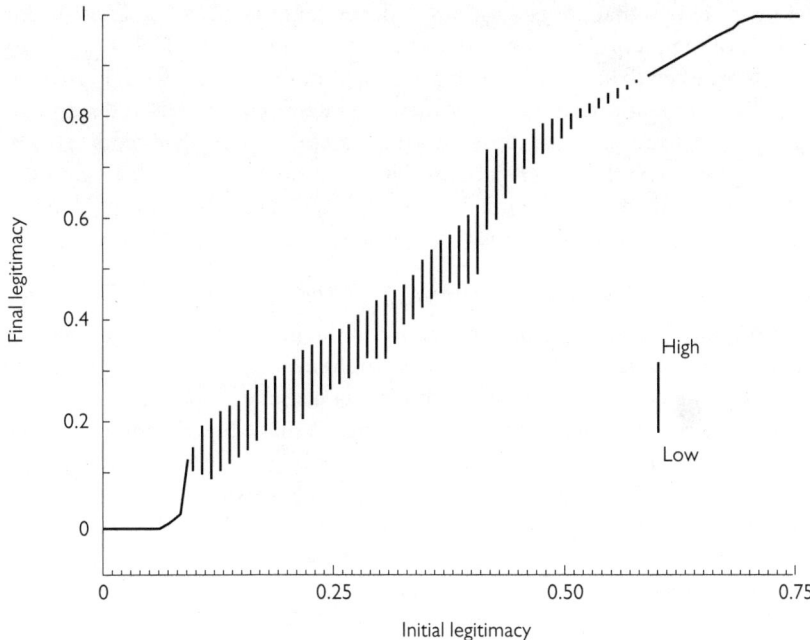

FIGURE A.7. Initial and final legitimacy.

according to the theory. The range of outcomes in such a system is not apparent, and its exploration by simulation would be a substantial undertaking.

We have chosen a conservative and state-centered view of the motives for imperial expansion. In the current theory, if the ruler is satisfied, no conflict is initiated, even where there is a total fusion of economy and state and a history of bellicosity. A more radical suggestion is that the legitimacy goal that rulers pursue may ratchet upward as a result of economic dependency on the state created by past imperial success. To the extent that this is a more empirically realistic view, all imperialist expansions must inevitably lead to overexpansion and instability. This alternative view has an interesting obverse (also suggested indirectly by Weber in discussing nations that choose neutrality such as Switzerland) that lack of imperial expansion, or failure to attain or maintain empire, may lead to a downward ratcheting of legitimacy needs of the ruler.[5]

In the theory examined here, the legitimacy of rule results solely from the status attainment of the political community in the international power-prestige order. This is a considerable simplification. The legitimacy of rule and rulers arises from multiple sources.[6] Successful foreign conflict and the attainment of power-prestige in the world order are critical in legitimating rule with classes that are economically dependent on the state. The current version of the theory, however, treats all other groups as residual (e.g., trade-oriented rather than imperialist capitalists, economic masses, and religious and cultural communities). Bureaucratic interference with independent capitalism, taxes on and casualties among the masses, and competition among the elites of different communities within the nation may all place active rather than passive limits on expansion. The elaboration of more complex and realistic models is the next step in theory development.

THEORY SIMULATION AS A STEP TOWARD APPLIED SOCIAL THEORY

In using simulation experiments to explore the implications of theories, we begin with a model based on explicitly simplified assumptions. After the dynamics of the core model become visible, we elaborate by making constants into variables and adding additional variables to make the system more realistic. A further step becomes possible for sociology once we have dynamic models that, properly specified, produce good approximations to empirical patterns found in the past. A realistic model of some basic social processes enables us to carry out thought-experiments of a different sort. It becomes possible to plug in hypothetical conditions and project the outcomes in a simulated world. This world may be our own long-term future. The initial conditions may be various policy options, or they may be real conditions that we observe in the present or anticipate will exist.

Sociology's record of practical application in the past has not been impressive. In part this has been because of the split between theory and empirical research. Theories have rarely been formulated in ways that are conducive to accounting for processes in a multicausal world, complicated by time effects and feedbacks. As a result, abstract verbal theories have not usually offered much beyond retrospective interpretations. Extrapolation of empirical trend data, however, unguided by theoretical models of underlying causal mechanisms, has been vulnerable to unforeseen shifts, such as those that have undermined population projections in the past. The technique of experimenting with computer simulations holds promise for sociology to become a useful applied science, at a level of precision and nonobviousness that goes beyond trend extrapolations and simple statements of short-run tendencies.

Since sociological prediction raises feelings of uneasiness in some quarters, it is worthwhile in conclusion to clear away a few misconceptions. Policy-oriented prediction does not automatically imply a social-science elite manipulating the world. It is more likely to be a means of generating information that can enter the usual debates within the political process. There is nothing intrinsic in the nature of running simulation models that would keep sociologists from investigating the consequences of policy options that they consider to be in the democratic interest. When and if sociological theory becomes more successful, we would expect competing interest groups to have their own teams of sociologists doing simulations. Perhaps their performance might not be any better than economists' predictions have been in the recent past. At any rate, that would be a step toward a higher level of social usefulness for sociological theory.

Questions of another order involve the possible limits of realistic social prediction. Even at its best, dynamic theory simulation might be doomed to be no more successful than meteorology, which has poor forecasting accuracy beyond a few days. That is to say, do most social processes that are of policy interest take place in regions where chaos prevails? If this is so, no amount of improvement in our theories will get us past the predictive barrier. As yet, we know little about what can be done or not done with dynamic theory simulation. It seems implausible that simulations will tell us nothing useful. (For example, what would be the social consequences of legalizing various drugs? What would follow from totally cutting off immigration or throwing open a state's borders to all comers?) Useful answers to such questions depend on concerted efforts to frame them adequately in terms of a general theory. The improvement of applied simulation thus depends on the improvement in dynamic theoretical models generally.

Borkenau's Geopolitics of Language and Cultural Change

FRANZ BORKENAU DIED in Vienna in 1957 at the comparatively early age of 56. Richard Lowenthal brought out a posthumous collection of his papers, most previously unpublished, under the title *End and Beginning: On the Generations of Cultures and the Origins of the West* (Borkenau 1981). The papers were written in the late 1940s and early 1950s by a man trained before and just after World War I. They are an intellectual throwback to an earlier generation. In many ways this is an advantage, particularly in Borkenau's use of historical and comparative linguistics, a form of linguistics that has fallen out of fashion. Borkenau leads us to places where few other thinkers have been before, especially in his reversal of our usual perspective on the fall of the Roman Empire. Instead of seeing the change from the side of "civilization," he looks at it from the point of view of the Germans. It is in the crisis of German tribal society, he argues, that we must find the origins of Western society.

Borkenau situates himself in intellectual argument with his near contemporaries Oswald Spengler and Arnold Toynbee. Borkenau too thinks that civilizations are born and die; that the West was born around A.D. 400 and is now coming to an end. Its successor is in sight, he thinks, in the new spirit visible in Russia (keep in mind, of course, when he was writing). One might attribute Borkenau's opinion to the viewpoint of a central European, an ex-member of the Communist Internationale, contemplating from Vienna the newly arisen prospect of atomic war while glancing at the Soviet armies over his shoulder.

In another respect, there is nothing anachronistic about Borkenau's contribution. The recent Golden Age of historical sociology has revamped our ideas about when the "modern" era begins. The economic transformation of modern capitalism is now understood to be implicated in a prior political transformation, and both of these take us back behind the usual seventeenth-and eighteenth-century "dividing line." How far back? Macfarlane (1978) claims that in England, at least, there is evidence that "modern" structures already existed in the High Middle Ages, and others have argued that the same applies to all of northwestern Europe. I have argued that it was a revolution in the structural and economic organization of the medieval church that set off the change (Collins 1986). Goody (1983), focusing on the modernization of the family, argues that the change is rooted even further back, in the centuries after the establishment of Christianity as state-supported religion (initially in Rome after A.D. 300).

Borkenau throws his weight into the discussion at this point with a date similar to Goody's but a more complex argument. What is distinctive about the West arises from the breakdown of Germanic tribal society during the great migrations and invasions, especially the seaborne invasions of Britain and Ireland, thereafter spreading southward through the Continent. Borkenau's data are largely about religion, both medieval Christianity and the Germanic myths. He also has striking evidence from the history of languages. Borkenau's criterion for modernity is cultural, but he also seems to believe that culture is produced by social conditions. Thus he opens the way to a widened theory of culture, as well as to an interpretation of the processes that produced Western society. His argument can be seen to converge, too, with that of Perry Anderson in *Passages from Antiquity to Feudalism* (1974a), except that for Borkenau the crucial feature is not what the West has inherited from Rome but the crisis experienced by Germanic societies as they took advantage of geopolitical opportunities resulting from disintegration of the empire.

I shall sketch some parts of this argument, but first a word about how to read Borkenau's book. It is a collection in three parts, the first and third consisting of Borkenau's already published essays, the middle and longest part consisting of unpublished manuscripts, apparently intended as the basis for a book. The opening and closing sections, with their reflections on Spengler and Toynbee, now seem somewhat antiquated. The central section, a 300-page book within a book, is one of the most brilliant pieces of historical interpretation I have ever seen.

Within this inner book is a 70-page chapter labeled a "linguistic prelude" and entitled "The Rise of the I-form of Speech." This is the finest piece of comparative language analysis that I know of. Most of the rest of this appendix is devoted to spelling out its argument.

THE EMERGENCE OF WESTERN SPEECH

The first use of the isolated pronoun "I" in northern Europe is found in a runic inscription of about A.D. 400 from Denmark: "I, Hlegestr from Holt, made this horn." This statement contrasts sharply with the spirit of Greek and Latin expression. A Roman craftsman would not have intruded this emphatic first person, but would have written: "*Gn. Manlius faber hoc cornu fecit*" —(The craftsman Gn. Manlius made this horn) (pp. 134–35). What we have here, says Borkenau, is the rise of the distinctively Western attitude toward the world (and toward society): individualism amounting to egoism, self-assertion, activism. Linguistic evidence shows this attitude spreading through the northern languages. Use of the first-person pronoun became obligatory by A.D. 1000 in the Scandinavian languages and later spread to English, German, and French (the last resisted until the 1600s).

Borkenau wishes to provide a sociological explanation of this linguistic change. To make his case, he must dispose of alternative explanations. There is a purely linguistic argument that separate pronouns are introduced because phonetic changes made it impossible to distinguish the sounds of various endings (e.g., French *je fais, il fait*). Borkenau, drawing on an impressive range of language comparisons, dismisses this explanation as failing to capture the time sequence in which the two changes (pronouns, sound shifts) occurred in different languages. The second alternative is to explain the rise of pronouns as part of a general shift from the "synthetic" languages of traditional Indo-European toward the modern "analytical" type. Borkenau's treatment of this hypothesis is a marvel of erudition. He ranges through the languages of the Balkans and the Middle East in a fashion that only a Central European of that generation could have done. The upshot is as follows.

The "synthesizing" languages, such as ancient Greek, condensed meanings by means of inflections on a limited number of roots. These forms began to disintegrate with the political decline of ancient civilization, and by the eleventh century A.D. analytical forms, such as composite tenses ("I am going to be moving"), were far advanced almost everywhere. (This is a reason to find the "dark ages," rather than some later period, pivotal in the history of the West.) There were variations: Slavonic and Celtic languages have kept nearer the synthetic style, the German languages have departed furthest from it, while the southern European languages have moved to an intermediate position. Borkenau argues that the I-form of speech is merely one indicator of a shift in the entire social outlook: "Such a separation of the individual from its acts is rarely expressed in Greek and Latin, and only for the sake of special emphasis. Where all modern languages are essentially psychological, classical antiquity is entirely and unreservedly given to the expression of the outward event" (p. 146). Composite tenses for expressing the future are particularly revealing of this attitude change. English and Scandinavian use "shall" and "will," auxiliaries that express the obligation or decision of an agent, the realm of intention, forethought, and resistance. The more inflected languages of the Mediterranean continue to use an ending that merely notes the time rather than stressing the agent.

I cannot reproduce the cleverness and breadth of Borkenau's comparisons of numerous aspects of language ranging from Iceland to Arabia. Two main points must suffice. First, the underlying theory is sociological, even to a large extent political (and geopolitical). Language reflects changes in the society. Borkenau makes sense, for example, out of the varieties of grammatical forms among Balkan languages by indicating how their parallels follow not from the historical antecedents of these language groups, but from the political boundaries of incorporation into the Byzantine Empire. Similar results follow from the Hellenistic conquests that brought Greek into a political unity with Middle Eastern languages. Though his theory of language is not systematized, Borkenau gives politics an important place in chains of events that lead to shifts in language. The second point is one that brings Borkenau surprisingly close to the ideas of Noam Chomsky: syntax is more important than phonetics or vocabulary for establishing the underlying social and historical dimensions of language (p. 152). This emphasis contrasts with most historical philology and sociolinguistics, which concentrate on the more superficial aspects of language change.

Let us return to Borkenau's specific argument on the rise of the Western outlook. What major social events centered in northern Europe occurred during the period A.D. 400 to 1000? This was the period of the "Völkerwanderung," the military migrations that rearranged the political and linguistic map. The only premigration language known to us, Gothic, lacked the independent pronoun, but all the postmigration languages have it. But why should this particular migration have given rise to language change indicative of individualistic assertion when other migrations (such as those of the ancient Italic peoples or the Mongols) did not? Borkenau points out that the Teutonic migrations especially were movements of ad hoc war leaders with personal followings. Seaborne raids and invasions in particular were organized as collections of young men, moving without women, who had broken their tribal kinship ties. By contrast, the other migrations Borkenau considers were movements of entire tribes, who transferred their traditional kinship groupings to new territories. It is this freely recruited, voluntarist war-following of the Scandinavians that gave rise to the individualist, self-assertive attitude expressed in their language.

There are further complexities to the argument. Of all the Celtic tongues, only Irish had independent pronouns. These developed in roughly the eighth century A.D.. Again, Borkenau proposes, this happened in an island society during a period of individualistic migrations of personal followings, although later political pressures resurrected the local clan in counterpoise to any centralized kingship. England was culturally colonized by Christian missionaries from Ireland during this period (a point that Borkenau develops in later chapters) and was the focal point from which monastic settlements with the ascetic "reforming" activism spread back to the Continent. But England was also above all the land of the Teutonic invasions, from the Anglo Saxon period (400s to 500s) through the Normanized Viking era six centuries later. English, Borkenau asserts, is the most "Western" of languages. Not only has synthesis (inflection) most thoroughly disappeared in English, but it is the only language that capitalizes the "I." Fittingly, the first instance we have of the use of the detached "I," Hlegestr's horn, was found in the very bay of the Danish coast from which the Anglo Saxon invaders set out for Britain.

Borkenau adds a charming countertheme. He traces the rise of the polite second-person plural (Italian *lei*, French *vous*, Spanish *usted*, and German *Sie*) rather than the singular (*voi*, *tu*, *tu*, and *du*). The social attitude that led to this development is the opposite of that involved in the use of the emphatic "I." Before the abrasive first person came into currency, the second-person singular had no special connotation of social relationship; afterward, it came to smack of subordination to the speaker. To counteract this impression, the polite second-person "you" came into use.[1] Furthermore, it began in the territories that had the longest resistance to the spread of the new northern form. The I-form spread from Scandinavia to the Mediterranean; when it hit Provence and Catalonia in the 1100s, it was answered by the polite you-form, which spread in reverse order, finally reaching Scandinavia in the 1500s. Again England provides the most extreme example. There the singular second person ("thou") disappeared entirely in polite speech (though not without some political resistance, as among the Quakers), leaving only the self-assertively capitalized "I" to deal nonintimately with a universally depersonalized "you."[2]

Borkenau sums up his linguistic arguments: "Features such as 'I' and 'you,' the loss of case endings, the growth of composite and the loss of simple tenses, the ever more important role of transitive verbs and active expressions, indicate clearly enough the general character of our Western civilization. The structures of languages provide some general clues pointing to the salient features of a civilization. But only the direct study of its ideas and institutions can give us certainty about how to interpret the clues" (p. 201). Borkenau proceeds to do this in the rest of his "book within a book" on the origins of the West. Before turning to this, I would add the following comments.

Implicit in Borkenau's work is a theory about language change that roots it in social organization. But there are problems with Borkenau's use of this conception. There is some conflict between the premise that society produces language forms and the notion of a germ of civilization, the notion that once the spirit of an era is given birth it continues to be efficacious. If society creates personal and linguistic attitudes, it must be society that sustains those attitudes and replace them with something else. A "spirit" does not die of its own accord, although Borkenau's vestigial Spenglerism sometimes implies that it does after its allotted time is up. Borkenau has interesting things to say in this regard about the structure of the Russian language. Russian's emphasis on aspect instead of tense orient it toward permanences rather than actions in time. Russian shrinks from expressing direct personal ownership and "avoids representing the individual as the center of things" (p. 197). The characterization may be accurate, but the implication of a world-historical transition is Borkenau's brooding over the replacement of one civilization by another, part of the mood of Vienna in 1950. I think that the sociological explanation of language is the right one. This means that language does not indicate an autonomous "spirit," even though there are long-run mechanisms of both inertia and change that we do not well understand. But it will necessitate a more complex theory than Borkenau affords it.

The linguistics and social science of the later twentieth century have not been well positioned to provide such a theory. The "linguistic turn" evident in philosophy, anthropology, and psychology has privileged formal analysis of ahistorical structures. In my opinion, if a historical theory of language is to be developed, it will take a comparative sociologist to do it.

GERMANIC RELIGION AND NIHILISM

Borkenau indicates that Western culture has multiple roots, all stemming from the early medieval period after the breakdown of the Roman Empire. He examines the Pelagian heresy that emanated from Britain just as it broke free from Rome, with its stress on the archetypical Western theme of salvation through one's own efforts. He traces the politics of monasticism in the Irish Far West and its break from the Mediterranean monastic tradition. All this, although creatively handled, is still within the themes of traditional interpretation, which place Western civilization as an extension of classical culture traced through Christianity. What is most distinctive in Borkenau's argument, though, is his treatment of German mythology and religion during this period.

Borkenau asks a question rarely if ever before raised: what did the breakdown of the Roman Empire look like from the German side? Already at the time of Caesar the empire was creating a crisis in German society. A "party" split arose between pro-Roman and anti-Roman factions owing to the Roman policy of buying alliances with certain tribes against their fellows, a split that grew even wider as Germans came to man most of the Roman frontier legions. This split is usually seen as a sign that the more primitive society felt culturally inferior when confronted with the more advanced civilization. But that civilization was visibly crumbling militarily. Hence a genuine choice within the German world: adopting Mediterranean culture, especially Christianity, or pushing the opposite way, for a German counterculture.

In this context, Borkenau points to a little-recognized pattern in the history of Teutonic religions. There were actually two sets of gods: the older Wanic deities (or "Vanir": Freya, Freyr, Njord) who were objects of chthonic, seasonal cults; and the Ase deities (or "Aesir": Odin, Thor, and others), masculine war gods whose worship required bloody human sacrifices. The Wanic cults, which practiced vague animistic forest rites, were already falling into decay at the time of Caesar's campaigns; the Ase cults *did not appear until about the sixth century A.D.* and flourished for several centuries before giving way to Christianity.[3] Borkenau draws two dramatic conclusions for the origins of Western culture.

First, the Germanic tribes went through the crucial period of overrunning and replacing the Roman Empire as a *predominantly irreligious culture.* The ancient German sagas are notable, in contrast to Greek, Hindu, or Celtic myths, for the absence of deities intervening in human heroes' lives. Western culture formed itself not under the benediction of projected moral symbols but as a saga of godless egos. For this is exactly the time of the language shift, of the migrations of personal followerships and the breaking of old tribal ties. Borkenau searches myths and later literature for remnants of this period, producing an impressive set of interpretations of the Siegfried saga and other works that should make Lévi-Strauss envious. Borkenau's conclusions, too, are more powerful than the static archetypes of the sort Dumézil brings out, for he finds evidence of a severe moral crisis in the period of migrations and wars among the Germanic coalitions: guilt over the breaking of kinship ties in new political alliances, horrible visions of the consequences of leaving unburied the victims of their massive battles in a society for whom the funeral rite was central. When the Ase pantheon finally appeared midway through this period, it presents us with the least supportive, most pessimistic religion. Odin, god of the battlefield, is also the god of treachery, of the hangman, and of death. Thor and the other divine heroes are nevertheless doomed to fight a battle at the end of the world—and lose. An existentialist despair, Borkenau proposes, is at the root of the West's first advanced culture, linked to Western individualism, striving, and self-reliance.[4]

Second, this culture was nevertheless an advanced culture. It was not the product of illiterate tribes but grew up in the times and places that an indigenous alphabet—the runes—was invented. It was a culture formed in explicit war against Christianity for control of the new states of the north, a long struggle marked by the pagan Saxon revolt in Germany against the Frankish converts to Christianity and not ended until the forced conversion of the last Scandinavians after 1100.[5] In this context fits the curious legend of Odin, sacrificed on a holy tree for nine days and nights but finally tearing himself loose—simultaneously emulating, repudiating, and outdoing the Christian Jesus. It was a culture that seemed to know it was going to die but was determined to fight: the most historically aware consciousness until modern secular times.

Borkenau's manuscript was left unfinished at his death, and there remains the problem of putting together the pieces of his argument: the linguistic revolution with its most extreme forms in the seafaring warrior societies of the north; the sense of "primal crime of the dark ages" in the treachery to tribal loyalties and rites in the mass migrations and wars on the Continent; the transformation of Christianity as both enemy and inheritor of these northern societies as evidenced by its Pelagianism and its monasticism. This is a job for a historical sociologist with sufficient insight into the political sociology of religion, the transformation of kinship systems, the sociology of language change, and above all enough independence of mind to escape the usual evolutionist and Mediterranean-oriented clichés about the medieval era. In short, it would take someone with the unique talents of a Franz Borkenau. One can only hope he will find adequate successors.

A contemporary called Borkenau "an argonaut of the human spirit." The image could hardly be more fitting.

Notes

INTRODUCTION: THE GOLDEN AGE OF MACROHISTORICAL SOCIOLOGY

1. There is related work in the field of international relations, especially in the branch now called security studies (leading works include Waltz 1979, Gilpin 1981, Keohane 1986, Walt 1987). Here we see an odd effect of academic Balkanization, the divergence between work in political science and in historical sociology. The two disciplinary camps operate on overlapping terrain but with different conceptual tools and concerns. The international relations field has debated the premises of neorealism, the extent to which behavior of states can be reduced to calculations of self-interest, whether these interests are economic or sheer power, and whether the interstate arena is a place of normless anarchy. From a sociological viewpoint, the debate over international anarchy mixes analytical theorizing and normative evaluation so as to obscure the focus on the geopolitical principles that simultaneously structure the interstate arena and the states within it. The older balance-of-power school (Morgenthau 1948) took British strategy in the early modern period as its normative model of the desirable and overgeneralized it into an analytical theory of all geopolitics. The newer hegemonic stability theory similarly bases itself on modern European history and confines itself to arguing for the desirable effects of a hegemon in enforcing the rules of world order (an argument that overlaps analytically with sociological world-system theory while diverging from it in normative emphasis). In general, international relations theory has been more concerned with policy questions and with the causes of outbreaks of war and what can be done to prevent them. Sociological geopolitics is more concerned with how states are shaped, both in their borders and in their internal organization, by long-term patterns of war and threats of war.

CHAPTER 1: MATURATION OF THE STATE-CENTERED THEORY OF REVOLUTION AND IDEOLOGY

1. Mann (1986, 1993) uses the image of crystallization for the formation of power structures that dominate particular historical epochs. The image is highly appropriate for his model in which social structures are not fixed entities but four overlap-

ping networks of concrete relationships: military, political, economic, and cultural. In Mann's vision of world history, the sizes and shapes of these several networks across the global landscape do not generally coincide; the very overlapping of the networks (e.g., the greater extension of religious networks outside the military networks of the Roman Empire) is a key to social change. A similar model of networks of different sizes is documented in Chase-Dunn and Hall (1997) for long periods of world history.

2. Another way to say this is that temporarily fixed identities at a lower level can become nodes of a network that crystallizes certain social identities (organizations, groups, states) at a higher level, and that this process can proceed recursively to yet higher levels of network relationship. Dissolution of the network of relations constituting identities can occur at any level as this process goes on. For a concrete example, see my argument that collegial democracy can emerge from alliance structures in certain geopolitical configurations (Chapter 4).

3. Goldstone's strategy of confining his analysis to comparisons across time within each state is highly appropriate. It would be impossible (as well as unproductive) to sample all states at all times and places. As Li (1998) points out, the method of studying the independent variable over a long period of time within the same state should be regarded as a virtue because it holds extraneous features of the cases constant to a considerable extent. The method yields a relatively pure test and opportunity to falsify the model in the classic Popperian sense.

CHAPTER 2: THE GEOPOLITICAL BASIS OF REVOLUTION: THE PREDICTION OF THE SOVIET COLLAPSE

1. Collins 1978 is the source for materials below not otherwise cited. The general model formulated therein was based on a synthesis of previous GP literature together with research using historical atlases covering 3,000 years of the Middle East and Europe and an independent series covering China. This is a broader basis than is cited by most of the international relations and GP literature, in which evidence is drawn primarily from post-1500 Europe and secondarily from the classic phase of Greco-Roman antiquity.

2. In contrast, one limit on much international relations literature is that it is concerned with the incidence of war and the conditions for stability or transition in the interstate system. The broader problem, however, is to explain the conditions that determine the changing power of states, and especially the power that results from the outcomes of wars.

3. Boulding formally derived cumulative advantage in the case of two-person games (1962: 237–39).

4. The last is the type of simplification that emerged from the multistate fragmentation of medieval Europe. A series of three large empires/coalitions have fought for hegemony: the Spanish/Habsburg Empire against a coalition centered on France; French military/diplomatic expansion culminating in the Napoleonic Empire; the German-centered axis against the allied periphery in World Wars I and II. The recurrence of this pattern, with different actors in the roles, suggests structural conditions such as those set forth in the cumulative dynamics of principles 1–

3, as well as random factors that determine who plays which roles. In each case the most expansionary coalition fell to defeat through military exhaustion.

5. Wars between Roman and Persian empires culminating in the early seventh century left both exhausted in a power vacuum into which the Arab conquest coalition suddenly expanded under the new ideology of Islam. Other examples from Chinese history are cited in Collins 1978. The exhaustion of Germany, Britain, and France in World War II left the world under the dominance of the two marchland states, the United States and Russia. A principal discussion in international relations literature concerns whether multisided balance-of-power situations or two-sided polarization leads to greater stability or to the likelihood of major war (Waltz 1979; Gilpin 1981). The empirical materials cited are inconclusive, in part because of the relatively short time spans examined. Over periods of 250 years or more that I have examined in historical atlases, the GP situation has typically simplified eventually and culminated in showdown war.

6. The second part of this empirical pattern fits the Simmel-Coser principle: cross-cutting ties reduce the intensity of conflict (Coser 1956: 78–80).

7. That is to say, modern technology makes possible a very large increase in the distance at which military force can be projected for very short periods of time. Against sustained resistance (even of a much lower military resource level), however, logistical costs at long distance are determinative, as the United States found in Vietnam during the period 1963–75. In the long run of the past 2,000 years, there has been only a modest increase in the maximal size of empires and no tendency to increase the frequency of approaches to world empires. This bolsters the inference that the ratio between transportation range and logistical cost has not changed greatly. Logistical constraints on the movement of effective military power under various historical conditions have been examined by Van Creveld (1977, 1991).

8. Formally stated, the five principles may be combined into a single, complex expression. Marchland advantage is weighted by the relative resource levels of adjacent states; overextension is the fundamental principle for stating the relative vulnerability of particular geographical points to states with given resources and logistical loads. Showdown wars result from long-term cumulation of resource and geopositional advantages and disadvantages. The technical difficulty in investigating this formalism is that mathematical and computer simulation methods are straightforward only in calculating the geopolitical strength of a single state with arbitrary values set for its external environment. There is no simple way to model the general pattern of systems of multiple states in topological space—that is, the variety of possible spatial configurations that affect the marchland advantage. So far, computer simulations have been carried out only on simplified versions of geopolitical principles; see Hanneman, Collins, and Mordt 1995, a short version of which is printed here as Appendix A.

9. I leave aside here consideration of the various kinds of revolutionary coalitions and countercoalitions, since these are to a large extent outside the realm of the state. In this part of her model, Skocpol draws upon Moore (1966). Moore's analysis of the varying structural consequences of different types of class relations in capitalist agriculture have been tested on a further range of historical cases by Paige (1975); it converges as well with the early formulation of Stinchcombe (1961). Moore revives

Marxian class analysis of revolutions by shifting the focus from industrial to agricultural property relations. Skocpol opens another direction by adding a focus on the autonomous dynamics of the state. These lines of theory are not necessarily alternatives. The state-breakdown model is crucial for the initiation of revolution; the actors in the conflict and the directions it takes, especially after the revolution, are affected by economic property relations (see Figure 7). The relative weight of these in relation to other factors remains to be clarified by future research.

10. A key comparison is the Meiji Restoration, in which a period of population stability rather than growth played into state fiscal crisis and other aspects of strain (see Goldstone 1991: 404–14). This occurred because incomes were fixed in kind while cash prices rose with economic expansion. For a more detailed comparison of the Skocpol and Goldstone models, see Chapter 1.

11. Although this has not been tested systematically, historical evidence would seem to support it. It is difficult to cite any instance in which an entire political (or religious) order became delegitimated and overturned while the ruler remained personally popular. Conversely, there appear to be no instances in which a new institutional order was instituted by a leader who was very unpopular. The distinction between personal and institutional legitimacy appears to be operative empirically only in the middle of the continuum. This is not to say that the intense personal unpopularity of a ruler is the only pathway to institutional delegitimation (an aspect of what we commonly call revolution), although in some instances it has been: personal dislike of the religion and sexual morality of King Charles I was a prelude to the English revolution of 1640; swings in the personal popularity of Gorbachev were part of the dynamic of delegitimation of the Soviet regime. But victims of revolution such as Louis XVI in France and Nicholas II in Russia were neither especially hated nor especially popular figures (Stone 1979: 335). In all these cases the halo of regime crisis accelerated personal unpopularity.

12. Data here and in the following text are from Collins 1986, *Facts on File*, and *Keesing's Record of World Events* unless otherwise specified.

13. "Thus it is highly likely that, once a first round of serious crises caused the loss of Eastern Europe or other distant territory, there would be set in motion cumulative processes of internal weakening, culminating in the eventual loss of the next tier of ethnically distinct conquest: the Baltic states, the Ukraine, the Caucasus, and the central-Asian Moslem territories" (Collins 1986: 203).

14. A third subpath, victory by one state that leads to world domination, was ruled out by the likelihood that nuclear war itself would result in extreme resource destruction (Office of Technology Assessment 1979). In addition, principles 1–3 and 5 indicated that Russia would not be the victor in a war with the entire enemy coalition.

15. This is not to say there that were no other sources of intra-elite conflict before the period of GP crisis in the 1980s. As noted below (in the section "Capitalism Versus Socialism"), disputes over economic inefficiency and market-oriented reforms also split the Communist elite; but comparisons among China, the USSR, and Eastern Europe indicate that those cannot have been the key to the breakdown of the Soviet Empire.

16. See Collins and Waller (1992) and Gaddis (1992) for more extensive review of theories that mispredicted the Soviet collapse.

17. Applied to the United States, d'Encausse's model would imply that the United States too, with its increasing disparity in ethnic birthrates, is heading toward disintegration along ethnic lines. GP theory, applied to the current conditions that predict high power-prestige for the United States in the middle-range future, predicts no such ethnic disintegration.

18. For similar reasons, the prediction of downfall made by the Soviet dissident Andrei Amalrik (1970) must be taken as an ad hoc claim, since it was not based on principles of widely valid applicability.

19. It should be noted that Goldstone (1992), in applying his state-breakdown model with emphasis upon the causal chain initiated by population growth, concludes that China in the late twentieth century is in a prerevolutionary phase. We thus have a direct confrontation between the predictions of GP theory and the population-centered variant of state breakdown theory. Li (1998), who compares the two components through a series of quantitative indicators for the full model for the Qing dynasty across four periods of rebellion (the Rebellion of the Three Feudatories, 1673–81; the White Lotus Rebellion, 1792–1804; the Taiping Rebellion, 1851–64; and the 1911 Revolution), shows that the population dynamic leading to state breakdown was strongest for the Taiping Rebellion, whereas the 1911 Revolution was largely caused by geopolitical strain. Future events will provide further grounds for assessing the validity of these theories.

20. A variant on the capitalist-superiority model is a stage theory of development, in which all other kinds of economies eventually give way to capitalism. Such theorizing may well be guided by the ideological euphoria of the period of anticommunist revolt. Empirically, there is as yet no clear evidence that a transition from socialism to capitalism is under way. As of the late 1990s, it is not clear that many of the ex–Soviet bloc states are becoming full-fledged market capitalist economies. It is possible that hybrid or other forms will prevail, perhaps for long periods of time. A predominant form deriving from the disintegration of socialism seems to be industrial-enterprise feudalism (Burawoy and Krotov 1992). The development of a well-supported theory of economic transition still has a long way to go. In its absence, we have little to rely on for systematic predictions.

21. Thus Gorbachev's visit to China in May 1989, in an effort to reduce GP confrontation, was the catalyst for the mass demonstration at Tiananmen Square. The failure of that uprising shows that individual charisma alone is insufficient to produce structural change in the absence of the factors listed in state breakdown theory (see Li 1993).

22. The ideological prestige of capitalism throughout its existence may thus be as connected with its geopolitical associations as with its economic performance. It is consistent with this argument that the ideology of capitalism spread around the world in conjunction with British and then U.S. geopolitical strength and came under attack at just the times and places geopolitical control weakened. The issue demands more systematic investigation.

23. Wuthnow's (1989) systematic comparisons of which European states adopted or rejected Protestantism, the Enlightenment, and the nineteenth-century socialist

movements provide perhaps our most advanced model. Wuthnow's state-centered theory bears a kinship to the Skocpol-Goldstone-Tilly model of state resource extraction. A central process behind major new ideological movements is the emergence of new economic and organizational resources that strengthen the state sector. When these emerge in conjunction with a stalemate between state actors and the property-controlling conservatives (a variant on the Skocpol model), opportunity is opened up for a third faction of cultural entrepreneurs. Their success depends on the degree of stalemate among the two branches of the intra-elite conflict, together with the extent of expansion of new material/organizational means of cultural production.

24. There has been some success in predicting outbreaks of war, given the existence of identifiable starting points at which international disputes occur. An empirically successful model builds on the relative resources and alliance patterns of the opposing states (Bueno de Mesquite and Lalman 1992).

25. Portes (1995), commenting on the symposium volume in which the original version of this chapter was published, has argued that GP theory is imprecise to the point of making no predictions at all. His argument is that the principles of marchland advantage and fragmentation of the interior can be applied only after the fact, since every state is in the middle with regard to some other states if one looks far enough. The objection rests on a misunderstanding of how GP principles are applied. The basic principles of GP theory are that, all other things being equal, resource-rich states expand territorially at the expense of resource-poor states; "marchland" or "edge" states expand at the expense of interior states; logistical loads increase with the distance that military power is projected from the home base, resulting at a calculable point in military overextension and loss of territorial power. These analytical principles interact with each other. The result is a cumulative pattern of growth or decline in resources, in geopositional advantage or disadvantage, and in logistical loads.

How do we determine whether a state is an "interior" or a "marchland" state? Historically, this condition is always relative to how densely settled and wealthy the population is on a state's borders. For example, Moscow was a marchland state in northern Russia in the fourteenth century because effectively there was no military power north of it, although there were small tribal coalitions in the area. Similarly, what counts as "on one's borders" depends on the level of long-distance transportation technology. The United States and Russia could not have been territorial enemies effectively in the early nineteenth century because it was a terrific logistical overextension for both to come into military contact. (There were small standoffs in northern California, but both sides quickly realized neither could wield much power against the other.) Thus a state is an interior state to the extent that it has enemies on its borders in several directions, its enemies' relative level of resources is high enough to pose a threat, and its enemies are within effective logistical range. At any point in time, it is possible to measure a state's resources, territorial configuration, and logistical loads in relation to those of its neighbors. In "The Future Decline of the Russian Empire" I used the formula based on Stinchcombe 1968 to calculate the military vulnerability of the USSR's borders to its neighbors such as China (see Collins 1986: 190, 198–99; Stinchcombe 1968: 218–30).

26. Not every aspect of the Soviet breakdown was included in my GP prediction.

It has been pointed out that the transition was relatively bloodless, with prolonged revolutionary fighting in only one instance (Romania). The implication seems to be that this pattern invalidates a theory of revolutionary change, or at any rate that theory embodied in Marx's adage "force is the midwife of every old society pregnant with a new one." GP/state-breakdown theory, however, does not imply that every transition is violent, but only that the accumulation of resource strains based on the organized means of violence sets in motion processes that eventuate in regime change.

27. These recent cases appear to be part of a more general process of revolt contagion in interlinked states. A prime example is the chain of revolts in the spring and summer of 1848 that spread from Switzerland, Italy, and France through the German states, Austria, and Hungary and then demobilized during the next year. Another such wave of revolts happened in cities throughout Germany and Central Europe at the close of World War I (Kinder and Hilgemann 1968: 328, 406). A theory of revolt contagion has yet to be formulated.

28. Kuran (1995) argues that revolutionary surprises are structurally inevitable because disgruntled citizens always misrepresent their preferences under social pressure from above and hence mislead not only their rulers but also each other. This theory provides a good explanation of the tipping-point process, while overgeneralizing mesolevel indeterminacy to the macrolevel as well.

29. I refer to this as *lower-meso*, reserving *micro* for the truly small slices of interaction between a few face-to-face actors, down to the ultra-micro level of conversational and emotional/nonverbal rhythms.

30. The issue of the inhumaneness or immorality of predictions must be discussed elsewhere. In the present case, I feel there was nothing immoral about attempting to make a contribution in 1980 to surviving the nuclear arms race.

CHAPTER 3: "BALKANIZATION" OR "AMERICANIZATION": A GEOPOLITICAL THEORY OF ETHNIC CHANGE

1. Hobsbawm and Ranger (1983) refer to this as "the invention of tradition." In the African context it has been referred to as "the invention of the tribe" (Vail 1989). Barth (1969) and Gellner (1983) critique primordialism from the point of view of political construction of ethnicity and nationalism. In contrast, Anthony Smith (1986) emphasizes long-standing communities maintained by cultural memory, religious institutions, and the activities of intellectuals; such ethnic traditions provide both the core of nationalist states and resistance against incorporation into an alien nationalism. In Smith's account, collective political mobilization in the past may have been a component of the formation of ethnic traditions, whereafter the tradition became self-perpetuating.

2. The relationship between sociology and biology is fraught with polemic. I would like to state clearly that my discussion of the social construction of somatotypes differs from that of contemporary sociobiology. As I read that position, it speculates on the natural selection of human and animal characteristics by their contribution to evolutionary fitness (i.e., the enhancement of the breeding success of the species). My argument does not hinge on natural selection or reproductive fitness

but on geopolitical relations that keep breeding pools separate or move them closer together. Most sociologists who disapprove of sociobiology tend to avoid the topic entirely. This avoidance has the consequence of ceding an empirical reality (somatic differences in physical appearance) to disciplines that explain these features in an unsociological manner. My argument is that sociology is intellectually strong enough to take this topic back from the biologists. In important respects, sociology shapes biology.

3. The folk distinction between race and ethnicity has become incorporated into U.S. sociology because, it is argued, the difference between assimilation patterns for white European ethnics and black African Americans show two different social processes at work. Nevertheless, the explanatory question can only be solved within the framework of an analytically unifying theory of what determines variations in the sharpness of ethnic distinctions. We should avoid reproducing the segregation of groups in the segregation of theories.

4. The interacting causes of change in ethnic divisions in both directions on the continuum could be modeled by simulation methods exemplified in Appendix A.

5. In the United States, legitimate ethnic recognition is enacted in the ceremonial naming of the ethnic group on public occasions, invitations for individuals to appear as ethnic representatives in parades, receipt of ethnic slots on an election ticket or party convention, and the like.

6. The term comes from *ethnos*, which the classical Greeks used to refer to a political unit less formally structured than a city-state. Earlier it referred to a military host or war band, sometimes to a tribe or nation (Snodgrass 1980; Smith 1986: 21).

7. Nationalism has often been connected with the rise of universal military conscription and with tuition-free and compulsory mass public education. These are related phenomena; the first states to produce one tended to develop the other.

8. The Homeric poems, which became the staple of education around 600 B.C.E., depict an earlier and somewhat more limited pan-Greek war coalition, the Achaeans; this can be regarded as propaganda for translocal identity that touted the archetype of the panethnic military alliance.

9. The ascendancy of a national culture does not imply cultural uniformity in every respect. Cultures also differ by social class. Formation of a national culture means only that the culture of the upper classes becomes successfully institutionalized in the public sphere as the high-status, legitimate culture for respectable activity. The national language becomes that which is spoken for politics and business; it becomes the medium of instruction in the schools, promoted along with its standards of "proper" pronunciation and idiom. Variations may exist (such as the working-class cockney and other regional dialects of Britain) but in a delegitimated form, as the butt of public humor and signs of imperfect membership in the high-status culture. George Bernard Shaw's 1912 comedy contrasting Professor Henry Higgins and Eliza Doolittle is superficially a satire on social class but implicitly indicates the success of ethnolinguistic nationalism.

10. This is borne out even on the level of uniformity in sexual behavior, which Watkins reveals as a form of national culture. The major exceptions to her model, states where demographic diversity increased rather than decreased between 1870

and 1960, were places where much ethnic strife took place over the shape of state sovereignty: Belgium and Ireland (Watkins 1991: 5).

11. Here, I calculate the period from the conquest of the Etruscans around 270 B.C.E. up to the civil war (or "Social War") in 91–88 B.C.E. on behalf of the ethnic groups of the Italian peninsula, which led to their being granted full Roman citizenship.

12. This contrasts with the historical myth that traces the origins of China back through a series of dynasties, the first of which was allegedly founded in 2698 B.C.E. The latter, if it had any historical basis, was doubtless a small kingdom of little more than tribal size. Even the Shang, the first well-attested Chinese state ca. 1500 B.C.E., covered no more than a segment of the Yellow River valley in the north (Eberhard 1977). Ethnonationalism is intrinsically a process of myth-making.

13. On the sense of impending doom in the Austrian Empire, see Wank 1997: 47.

14. The Austro-Hungarian Empire at the end of the nineteenth century was K & K, *Kaiserlich-Königlich*, a reference to the holder of the joint crown as emperor of Austria and king of Hungary. The identity was mocked by Robert Musil in *The Man Without Qualities* as Kakania, a play on the letter "k" and baby talk for excrement.

15. The *Lernfreiheit* institutionalized around 1810, which allowed students to transfer freely among the universities of the German states, foreshadowed the customs union and ensuing economic integration twenty years later.

16. Brubaker (1992) suggests that Germany had a culturally distinctive model of citizenship, based on family descent ("blood"), which contrasted with the territorially based French model, which gave automatic citizenship to those born on French soil. But the German law on citizenship by descent was weak until 1913; it was strengthened at the height of German military power and in the context of Pan-German agitation. The descent-based definition of an ethnic community fit the upward geopolitical trajectory of unification of German speakers into a strong state surrounded by weak states containing many pockets of linguistic compatriots. The renewed partition of Germany after its 1945 defeat, and the movement of refugees at that time and again after the fall of the Soviet bloc in 1989–91, has kept the descent criterion of ethnonational citizenship salient in later geopolitical situations.

17. "Italy" should not automatically be assumed to have occupied its present borders. The Po valley was regarded as Cisalpine Gaul as late as 270 B.C.E. and as colonial territory for centuries thereafter.

18. Borkenau (1981) gives evidence that the very process of forming intertribal coalitions for long-distance migration and conquest led to major syntactical changes. Among these were what Borkenau calls "the I-form of speech," the northern European linguistic pattern of separating out pronouns, especially first-person pronouns, for special emphasis instead of conveying agency merely by inflection (see Appendix B).

19. Similarly, after the breaking away of the American colonies from Britain, the rejection of formal British speaking traditions in favor of a more informal American style occurred quite abruptly at the turn of the nineteenth century (Cmiel 1990).

20. Hence Tuscan became the standard Italian literary language beginning around

1450, because Tuscan cities like Florence were the center for the high-prestige cultural export of art (Burke 1986: 237–38).

21. A more minor difficulty for the GP theory of ethnonationalism is the strengthening of French national identity after the 1871 defeat by Prussia. But other factors were also at work. State penetration accelerated after this period; and France's overall geopolitical trajectory rose when France expanded as a colonial power from 1830 to 1930.

22. There is a large literature on structural conditions for occupational mobility, of which the strongest condition is expansion in the size of nonagricultural, white-collar, and professional occupations (Bendix and Lipset 1959; Blau and Duncan 1967). These conditions for occupational mobility cut across societies, whether geopolitical power-prestige is high or low. My point here is not that GP trajectory determines the amount of upward occupational mobility, but rather that geopolitics determines ethnic identification even when different classes are encompassed within the same ethnic group. An ethnonational identity in which everyone is regarded as belonging to the same ethnic group necessarily includes class distinctions within it.

23. Hence even with the late-twentieth-century mobilization of nonwhite ethnic minorities demanding separate pieces of the educational pie, the pieces demanded are for credentials within the unified schooling sequence, rather than for ethnically distinct school systems. Educational credentials are standardized because they have become legitimate gatekeeping requirements throughout the job market. Establishing ethnically separate education would be tantamount to creating a currency that could not be cashed in for jobs in the mainstream economy.

24. The first several generations of militant Irish nationalists, including Wolfe Tone and Charles Parnell, were Protestant landowners; so were literary nationalists like William Butler Yeats.

25. The United States took the geopolitical lead from the former Great Powers and shaped the postwar order by promoting the dismantling of their empires, along with those of smaller colonial lords. The promotion of ethnic nationalism in ex-colonial Asia and Africa by a U.S.-led United Nations in the 1950s and 1960s fed the atmosphere in which oppressed ethnicities became culturally defined and politically mobilized in the United States as well.

26. Within the cosmopolitan white upper-middle class, from the 1960s to the present, moral and cultural prestige has come to be defined by one's support for the black movement. This is one source of the so-called "political correctness" of the 1980s and 1990s.

27. See Moskos and Butler 1996 for evidence that the strongest black-white solidarity and integration is found within the U.S. army in the post–Vietnam War era.

28. The same may be said for the components of ethnonational identity. The history of languages has not come to an end. Languages of the future will be shaped not only by migration and contact but also by geopolitical domination and stable lines of conflict. There is room here for a macrohistorical, state-centered sociology of languages.

29. Thus far, UN troops have fought only as separate national formations, unified only at the top level of military staff. There has been no experience of nationally diverse soldiers fighting in mixed ranks in a world army.

30. The primordialist interpretation of ethnic strife in the former Yugoslavia is wrong for another reason besides the neglect of the changing geopolitical configuration. Primordialist interpretations are most defensible in situations where the state has not penetrated into society but remains a thin layer at the top. Even this is not a good interpretation of ethnic hostility, however, since protoethnic groups typically lived peaceably with each other in this nonmobilized situation before state penetration (Barkey makes this point explicitly on the Austrian and Ottoman Empires; see Barkey 1997: 103). I suggest that the former Yugoslavia is not an example of lack of state penetration, but just the reverse: as a communist society it was the most deeply penetrated of systems. The downfall of communism was a double blow that brought the destruction of geopolitical prestige (including its interstitial niche version) as well as the destruction of the major structure of state penetration. The result is the worst of both worlds: just enough centralizing state and economic structures remain so that there is an arena for groups to fight in, along with delegitimation of state penetration that would be thorough enough to keep them from fighting.

CHAPTER 4: DEMOCRATIZATION FROM THE OUTSIDE IN: A GEOPOLITICAL THEORY OF COLLEGIAL POWER

1. Other, more complex, typologies are available. For example, Tilly, McAdam, and Tarrow (1997) propose four dimensions, each a continuum: breadth of citizenship, equality of citizenship, binding consultation, and protection from arbitrary action by state agents. I use a simpler typology because I wish to stress a structure that is both key and badly undertheorized, collegial power-sharing.

2. I forgo documentation of this point in order to concentrate on the structural dimensions. An examination of the comparative history of political rights would show that even the Anglo-American tradition includes the lack or violation of such rights for particular periods and particular sections of the population. A comprehensive sociological analysis of this dimension of democracy has yet to be written.

3. The institutionalized tradition of peaceful party alternation in office was not clearly accepted until the 1740s. In 1715, Lord Bolingbroke, who led Tory ministries in 1704–8 and 1710–14, was accused of plotting to bring back the old Catholic dynasty and fled to exile in France until he was pardoned in 1723. The last attempt to restore the Stuart monarchy occurred in 1745–46 when a Scottish army invaded England.

4. Rueschemeyer (private communication) points out that this is an ideal-typical statement. The development of the state, especially as it shifted in the nineteenth and twentieth centuries from taxation and warmaking to social and economic regulation and services, not only mobilized previously subordinated groups to demand an expansion of the franchise but also created new organs of collegial power-sharing. My emphasis is on long-term geopolitical processes that set the framework within which this could happen.

5. A contemporary version is given by Burton and Higley (1987): arrangements among elites, rather than a pervasive cultural ethos, produced democracies.

6. Weber further distinguishes between self-armed independent knights and a

self-armed disciplined infantry. The latter are typically recruited from the non-wealthy masses and become banded together as a conscious community because their tactic of fighting as a unit is their source of strength. Weber confines the term "democracy" to the cases of ancient Greco-Roman and medieval Italian city-states, where the popular infantry wrested political rights from the aristocracy. Nevertheless, his military argument in its most general form also helps explain the feudal assemblies of knights that were the bases for collegial democracy in the large territorial states of northern Europe. See Weber 1961: 237, 240.

7. We shall see some further complexities, in which GP weaknesses resulting from dynastic alliances provided an opening for collegial structures on the rebound.

8. Lévi-Strauss (1969) conjectured that the primitive state could have arisen by a similar process. In tribal marriage politics, a policy of pursuing far-flung alliances results in accumulating advantages for some families: the "marriage-rich" become still richer in their alliances, while the "marriage-poor" eventually have to drop out of the competition or confine themselves to local exchanges. Eventually there is "kinship revolution" in which the leading families shift to outright military rule using a nonkinship apparatus of control.

9. Thus in 1328 an anti-Pope was elected by a committee of thirteen Roman clergy chosen by the German emperor to challenge the French-controlled Avignon Pope. The anti-Pope in turn chose nine cardinals to act as his supporters and to reward dissident clergy (Kelley 1986: 216). Anti-Popes were common in the Middle Ages: there were two or more Popes during 125 of the 514 years between 999 and 1513, including a total of 77 Popes and 21 anti-Popes. Most of the anti-Popes were concentrated in the periods 1060–1180 and 1328–1449, just the times when collegial structures were growing. On a lower level of authority, the collegial power of monks to choose their abbots was supported by reforming Popes as a remedy to appropriation of those offices by lay aristocrats (ibid.: 137).

10. As the result of King John's concessions, England became a fief of the Pope during this period, a time when the papacy was approaching its maximal theocratic claims (Kelley 1986: 187). On the whole, however, the English king became successful comparatively early in gaining control over church resources on his island. The crown became a relatively strong administration in a way that the German emperor did not and provided a centripetal pole in the balance of forces that was lacking in Germany.

11. As Wallerstein has noted, there were 30 British colonies in the Americas, most of which had similar fiscal grievances with Britain (1989: 210–11). Many of these vacillated but ultimately did not join the revolt. Nova Scotia, for example, was too exposed to British naval power to see any prospect for success.

12. A similar analysis could be carried out for China. The key to possible future Chinese democracy, from the viewpoint of GP theory, would be whether federated structures emerge: possibly as the result of decentralization into a regional balance of power, possibly through a coalition with offshore Chinese regimes. Straightforward growth in Chinese GP power in East Asia, on the other hand, would offer increased legitimacy through power-prestige for the ruling regime, which could continue to be autocratic. This diagnosis contrasts with more conventional approaches to

democracy that stress Chinese cultural heritage (negative) or economic growth (positive).

CHAPTER 5: GERMAN-BASHING AND THE THEORY
OF DEMOCRATIC MODERNIZATION

1. Schnädelbach 1984: 13; Willey 1978: 28, 184–85; Köhnke 1991. Helmuth Plessner's *Die verspätete Nation* (The Retarded Nation) states characteristically: "As the nation which came on the scene too late, referred from the outset to models which were the opposite of theirs, the German people distances itself from the norms of latinity and urbanity which it nevertheless feels to be authoritative, while in its own *élan* it gives priority to spontaneity and originality, and thus also inner depth: that is, it flatters itself that it is like a volcano, erupting in extravagance and wildness" (quoted in Schnädelbach 1984: 20). Plessner's book was originally published while he was in exile during the shock of the Nazis in 1935. The massive literature of the *Sonderweg* thesis will not be reviewed here.

2. Stalin's joke that the Germans would never make a revolution of their own because they were afraid to walk on the grass is widely known. The Marxist picture of Germans as authoritarian conformists continues the originating traditions of Marxism. In the 1840s, Marx joined in the Young Hegelian criticism of the Germans as laggards behind the French. In his later writings, Marx came to see English industrialism as showing Germany the face of its future. Non-Marxist analysis, however, tends to put the divergence of Germany further back; for Elias (1989) it was the destructive wars of the 1600s that turned Germany into the path of depression and nostalgia for the medieval empire and carried over into the militarism of status cultures during the Wilhelmine era, even among the bourgeoisie.

3. It is conventional to include Austria within the German cultural orbit. This is justified on structural grounds: German-speaking intellectuals, artists, and musicians moved freely among the states of Germany and Austria and parts of Switzerland; the network of universities in these places made a common career pool; structurally the institutions of Austria were similar to those of the German states, with the added complication of Austria's multiethnic empire. The institutional similarity is based on the fact that in the Middle Ages all these states were within the Holy Roman Empire under a German-speaking emperor. In modern times, politicians too have flowed across the borders: Hitler was an Austrian by birth. Oddly, although Austria was notably more conservative than Germany, it has escaped Austria-bashing, the sort of bashing suffered by Germany, perhaps by sloughing its cultural identity off onto Germany.

4. Foreign existentialists almost uniformly received their philosophical training in Germany. The Dane Søren Kierkegaard was a student at Berlin in the 1840s; Franz Kafka studied at the German university of Prague; Jean-Paul Sartre developed French existentialism after studying in 1933–34 at the Maison Française in Berlin, while others of his circle (e.g., Raymond Aron) had sojourned at Cologne, and migrants like Alexandre Kojève and Alexandre Koyré introduced Hegelian and Diltheyian philosophy from the German intellectual network. Data on these network connections are drawn from Collins 1998.

5. I use the term "modern" and its cognates throughout, despite the popularity of referring to an era of "postmodernity" that emerged sometime after the end of the eighteenth-century Enlightenment. Virtually all features of "postmodernism" are intensifications of the structural features of modernization. If special emphasis is wanted for some trends in the late twentieth century, the term "hypermodernism" would be preferable.

6. Parsons (1964) attempted to account for democracy as the differentiation of executive administration from juridical pattern maintenance and legislative goal-setting and held that democracy is a universal evolutionary stage. The theory is not convincing in terms of causality. It is not clear what selective advantages follow from this type of differentiation, especially since the democratic division of powers can promote deadlock rather than efficient action. In contrast, Runciman (1989) argues on the basis of a wide-ranging historical comparison that industrial/bureaucratic societies can exist in a number of political forms. In a more limited way, and ignoring premodern forms of democracy, Lipset (1994) argues that capitalism is a necessary but not sufficient condition for democracy.

7. H. Rosenberg 1958; Bruford 1965; Brunschwig 1947; Bendix 1978. Strictly speaking, the earliest bureaucracy in Europe since the end of Roman times was the papal chancery after 1100 (Southern 1970: 105–24). This too was a political organization, during a period when the papacy made strong claims for secular power against the fragmented feudal states. The carrying out of paperwork by an administrative chancery spread into secular administration in the 1200s (Bartlett 1993: 283–85), resulting in a patrimonial/bureaucratic mixture. Bureaucratization of the private sector did not occur until big business corporations were formed in the 1880s and later. This happened more or less simultaneously in all the major societies, and especially in Germany and the United States. French business organization lagged in a familistic direction well into the twentieth century (Torstendahl 1991; Granick 1962).

8. Kiser and Schneider (1994) argue that Prussian bureaucracy in the eighteenth-century tax administration contained a number of nonbureaucratic elements, including a rather flat hierarchy, considerable direct interference from the top, and some hiring through nepotistic personal connections. In this account, full-scale bureaucracy emerged around 1800. Mann also refers to limitations on German bureaucracy, especially at the top levels and in the lack of integration among different administrative departments (1993: 450–52). But these kinds of failures to realize the Weberian ideal type are virtually universal; twentieth-century bureaucracies continue to have their politicized and chaotic elements.

9. As Kiser (1991) points out, however, the administration of the tax farmers in eighteenth-century France had become internally bureaucratic, because the tax farmer himself resisted corruption by his own employees. When the government took over direct tax collection again after the Revolution, the bureaucratic structure of the previous tax farmers was generally incorporated into the state structure. On the whole, the ancien-regime French government was nonbureaucratic; Mann estimates that only 5 percent of officials could be called bureaucrats in the Weberian sense of the term (1993: 452–54).

10. CMH 1910, 7: 649–50, 670. Mann notes that the original United States formally had a salaried bureaucracy at the federal level, but it was undermined by the political spoils system and personal patronage that became increasingly *non*bureaucratic through the 1870s (1993: 457–9, 468–70).

11. The rural South in the United States was largely controlled by personalistic politics that Weber would have described as patrimonial until 1950 and beyond (Key 1949).

12. The bureaucracy of imperial China, which predates the bureaucracies of Europe, mitigated the severe punishments of torture and mutilation inflicted on the general populace in the case of offenses by officials. In Europe, ritual public torture and execution was a common practice through the 1600s and later. Torture during judicial investigations was partially abolished in France by royal decree in 1780, and completely by the revolutionary code. The humanizing effects of bureaucracy are suggested by the abolition of corporal punishment in the Prussian army by the reform of 1808. In contrast, in the British navy through the 1820s, discipline (primarily of sailors, who were generally enrolled forcibly by armed press-gangs) was enforced by public whipping, which amounted in many cases to death by prolonged torture. Not surprisingly there were several mutinies in the British fleet in 1797, which were repressed with great brutality. Through the 1860s, the British army in India engaged in ritual executions by draping malefactors over the muzzle of a cannon. In civilian life, the Dickensian horrors of British criminal law were only gradually mitigated after 1830. Up to that time, the death penalty and overseas transportation into penal servitude were the principal penalties for virtually all offenses. Lea 1973; CMH 1910, 8: 452–53, 476–80, 744–55; Kinder and Hilgemann 1968: 307.

13. My conception of secularization differs somewhat from that used by some leading sociologists of religion. Stark and Bainbridge (1985) argue that there is an ongoing process in which all religious movements, starting out at a high level of supernatural orientation and hence of tension with secular society, gradually accommodate to society as the social class level of their membership rises. The result is not an irreligious society but the active religious market found in the twentieth-century United States, in which new, supernaturally oriented religious movements continuously reappear, recruiting from the disaffected or unchurched population whose spiritual demands are unmet by the liberalized churches (see also Warner 1993). In contrast to this model of secularization, I would point out that the cycle of worldly accommodation by the dominant church, with periodic renewal movements, also occurred in medieval Christendom, without bringing about doctrinal tendencies away from supernaturalism. The medieval cycle fluctuated between formally ritualistic church observance and movements of mysticism or piety. The Stark-Bainbridge cycle should not be called so much secularization-and-counter-secularization as social-tension-and-accommodation. Thus the key aspects of secularization over the past few centuries have been the decline of the institutional centrality of the church among social organizations, and especially the emergence of secular forms of legitimation for the state and lay-controlled public education.

14. Benjamin Disraeli, prime minister in 1868 and again from 1874 to 1880, was not an exception; he was baptized as a Christian in 1817.

15. Heer 1968: 134, 194–203; CMH 1910, 8: 56, 733; 9: 185. D'Holbach, a German baron residing in Paris, set off a debate between deists and atheists in the 1770s. Voltaire wrote his antireligious treatises while in exile in Switzerland, and they were intermittently repressed in France; his principal supporter was Frederick the Great, who made him a member of the Berlin Academy in the 1750s. The 1760s publication of the *Encyclopédie*, with its guardedly secular slant, was suspended by the French government. Baudelaire was prosecuted for public impropriety in 1864.

16. The Jesuits flourished by absorbing both humanism and science into Christian education. Although humanists during the 1400s occasionally promoted paganism, the Protestant reformers (Erasmus, Luther, Calvin, and others) came from Humanist circles. Again during the scientific revolution, priests like Marin Mersenne and Pierre Gassendi were at the center of the network structure, and on the whole there was little difficulty in giving a religious legitimation to the new science.

17. Rothblatt 1981; Green 1969; Richter 1964; CMH 1910, 12: 24–25, 57–58; Marsden and Longfield 1992. At the same time (1872), Britain established compulsory elementary schooling supported by government financial grants and regulated by government inspection. The majority of these schools were run by the Church of England, however, and free nondenominational education was not mandated until 1902. By contrast, Prussia established state-supported universal compulsory schooling in 1717, which was gradually made effective around 1763.

18. After the suppression of the liberal student movement in 1819, a number of professors were deprived of their posts until 1824. Others were casualties of the Young Hegelian agitation. Ludwig Feuerbach lost his position in 1830; D. F. Strauss was dismissed in the scandal over his *Life of Jesus* in 1837; Arnold Ruge's academic journal was suppressed, and Bruno Bauer was dismissed for atheism in 1842. After the failure of the 1848 revolution, several outspoken materialists as well as religiously liberal neo-Kantians lost their licenses to teach in 1853. Antisocialist laws were in force from 1878 to 1890 after an attempted assassination of the Kaiser. But penalties were not usually long or severe; most of those prohibited from teaching in 1853 were back at academic posts in 1857. Strauss, Feuerbach, and the materialist Ludwig Büchner became best-selling authors (Willey 1978: 61–63, 70, 89, 96; Köhnke 1991: 64, 79, 83, 91). These controls were mild in comparison with the ritual executions for heresy through the 1600s or the banishment and imprisonment meted out for unorthodoxy in much of Europe during Voltaire's day. At their worst, infringements on academic freedom in German universities were comparable to standard contemporary practices elsewhere. In the 1840s the Tractarian leader John Henry Newman was forced out of Oxford for his unorthodox stance on the state church. In France academic freedom did not exist before the 1870s. In the United States there were no research universities at all until late in the century. In practice, German academics acquired de facto autonomy, whatever the political regime, as long as their innovation stuck to scholarly subjects and stayed out of political activism. The result was a series of

scholarly innovations that liberalized and eventually completely secularized Christian doctrine.

19. A traveling companion of George Herbert Mead's in 1889 compared the pressures of religious compulsion in America with the freedom of thought in Germany: " In America, where poor, hated unhappy Christianity, trembling for its life, claps the gag in the mouth of Free Thought and says, 'Hush, hush, not a word or nobody will believe in me anymore,' he [Mead] thinks it would be hard for him to get a chance to utter any ultimate philosophical opinions savoring of independence" (quoted in Miller 1973: xvii).

20. The term "industrial revolution" was coined not in England but in France by Auguste Blanqui in 1837.

21. The first railroad line in England was built in 1828, the first in Germany in 1835. By 1850, railroads in Germany were comparable to those in England and considerably more extensive than in France. Even earlier, there was much less difference between German and English economic modernization than is imposed by our retrospective imagery. An observer in 1809 called the Ruhr factory district "a miniature England" (Barraclough 1979: 210). *Frankenstein*, written by the Englishwoman Mary Shelley in 1818, is the first notable work of science fiction and a warning against the dangers of the new technology. The dangerous modernizer in the story is not English, but a German scientist.

22. Blackbourn and Eley (1984) reject the *Sonderweg* thesis as it applies to Germany by taking a Marxist view on the actual level of democracy attained in England during this period. On the political dimension the materials cited by Blackbourn and Eley support my argument here. Their weakness is that they adhere to a unidimensional model of modernity and fail to recognize the dimensions on which Germany was a leader in modernization.

23. As late as 1898–1901, Joseph Chamberlain as British colonial minister continued to advocate the policy of alliance with Germany and lost his office over the issue.

24. Goldhagen (1996), in documenting the complicity of the entire German population in the Holocaust, rests his argument on the assumption that national culture is the underlying cause. His too narrow focus on Germany (sampling on a truncated dependent variable) ignores the comparative dimension of anti-Semitic violence. For a useful correction, see Brustein 1996 and Michael Mann's forthcoming work, *Fascists*.

25. During Hitler's last days in his bunker, as Russian troops stormed Berlin, what did he read? Nietzsche? Heidegger? Hegel? None of these; it was the British admirer of heroes, Thomas Carlyle (Liddell-Hart 1970: 679).

CHAPTER 6: MARKET DYNAMICS AS THE ENGINE OF HISTORICAL CHANGE

1. Generally speaking, slave markets are a subtype within agrarian-coercive societies. I treat them first because it is convenient to deal with Rome before medieval Europe and China.

2. "Generalized exchange seems to be in particular harmony with a society with feudal tendencies. . . . One comes to the conclusion that generalized exchange leads

almost unavoidably to anisogamy, i.e. to marriage between spouses of different status; and that this must appear all the more clearly when the cycles of exchange are multiplied or widened; but that at the same time it is at variance with the system, and must therefore lead to its downfall. . . . The disorder . . . is inherent in the system, viz., the conflict between the egalitarian conditions of generalized exchange, and its aristocratic consequences." Lévi-Strauss 1969: 265–67.

3. Stinchcombe (1983: 252) has suggested that in a patrilineal, patrilocal mixed herding and gardening economy women are objectively exploited by the criterion of the appropriation of surplus value from their labor.

4. On Heian Japan, see Lévi-Strauss 1984, and Collins, "Courtly Politics and the Status of Women" in Collins 1986. On Greece and Italy, see Fustel de Coulanges 1980; Polignac 1995. On the Norman state, see Searle 1988. Searle claims that the Vikings' "predatory kinship" was a longer-surviving version of an older kinship dynamic found throughout the Germanic world (1988: 8).

5. This was a long and slow process. As Mann shows, primitive peoples evaded the state, time and again increasing the scale of organization and production, then migrating away when a coercive state appeared. It was only when ecological and geopolitical patterns "caged" some groups on territories from which they could not escape that the state became permanent. This caging in turn would have been due to geopolitical alliances and population growth that resulted from kinship markets (see Mann 1986: 34–72).

6. This is a second dynamic, in addition to the kinship-alliance market already described, by which state organization has arisen among stateless peoples. Both dynamics may overlap in any particular instance. The indigenous dynamics of kinship markets is apparently much slower than the external tentacles of the slave market.

7. As Patterson (1982) has shown, manumission was an essential part of the incentive system of slave labor. The system constituted a self-reinforcing loop: slaves could amass money to buy their freedom and thus had an incentive to enter the monetized market economy. Rather than undermining slavery, ex-slaves themselves became handlers and petty owners of other slaves, since this was the labor force available for entrepreneurial production.

8. Weber overstates the identification of the equestrian order (knights) with the capitalist class. Runciman points out that the senatorial aristocracy and the *equites*, although political rivals, overlapped considerably in their economic activities in landowning, money-lending, and investments (1983: 167–68).

9. Finley (1973) and Polanyi (1977) criticize the idea that there was any substantial market economy in the ancient world. Trade was carried out according to traditional terms, not market-responsive prices. Long-distance trade (especially in grain supplies) was part of the international politics of cities administered by compulsion or alliance. Polanyi argues that a true market, in which goods move in response to price differences, existed only in the eastern Mediterranean ca. 325 B.C.E. until the time of Augustus, while grain traders in Rhodes collected information and directed ships to ports where payoff was highest (1977: 228–51). This is an overly restricted view of markets. The dynamics I listed at the beginning of this chapter apply to exchange systems even when information is restricted; they do not require that there be a market-clearing price. Neither Finley nor Polanyi includes the slave market in

his generalization about the lack of markets in antiquity. Because slaves had the advantage of being a self-transportable commodity, they could circumvent the limitations of land transport that Finley stresses were a restriction on markets. The price of slaves varied with supply and demand, and investment in slaves was often a subject of calculation.

10. In Greece, a similar outcome was reached by a somewhat different route. Smallholders survived as a rent- and tax-paying peasantry in the eastern much more than the western Mediterranean. The spread of the slave economy and the replacement of citizen-soldiers with mercenaries nevertheless came to dominate. The result was an organization of the upper classes much as existed in Rome, and the downfall of Greek democracy (Ste. Croix 1983).

11. Weber did, however, see the end of political investment capitalism by military entrepreneurs as the major transformation of the later Roman Empire: "The freedom of the cities was swept away by a bureaucratically organized world empire within which there was no longer a place for political capitalism. In the beginning the emperors were forced to resort to the financial power of the knighthood but we see them progressively emancipate themselves and exclude the knightly class from the farming of taxes and hence from the most lucrative source of wealth. . . . The provision for the economic needs of the state was taken care of through compulsory contributions and compulsory labor of servile persons instead of competitive contracts [These would have been contracts for suppliers of slave labor. —R.C.]. . . . This development means the throttling of ancient capitalism. A conscript army takes the place of the mercenaries" (Weber 1961: 247–48).

12. Geopolitical principles include the cumulative growth of resource advantages over one's neighbors and its negative counterpart, cumulative disadvantage; geopositional advantage or disadvantage (marchland vs. central locations, determining the number of enemies to be faced); and overextension, logistical and political strains that increase as armies operate further from home base (see Chapter 2). For Rome, the point of sharply diminishing returns and accelerating costs was reached at the German frontier. In addition, cumulative resource advantages build up for rival states as military powers consolidate in different parts of the globe. Such states eventually destroy the smaller intermediaries until these giants directly confront one another at locations where neither has a decisive advantage. That is what happened in the long, expensive stalemate between Rome and Parthia/Persia in the centuries after 40 B.C.E.

13. Slaves were also used in harems, both as concubines and as eunuch guards (Hodgson 1974, 2: 143–44). In those circumstances slavery was a form of luxury consumption rather than production.

14. An extreme version of this purchase of military force was Islamic slave-soldiery, which rulers turned to as a counterweight against the threat of feudal decentralization.

15. These contingencies of state power are ultimately determined by geopolitics, which is another layer of causality, in addition to market dynamics, on the divergent paths of world history. Just as the geopolitical factor plays a role in the downfall of the military/slave economy, it plays a part as well in the downfall of the socialist enclave in twentieth-century world capitalism (described below).

16. Islamic societies too had a version of corporate religious capitalism. Islam

lacked monasticism, but religious endowments (*waqf*) in the form of schools, hospitals, or charities could own property (Hodgson 1974, 2: 51, 136). Wealthy patrons used this device to shield their property from restrictions on inheritance by officials as well as to evade Koranic constraints on investment. *Waqf* investments extended to urban apartment blocks and shops for rental income and mills and factories that produced oil, sugar, and textiles (Garcin 1988: 121–23). Buddhist monasteries in medieval China had been used similarly by the Chinese gentry as a device for withdrawing land from government taxation and for circumventing restrictions on profit-making enterprises. Lacking the autonomous organizational force of monastic corporations, *waqf* structures did not constitute a separate religious economic sector as much as they did an adjunct to the Islamic market structures I have described above in connection with slave markets.

17. As I argued in "The Future Decline of the Russian Empire," the political crisis of the Soviet states was predictable from the geopolitical dynamic. Without that dynamic, economic penetration by world capitalism would still have been proceeding, but against greater resistance (Collins 1986: 185–209).

CHAPTER 7: AN ASIAN ROUTE TO CAPITALISM

1. In Chapter 6, I listed four types of market structures rather than the three types of economies given here. The game I was playing in the previous chapter was to see how far I could go with the classic Marxian historical stages; in this list of three economies, slave markets are a subtype of agrarian-coercive exchange.

2. Historically markets grew up around capital cities and other central places in agrarian-coercive empires (Finley 1973; Nishijima 1986). These markets were based on the delivery of coerced goods from the estates of the resident aristocracy, a system that sometimes devolved into independent modes of transport and delivery, together with local truck-farming and handcrafts for aristocratic consumption.

3. This latter obstacle was stressed by Thompson 1967 for Europe; for Japan, see Smith 1988b. The Weberian concept of an economic ethic does not simply mean hard work and frugality; poor peasants had to live this way if they were to stay alive, but this was not the same thing as having a calculating attitude toward investment in long-term growth of production.

4. Weber recognized monasticism as the first thoroughly disciplined and rationalized organization of life, citing both medieval Catholicism and Buddhist Tibet (1961: 267–69). But Weber saw the monasteries' resulting accumulation of wealth merely as a form of corruption, without consequences for economic growth in general. See especially his dismissal of Chinese Buddhism in Weber 1958: 268–69.

5. The main distinctions are among the older ceremonial Buddhism of the court-related monasteries (especially Shingon and Tendai), the Zen movement, and movements of the Pure Land type. Strictly speaking, Nichiren Buddhism was not a Pure Land doctrine, but its practices and social relations were similar. As time went on, the various branches influenced one another; the chanting of *nembutsu* prayers was often combined with Zen meditation. Similarly on the material side, all of the branches of Buddhism eventually became commercialized. The Pure Land sects

were instrumental in spreading market relations among the common people, and the Nichiren sect was particularly associated with the merchant towns of the late Middle Ages. By the Sengoku period, all the Buddhist branches, including the oldest sects, had become part of the productive religious economy.

6. By 1600, Japan was more populated than the comparably sized territories of Britain and France. In ratio of population to land area, Japan had the world's most densely settled population—about 50 percent greater than that of the Netherlands, the second most densely populated country at the time (calculated from McEvedy and Jones 1978).

7. The first Japanese commoners to rise to social prominence were leaders of Buddhist evangelical movements; Nichiren was the son of a fisherman.

8. Dumoulin 1990; Kitagawa 1990. Collcutt provides a succinct overview of the economic activities of the dominant *gozan* (Five Mountains) monasteries of Rinzai Zen (1990: 632, 637–42).

9. *Za* were also created under the protection of aristocrats. It would appear from the relative frequency of reference to temple-sponsored *za* that this was the most common form; see Yamamura 1990a.

10. Collcutt 1990: 604–9, 613. Likewise in late T'ang and Sung China, certificates of monastic ordination (for ordinary monks, not only for abbots) were sold in official revenue-raising campaigns; in the Sung period these certificates circulated for private resale. In China the certificates became used as a paper currency and were items of investment on a speculative market (Ch'en 1964: 241–44).

11. This is the figure for Yamato province (the hinterlands of the old capital Nara) in the late 1100s. The proportion of temple land varied across Japan; one overall estimate is that temples owned 60 percent of productive land in the early 1200s. A conservative estimate for the medieval period is 25 percent. McMullin 1984: 22–23, 33.

12. The mobilization of massive military force reached its peak in the early Tokugawa period, when in 1634 the shogun Iemitsu marched 307,000 troops through Kyoto in a show of strength: an army considerably larger than virtually all European armies to date, which were just then undergoing their own expansionary revolution (McMullin 1984: 212; Ooms 1985: 54; Parker 1988).

13. By 1800, Japanese workers' standard of living was not far below that of English workers, who were themselves exceptional within Europe (Yasuba 1986; Hanley 1986). Tokugawa Japan also had the world's highest popular literacy rate and one of the earliest and largest commercial markets for books (Dore 1965; Moriya 1990). On economic growth in the Tokugawa, see Hanley and Yamamura 1977; Nakane and Oishi 1990; Totman 1993; Hauser 1974; Nakai and McClain 1991; T. Smith 1959; Toby 1984; and Crawcour 1963, 1989.

APPENDIX A: HOW SIMULATING A COMPACT THEORY CAN REPRODUCE THE TANGLED PATHWAYS OF HISTORY

This is a revised version of a paper originally written with Robert Hanneman and Gabriele Mordt.

1. Technical detail on the simulation experiments presented here, along with references to the growing literature on computer simulation in sociology, may be found in Hanneman, Collins, and Mordt 1995.

2. In this analysis we do not distinguish between legitimacy of the legal order as a whole and legitimacy of incumbent power holders. In practice, the dynamics of legitimacy flow along a continuum: after legitimacy falls to low levels for particular incumbents, further shifts result not only in revolutions of personnel but also in revolutions of structure. Legitimacy theory, like all theories, is most useful when it explains a range of variations by means of dynamic processes. For this reason, treating legitimacy as a continuum encompassing both individuals and structures is more useful than the emphasis on static structural typology predominant in the literature.

3. We hold that there is no sharp distinction between the political popularity and legitimacy of particular rulers. Popularity polls give an indication of relative standing along one portion of the continuum of personal legitimacy. Such polls usually do not tap the extreme low end of the legitimacy continuum, but extremely low popularity of leaders is the next step to denying them legitimacy to rule at all. Available data using popularity measures suggest that war-related feelings are the strongest source of legitimacy and that economic prosperity or discontent is a weaker source (Ostrom and Simon 1985; Norpoth 1987). A notable finding is that war-based legitimacy has both a positive swing—with the initiation of conflict and with victory—and a negative swing, as casualties mount. Gallup polls show that the highest popularity ratings of U.S. presidents are war-related: 89 percent for George Bush in March 1991 (after victory in the Gulf War), 87 percent for Harry Truman in June 1945 (after V-E Day), 84 percent for Franklin Roosevelt in January 1942 (immediately after the Japanese attack on Pearl Harbor).

4. The cost to the United States of propping up allied regimes in South Vietnam in the 1960s and 1970s is an example. Again Athens and Rome provide good parallels to the U.S. and to some extent the British empires of modern times. The Athenian coalition against the Persians ca. 480–360 B.C.E. operated in effect as an empire, with Athens demanding military contributions to its fleet and militarily punishing disobedience. The Romans expanded (after the conquest of Carthaginian territories in the western Mediterranean ca. 200 B.C.E.) largely by enrolling an increasing number of "friends" whose side it took in the conflicts among the smaller states of the Aegean and the East, as well as among the German tribes. Rome shows the gradations between primacy-in-alliance and direct rule; after two centuries of informal rule, a formal empire was established.

5. That is to say, a realistic general theory of state belligerence should give the conditions under which states avoid international conflict. One suggestion is that states that are neutrals in conflicts among major power blocs are likely to be too weak to win against either coalition but strong enough to lose prestige by entering into an alliance as a junior partner. Switzerland after 1520 and Sweden after 1815 are modern neutrals that arrived at their positions after periods in which they demonstrated their military strength, which left them with fairly high degrees of legitimacy.

6. Evidence on violent regime changes between 1816 and 1975, however, indicates that war defeats and costs are primary determinants of domestic legitimacy (Bueno de Mesquite, Siverson, and Woller 1992).

APPENDIX B: BORKENAU'S GEOPOLITICS
OF LANGUAGE AND CULTURAL CHANGE

1. " 'I made this piece of craftsmanship, not you,' the runic inscriptions seem to say. The idea of politeness does not fit with the idea of a Viking" (p. 190).

2. "The country which only uses 'you' is also the country where 'never show your feelings' is an essential educational precept, a precept unintelligible to all Continentals. England has gone much farther than any other part of the Western world in developing the sense of distance and reserve" (p. 192).

3. Borkenau's position would be controverted by some specialists, especially the Dumézil school, which regards all German gods as variants on an ancient Indo-European three-function scheme. The fashionableness of structuralist interpretations in recent years has largely evaded the issue of historical changes and left the state of evidence much where it was when both Borkenau and Georges Dumézil wrote in the 1950s. (See Strutynski's introduction to Dumézil's *Gods of the Ancient Northmen*, University of California Press, 1973). Borkenau's dating is based on a careful overview of runic inscriptions and sticks closer to the actual facts than the opposing school. Some of Borkenau's particular interpretations, such as the identification of Balder as a Wanic god, may be inaccurate. But in the absence of any other politically oriented look at Germanic religious history, Borkenau's arguments seem to me to hold precedence.

4. "Godless did Germanic history begin [after the collapse of the fertility cults], and that fact has determined decisively not only the character of ancient German paganism, but also of Germanic Christianity and subsequently of Western Christianity—and with it of Western civilization" (p. 256).

5. During Charlemagne's 30-year conquest of the Saxons (772–804), the high point was cutting down the sacred tree of the pagan sacrificial cult and mass baptism of the surrendering nobles. Christian territory was truncated again by revolt in the tenth century (Kinder and Hilgemann 1968: 119; Bartlett 1993).

Bibliography

Abu-Lughod, Janet L. 1989. *Before European Hegemony. The World System A.D. 1250–1350*. New York: Oxford University Press.

Adcock, F. E. 1957. *The Greek and Macedonian Art of War*. Berkeley: University of California Press.

Aitchison, Jean. 1991. *Language Change: Progress or Decay?* Cambridge: Cambridge University Press.

Akamatsu Toshihide and Philip Yampolsky. 1977. "Muromachi Zen and the Gozan System." In Hall and Toyoda 1977.

Amalrik, Andrei. 1970. *Will the Soviet Union Survive Until 1984?* New York: Harper and Row.

Anderson, Benedict. 1983. *Imagined Communities: Reflections on the Origins and Spread of Nationalism*. London: Verso.

Anderson, Perry. 1974a. *Passages from Antiquity to Feudalism*. London: Verso.

———. 1974b. *Lineages of the Absolutist State*. London: Verso.

Andreski, Stanislav. 1971. *Military Organization and Society*. Berkeley: University of California Press.

Angermeier, Heinz. 1984. *Die Reichsreform 1410–1555: Die Staatsproblematik in Deutschland zwischen Mittelalter und Gegenwart*. Munich: C. H. Beck.

Arrighi, Giovanni. 1994. *The Long Twentieth Century*. London: Verso.

Barkey, Karen. 1997. "Thinking About the Consequences of Empires." In Barkey and Von Hagen 1997.

Barkey, Karen, and Mark Von Hagen, eds. 1997. *After Empire: Multiethnic Societies and Nation-Building*. Boulder, Colo.: Westview Press.

Barkin, Kenneth. 1987. "Germany and England: Economic Inequality." *Tel Aviver Jahrbuch für deutsche Geschichte* 16: 200–211.

Barraclough, Geoffrey. 1963. *The Origins of Modern Germany*. New York: Capricorn Books.

———. 1979. *The Times Atlas of World History*. Maplewood, N.J.: Hammond.

Barth, Fredrick. 1969. *Ethnic Groups and Boundaries*. London: Allen and Unwin.

Bartlett, Robert. 1993. *The Making of Europe: Conquest, Colonization and Cultural Change, 950–1350*. Princeton, N.J.: Princeton University Press.

Becker, Abraham S. 1986. *Sitting on Bayonets: The Soviet Defense Budget and the*

Slowdown of Soviet Defense Spending. Santa Monica, Calif.: Rand / UCLA Center for the Study of Soviet International Behavior.

―――. 1987. *Ogarkov's Complaint and Gorbachev's Dilemma: The Soviet Defense Budget and Party-Military Conflict*. Santa Monica, Calif.: Rand.

Bellah, Robert. 1957. *Tokugawa Religion: The Cultural Roots of Modern Japan*. New York: Free Press.

Bendix, Reinhard. 1967. "Tradition and Modernity Reconsidered." *Comparative Studies in Society and History* 9: 292–346.

―――. 1977. *Nation-Building and Citizenship*. Berkeley: University of California Press.

―――. 1978. *Kings or People: Power and the Mandate to Rule*. Berkeley: University of California Press.

Bendix, Reinhard, and S. M. Lipset. 1959. *Social Mobility in Industrial Society*. Berkeley: University of California Press.

Berelson, Bernard. 1960. *Graduate Education in the U.S.* New York: McGraw-Hill.

Berman, Harold. 1983. *Law and Revolution: The Formation of the Western Legal Tradition*. Cambridge, Mass.: Harvard University Press.

Bernstein, Alvin H. 1989. *Soviet Defense Spending*. Santa Monica, Calif.: Rand.

Bessinger, Mark R. 1990. *Nonviolent Public Protest in the USSR, December 1, 1986– December 31, 1989*. Washington D.C.: National Council for Soviet and East European Research.

Black, Antony. 1979. *Council and Commune*. London: Burns and Oates.

Blackbourn, David, and Geoff Eley. 1984. *The Peculiarities of German History*. New York: Oxford University Press.

Blau, Peter M., and Otis Dudley Duncan. 1967. *The American Occupational Structure*. New York: Wiley.

Blockmans, Wim P. 1978. "A Typology of Representative Institutions in Late Medieval Europe." *Journal of Medieval History* 4: 189–215.

Blumberg, Rae Lesser. 1984. "A General Theory of Gender Stratification." In Randall Collins, ed., *Sociological Theory 1984*. San Francisco: Jossey-Bass.

Bonacich, Edna. 1972. "A Theory of Ethnic Antagonism: The Split Labor Market." *American Sociological Review* 37: 547–59.

Borkenau, Franz. 1981. *End and Beginning: On the Generations of Cultures and the Origins of the West*. New York: Columbia University Press.

Boulding, Kenneth. 1962. *Conflict and Defense*. New York: Harper and Row.

Brady, Thomas A. 1985. *Turning Swiss: Cities and Empire, 1450–1550*. Cambridge: Cambridge University Press.

Braudel, Fernand. [1949] 1972. *The Mediterranean and the Mediterranean World in the Age of Philip II*. New York: Harper and Row.

―――. [1967–79] 1981–84. *Material Civilization and Capitalism, 1400–1800*. 3 vols. Harper and Row.

―――. 1977. *Afterthoughts on Material Civilization and Capitalism*. Baltimore: Johns Hopkins University Press.

Brinton, Crane. 1938. *The Anatomy of Revolution*. New York: Random House.

Browning, Christopher. 1992. *Ordinary Men: Reserve Police Battalion 101 and the Final Solution in Poland*. New York: HarperCollins.

Brubaker, Rogers. 1992. *Citizenship and Nationhood in France and Germany.* Cambridge, Mass.: Harvard University Press.

Bruford, W. H. 1965. *Germany in the Eighteenth Century: The Social Background of the Literary Revival.* Cambridge: Cambridge University Press.

Brunschwig, Henri. 1947. *Le Crise de l'état Prussien à la fin de XVIIIe siècle.* Paris: Presses Universitaires de France.

Brustein, William. 1996. *The Logic of Evil: The Social Origins of the Nazi Party, 1925–1933.* New Haven, Conn.: Yale University Press

Bryant, Joseph M. 1990. "Military Technology and Socio-Cultural Change in the Ancient Greek City." *Sociological Review.*

Bueno de Mesquite, Bruce, and David Lalman. 1992. *War and Reason.* New Haven, Conn.: Yale University Press.

Bueno de Mesquite, Bruce, Randolph M. Siverson, and Gary Woller. 1992. "War and the Fate of Regimes: A Comparative Analysis." *American Political Science Review* 86: 638–46.

Burawoy, Michael, and Pavel Krotov. 1992. "The Soviet Transition from Socialism to Capitalism." *American Sociological Review* 57: 16–38.

Burke, Peter. 1986. *The Italian Renaissance: Culture and Society in Italy.* Princeton, N.J.: Princeton University Press.

Burton, M. G., and J. Higley. 1987. "Elite Settlements." *American Sociological Review* 52: 295–307.

Calhoun, Craig. 1982. *The Question of Class Struggle.* Chicago: University of Chicago Press.

Cameron, Euan. 1991. *The European Reformation.* Oxford: Clarendon Press.

Chadwick, Owen. 1966. *The Victorian Church.* Oxford: Oxford University Press.

Chafetz, Janet Saltzman. 1984. *Sex and Advantage: A Comparative Macro-Structural Theory of Sexual Stratification.* Totowa, N.J.: Rowman and Allanheld.

Chaffee, John W. 1985. *The Thorny Gates of Learning in Sung China.* Cambridge: Cambridge University Press.

Chase-Dunn, Christopher. 1989. *Global Formation: Structures of the World Economy.* Oxford: Blackwell.

Chase-Dunn, Christopher, and Thomas D. Hall, eds. 1991. *Core/Periphery Relations in Precapitalist Worlds.* Boulder, Colo.: Westview Press.

———. 1997. *Rise and Demise: Comparing World-Systems.* Boulder, Colo.: Westview Press.

Chaudhuri, K. N. 1990. *Asia Before Europe: Economy and Civilisation of the Indian Ocean from the Rise of Islam to 1750.* Cambridge: Cambridge University Press.

Ch'en, Kenneth. 1964. *Buddhism in China.* Princeton, N.J.: Princeton University Press.

Chesterfield, Lord. 1992. *Letters.* New York: Oxford University Press.

CMH (*Cambridge Modern History*). 1910. Cambridge: Cambridge University Press.

Cmiel, Kenneth. 1990. *Democratic Eloquence.* Berkeley: University of California Press.

Collcutt, Martin. 1981. *Five Mountains: The Rinzai Zen Monastic Institution in Medieval Japan.* Cambridge, Mass.: Harvard University Press.

———. 1990. "Zen and the *Gozan.*" In Yamamura 1990b.

Collins, Randall. 1978. "Long-Term Social Change and the Territorial Power of States." In Louis Kriesberg, ed., *Research in Social Movements, Conflicts, and Change.* Vol. 1. Greenwich, Conn.: JAI Press.

――――. 1979. *The Credential Society: An Historical Sociology of Education and Stratification.* New York: Academic Press.

――――. 1980. "The Future Decline of the Russian Empire: An Application of Geopolitical Theory." In Collins 1986.

――――. 1981a. "Crises and Declines in Credential Systems." In *Sociology Since Midcentury: Essays in Theory Cumulation.* New York: Academic Press.

――――. 1981b. "Does Modern Technology Change the Rules of Geopolitics?" *Journal of Political and Military Sociology* 9: 163–77.

――――. 1986. *Weberian Sociological Theory.* New York: Cambridge University Press.

――――. 1998. *The Sociology of Philosophies.* Cambridge, Mass.: Harvard University Press.

Collins, Randall, and David V. Waller. 1992. "What Theories Predicted the State Breakdowns and Revolutions of the Soviet Bloc?" In Louis Kriesberg, ed., *Research in Social Movements: Conflicts and Change.* Vol. 14. Greenwich, Conn.: JAI Press.

Coser, Lewis A. 1956. *The Functions of Social Conflict.* Glencoe, Ill.: Free Press.

Crawcour, E. Sydney. 1963. "Changes in Japanese Commerce in the Tokugawa Period." *Journal of Asian Studies* 23: 387–400.

――――. 1989. "Economic Change in the Nineteenth Century." In Marius B. Jansen, ed., *The Cambridge History of Japan.* Vol. 5. Cambridge: Cambridge University Press.

Crone, Patricia. 1980. *Slaves on Horses: The Evolution of the Islamic Polity.* Cambridge: Cambridge University Press.

Curtin, Philip P. 1984. *Cross-Cultural Trade in World History.* Cambridge and New York: Cambridge University Press.

Dore, Ronald P. 1965. *Education in Tokugawa Japan.* Berkeley: University of California Press.

Downing, Brian M. 1992. *The Military Revolution and Political Change: Origins of Democracy and Autocracy in Early Modern Europe.* Princeton, N.J.: Princeton University Press.

Dumoulin, Heinrich. 1988. *Zen Buddhism: A History.* Vol. 1, *China.* New York: Macmillan.

――――. 1990. *Zen Buddhism: A History.* Vol. 2, *Japan.* New York: Macmillan.

Eberhard, Wolfram. 1977. *A History of China.* Berkeley: University of California Press.

Eley, Geoff. 1986. *From Unification to Nazism: Reinterpreting the German Past.* London: Allen and Unwin.

Elias, Norbert. 1989. *Studien über die Deutschen: Machtkämpfe und Habitusentwicklung im 19. und 20. Jahrhundert.* Frankfurt: Suhrkamp.

Elkin, A. P. 1979. *The Australian Aborigines.* Sydney: Angus and Ferguson.

Elvin, Mark. 1973. *The Pattern of the Chinese Past.* London: Methuen.

――――. 1984. "Why China Failed to Create an Endogenous Industrial Capitalism: A Critique of Max Weber's Model." *Theory and Society* 13: 379–92.

d'Encausse, Helene C. 1979. *Decline of an Empire: The Soviet Socialist Republics in Revolt*. New York: Harper and Row.

Enggass, P. M. 1986. *Geopolitics: A Bibliography of Applied Political Geography*. Monticello, Ill.: Vance Bibliographies.

Evans, Peter B., Dietrich Rueschemeyer, and Theda Skocpol, eds. 1985. *Bringing the State Back In*. New York: Cambridge University Press.

Fabiani, Jean-Louis. 1988. *Les Philosophes de la Republique*. Paris: Editions de Minuit.

Facts on File World Political Almanac. Published annually. New York: Facts on File.

Fein, Helen. 1979. *Accounting for Genocide*. New York: Free Press.

Finke, Roger, and Rodney Stark. 1992. *The Churching of America, 1776–1990*. New Brunswick, N.J.: Rutgers University Press.

Finley, Moses I. 1973. *The Ancient Economy*. Berkeley: University of California Press.

———. 1982. *Economy and Society in Ancient Greece*. New York: Viking.

Fleming, Donald, and Bernard Bailyn. 1969. *The Intellectual Migration: Europe and America, 1930–1960*. Cambridge, Mass.: Harvard University Press.

Flexner, Abraham. 1930. *Universities: American, English, German*. New York: Oxford University Press.

Foley, Vernard, and Werner Soedel. 1981. "Ancient Oared Warships." *Scientific American* 244 (April): 148–63.

Foster, R. F. 1989. *The Oxford History of Ireland*. Oxford: Oxford University Press.

Frank, André Gunder. 1966. "The Development of Underdevelopment." *Monthly Review* 18: 17–31.

Fung Yu-lan. 1952. *A History of Chinese Philosophy*. Princeton, N.J.: Princeton University Press.

Fustel de Coulanges, Numa Denis. [1864] 1980. *The Ancient City*. Baltimore: Johns Hopkins University Press.

Gaddis, John Lewis. 1992. "International Relations Theory and the End of the Cold War." *International Security* 17, no. 3: 5–58.

Garcin, Jean-Claude. 1988. "The Mamluk Military System and the Blocking of Medieval Moslem Society." In Jean Baechler, John A. Hall, and Michael Mann, eds., *Europe and the Rise of Capitalism*. Oxford: Blackwell.

Gay, Peter. 1968. *Weimar Culture*. New York: Harper and Row.

Gelman, Harry. 1989. *The Soviet Turn Toward Conventional Force Reduction: The Internal Struggle and the Variables at Play*. Santa Monica, Calif.: Rand.

Gellner, Ernst. 1983. *Nations and Nationalism*. Ithaca, N.Y.: Cornell University Press.

Gernet, Jacques. 1962. *Daily Life in China on the Eve of the Mongol Invasion, 1250–1276*. Stanford, Calif.: Stanford University Press.

———. 1982. *A History of Chinese Civilization*. Cambridge: Cambridge University Press.

Gills, Barry K., and André Gunder Frank. 1991. "The Cumulation of Accumulation: Theses and Research Agenda for 5,000 Years of World System History." In Chase-Dunn and Hall 1991.

Gilpin, Robert. 1981. *War and Change in World Politics*. New York: Cambridge University Press.

Gimpel, Jean. 1976. *The Medieval Machine*. Baltimore: Penguin.

Girouard, Mark. 1978. *Life in the English Country House.* New Haven, Conn.: Yale University Press.

Gleick, James. 1987. *Chaos: Making a New Science.* New York: Penguin.

Goitein, Solomon. 1967. *A Mediterranean Society.* Berkeley: University of California Press.

Goldhagen, Daniel. 1996. *Hitler's Willing Executioners: Ordinary Germans and the Holocaust.* New York: Knopf.

Goldscheider, Calvin, and Alan S. Zuckerman. 1984. *The Transformation of the Jews.* Chicago: University of Chicago Press.

Goldstone, Jack A. 1991. *Revolution and Rebellion in the Early Modern World.* Berkeley: University of California Press.

———. 1992. "Immanent Political Conflicts Arising from China's Environmental Crisis." Occasional Papers Series of the Project on Environmental Change and Acute Conflict. Cambridge, Mass.: American Academy of Arts and Sciences.

Goody, Jack. 1983. *The Development of the Family and Marriage in Europe.* Cambridge: Cambridge University Press.

Gouldner, Alvin W. 1976. *The Dialectic of Ideology and Technology.* New York: Seabury Press.

Granick, David. 1962. *The European Executive.* New York: Doubleday.

Green, V. H. H. 1969. *The Universities.* Baltimore: Penguin.

Greenberg, Joseph H. 1970. *The Languages of Africa.* Bloomington: University of Indiana Press.

———. 1974. *Language Typology. A Historical and Analytical Overview.* The Hague: Mouton.

———. 1987. *Language in the Americas.* Stanford, Calif.: Stanford University Press.

Greenfeld, Liah. 1992. *Nationalism.* Cambridge, Mass.: Harvard University Press.

Gusfield, Joseph R. 1958. "Equalitarianism and Bureaucratic Recruitment." *Administrative Science Quarterly* 2: 521–41.

Hagen, Willilam W. 1980. *Germans, Poles and Jews: The Nationality Conflict in the Prussian East, 1772–1914.* Chicago: University of Chicago Press.

Hall, John. 1986. *Powers and Liberties: The Causes and Consequences of the Rise of the West.* Berkeley: University of California Press.

Hall, John Whitney, and Toyoda Takeshi, eds. 1977. *Japan in the Muromachi Age.* Berkeley: University of California Press.

Hall, John Whitney, Keiji Nagahara, and Kozo Yamamura, eds. 1981. *Japan Before Tokugawa: Political Consolidation and Economic Growth, 1500 to 1650.* Princeton, N.J.: Princeton University Press.

Hamashita, Takeshi. 1994. "The Tribute Trade System and Modern Asia." In A. J. H. Latham and H. Kawakatsu, eds., *Japanese Industrialization and the Asian Economy.* London: Routledge.

Hanley, Susan B. 1986. "Standard of Living in Nineteenth Century Japan: Reply to Yasuba." *Journal of Economic History* 46: 225–26.

Hanley, Susan B., and Kozo Yamamura, eds. 1977. *Economic and Demographic Change in Preindustrial Japan, 1600–1868.* Princeton, N.J.: Princeton University Press.

Hannan, Michael T. 1979. "Dynamics of Ethnic Boundaries in Modern States." In

John W. Meyer and Michael T. Hannan, eds., *National Development and the World System*. Chicago: University of Chicago Press.

Hanneman, Robert A., Randall Collins, and Gabriele Mordt. 1995. "Discovering Theory Dynamics by Computer Simulation: Experiments on State Legitimacy and Imperialist Capitalism." *Sociological Methodology* 25 (1995): 1–46.

't Hart, Marjolein C. 1993. *The Making of a Bourgeois State: War, Politics and Finance During the Dutch Revolt*. Manchester: Manchester University Press.

Hauser, William B. 1974. *Economic Institutional Change in Tokugawa Japan: Osaka and the Kinai Cotton Trade*. Cambridge: Cambridge University Press.

Hechter, Michael. 1974. "The Political Economy of Ethnic Change." *American Journal of Sociology* 79: 1151–78.

Heer, Friedrich. [1953] 1968. *The Intellectual History of Europe*. New York: Doubleday.

Hellie, Richard. 1982. *Slavery in Russia, 1450–1725*. Chicago: University of Chicago Press.

Henderson, D. F. 1968. "The Evolution of Tokugawa Law." In John Hall and Marius Jansen, *Studies in the Institutional History of Early Modern Japan*. Princeton, N.J.: Princeton University Press.

Hepple, Leslie W. 1986. "The Revival of Geopolitics." *Political Geography Quarterly* 4, no. 4 (supplement): s21–36.

Hobsbawm, Eric, and Terence Ranger, eds. 1983. *The Invention of Tradition*. Cambridge: Cambridge University Press.

Hockett, Charles F. 1979. "Introduction." In Whitney [1875] 1979.

Hodgson, Marshall G. 1974. *The Venture of Islam*. 3 vols. Chicago: University of Chicago Press.

Hoffman, Philip T., and Kathryn Norbert, eds. 1994. *Fiscal Crises, Liberty, and Representative Government, 1450–1789*. Stanford, Calif.: Stanford University Press.

Holborn, Hajo. 1959–69. *A History of Modern Germany*. New York: Knopf.

Hopkins, Keith. 1977. "Economic Growth and Towns in Classical Antiquity." In P. Abrams and E. A. Wrigley, eds., *Towns in Societies*. Cambridge: Cambridge University Press.

―――. 1980. "Taxes and Trade in the Roman Empire, 200 B.C.E.–A.D. 400." *Journal of Roman Studies* 70: 301–24.

Howe, Christopher. 1996. *The Origins of Japanese Trade Supremacy*. Chicago: University of Chicago Press.

Ikegami, Eiko. 1995. *The Taming of the Samurai: Honorific Individualism and the Making of Modern Japan*. Cambridge, Mass.: Harvard University Press.

Jencks, Christopher, and David Riesman. 1968. *The Academic Revolution*. New York: Doubleday.

Jochmann, Werner. 1988. *Gesellschaftskrise und Judenfeindschaft in Deutschland 1870–1945*. Hamburg: Christians.

Johnson, Allen W., and Timothy Earle. 1987. *The Evolution of Human Societies: From the Foraging Group to the Agrarian State*. Stanford, Calif.: Stanford University Press.

Jones, Eric L. 1988. *Growth Recurring: Economic Change in World History*. Oxford: Clarendon Press.

Katsumata Shizuo and Martin Collcutt. 1981. "The Development of Sengoku Law." In Hall, Nagahara, and Yamamura 1981.

Kawakatsu, Heita. 1994. "Historical Background." In A. J. H. Latham and H. Kawakatsu, eds., *Japanese Industrialization and the Asian Economy*. London: Routledge.

Keesing's Record of World Events. Published annually. London: Longman.

Kelley, J. N. D. 1986. *The Oxford Dictionary of Popes*. New York: Oxford University Press.

Kennedy, Paul. 1987. *The Rise and Fall of the Great Powers: Economic Change and Military Conflict from 1500 to 2000*. New York: Random House.

Keohane, Robert O. 1986. *Neorealism and Its Critics*. New York: Columbia University Press.

Key, V. O. 1949. *Southern Politics*. New York: Knopf.

Kinder, Hermann, and Werner Hilgemann. 1968. *Atlas historique*. Paris: Stock.

King, Gary, Robert O. Keohane, and Sidney Verba. 1994. *Designing Social Inquiry: Scientific Inference in Qualitative Research*. Princeton, N.J.: Princeton University Press.

Kirschner, Julius, ed. 1995. "The Origins of the State in Italy, 1300–1600." *Journal of Modern History* 67(supplement).

Kiser, Edgar. 1991. "Markets and Hierarchies in Early Modern Tax Systems: A Principal-Agent Analysis." Paper presented at annual meeting of the American Sociological Association.

Kiser, Edgar, and Joachim Schneider. 1994. "Bureaucracy and Efficiency: An Analysis of Taxation in Early Modern Prussia." *American Sociological Review* 59: 187–204.

Kitagawa, Joseph M. 1987. *On Understanding Japanese Religion*. Princeton, N.J.: Princeton University Press.

———. 1990. *Religion in Japanese History*. New York: Columbia University Press.

Köhnke, Klaus Christian. 1991. *The Rise of Neo-Kantianism*. Cambridge: Cambridge University Press.

Kornai, Janos. 1992. *The Socialist System: The Political Economy of Communism*. Princeton, N.J.: Princeton University Press.

Kroeber, A. L. 1963. *Anthropology: Culture Patterns and Processes*. New York: Harcourt.

Kuran, Timur. 1995. "The Inevitability of Future Revolutionary Surprises." *American Journal of Sociology* 100: 1528–51.

Labov, William. 1971. *Sociolinguistic Patterns*. Philadelphia: University of Pennsylvania Press.

Labov, William, and Wendell A. Harris, 1986. "De Facto Segregation of Black and White Vernaculars." In David Sankoff, ed., *Current Issues in Linguistic Theory 53: Diversity and Diachrony*. Amsterdam: Benjamins.

Lane, Frederic C. 1973. *Venice: A Maritime Republic*. Baltimore: Johns Hopkins University Press.

Lea, Henry Charles. 1973. *History of Judicial Torture*. Philadelphia: University of Pennsylvania Press.

Lenski, Gerhard E. 1966. *Power and Privilege: A Theory of Stratification.* New York: McGraw-Hill.

Levi, Margaret. 1988. *Of Rule and Revenue.* Berkeley: University of California Press.

Lévi-Strauss, Claude. [1949] 1969. *The Elementary Structures of Kinship.* Boston: Beacon Press.

———. 1984. "The Origin of Historical Societies." Public lecture, UCLA.

Li, Jie-li. 1993. "Geopolitics of the Chinese Communist Party in the Twentieth Century." *Sociological Perspectives* 36: 315–33.

———. 1996. "State Fragmentation: A Comparative Analysis of the British North American Empire, the United States, and Qing China, 1600–1900." Ph.D. diss., Department of Sociology, University of California, Riverside.

Li, Rebecca. 1998. "Alternative Routes to Revolution: An Integrated Model of Societal Disintegration in Qing China." Ph.D. diss., Department of Sociology, University of California, Riverside.

Liddell-Hart, B. H. 1970. *History of the Second World War.* New York: Putnam.

Lieberson, Stanley. 1980. *A Piece of the Pie: Blacks and White Immigrants Since 1880.* Berkeley: University of California Press.

Light, Ivan, and Stavros Karageorgis. 1994. "The Ethnic Economy." In Neil J. Smelser and Richard Swedberg, eds., *Handbook of Economic Sociology.* Princeton, N.J.: Princeton University Press.

Lipset, Seymour Martin. 1994. "The Social Requisites of Democracy Revisited." *American Sociological Review* 59: 1–22.

Löwith, Karl. [1941] 1967. *From Hegel to Nietzsche.* New York: Doubleday.

Luttwak, Edward. 1976. *The Grand Strategy of the Roman Empire—From the First Century A.D. to the Third.* Baltimore: Johns Hopkins University Press.

Macfarlane, Alan. 1978. *The Origins of English Individualism.* Oxford: Blackwell.

MacLeod, William Christie. 1967. "Celt and Indian: Britain's Old World Frontier in Relation to the New." In Paul Bohannan and Fred Plog, eds., *Beyond the Frontier.* Garden City, N.Y.: American Museum Sourcebooks in Anthropology.

Mann, Michael. 1986. *The Sources of Social Power.* Vol. 1, *A History of Power from the Beginning to A.D. 1760.* Cambridge: Cambridge University Press.

———. 1989. "Comments on Paul Kennedy's *The Rise and Fall of the Great Powers.*" *British Journal of Sociology* 40: 331–35.

———. 1993. *The Sources of Social Power.* Vol. 2, *The Rise of Classes and Nation-States, 1760–1914.* Cambridge: Cambridge University Press.

Mardin, Serif. 1997. "The Ottoman Empire." In Barkey and Von Hagen 1997.

Marsden, George M., and Bradley J. Longfield. 1992. *The Secularization of the Academy.* Oxford: Oxford University Press.

Marwell, Gerald, and Pamela Oliver. 1993. *The Critical Mass in Collective Action: A Micro-Social Theory.* New York: Cambridge University Press.

Massey, Douglas S., and Nancy A. Denton. 1993. *American Apartheid: Segregation and the Making of the Underclass.* Cambridge, Mass.: Harvard University Press.

Mauss, Marcel. [1914] 1969. "Les Origines de la Notion de Monnaie." In *Oeuvres,* Vol. 2. Paris: Editions de Minuit.

———. [1925] 1967. *The Gift.* New York: Norton.

McCormack, Gavan, and Yoshio Sugimoto, eds. 1984. *The Japanese Trajectory: Modernization and Beyond.* Cambridge: Cambridge University Press.

McEvedy, Colin. 1961. *The Penguin Atlas of Medieval History.* Baltimore: Penguin.

———. 1967. *The Penguin Atlas of Ancient History.* Baltimore: Penguin.

———. 1972. *The Penguin Atlas of Modern History.* Baltimore: Penguin.

———. 1982. *The Penguin Atlas of Recent History: Europe Since 1815.* Baltimore: Penguin.

McEvedy, Colin, and Richard Jones. 1978. *Atlas of World Population History.* Baltimore: Penguin.

McMullin, Neil. 1984. *Buddhism and State in Sixteenth Century Japan.* Princeton, N.J.: Princeton University Press.

McNeill, William H. 1963. *The Rise of the West: A History of the Human Community.* Chicago: University of Chicago Press.

———. 1976. *Plagues and Peoples.* New York: Doubleday.

———. 1982. *The Pursuit of Power.* Chicago: University of Chicago Press.

———. 1986. *Polyethnicity and National Unity in World History.* Toronto: University of Toronto Press.

McPhail, Clark. 1991. *The Myth of the Madding Crowd.* New York: Aldine de Gruyter.

McRae, John R. 1986. *The Northern School and the Formation of Early Ch'an Buddhism.* Honolulu: University of Hawaii Press.

Merkl, Peter H. 1975. *Political Violence Under the Swastika.* Princeton, N.J.: Princeton University Press.

Meyer, John W. 1987. "The World Polity and the Authority of the Nation-State." In George M. Thomas, John W. Meyer, Francisco O. Ramirez, and John Boli, eds., *Institutional Structure: Constituting State, Society and the Individual.* Newbury Park, Calif.: Sage.

Miller, George. 1973. *George Herbert Mead.* Chicago: University of Chicago Press.

Mitchell, Allan. 1979. *German Influence in France After 1870: The Formation of the French Republic.* Chapel Hill: University of North Carolina Press.

Moaddel, Mansoor. 1992. "Ideology as Episodic Discourse: The Case of the Iranian Revolution." *American Sociological Review* 57: 357–79.

Modelski, George, and W. R. Thompson. 1988. *Sea Power and Global Politics Since 1494.* Seattle: University of Washington Press.

Moore, Barrington, Jr. 1966. *Social Origins of Dictatorship and Democracy.* Boston: Beacon Press.

Morgenthau, Hans J. 1948. *Politics Among Nations.* New York: Knopf.

Moriya, Katsuhisa. 1990. "Urban Networks and Information Networks." In Nakane and Oishi 1990.

Morris-Suzuki, Tessa. 1994. *The Technological Transformation of Japan: From the Seventeenth to the Twenty-first Century.* Cambridge: Cambridge University Press.

Moskos, Charles C., and John Sibley Butler. 1996. *All That We Can Be: Black Leadership and Racial Integration the Army Way.* New York: Basic Books.

Mosse, George L. 1964. *The Crisis of German Ideology.* New York: 1964.

Mueller, Detlef K. 1987. "The Process of Systematization: The Case of German Secondary Education." In Detlef K. Mueller, Fritz Ringer, and Brian Simon, *The*

Rise of the Modern Educational System: Structural Change and Social Reproduction 1870–1920. Cambridge: Cambridge University Press.

Mueller, Hans-Eberhard. 1984. *Bureaucracy, Education and Monopoly: Civil Service Reforms in Prussia and England*. Berkeley: University of California Press.

Murphy, Raymond. 1988. *Social Closure: The Theory of Monopolization and Exclusion*. Oxford: Clarendon Press.

Murray, Alexander. 1978. *Reason and Society in the Middle Ages*. Oxford: Clarendon Press.

Nagahara Keiji. 1990. "The Medieval Peasant." In Yamamura 1990b.

Nakai Nobuhiko and James L. McClain. 1991. "Commercial Change and Urban Growth in Early Modern Japan." In John W. Hall, ed., *The Cambridge History of Japan*. Vol. 4, *Early Modern Japan*. Cambridge: Cambridge University Press.

Nakamura Hajime. 1967. "Suzuki Shosan and the Spirit of Capitalism in Japanese Buddhism." *Monumenta Nipponica* 22: 1–14.

Nakane, Chie, and Shinzaburo Oishi, eds. 1990. *Tokugawa Japan: The Social and Economic Antecedents of Modern Japan*. Tokyo: University of Tokyo Press.

Nee, Victor, and Peng Lian. 1994. "Sleeping with the Enemy: A Dynamic Model of Declining Political Commitment in State Socialism." *Theory and Society* 23: 253–96.

Needham, Joseph. 1954–. *Science and Civilization in China*. Multiple vols. Cambridge: Cambridge University Press.

Nipperdey, Thomas. 1986. *Nachdenken über die deutsche Geschichte: Essays*. Munich: C. H. Beck.

Nishijima Sadao. 1986. "The Economic and Social History of Former Han." In *Cambridge History of China*. Vol. 1., *The Ch'in and Han Empires*, ed. Denis Twitchett and Michael Loewe. Cambridge: Cambridge University Press.

Nolte, Ernst. 1969. *Three Faces of Fascism: Action Francaise, Italian Fascism, National Socialism*. New York: New American Library.

Norpoth, Helmut. 1987. "Guns and Butter and Government Popularity in Britain." *American Political Science Review* 81: 949–70.

Oakley, Francis. 1979. *The Western Church in the Later Middle Ages*. Ithaca, N.Y.: Cornell University Press.

Office of Technology Assessment, U.S. Congress. 1979. *The Effects of Nuclear War*. Washington, D.C.: Government Printing Office.

Olzak, Susan. 1992. *The Dynamics of Ethnic Competition and Conflict*. Stanford, Calif.: Stanford University Press.

Olzak, Susan, and Joane Nagel, eds. 1986. *Competitive Ethnic Relations*. Orlando, Fla.: Academic Press.

Ooms, Herman. 1985. *Tokugawa Ideology: Early Constructs, 1570–1680*. Princeton, N.J.: Princeton University Press.

Ostrom, Charles W. Jr., and Dennis M. Simon. 1985. "Promise and Performance: A Dynamic Model of Presidential Popularity." *American Political Science Review* 79: 334–58.

Paige, Jeffrey M. 1975. *Agrarian Revolution*. Berkeley: University of California Press.

Parker, Geoffrey. 1988. *The Military Revolution: Military Innovation and the Rise of the West*. New York: Cambridge University Press.

Parsons, Talcott. 1964. "Evolutionary Universals in Society." In Talcott Parsons, *Sociological Theory and Modern Society*. New York: Free Press, 1967.

Patterson, Orlando. 1982. *Slavery and Social Death: A Comparative Study*. Cambridge, Mass.: Harvard University Press.

———. 1987. "Comparing Slave Societies." Paper delivered at Annual Meeting of the American Sociological Association, Chicago.

Perrow, Charles. 1984. *Normal Accidents*. New York: Basic Books.

Pipes, David. 1981. *Slave Soldiers and Islam*. New Haven, Conn.: Yale University Press.

Polanyi, Karl. 1977. *The Livelihood of Man*. New York: Academic Press.

Polignac, Francois de. [1984] 1995. *Cults, Territory and the Origins of the Greek City-State*. Chicago: University of Chicago Press.

Portes, Alejandro. 1994. "The Informal Economy and Its Paradoxes." In Neil J. Smelser and Richard Swedberg, eds., *Handbook of Economic Sociology*. Princeton, N.J.: Princeton University Press.

———. 1995. "On Grand Surprises and Modest Certainties: Comment on Kuran, Collins and Tilly." *American Journal of Sociology* 100: 1620–26.

Richter, Melvin. 1969. *The Politics of Conscience: T. H. Green and His Age*. Cambridge, Mass.: Harvard University Press.

Roeder, Philip G. 1991. "Soviet Federalism and Ethnic Mobilization." *World Politics* 43: 196–232.

Roemer, John. 1982. *A General Theory of Exploitation and Class*. Cambridge, Mass.: Harvard University Press.

———. 1986. "New Directions in the Marxian Theory of Exploitation and Class." In John Roemer, ed., *Analytical Marxism*. Cambridge: Cambridge University Press.

Rosenberg, Arthur. 1964. *Imperial Germany: The Birth of the German Republic*. Boston: Beacon Press.

Rosenberg, Hans. 1958. *Bureaucracy, Aristocracy, and Autocracy*. Cambridge, Mass.: Harvard University Press.

Rosovsky, Henry. 1961. *Capital Formation in Japan, 1868–1940*. Glencoe, Ill.: Free Press.

Rothblatt, Sheldon. 1981. *The Revolution of the Dons: Cambridge and Society in Victorian England*. Cambridge: Cambridge University Press.

Rozman, Gilbert, ed. 1991. *The East Asian Region: Confucian Heritage and Its Modern Adaptation*. Princeton, N.J.: Princeton University Press.

Rueschemeyer, Dietrich, Evelyn H. Stephens, and John D. Stephens. 1992. *Capitalist Development and Democracy*. Chicago: University of Chicago Press.

Runciman, W. G. 1983. "Capitalism Without Classes: The Case of Classical Rome." *British Journal of Sociology* 34: 157–77.

———. 1989. *A Treatise on Social Theory*. Vol. 2., *Substantive Social Theory*. Cambridge: Cambridge University Press.

Russell, Bertrand. 1957. *Why I am Not a Christian*. London: Allen and Unwin.

Sabel, Charles F. 1994. "Learning by Monitoring: The Institutions of Economic Development." In Neil J. Smelser and Richard Swedberg, eds., *Handbook of Economic Sociology*. Princeton, N.J.: Princeton University Press.

Sahlins, Marshall. 1972. *Stone Age Economics*. Chicago: Aldine.

Sanderson, Stephen K. 1994. "The Transition from Feudalism to Capitalism: The Theoretical Significance of the Japanese Case." *Review* 13: 15–55.

————. 1995. *Social Transformation: A General Theory of Historical Development*. Oxford: Blackwell.

Sansom, George B. 1961. *A History of Japan, 1334–1615*. Tokyo: Charles Tuttle.

Sapir, Edward. 1921. *Language: An Introduction to the Study of Speech*. New York: Harcourt.

Schelling, Thomas C. 1962. *The Strategy of Conflict*. Cambridge, Mass.: Harvard University Press.

Schnädelbach, Herbert. 1984. *Philosophy in Germany, 1831–1933*. Cambridge: Cambridge University Press.

Schorske, Carl E. 1980. *Fin-de-Siècle Vienna*. New York: Knopf.

Schumpeter, Joseph A. [1911] 1961. *The Theory of Economic Development*. New York: Oxford University Press.

————. 1939. *Business Cycles: A Theoretical, Historical, and Statistical Analysis of the Capitalist Process*. New York: McGraw-Hill.

Searle, Eleanor. 1988. *Predatory Kinship and the Creation of Norman Power, 840–1066*. Berkeley: University of California Press.

Sedaitis, Judith B., and Jim Butterfield, eds. 1991. *Perestroika from Below: Social Movements in the Soviet Union*. Boulder, Colo.: Westview Press.

Sheehan, James J. 1990. *German History, 1770–1866*. Oxford: Oxford University Press.

Simmel, Georg. [1908] 1955. *Conflict and the Web of Group-Affiliations*. New York: Free Press.

Singer, J. David, and associates. 1979. *Explaining War*. Beverly Hills, Calif.: Sage.

Singer, J. David, and Paul F. Diehl. 1990. *Measuring the Correlates of War*. Ann Arbor: University of Michigan Press.

Skocpol, Theda. 1979. *States and Social Revolutions*. New York: Cambridge University Press.

Smith, Anthony D. 1986. *The Ethnic Origins of Nations*. Oxford: Blackwell.

Smith, Thomas C. 1959. *Agrarian Origins of Modern Japan*. Stanford, Calif.: Stanford University Press.

————. 1988a. *Native Sources of Japanese Industrialization, 1750–1920*. Berkeley: University of California Press.

————. 1988b. "Peasant Time and Factory Time in Japan." In Smith 1988a.

Snodgrass, Anthony. 1980. *Archaic Greece*. Berkeley: University of California Press.

Southern, R. W. 1970. *Western Society and the Church in the Middle Ages*. Harmondsworth: Penguin.

Spaulding, Robert K. 1943. *How Spanish Grew*. Berkeley: University of California Press.

Sperber, Hans, and Wolfgang Fleischhauer. 1963. *Geschichte der deutschen Sprache*. Berlin: de Gruyter.

Stark, Rodney, and William Sims Bainbridge. 1985. *The Future of Religion*. Berkeley: University of California Press.

Ste. Croix, Geoffrey de. 1983. *The Class Struggle in the Ancient Greek World*. London: Duckworth.

Stinchcombe, Arthur L. 1961. "Agricultural Enterprise and Rural Class Relations." *American Journal of Sociology* 67:165-76.

————. 1968. *Constructing Social Theories*. New York: Harcourt.

————. 1983. *Economic Sociology*. New York: Academic Press.

————. 1984. "Class in Marx's Conception of History." *New Left Review* 146: 94–III.

————. 1995. *The Political Economy of the Caribbean, 1750–1900: A Sociology of Slavery and Freedom*. Princeton, N.J.: Princeton University Press.

Stolz, Friedrich, and Albert Debrunner. 1966. *Geschichte der lateinischen Sprache*. Berlin: de Gruyter.

Stone, Lawrence. 1979. *The Family, Sex and Marriage in England, 1500–1800*. London: Weidenfeld and Nicolson.

Strauss, Gerald. 1972. *Pre-Reformation Germany*. London: Macmillan.

de Swaan, Abram. 1988. *In the Care of the State: Health Care, Education and Welfare in Europe and the USA in the Modern Era*. Cambridge, Mass.: Polity Press.

Szelenyi, Ivan, and Balazs Szelenyi. 1994. "Why Socialism Failed: Toward a Theory of System Breakdown—Causes of Disintegration of East European State Socialism." *Theory and Society* 23: 211–31.

Thompson, E. P. 1963. *The Making of the English Working Class*. London: Gollancz.

————. 1967. "Time, Work Discipline, and Industrial Capitalism." *Past and Present* 38: 57–93.

Thompson, William R. 1988. *On Global War: Historical-Structural Approaches to World Politics*. Columbia: University of South Carolina Press.

Thomson, J. A. F. 1980. *Popes and Princes 1417–1517: Politics and Piety in the Late Medieval Church*. London: Allen and Unwin.

Tilly, Charles. 1978. *From Mobilization to Revolution*. Reading, Mass.: Addison-Wesley.

————. 1990. *Coercion, Capital, and European States, AD 990–1990*. Oxford: Blackwell.

————. 1993. *European Revolutions, 1492–1992*. Oxford: Blackwell.

————. 1995. *Popular Contention in Great Britain, 1758–1834*. Cambridge, Mass.: Harvard University Press.

Tilly, Charles, Douglas McAdam, and Sidney Tarrow. 1997. "Moral Equivalents of Social Movements." Paper delivered at annual meeting of the American Sociological Association, Toronto.

Toby, Ronald P. 1984. *State and Diplomacy in Early Modern Japan: Asia in the Development of the Tokugawa Bakufu*. Princeton, N.J.: Princeton University Press.

Torstendahl, Rolf. 1991. *Bureaucratisation in Northwest Europe, 1880–1985*. London: Routledge.

Totman, Conrad. 1993. *Early Modern Japan*. Berkeley: University of California Press.

Toyoda Takeshi and Sugiyama Hiroshi. 1977. "The Growth of Commerce and Trades." In Hall and Toyoda 1977.

Udovitch, Abraham. 1970. *Partnership and Profit in Medieval Islam*. Princeton, N.J.: Princeton University Press.

Vail, Leroy. 1989. *The Creation of Tribalism in Southern and Central Africa*. London: James Currey.

Van Creveld, Martin. 1977. *Supplying War: Logistics from Wallenstein to Patton*. New York: Cambridge University Press.

———. 1991. *Technology and War: From 2000 B.C. to the Present*. New York: Free Press.

Varley, H. Paul. 1977. "Ashikaga Yoshimitsu and the World of Kitayama: Social Change and Shogunal Patronage in Early Muromachi." In Hall and Toyoda 1977.

Vesey, Lawrence R. 1965. *The Emergence of the American University*. Chicago: University of Chicago Press.

Von Hagen, Mark, and Karen Barkey. 1997. *After Empire: Multiethnic Societies and Nation-Building*. Boulder, Colo.: Westview.

Wakita Haruko and Susan B. Hanley. 1981. "Dimensions of Development: Cities in Fifteenth- and Sixteenth-Century Japan." In Hall, Nagahara, and Yamamura 1981.

Walder, Andrew G. 1994. "The Decline of Communist Power: Elements of a Theory of Institutional Change." *Theory and Society* 23: 297–324.

Waldinger, Roger. 1996. *Still the Promised City? African-Americans and New Immigrants in Postindustrial New York*. Cambridge, Mass.: Harvard University Press.

Waller, David V. 1992. "Ethnic Mobilization and Geopolitics in the Soviet Union: Toward a Theoretical Understanding." *Journal of Political and Military Sociology* 20: 37–62.

Wallerstein, Immanuel. 1974. *The Modern World System: Capitalist Agriculture and the Origins of the European World-Economy in the Sixteenth Century*. New York: Academic Press.

———. 1980. *The Modern World System II. Mercantilism and the Consolidation of the European World-Economy*. San Diego, Calif.: Academic Press.

———. 1989. *The Modern World System III. The Second Era of Great Expansion of the Capitalist World-Economy, 1730–1840s*. San Diego, Calif.: Academic Press.

Walt, Stephen M. 1987. *The Origins of Alliances*. Ithaca, N.Y.: Cornell University Press.

Waltz, Kenneth N. 1979. *Theory of International Politics*. New York: Columbia University Press.

Wank, Solomon. 1997. "The Habsburg Empire." In Barkey and Von Hagen 1997.

Warner, R. Stephen. 1993. "Work in Progress Toward a New Paradigm for the Sociological Study of Religion in the United States." *American Journal of Sociology* 98: 1044–93.

Waters, Mary C. 1990. *Ethnic Options: Choosing Identities in America*. Berkeley: University of California Press.

Watkins, Susan Cotts. 1991. *From Provinces into Nations: Demographic Integration in Western Europe, 1870–1960*. Princeton, N.J.: Princeton University Press.

Weber, Eugen. 1976. *Peasants into Frenchmen: The Modernization of Rural France, 1870–1914*. Stanford, Calif.: Stanford University Press.

Weber, Max. [1909] 1976. *The Agrarian Sociology of Ancient Civilizations*. London: New Left Books.

————. [1917] 1958. *The Religion of India*. New York: Free Press. [Original title: *Die Wirtschaftsethik der Weltreligionen: Hinduismus und Buddhismus*.]

————. [1922] 1968. *Economy and Society*. New York: Bedminster Press.

————. [1922] 1991. *The Sociology of Religion*. Boston: Beacon Press.

————. [1923] 1961. *General Economic History*. New York: Collier.

Weinstein, Stanley. 1977. "Rennyo and the Shinshu Revival." In Hall and Toyoda 1977.

Weisz, George. 1983. *The Emergence of Modern Universities in France, 1863–1914*. Princeton, N.J.: Princeton University Press.

White, Harrison C. 1981. "Where Do Markets Come From?" *American Journal of Sociology* 87: 517–47.

————. 1992. *Identity and Control: A Structural Theory of Social Action*. Princeton, N.J.: Princeton University Press.

Whitney, William Dwight. [1875] 1979. *The Life and Growth of Language*. New York: Dover.

Wickham, Chris. 1984. "The Other Transition: From the Ancient World to Feudalism." *Past and Present* 103: 3–36.

Willey, Thomas E. 1978. *Back to Kant: The Revival of Kantianism in German Social and Historical Thought, 1860–1914*. Detroit, Mich.: Wayne State University Press.

Williams, Eric. 1966. *Capitalism and Slavery*. New York: Putnam.

Williamson, C. 1960. *American Suffrage: From Property to Democracy, 1760–1860*. Princeton, N.J.: Princeton University Press.

Wuthnow, Robert. 1989. *Communities of Discourse: Ideology and Social Structure in the Reformation, the Enlightenment, and European Socialism*. Cambridge, Mass.: Harvard University Press.

Yamamoto, Shichihei. 1992. *The Spirit of Japanese Capitalism*. New York: Madison Books.

Yamamura, Kozo. 1981. "Returns on Unification: Economic Growth in Japan, 1550–1650." In Hall, Nagahara, and Yamamura 1981.

————. 1990a. "The Growth of Commerce in Medieval Japan." In Yamamura 1990b.

Yamamura, Kozo, ed. 1990b. *The Cambridge History of Japan*. Vol. 3, *Medieval Japan*. Cambridge: Cambridge University Press.

Yasuba, Yasukichi. 1986. "Standard of Living in Japan Before Industrialization: From What Level Did Japan Begin?" *Journal of Economic History* 46: 217–24.

Index

In this index an "f" after a number indicates a separate reference on the next page, and an "ff" indicates separate references on the next two pages. A continuous discussion over two or more pages is indicated by a span of numbers, e.g., "57–59."

Library of Congress Cataloging-in-Publication Data

Collins, Randall
    Macrohistory : essays in sociology of the long run / Randall Collins.
       p.   cm.
    Includes bibliographical references and index.
    ISBN 0-8047-3523-9 (cloth : alk. paper).
    ISBN 0-8047-3600-6 (paper : alk. paper)
    1. History—Philosophy.   2. History—Methodology.   I. Title.
  D16.8.C5925   1999
  901—DC21   99-31771

♾ This book is printed on archival-quality paper.

Original printing 1999
Last figure below indicates year of this printing:
08 07 06 05 04 03 02

Typeset by BookMatters in 10.5/12.5 Bembo and Gill Sans